James Joyce and Cultural Genetics

Historicizing Modernism

Series Editors
Matthew Feldman, Professorial Fellow, Norwegian Study Centre, University of York, UK; and Erik Tonning, Professor of British Literature and Culture, University of Bergen, Norway

Associate Editor
Natasha Periyan, Lecturer in Literature, King's College London, UK

Editorial Board
Professor Chris Ackerley, Department of English, University of Otago, New Zealand; Professor Ron Bush, St. John's College, University of Oxford, UK; Dr Finn Fordham, Department of English, Royal Holloway, UK; Professor Steven Matthews, Department of English, University of Reading, UK; Dr Mark Nixon, Department of English, University of Reading, UK; Professor Janet Wilson, University of Northampton, UK; Santanu Das, University of Oxford, UK; Nan Zhang, The University of Hong Kong; and Kevin Andrew Riordan, Nanyang Technological University, Singapore.

Historicizing Modernism challenges traditional literary interpretations by taking an empirical approach to modernist writing: a direct response to new documentary sources made available over the last decade.

Informed by archival research, and working beyond the usual European/American avant-garde 1900–45 parameters, this series reassesses established readings of modernist writers by developing fresh views of intellectual contexts and working methods.

Series Titles
Arun Kolatkar and Literary Modernism in India, Laetitia Zecchini
British Literature and Classical Music, David Deutsch
Broadcasting in the Modernist Era, Matthew Feldman, Henry Mead and Erik Tonning
Charles Henri Ford, Alexander Howard
Chicago and the Making of American Modernism, Michelle E. Moore
Christian Modernism in an Age of Totalitarianism, Jonas Kurlberg
Ezra Pound's Adams Cantos, David Ten Eyck
Ezra Pound and His Classical Sources, Jonathan Ullyot

Ezra Pound's Eriugena, Mark Byron
Ezra Pound's Washington Cantos and the Struggle for Light, Alec Marsh
Great War Modernisms and The New Age Magazine, Paul Jackson
Historical Modernisms, Jean-Michel Rabaté and Angeliki Spiropoulou
Historicizing Modernists, Edited by Matthew Feldman,
Anna Svendsen and Erik Tonning
James Joyce and Absolute Music, Michelle Witen
James Joyce and Catholicism, Chrissie Van Mierlo
James Joyce and Photography, Georgina Binnie-Wright
Jean Rhys's Modernist Bearings and Experimental Aesthetics, Sue Thomas
John Kasper and Ezra Pound, Alec Marsh
Judith Wright and Emily Carr, Anne Collett and Dorothy Jones
Katherine Mansfield: New Directions, Edited by Aimée Gasston,
Gerri Kimber and Janet Wilson
Katherine Mansfield and Literary Modernism, Edited by Janet Wilson,
Gerri Kimber and Susan Reid
Late Modernism and the English Intelligencer, Alex Latter
The Life and Work of Thomas MacGreevy, Susan Schreibman
Literary Impressionism, Rebecca Bowler
The Many Drafts of D. H. Lawrence, Elliott Morsia
Modern Manuscripts, Dirk Van Hulle
Modernist Authorship and Transatlantic Periodical Culture, Amanda Sigler
Modernist Lives, Claire Battershill
Modernist Wastes, Caroline Knighton
The Politics of 1930s British Literature, Natasha Periyan
Reading Mina Loy's Autobiographies, Sandeep Parmar
Reframing Yeats, Charles Ivan Armstrong
Samuel Beckett and Arnold Geulincx, David Tucker
Samuel Beckett and the Bible, Iain Bailey
Samuel Beckett and Cinema, Anthony Paraskeva
Samuel Beckett in Confinement, James Little
Samuel Beckett and Experimental Psychology, Joshua Powell
Samuel Beckett's 'More Pricks than Kicks', John Pilling
Samuel Beckett's German Diaries 1936-1937, Mark Nixon
Samuel Beckett and the Second World War, William Davies
T. E. Hulme and the Ideological Politics of Early Modernism, Henry Mead
Virginia Woolf's Late Cultural Criticism, Alice Wood

James Joyce and Cultural Genetics

The Joycean Genome

Wim Van Mierlo

BLOOMSBURY ACADEMIC
LONDON • NEW YORK • OXFORD • NEW DELHI • SYDNEY

BLOOMSBURY ACADEMIC
Bloomsbury Publishing Plc
50 Bedford Square, London, WC1B 3DP, UK
1385 Broadway, New York, NY 10018, USA
29 Earlsfort Terrace, Dublin 2, Ireland

BLOOMSBURY, BLOOMSBURY ACADEMIC and the Diana logo
are trademarks of Bloomsbury Publishing Plc

First published in Great Britain 2023
This paperback edition published 2025

Copyright © Wim Van Mierlo, 2023

Wim Van Mierlo has asserted his right under the Copyright, Designs
and Patents Act, 1988, to be identified as Author of this work.

For legal purposes the Acknowledgements on p. xii constitute
an extension of this copyright page.

Cover design: Rebecca Heselton

All rights reserved. No part of this publication may be reproduced or
transmitted in any form or by any means, electronic or mechanical,
including photocopying, recording, or any information storage or retrieval
system, without prior permission in writing from the publishers.

Bloomsbury Publishing Plc does not have any control over, or responsibility
for, any third-party websites referred to or in this book. All internet addresses
given in this book were correct at the time of going to press. The author and
publisher regret any inconvenience caused if addresses have changed or sites
have ceased to exist, but can accept no responsibility for any such changes.

A catalogue record for this book is available from the British Library.

A catalog record for this book is available from the Library of Congress.

ISBN: HB: 978-1-3501-6988-3
PB: 978-1-3504-1893-6
ePDF: 978-1-3501-6989-0
eBook: 978-1-3501-6990-6

Series: Historicizing Modernism

Typeset by Integra Software Services Pvt. Ltd.

To find out more about our authors and books visit www.bloomsbury.com
and sign up for our newsletters.

For Chrissie

Contents

Editorial preface to *Historicizing Modernism*	x
List of abbreviations	xi
Acknowledgements	xii
Introduction	1
1 The Celtic note: *Chamber Music*	23
2 Over the dark sea: *Exiles*	53
3 Spiritual manifestations and genetic psychohistories: *Epiphanies*, *Stephen Hero* and *A Portrait of the Artist*	77
4 Creating the conscience: *Ulysses*	99
5 Sketching histories: *Finnegans Wake*	131
6 Bringing the dear prehistoric scenes all back again: *Finnegans Wake*	165
Bibliography	207
Index	222

Editorial preface to *Historicizing Modernism*

This book series is devoted to the analysis of late nineteenth- to twentieth-century literary Modernism within its historical contexts. *Historicizing Modernism* therefore stresses empirical accuracy and the value of primary sources (such as letters, diaries, notes, drafts, marginalia or other archival materials) in developing monographs and edited collections on modernist literature. This may take a number of forms, such as manuscript study and genetic criticism, documenting interrelated historical contexts and ideas, and exploring biographical information. To date, no book series has fully laid claim to this interdisciplinary, source-based territory for modern literature. While the series addresses itself to a range of key authors, it also highlights the importance of non-canonical writers with a view to establishing broader intellectual genealogies of Modernism. Furthermore, while the series is weighted towards the English-speaking world, studies of non-Anglophone modernists whose writings are open to fresh historical exploration are also included.

A key aim of the series is to reach beyond the familiar rhetoric of intellectual and artistic 'autonomy' employed by many modernists and their critical commentators. Such rhetorical moves can and should themselves be historically situated and reintegrated into the complex continuum of individual literary practices. It is our intent that the series' emphasis upon the contested self-definitions of modernist writers, thinkers, and critics may, in turn, prompt various reconsiderations of the boundaries delimiting the concept 'modernism' itself. Indeed, the concept of 'historicizing' is itself debated across its volumes, and the series by no means discourages more theoretically informed approaches. On the contrary, the editors hope that the historical specificity encouraged by *Historicizing Modernism* may inspire a range of fundamental critiques along the way.

Matthew Feldman
Erik Tonning

Abbreviations

BL	British Library, Additional Manuscripts
Buffalo	University of Buffalo, James Joyce Collection
Cornell	Cornell University Library, James Joyce Collection
E	*Exiles*
EB	*Encyclopaedia Britannica*
FW	*Finnegans Wake*
FW-R	*The Restored Finnegans Wake*
GJS	*Genetic Joyce Studies*
JJA	*James Joyce Archive*
JJDA	*James Joyce Digital Archive*
JJQ	*James Joyce Quarterly*
L-Corr	*James Joyce Correspondence*
LI, II, III	*Letters*
NLI	National Library of Ireland
OCPW	*Occasional, Critical, and Political Writing*
P	*A Portrait of the Artist as a Young Man*
PSW	*Poems and Shorter Writings*
SH	*Stephen Hero*
SL	*Selected Letters*
U	*Ulysses*
VI.B	Notebooks for *Finnegans Wake* at Buffalo

Acknowledgements

James Joyce and Cultural Genetics has had a long gestation period as its arguments quietly simmered in my mind. Some of its ideas go back to my PhD thesis, completed at the University of Miami in the late 1990s, on the early drafts notebooks for *Finnegans Wake*. These ideas were later expanded for a book ostensibly on *Finnegans Wake* and historiography, but the book never came together. Meanwhile, my interests expanded and took me into new directions of research in book history, textual scholarship and archival studies, until I saw my way back to the original project and how better to combine historiography and genetic criticism with the present volume as a result. I got here in no small part because of the generosity, kindness, advice, support and indulgence I received over the years from many Joyce scholars and enthusiasts, as well as uncountable stimulating conversations and exchanges I had the pleasure of having with them. Sadly, some great people who have been an influence and inspiration to me are no longer with us (marked by † in the list below).

Special thanks go to Chris Ackerley, Bernard Benstock†, Erik Bindervoet, Zack Bowen†, William S. Brockman, Viviana-Mirela Braslasu, Luca Crispi, Ronan Crowley, Vincent Deane, Mary E. Donnelly, Daniel Ferrer, Finn Fordham, Hans Walter Gabler, Andrew Gibson, Michael Groden†, Andrew Haggerty, David Hayman, Robbert-Jan Henkes, Cheryl Herr, Terence Killeen, Ingeborg Landuyt, Geert Lernout, Patrick A. McCarthy, Lesley McDowell, Len Platt, R.J. Schork†, Sam Slote, Dirk Van Hulle and my wife Chrissie Van Mierlo to whom this book is dedicated. I also want to thank my colleagues at Loughborough University and the members of the Charles Peake *Ulysses* Seminar and the *Finnegans Wake* Research Seminar at the Institute of English Studies, University of London, as well as staff at the National Library of Ireland and the British Library.

Chapters 1 and 2 previously appeared in an earlier form as "'I have met you too late": James Joyce, W.B. Yeats, and the Making of *Chamber Music*', in *Writing Modern Ireland*, special 2010 issue of *South Carolina Review*, 43(1): 50–73, edited by Catherine Paul, and 'The Greater Ireland beyond the Sea: Joyce, Exile and Irish Emigration', in *Joyce, Ireland and Britain*, eds Len Platt and Andrew Gibson (Gainesville: University Press of Florida, 2007), pp. 178–97. Although some of the arguments remain the same, the text has been significantly overhauled, revised and corrected.

Introduction

James Joyce and Cultural Genetics unravels the DNA (so to speak) of James Joyce's authorship. Authorship studies have seen a surge in the last decade or so as a field of inquiry operating within and alongside the history of the book. Concerned with the writer as a 'professional' author, authorship studies have seen a wide range of applications, such as authorship attribution in the Early Modern period or the analysis of author–publisher relations in the nineteenth and twentieth centuries. As such, authorship studies engage with the complete life-cycle of a literary work, from creation and composition to the institutions (publishers, magazines, literary events and so on) that shape the work's reception. Authorship can be understood in several different ways. In the most general sense, it refers to the 'practice or activity of literary writing, especially of writing for publication'. This practice, however, is subject to, on the one hand, different forms of 'textual control' (editing, censorship) and, on the other, 'a complex of values' that include legal and moral rights (sincerity, authority, copyright and so on). Crucially for my project, creativity is as much about the shaping of words as it is about 'turning the author's life into an artistic experiment that (re-)shapes both life and work, style and man' (Berensmeyer et al. 2019, 2). The overly Romantic inflection notwithstanding, the shaping of life and work is important because of the autobiographical nature of Joyce's work. Joyce pursued life as an artistic experiment in *Exiles* and *A Portrait of the Artist as a Young Man*. What concerns me in particular, however, is the interaction between authorial agency and the time and place in which the author was active. To understand this interaction calls for a deeply historicizing method.

The present book uses James Joyce's manuscripts and notebooks for its genealogical exploration of Joyce's life and work, but it goes beyond the traditional scope of genetic studies in taking in this broader purview of Joyce's authorship. *James Joyce and Cultural Genetics* moves along the double helix of genetic criticism and the 'Irish Joyce'. Its aim in fact is to bring these quite disparate fields together in a combined approach. The questions my book explores relate to how Joyce 'made' his work in terms of their composition history, but also how he fashioned them, and by extension fashioned himself, in terms of the place he wanted his books to occupy in the world. There is little doubt that Joyce wanted to reach Irish readers, and it is the steps in this process, how he evolved as a writer, which I seek to uncover.[1] Part of this endeavour involves a fresh look at Joyce's Irishness itself, how he simultaneously placed himself outside mainstream Irish nationalist culture but sought to remain Irish at heart. As has been noted many times before, the struggle with identity is central in Joyce's writing; how he explored, constructed and inserted his versions of Irish cultural identity in his writing have not yet been explored genetically. To find where all of this started, I will look at Joyce's beginnings: the writing of *Chamber Music*, his self-styled exile, the invention of the epiphanies, and the thematic beginnings and political points of departure of both *Ulysses* and *Finnegans Wake*. In tracing Joyce's development as a writer, I will bring to the fore the transformations that took place in his thought and his writing. These transformations include the development of his aesthetic theories between *Stephen Hero* and *A Portrait* and the creative economies they engendered within his own writing practice, his ambivalent stance on the Irish Revival, his protean attitudes towards Irish nationalism, and the narrative and thematic transfigurations that took place during the lengthy period of gestation of his final two books.

To encapsulate the concerns of the double helix of Joyce's authorship, I have invented the term 'cultural genetics'. Cultural genetics is really the missing link between genetic criticism and historicist/postcolonial criticism. Genetics – especially *Wakean* genetics – has unearthed a fantastic number of sources, books that Joyce read and took notes from in preparation for writing, and that have altered our understanding of Joyce's intertextuality. Scholarship in this area has focused primarily on the detail in the notebooks and where he used his notes in the text. These efforts resulted in an invaluable set of glosses that have been useful in gaining a deeper understanding of Joyce's meaning. However, often missing from this work are the wider cultural connections this reading elicits. Especially with Irish materials, these wider connections are hugely important, both in terms of Joyce's motivation and the context in which the books were produced. The reason for this absence is due in part to a misunderstanding about Joyce's reading practices. For a long time, the perception was that Joyce

---

[1] A surprising aspect of Joyce criticism is the extent to which his work is treated as a unit or a whole with little sense of its aesthetic and political developments.

was a 'high-strung, well-read, mnemonically retentive' who possessed a neurotic sensibility to weave 'as many details and facts as possible' into his writing (Herr 1986, 2). Likewise, the idea persists that Joyce's sources, not least during the composition of *Finnegans Wake*, consisted of books on esoteric, eccentric and unusual topics that came to his attention serendipitously. The books were usually far from rare or abstruse, but consisted of publications produced by some of the best known intellectuals of their day, such as Victor Bérard, E.A. Wallis Budge, J.B. Bury, Irjö Hirn, Otto Jespersen, Henry Vizetelly and so on. Without doubt, he also made many fortuitous discoveries. But equally, Joyce's reading showed purpose and strategy. This is evident, for instance, from the large number of books on Saint Patrick that he read during the early years of 'Work in Progress', as well as from the books he asked Sylvia Beach or Harriet Shaw Weaver to order for him. Again, none of these titles were hard to find; Joyce likely came across them in reviews and advertisements in the daily and weekly press. Finally, there is Joyce the textual *bricoleur* who borrowed verbal elements for the purposes of pastiche with only a minimal sense of context, as if Joyce had little sense or interest in what he was reading.

Conversely, much of the historicist work on Joyce has been excellent in examining the relevance of the broader cultural and political connections, opening up Joyce's attitudes towards Irish nationalism and the postcolonial nation. Examining a wide array of cultural forms contemporary to Joyce that incontrovertibly illuminate his work, this scholarship largely works with the 'ideologically charged conventions and assertions' within a culture that manifest themselves 'at the level of institutional discourse' (Herr 1986, 4, 8). But despite asking 'what historical, political and cultural specifics did Joyce really engage with?', these historicist and postcolonial studies often lacked 'exactitude' (Gibson and Platt 2006, 4, 19). In explaining how Joyce's work responded to these discourses, not enough attention was paid to the ideas, texts and materials that Joyce had access to, read, absorbed and incorporated in his writing and for which his notebooks and personal library provide evidence.

It is worth acknowledging, of course, that the historical turn in Joyce studies in the 1990s coincided more or less with the genetic turn that resulted, among others, in the uncovering of a vast number of new sources. What these sources tell us about Joyce's work beyond their local, textual use remains unexplored. In that respect, Herr's call that 'we still need to understand the relationship among allusion, narrative form, and cultural operations' (1986, 3) remains not as valid as it was in 1986, but it also shows the way for genetic work to expand its relevance and function into cultural genetics, which I understand as a historicist approach concerned with the origins and genealogies of both Joyce's writing and Joyce's thinking. However, before defining more precisely what I mean by the term, I want to explain further how I use textual genetics and cultural studies in this book.

Genetic criticism decentralizes the finished 'text' in favour of a dynamic model of textual production that lays bare the creative process. The purpose in tracing the coming-into-being of the literary work through the archive was to correct conventional forms of formalist criticism that turned away from recognizing there was a living and breathing individual behind the 'text' who had devoted considerable time and effort planning, researching, writing, expanding, correcting and polishing her writing (de Biasi 2011, 11). Since the rise of book history and archival studies, Pierre-Marc de Biasi's position is less controversial than it once was. But while the critical relevance of genetic studies is no longer in doubt, it is worth pausing on the question *how* one understands the archive in relation to the final work. According to de Biasi (2011, 11), the central hypothesis of genetic criticism is that the effects of its coming-into-being can be found in the literary work, which therefore 'contains the memory of its own genesis'. The fault lines of composition are present, although not necessarily visible, in the final text; we need drafts and manuscripts to see them. When the archive, the process of the work's own making, is part of the work, the work itself is no longer an entity that is closed and finite (2011, 182), but something without edges, epistemologically fluid, and always open to the potential of what could have been.

That Joyce had a predilection for what could have been is as relevant as the fact that he was attuned to the evolutionary nature of the literary work. A key aspect of Joyce's genealogy is that he rarely wrote with a clear plan in mind. Instead, he proceeded along several unforeseen turning points, moments when the writing would gel by way of osmosis or when Joyce saw connections that he could not see before. Likening writing to boring through a mountain from two sides was one of his favourite metaphors (*Letters* III, 110), as was the expression that 'the ingredients will not fuse until they have reached a certain temperature' (*L-Corr*, #L68393; see also *Letters* I, 205). This he wrote to Pound on 24 July 1917, three months before the compilation of the 'Subject Notebook' and serialization of his new book in *The Little Review*, which were both major turning points in the early genesis of *Ulysses*. For that reason, my approach departs also from the traditional linear ontogeny to include what one might call 'polygenetic processes', in which the writing proceeds along multiple or parallel lines.

If there is one overarching concern in tracing the evolution of Joyce as a writer, it lies in his own preoccupation with the desire for origins and the construction or uncovering of genealogies that make Joyce's art 'genetic'. At every level, *Finnegans Wake* especially is obsessed with origins. Its narratives are an attempt to unravel the circumstances behind the incident in the park involving HCE's alleged exposure. This incident becomes a pretext to scrutinize who Earwicker is and where he comes from, in the course of which every event in which he is involved blends with the history of every other event from the past, significant and trivial. Joyce's interest in origins, however, enters his writing quite early on. The 'old phrases' (*P* 233) from Elizabethan songs that Stephen delights in, which embody an unexpected authenticity and purity of language, is also the phraseology of *Chamber Music*. In tone and sentiment Joyce's lyrics are built on precedence (Campbell 2012, 57–8), while its language and themes derive from earlier lyrical traditions, both Irish and English. From *Stephen Hero* to *Ulysses*, Stephen is absorbed by the cultural traditions that he is part of and that have ineluctably shaped who he is. Even if he resents it, he is 'a product of Catholicism' (*SH* 139), of colonial Ireland, and of the political movements active around him. His creator, too, is ineluctably shaped by these origins (Tymoczko 1994, 12–13).

This book focuses on the creative beginnings and transformations in Joyce's evolution as a writer. The composition of his works reveals plenty of turning points that frequently coincide with, or indeed result from, ruptures in his aesthetics or politics. The example readers are most familiar with is the rewriting of *Stephen Hero* as *A Portrait*, when Joyce reshaped the narrative of his aborted autobiographical novel to make it more economic and pliable, inventing a new brand of *Bildungsroman* in the process. Other turning points may be less obvious, such as the one of *Exiles*. Even more so than his autobiographical novel, Joyce's play is an experiment in turning life into art. *Exiles* is a speculative exercise in what might have been, as Joyce probes the consequences of what might happen if he returned to Ireland. Because only the fair copy survives, we know little about the play's composition. The notes that Joyce produced, however, reveal quite a bit about the play's conception beyond its actual writing. On the one hand, the notes meticulously explore the protagonists' state of mind in a way that goes far beyond the actual play; on the other, they also reflect retrospectively on a play already written.

The genetic beginnings I am particularly interested in are Joyce's notes, for it is here that we find Joyce's engagement with cultural and historical materials before they become, strictly speaking, part of the creative work. This area is called *exogenetics*, the domain of reading notes and writers' libraries, that indicates the stages preparatory to the writing when a writer is undertaking orientational and exploratory research during the initial stages of conceiving and planning the work (de Biasi 1996, 42, 44). This planning is not purely functional, however; notebooks and libraries are mental spaces (Van Hulle 2014, 8) where the creative process takes hold for the first time. A writer's sources therefore are never *just* sources that explain the work; they are part of the intertextual genealogy of the work whose processes require interpretation (Debray-Genette 1977, 24–30). A careful analysis of the creative transformation of the sources into the writing is crucial for our understanding of Joyce's writing precisely because exogenetics are integral to his creative economy.

To a large degree, Joyce's notetaking practices, and how he used his notes during compositions, are understudied and poorly understood. No doubt this is due to the overwhelming body of extant material as well as the puzzling nature of the notes themselves. The mechanical nature of their collection and use in particular makes them resistant to interpretation. The common view is that Joyce lifted words and phrases from his sources and then stored this 'verbiage' in his notebooks until he found an appropriate place for it in his text. Even though the amassing and stockpiling of verbal and thematic detail is part and parcel of Joyce's method, 'trusting to genius for transforming trivia into the sublime' (Herring 1977, 4–5), the process was not just a mechanical one. David Hayman is one of the few critics who recognizes a creative impulse in Joyce's method. In the *Finnegans Wake* notebooks he identifies a special class of notes that he calls 'epiphanoids', defining these as 'highly charged personal observations' whose historical or biographical connections 'provide direct, though admittedly coded, links between his life experiences and certain creative decisions' (1990, 93, 1999, 34). They are moments of 'radiance' that turn life into art. Hayman overstates the special nature of these notes, and the modernist aesthetic that he attributes to them, particularly when the epiphanoids turn out to be reading notes. Nonetheless, Hayman helps us see a creative aspect in the notes as well as in their use. His claim that the 'epiphanoids', when used in *Finnegans Wake*, inflect the voice of the narrative (1999, 35) is correct, albeit that this applies to all notes. One might even say that there is a moment of 'radiance' in the reading notes as such, in that they reflect what captured Joyce's attention.[2] The connection between Joyce's

---

[2] Joyce's exogenetic process consists of three stages of intention and decision-making. The first stage is the impulse to take down a note while reading. The second is the form of the note itself, whose words can be verbatim, a condensation of the source text, or a discursive transformation that matches the source to intended use. The third stage is the transference of the note to the draft, when the original text can be further altered and revised to fit the narrative (in which case the intertextual link with the text may become irrevocably obscured in the final text).

notetaking practice, the aesthetics of observational 'radiance' and the epiphanies is one I discuss in Chapter 3. Joyce thus draws 'inspiration' from his reading. But his sources are not always creative starting points in the strict sense. Frequently, Joyce's reading follows, and is directed by, the writing, so that new sources affirm and bring into relief the discursive, thematic or political parameters already inscribed in the work.

Furthermore, exogenetics is also a form of cultural genetics. Without doubt, Joyce's reading was with equal measure 'indiscriminately important and unimportant' (Henkes 2011, 130), but that is not to say that he read his sources without regard to what they were aiming to communicate. Situated at the juncture between historicism and genetic criticism, cultural genetics therefore provides a new angle that redresses some of the more mechanistic approaches to Joyce's sources and notetaking to provide instead a view concomitant with the sociology of texts as adumbrated by D.F. McKenzie. The idea that Joyce was a 'lexical magpie' and a 'linguistic sponge' (Henkes 2011, 127), that he 'mine[d] his source-texts for lexical nuggets' (Slote 2016, 164), rightly acknowledges the sources as linguistic markers, but overlooks their value as cultural artefacts. Such a position is apt to assume that Joyce was indifferent to ideology or that he was reading against the grain. As a concept, the sociology of texts helps us to see this wider cultural context. In calling attention to the sociocultural conditions in which texts were produced and received, McKenzie highlights how the meaning of a literary work derives not only from interpreting its text but also from the 'physical forms, textual versions, technical transmission, institutional control, their perceived meanings, and social effects' (McKenzie 1999, 13). Joyce's sources are (inter-)texts, but they are also books that he encountered as products of their place and time.

Cultural genetics, therefore, seeks to understand not just how Joyce created his works and what their aesthetic import is but also how he created the political and cultural vision that we find in his writings. The number of previous studies that have looked at how Joyce viewed and responded to history is vast.[3] What these studies do not do, however, is ground their findings in the books Joyce read and used or trace the genealogy of his reading back to the creative process. My use of cultural genetics takes as its starting point Robert Spoo's observation that history is not just a theme in *Ulysses*, but 'a condition of the novel's aesthetic production' (1994, 4), and applies this to Joyce's composition practices. The

---

[3] Herr 1986, Spoo 1994, Nolan 1995, Fairhall 1993, Gibson 2002 and Gibbons 2015 are among the most influential studies.

aim is to understand the coming-into-being of Joyce's vision of history, culture and identity and how he impressed this vision in his books. It does this, on the one hand, by questioning the 'tribal' approach present in some types of Joyce criticism. This approach divides the political landscape into rudimentary ideological oppositions (British *v.* Irish; Catholic *v.* Protestant), depicting Joyce as someone who resists all forms of essentialism. This book pays attention rather to the finer positions and fault lines that play themselves out within the cultural field. It looks not at the big words that Stephen fears, but at the very specific historical conditions that surrounded him. History's particulars, the flotsam and jetsam of the past, is what *James Joyce and Cultural Genetics* is all about.

To bring cultural context and history more closely into focus within genetic criticism is critically a new departure. Genetic criticism traditionally operates within fairly conventional boundaries of literary formalism, looking mostly at how language, themes, motifs, structures and characterization develop within the *avant-texte*. It seemingly does not touch on those domains of inquiry that have informed literary criticism since the advent of new historicism and cultural studies. Nevertheless, cultural genetics is neither a new branch of genetic criticism, nor a necessary expansion of its methods and theoretical frameworks. In fact, genetic criticism has always acknowledged the social and cultural dimension of authorship and the creative act (Debray-Genette 1977, 25; Mitterand 2004, 117), although the matter has only more recently drawn analysis (Jurt 2007). What Mitterand calls cultural genetics is, like Jurt's Bourdieusian take, much wider than how I use the term. For him, genetic criticism is about extricating from the drafts something that lies 'beyond the author's individual expression', that is to say, the 'symptoms and earliest transformations' in culture itself. 'Cultural genetics', to his mind, therefore complements cultural history the way literary genetics complements literary history (2004, 117). Interestingly, new interdisciplinary research in cultural genomics has since developed on the correlation between DNA mutations, ancestry and cultural change (see, for example, Nash 2015; Nikolova 2018). Crucially, though, Mitterand's reflection on cultural genetics premises his concern with the way in which the language of the writer 'feeds on its environment and on the preimpositions and presuppositions of collective discourse' (1994, 117). The writer in question is Zola; Mitterand's object: the genesis of Zola's naturalism.

In *James Joyce and Cultural Genetics*, therefore, I am not just concerned with Joyce's work as aesthetic object, but with its creation as a cultural work, with the building of its 'network' of cultural and historical allusions, and Joyce's development of his identity politics and changing attitudes towards nationalism and the Irish Revival. Within this analysis, I will pay attention to Joyce's own preoccupation with change and genealogy, taking his oeuvre not as a statement, but as a permeable, evolving work. The points of entry are Joyce's notes, his personal library and his early drafts that form the creative mental spaces (Van Hulle 2014, 8) where he collected, absorbed and transformed the cultural and historical materials that he used in his writing.

Cultural genetics, consequently, is about applying the precepts of cultural studies and cultural memory to genetic criticism. Cultural studies are obviously important because of the specific connections between Joyce's work and its social, cultural and historical environment and the acts of cultural osmosis that Joyce performs in his writing. As Herr (1986, 2) puts it, Joyce 'teases us beyond the bounds of what seems necessary' in terms of ingesting the ideas, events, artefacts, texts and discourses from history and the world around him, not least the cultural and historical conditions that shaped Ireland as a nation in the late nineteenth and early twentieth century. But it needs bearing in mind that these conditions, and their outcomes, are fluid as well. The problem of cultural analysis, according to Clifford Geertz (1973, 407), is that it is easy to overestimate just how stable and interconnected the social order is at any given moment. In the case of Ireland, where cultural identity is highly contested, it is easy to see why this is problematic. By the same token, any literary response, let alone Joyce's, to the cultural mire is not necessarily seamless either. Whatever connections exist within a culture, or *mutatis mutandis* in a writer's reactions to culture, those connections, as Geertz advocates, must be somehow real and observable. Geertz's famous 'thick description' (1973, 26–8) is a suitable method for unpacking Joyce's notebooks.

Cultural studies are important also beyond the contextual and allusive nature of Joyce's writing. According to Stuart Hall (via Edward Said), cultural studies explore the affiliations and tension, between 'the text' and the 'institutions, offices, agencies, academies, corporations, groups, ideologically defined parties and professions, nations, races, and genders' that bear on it (Hall 1999, 106). Not coincidentally, these affiliations are similar to the ones McKenzie identifies for the sociology of texts. Precisely because the 'roles of institutions' and their own 'complex structures' affect 'the forms of social discourse, past and present' (McKenzie 1999, 15), we need to study the production, transmission, consumption of these 'texts' to gain the fullest understanding of their meaning.[4]

---

[4] Although as a book historian McKenzie does not explicitly consider the genesis of the work, the author's private production of his text in the manuscripts belongs to this purview too.

For a good part of his career, Joyce benefited from the support of several informal and semi-formal 'modernist' and avant-garde networks that surrounded him; they are part of the conditions in which he produced his work. The overlapping networks around Ezra Pound, Sylvia Beach, Harriet Shaw Weaver, Eugene Jolas and other literary figures from the 1910s, 1920s and 1930s have already been well documented, so I will not dwell on them in this book. Of greater interest are the figures clustered together in the Irish Revival. As an Irish writer living abroad, Joyce was mostly out of reach and of touch from the Revival, albeit not for a lack of good intentions on the part of Lady Gregory and W.B. Yeats. He kept himself informed, however, through friends and family at home, as well as through his reading. He kept abreast with the Irish papers and read widely on Irish history, economy and literature. In that respect, Joyce produced his work against the grain of the Revival as an institution, although not, as I argue, as a cultural project.

This is why the second of my precepts – cultural memory – is important too. Cultural memory emerges from a resistance to traditional historiography as a grand narrative of the past. The idea rather that history is read from 'the vantage point' of the present and thus becomes 'a history not of origins but of becomings, transformations, both material and immaterial' (Jones 2014, 126). It is a form of history in which the lived experiences of the subject, rather than the reconstruction of past events by the professional historian, are foregrounded. History and cultural memory are not necessarily each another's opposite, however. In disputing a strict dichotomy, Astrid Erll (2011, 45) posits historiography as only '*one* mode of cultural remembering', which sits alongside other 'symbolic forms' of representing the past, like religion, myth and literature, which 'contribute to the production of cultural memory'. This is important for Joyce who uses accounts of the past to create 'felt history' (Fairhall 1993, 32). While he draws on the history books for the writing, the past is primarily represented through his characters' lived experiences, recollections and responses to that past.[5] As Gibson (2002) has argued about 'Wandering Rocks', the effects of colonialism are everywhere visible in Dublin social life, but the characters appear oblivious to, and at times complicit with, the structures of power that surround them. The chapter's microcosmos is one of disintegration and alienation that results in a sense of 'false community' and 'false consciousness' (2002, 94). Gibson's reading of the 'false community' helpfully frames my own understanding in Chapter 3 of Stephen who positions himself in opposition to the nationalist mainstream

---

[5] See Frawley (2014, 2) for whom Joyce's work is 'a repository of cultural memory'.

while remaining a nationalist in his own right (Fairhall 1993, 34). In his writings, Joyce is astutely aware that Irish nationalism has different shades and meanings and that the Irish cultural project always consisted of multiple factions. In a sense – and this is what underpins the 'false community' – what unites the Irish is their antipathy to the British.

Joyce's work is hence not exactly an exercise in nation-building (this is where he differs from Yeats, especially Yeats's work on the Irish theatre) but rather corresponds to Maurice Halbwachs' take on the workings of collective memory in the creation of cultural identity. Collective memory, first of all, is a form of lived memory to which individuals in a community contribute in a piecemeal manner. This living memory is dependent on the social milieu (*cadres sociaux*, in Halbwachs' terminology) to which the individual belongs and which guide the perceptions and memories of the individual.[6] What the group remembers, collects, archives and passes on into tradition from the bottom up is what the group deems important for its self-image. Memories become mutually supportive of one another as the group feels that, looking back at its own past, it has stayed the same over time and 'becomes conscious of its identity' (Halbwachs 1980, 44–9, 85; see also Erll 2011, 15, 17). Halbwachs' ideas, developed in the 1930s, were enormously influential on later theories on intersubjectivity in memory studies. He laid the foundation for explanations that pointed out how, through convergence and aggregation, collective memory fed into tradition and, ultimately, nation-building (Erll 2011, 58–60). The way the Irish imagined migration as exile, the subject of my second chapter, is a good illustration of this principle, but so is Bloom's definition that 'a nation is the same people living in the same place' (*U* 12.1422–3). Although Bloom's definition is disparaged as naive, it is actually quite perceptive, pointing as it does to the process by which a community forms and develops. This process is in line with Halbwachs' theory about the formation of collective memory. The collective memory, or imagined community, is never quite homogeneous or monolithic, however, but is always evolving because the social frameworks of memory are in essence relational. Individuals in a group occupy a position in relation to others in respect of, for instance, their professional activity, social standing and so on (Halbwachs 1992, 62–3), but they are also part of different groups and therefore different frameworks.

---

[6] These frameworks consist of 'thought patterns, cognitive schemata, that guide our perception and memory in particular directions' (Erll 2011, 15). Halbwachs (1992, 59) describes them in terms of 'collective notions that cannot be placed in a particular place or at a definitive moment'.

The point about Gibson's 'false community' therefore is that these communities in Joyce's works are completely ad hoc (the people Molly Ivors goes to the Aran Isles with, the group gathered in Mr Best's back room in the National Library, the singers in the Ormond Hotel, the barflies in Barney Kiernan's, the 'fellowships' of medicals [*U* 14.187] in Holles street hospital) and, presumably, transitory. Groups, according to Halbwachs, 'change and segment continually' (1980, 85). They momentarily share experiences and a joint sense of Irish history constructed from stock narratives about the past greatness, valiant resistance and future hope. Again, Bloom's contention about the nation as community is remarkably apt for its insistence on the permeable, shifting nature of the community; nationalists, however, cannot accept the realism in Bloom's definition because for them the nation must be permanent and transcendental. The idea of 'fellowship' also puts into relief Stephen's desire to belong, even if for the most part he remains, like Bloom, an outsider, ostracized from Gogarty's tower, uninvited to George Moore's soirée, and an aspirational poet who has abandoned his studies among medical students. The disillusion that critics note in *Ulysses*, however, not only stems from Stephen's premature return to Ireland (has he really failed to become an artist?) but from the realization that he cannot entirely go it alone in creating the conscience of his race.

These ideas about fluid communities also illuminate Joyce's relationship with the Irish Revival. Recent studies have complicated the view that Joyce was simply an antagonist of the Revival and that we cannot understand Joyce's attitude towards the Revival if we place him outside its influence, especially with respect to the aim and method of nation-building that Joyce shared with Yeats (Castle 2001; McCourt 2015a). Nevertheless, while we now better acknowledge Joyce's affinity with Yeats, it is worth placing this relationship in a broader context. As a cultural movement that came to prominence in the 1880s, the Revival was, after all, so much more than Yeats and his immediate circle; it constituted a broad church comprising different strands, ideas and opinions whose exponents more often than not disagreed with one another on the purpose, meaning and direction of the cultural revival they strove to bring about (Foster 1993, 28 *et passim*; see also Hutton 2006, 123–9). The group centred around the writers of the Irish Literary Theatre was just one of those strands. Alongside it, we find a multitude of writers, thinkers and activists occupying different positions on the political spectrum. Catholic conservatives like D.P. Moran despised both the Protestant nationalists and Irish writers who sought their fame abroad. Yet a figure like the Protestant and politically more moderate Douglas Hyde narrowly advocated that literature could only be truly national if it were written in Irish, while intellectual Catholics like Thomas Kettle, Padraic and Mary Colum and (in later years) Thomas McGreevy resisted cultural isolationism. Yeats and his circle, finally, are themselves a conduit for different intellectual strands that links Celtic mythology, peasant culture and theosophy, but that also has its origins in the nineteenth century: Arthur Griffith and the United Irishman, the Irish Literary Society, and the academic work of liberal historians like Justin McCarthy and William O'Connor Morris. The Revival was, in other words, far from a coherent movement with a single agenda, but something rather more heterogeneous within which are found a wide variety of voices and personalities, and multiple, often conflicting, definitions of Irishness.

Within this plurality Joyce finds his place. As an artist he never aligned himself with any particular faction. In that respect, the common view is that he created his own Revivalist project. This book, Chapters 5 and 6 especially, argues for a similar position. But while Joyce eschewed the more reactionary conservatism of the Revival and criticized Yeats and Lady Gregory for their obsession with peasant drama, he does reveal a strong affiliation with the Revival's key aim: 'the Irish nation's desire to create its own civilization' (*OCPW* 111). It is worth reminding ourselves that in terms of its cultural self-definition and political self-determination, the Revival was a 'modern' project that has many parallels across Europe. The language of nationhood is decidedly progressive and forges new ideas and concepts about the national self. Yeats's writings in particular not only reflect this modernity but also echo some of Joyce's stances. In his Nobel acceptance speech, for instance, Yeats (1999, 406) said of Ireland: 'I think as I speak these words of how deep down we have gone, below all that is individual, modern and restless, seeking foundations for an Ireland that can only come into existence in a Europe that is still but a dream.' That such notions of modernity within the Revival could easily encompass Joyce's wayward writing is, I believe, more than just a rhetorical gesture; it is validated by the fact that several of Joyce's contemporaries saw him as one Irish voice within this larger field. Joyce, furthermore, also had great regard for economic arguments within the nationalist movements: those who believed that a politically and culturally independent Ireland could not thrive without economic independence. The cooperative movement, whose objective was to transform Irish farming into a modern system capable of sustaining itself and the Irish people, was clearly in Joyce's purview (O'Dea 2017).

The argument of this book is that Joyce's position changed over time as he developed as a writer. I will trace the trajectory of the shift in Joyce's attitudes towards the Irish Revival in particular, submitting that he successively adapted a stance within, against and complementary to the movement. During his early years in Dublin, while writing much of the verse for *Chamber Music*, Joyce may not have exactly sought to align himself with the Revival, but neither did he avoid association. Although 'The Day of the Rabblement' is Joyce's most outspoken attack, the essay's contents and the circumstances in which it composed are sufficiently equivocal so as not to signify a simple, total rupture with the Revival, even if he distanced himself from the direction in which Yeats and Lady Gregory were taking the Irish Literary Theatre. Coinciding with his self-fashioning as an exile, *Dubliners* and especially *Exiles* signalled the beginning of a new conception of himself as author. A deeply ambivalent play, *Exiles* was for Joyce an exercise in imagining what it would be like to return to Dublin; but while that option is closed off at the end of the play, Joyce adopts a diasporic Irish identity that, ironically, was deeply embedded in the Irish psyche. In *A Portrait* and *Ulysses*, Joyce is most deeply concerned with Irish politics, yet in these works he is farthest removed from the Revival in terms of its mainstream ambition: the recovery of an Irish past and investigation of its 'sources' or 'origins' that can be said to be constitutive of nationhood. As an autobiographical novel, *A Portrait* is far too concerned with the artistic self to fall within that purview, while *Ulysses*, although it has a much broader canvas, primarily deals with the quotidian (which is also the reason why these works have a less prominent place in this text). In *Finnegans Wake*, finally, with its emphasis on Catholic, pan-Celtic and Scandinavian influences, Joyce creates an alternative take on the Revival's politics of origins.

This idea of constant remaking sits at the heart of *James Joyce and Cultural Genetics* whose purpose is to provide a revisionist literary-historical, genetic perspective on Joyce's understanding and representation of Irish cultural identity and how Irish history, culture and politics are situated within his work. Since the aim of this book, furthermore, is to study the development of Joyce as a writer in cultural rather than aesthetic terms, the 'modernist' shift in the styles and discursive practices of *A Portrait* and *Ulysses* are of less importance than the changes in attitude towards questions of identity and history. As these questions are ordinarily treated with far less awareness of Joyce's changing attitudes and responses, it is crucial to hone in on the early as well as late moments in Joyce's life and creative output. For that reason, I begin this book with a chapter on *Chamber Music*, which reinvestigates Joyce's early, mutually appreciative connections with W.B. Yeats while contextualizing Joyce's first book publication as a modern, Irish project.

Joyce's relationship with W.B. Yeats was far more amicable than Joyce's biographers have led us to believe. Their correspondence tells a story of mutual admiration. Joyce submitted samples of his early poetry to Yeats for criticism. Yeats, cautiously positive, encouraged the young poet to write more; later he was instrumental in getting *Chamber Music* published with Elkin Mathews. Joyce, in turn, held a lifelong admiration for Yeats's work, especially the early stories in *The Tables of the Law* and the poetry from *The Wind among the Reeds*. Critics have noted affinities between Yeats's early work and Joyce's lyrics (see, for example, Campbell 2012). However, the main influence lies in the area of Yeats's rhythmical theories. Yeats's experiments with 'speaking to the psaltery' with Arnold Dolmetsch was what gave Joyce the idea to order a lute from the London instrument maker (Schuchard 2008, 173).

Joyce's ambition with *Chamber Music* was to engender a renaissance of the sentimental lyric captured in a modern verse experiment with strikingly simplified rhythms. Joyce turned to the Elizabethan and Jacobean lyricists for his model. The echoes are obvious and have been frequently noted before (see, for example, Paterson 2012, 120–1). The reason why Joyce felt the sixteenth- and seventeenth-century song was relevant for the modern Irish context has not yet been properly addressed. These reasons are manifold and bring into convergence a number of seemingly unrelated strands of thought and affinities in Joyce. At the simplest level, the Elizabethan song represented a form of popular lyricism that was a natural extension of the traditional music repertoire that, throughout his life, he was fond of performing, including Irish traditionals like 'The Croppy Boy'. On a political level, the songs represented a linguistic origin, which, although they may embody the language of the colonizer, is nonetheless part and parcel of Irish identity. In *A Portrait*, Stephen famously celebrates the 'old phrases' of Dowland, Byrd and Nash, the 'language of memory' (*P* 233) whose importation contributed to the hybridization of the language. One of his early notebooks attests to his sustained interest in these topics. Alongside his well-known notes on Aristotle and Aquinas, he takes down numerous quotations from Ben Jonson (as well as one from Yeats); notes an interest in the work on Celtic ballads by William Allingham and Thomas Percy's *Reliques of Ancient English Poetry*; and looks into the differences between poetic and musical rhythms.

That *Chamber Music* was, therefore, to all intents and purposes a Revivalist book is evinced by the conditions that led to its publication. As with its genesis, its publication and early reception took place within an Irish sphere. A number of Irish writers, including Lionel Johnson, Synge and Yeats himself, had already found an outlet for the work with the English publisher Elkin Mathews. It was on

Yeats's instigation that Arthur Symons introduced Joyce to Mathews. Although Symons did not particularly recognize the Irish qualities of Joyce's poetry, he did remind Mathews of Joyce's background. Those qualities, however, were noted by the reviewers who unwittingly furnished a striking echo with Little Chandler's secret hopes in 'A Little Cloud' to become the author of some lyrics that the critics would praise for their *'Celtic note'* (D 74).

Like *Chamber Music*, *Exiles* is a problematic work in Joyce's canon in that it does not easily fit into the modernist view of Joyce. Nonetheless, it deals with a particularly modern subject in Irish history: emigration. Chapter 2 presents an important stage in the making of Joyce's identity as an Irish writer. It aims to reinterpret Joyce's play, and the construction of his exilic identity, against the backdrop of the Irish perception of emigration and how crucial the idea of the diaspora is to Irish identity politics. It will argue that Joyce's play is not simply a confirmation of Joyce's ultimate rejection of Ireland, but rather that, as a personal fantasy of what a return to Ireland might entail, Joyce's play explores the exilic identity and the paradoxes surrounding its construction in the early decades of the twentieth century. Following the trauma of the Famine and British colonialism, emigration had become normalized in the course of the nineteenth century to such an extent that to leave the country was to be truly Irish.

Publicly and privately, Joyce promulgated the image of himself as a self-exile, which culminated early on in his fictional alter ego's pursuit of 'silence, exile and cunning' (P 247). As an aesthetic stance, Stephen's exhortation is compelling, but some of its political implications have gone unnoticed. The *Exiles* chapter will, therefore, first demonstrate how Joyce's view of himself as an exile was constructed gradually before investigating to what extent his decision to live abroad might initially have been determined by economic concerns: owing to financial difficulties caused by his father's profligacy, his prospects for a career as a writer and journalist (and even as a medical professional) would have been considerably hampered. The reimagining of emigration as exile and the notion that leaving is a need, not an opportunity, are crucial components in the Irish response to emigration (see Miller 1985, 93) that find their parallel in Joyce's own exile. Next, this chapter will briefly survey Joyce's treatment of exile and emigration in his other writings, with particular focus on 'A Little Cloud' from *Dubliners* whose evocation of the return migrant, and the concomitant crisis of identity, form a prelude to the more extensive treatment of this theme in *Exiles*. The character of the return migrant, who has become an 'other' for the indigenous population to which he returns, offers an important key to analyse more fully and deeply how the politics of migration are present in *Exiles*.

On the one hand, the politics of migration forged the imagining of a 'spiritual home' (Foster 1993, 91). On the other, the sense of placelessness that plagues the emigrant is supplanted by the awareness that the Irish have always been wanderers, starting with the medieval saints and scholars who left to spread Christianity across the seas. At the heart of the play are the ironies and highly ambivalent values that exist within these competing cultural responses – values that Joyce sardonically captures in the phrase 'over the dark sea' (Buffalo III A-36; *JJA* 11:36) as a metaphor for exile in his notes.

Chapter 3 explores some genetic lines that link Joyce's epiphanies, *Stephen Hero* and *A Portrait of the Artist as Young Man*. It weaves together two main strands in Joyce's aesthetic that are rarely connected in the criticism. The first of these strands deals with the development of Joyce's aesthetic theories. The focus is not so much on the philosophical influences that famously underpin these theories – Aristotle and Aquinas – but Joyce's appreciation of the creative process itself as it is filtered through Stephen's growth. The argument centres on a poetics of notetaking that brings Joyce's lifelong practice of notetaking together with the writing of epiphanies. As a genre rooted in observation and revelation, the epiphanies are akin to the creative potential provided by Joyce's notes and for which the 'Early Commonplace Book' provides illuminating evidence. With this in mind, I propose a genetic reinterpretation and reorientation of the epiphany theory in *Stephen Hero* that helps us understand better the genealogical connections between that theory and Stephen's aesthetic theories in *A Portrait*. These connections, at the same time, also reveal a genetic poetics within Joyce's art: he perceived creation as organic. The corollary of this postulate is Joyce's interest in origins which, in the early work, manifests itself in the elemental exploration of Irish nationalism and identity through the character of Stephen. What it means to be Irish is a question that Joyce develops, to a large extent, through Stephen's negative reaction to the mainstream nationalist movements. But in feigning to be apolitical, Joyce adeptly confronts the difficulty of what it means to be Irish without being nationalist (*SH* 54). Consequently, Stephen's rejection of nationalist politics necessitates a close analysis of cultural identity. Stephen is obsessed with etymology and voice and how the speech of people defines them as cultural beings. His author does as well, as the 'Alphabetical Notebook' bears witness. The second strand of the chapter comprises an analysis of Joyce's Irish notes in that notebook. Many of the materials in this notebook offer the raw materials for Stephen's anatomy of Irish culture. Heavily biographical in nature, it was compiled with a view to rewriting *Stephen Hero* as *A Portrait*. In this the poetics of notetaking is not far from the surface. The notes are there to turn observation into art. Specifically, they are a catalyst to realize both the stylistic condensation of the autobiographical narrative and the representation of Stephen's cultural politics.

Chapter 4 on *Ulysses*, which Joyce may have initially planned as a sequel to *A Portrait* plotting Stephen's return from Paris (Rose and O'Hanlon 1993, xv–xviii), continues along these lines. Perhaps it is a critical commonplace to think that *Ulysses* is the realization of Stephen's ambition in *A Portrait* 'to forge ... the uncreated conscience of my race' (*P* 253)? Whatever the answer, the portent of *Ulysses* is a reconciling of the past with the present, a process that had started in *A Portrait* (and its earlier version, *Stephen Hero*), but in more public manner. On the whole, the cultural politics of *Ulysses* call more explicitly on the postulates of cultural memory in the way that its characters experience and react to the past that has shaped them (see Frawley 2014, 1–2). Following the disillusion of his Parisian exile, Stephen knows he cannot simply fly by the nets of language, nation and religion; he realizes instead that to forge the uncreated conscience somehow involves a direct confrontation with the memory of Ireland's troublesome, and traumatic, colonial past. He is ready to engage in that process, but recognizes the paradoxes and pitfalls. The famous phrase, 'History is a nightmare from which I am trying to awake', is not about escape; it has an important, but often overlooked, afterthought: 'What if that nightmare gave you a back kick' (*U* 2.377–9). Leaving history behind, for the Irish, will come at a cost. Where Stephen's view is limited to contemplating the psychological enormity of this insight, Joyce the writer creates in *Ulysses* a work of epic proportions that reaches far beyond psychohistory into an archaeological exploration of Ireland's past. A core part of this chapter is again the thick description of an important document: the 'Subject Notebook'. On the one hand, this notebook contains extensive notes on theosophy and German philosopher Otto Weininger (1880–1903). Both significantly influence the development of Stephen's thinking (although Weininger not exclusively) and illuminate the heterodoxy with which he approaches the challenge he faces; they are the means by which he probes the end of history. At the same time, Joyce's interest in theosophy creates a surprising affiliation with the Irish Revival. On the other hand, the 'Subject Notebook' contains important evidence of Joyce's investigations in and views on Irish history and culture. A detailed examination of these creative onsets provides a richer appreciation of Joyce's historical concerns. It will reveal Joyce's fascination with the messiness of the Irish past. Ultimately, within the flotsam and jetsam of historical facts and narratives, and in the way they find their way into *Ulysses*, lie the contradictions and mixed allegiances of culture, identity and nationhood.

Despite its intensely Irish theme, *Ulysses* is rarely seen as a work in the tradition of the Irish Revival. Still, even though he never finished it, Yeats was impressed by what he had read and recognized 'the immense importance of the book' to the development of Irish literature in that it had 'our Irish cruelty' as well as 'our kind of strength' (Yeats 2002, #4152 and #4085). *Finnegans Wake*, by comparison, is probably Joyce's most explicit Revivalist work in its concern with roots and rootedness. Chapter 5, Sketching Histories, the first of two chapters on the *Wake*, will treat in detail the book's own origins and its preoccupation with an Irish past. The early fragments and sketches that Joyce produced in 1923, first of all, and the reading and notetaking that he undertook, reveal a deliberate intent to construct an alternative version of Revival narratives. For Joyce, the roots of Irish history and culture are not just rural and racially Celtic; they are, on the one hand, decidedly Catholic, and on the other, culturally diverse and (of course) urban. As the earliest iterations of *Wake*, the sketches adumbrate Ireland's cultural foundations: the myths and legends of the Irish saints and the Celtic fringe. Their subject matter spawned extensive reading on Joyce's part in hagiographical lore, Irish monastic traditions, Irish history and the Tristan and Isolde legend.

The first in the series is 'Roderick O'Connor', a narrative about the last High King of Ireland, which was followed by vignettes about Saint Kevin, Tristan and Isolde, Mamalujo (aka the 'Four Masters', the chroniclers of Irish medieval history), Saint Dympna and Saint Patrick. The suite is closed off with a final sketch, 'Here Comes Everybody', about a pseudohistorical Irish vassal of minor stature within the colonial nation, Humphrey Chimpden Earwicker. As discrete pieces, the sketches are not structurally or thematically related. However, they share some common features and characteristics, the most obvious of which is the hagiographical subject matter, but also their inherently hybridized view of history. The sketches show a marked reverence for a time gone by, but because of the grotesque nature of their intent, they are not purely enraptured in nostalgia, nor do they represent a simple yearning for a lost past. In any case, the past time is almost completely imaginary. None of the events in the sketches is strictly historical; they are narrative reimaginings of the past whose characters are reinvented wholly or in part in the present, *sub specie temporis nostri*. The sketches thus creatively exploit history to effect a displaced past.

The second *Wake* chapter will delve deeper into *Finnegans Wake*'s view about the retelling of the past as the invention of history.[7] Chapter 6 hinges

---

[7] An earlier treatment of history as invention in *Finnegans Wake* is found in Hofheinz (1995).

on another take on cultural genetics that is at the heart of the *Wake*: its preoccupation with origins and genealogical connections, how things came to pass as they did. In their attempt to bring 'the dear prehistoric scenes all back again' (*FW-R* 298.40–299.1; *FW* 385.19), the *Wake*'s narratives reveal 'morphological circumformation' (*FW-R* 468.2; *FW* 599.16–17) of history: how history itself came into being. This type of metahistoriography derives in no small way from Giambattista Vico's genetic view of history in *New Science*; Vico grounded his exposition of the principles of historical change in an investigation of specific historical practices. Chapter 6, therefore, starts with a consideration of the *Wake*'s paradoxical multiverse: the tension between its universal logic and its drowning in particulars (Fordham 2007, 35); between its ambition to be the history of all times and places and its desire for revelation. Because the *Wake*'s genesis coincided with the creation of the Irish Free State, one of the big questions that has preoccupied the *Wake*'s historicist critics is whether the book contains a vision of a new Ireland that emerges from Joyce's disappointment over the nation's failure in partition and the triumph of Catholic conservatism. The dislocation of time and place and the dislocation of language militate against a unifying principle at any level; the *Wake* thus stops short of serving up a clear vision. Nonetheless, Joyce's final work betrays at least a strong desire for cohesion. What drives the narratives is the desire of the 'actors' in the book to establish the truth (Fairhall 1993, 221). In terms of its scope, therefore, Chapter 6 combines Joyce's 'genealogical' composition method – his foraging of reading materials recorded in his notebooks – with that of the *Wake*'s characters and narrators who, sometimes quite literally, root through history. The *Wakean* morphology, composed of a surfeit of ultra-specific historical and cultural material, the flotsam and jetsam of historical and cultural production, is not only Joyce's upside-down, grassroots answer to the Irish Revival; it also counteracts the generalizations of universal history. The end of history, as Stephen knows, is impossible; one is always *in* history.

This rooting through history connects with the book's evocation of time and place (or space). As every reader knows, time and space are essential symbols in *Finnegans Wake*. It is of interest therefore to explore the specifically historiographical ramifications. For that reason, it is relevant to take a close look at the *Wakean* year 1132, which is simultaneously specific and outside time. Joyce's uses the specificity of historical annals, a minor motif in the *Wake*, to contrast it with an idealized moment, a time before the fall, before the nightmare of history began. The *Wake*'s concern with origins matches here some of the Revival's historiographical and ethnographic practices (see Castle

2001). Not only do its narratives obsessively trace the genealogical histories of people, places, institutions and customs, the idea of temporal change, historical eras coming to an end and new periods beginning, are an essential component. Obviously one thinks here of Vico's cycles. But the significance works more deeply as well at a political and cultural level. From the Anglo-Norman invasion to the Irish Civil War, epochal changes have marked Irish history; concomitant with these changes, and a core aspect of much mainstream Revival writing, is a yearning back to the time before the nightmare of history. The 'Roderick O'Connor' sketch, as I argue in Chapter 5, deals precisely with this narrative of epochal change. But Joyce returns to it throughout the *Wake*. This is why the figure of Saint Patrick, for instance, who heralded the end of pagan Ireland, is so important to him.

The cast of historical characters, which Joyce invented in the early sketches, continues to play their part as emblems of Irishness. The chapter will return to Roderick O'Connor, Saints Kevin and Patrick, Tristan and Isolde, and Mamalujo to set out their place in the book's historical constellation. Enveloping the early sketches into 'Work in Progress' was not merely a structural decision; before they found their place in the text, they had profoundly affected the direction of the work in terms of its creative economy. Unless one accepts the Finn's Hotel theory that they were discrete stories, the early sketches served as the basis for Joyce's 'historical method' in which he used the past as a trellis. The purview of the *Wake* is the past; its disposition nostalgia: 'Bringing the dear prehistoric scenes all back again' (*FW-R* 398.40–299.1; *FW* 385.18–19). The return of the historical cast of characters from the early sketches is the conduit through which Joyce creates this vision, not least Mamalujo. If in 'repeating' (*FW-R* 298.08; *FW* 384.16) the stories of history lies the key to 'not forgetting' (*FW-R* 301.10; *FW* 388.10), *Finnegans Wake* epitomizes the workings of cultural memory.

In the formation of the social frameworks that determine the collective notion of national identity, space and place play a crucial role. *Finnegans Wake* again probes these precepts. The analysis of places through maps, one of Mamalujo's tools, is a way of coming to terms with the history that made them. Conversely, the *Wake* also performs this making in a manner that is similar to the Irish tradition of 'dinnseanchas', the poetry of the naming of places. With great regularity, the book indulges in naming places with feigned exactitude. However, rarely noted in previous criticism, it is again the pervading sense of nostalgia that marks the *Wake*'s treatment of place. In its desire for a past unspoilt by history, the book is preoccupied with the Irish landscape. The preoccupation comes to the fore, among others, in its evocations of a decidedly premodern Dublin. The pastoral environs of Chapelizod, epitomized by Joyce's use of Sheridan Le Fanu's *The House by the Churchyard*, deserves especial attention in this respect as a place frozen in time. The novel's eighteenth-century setting serves as a reminder of an *idyllicized* phase of Irish history during the Parliament of Burke and Grattan. Its correlative is another landscape feature and a point of contention of Ireland's colonial past: the disappearance of its ancient woodlands lamented by the citizen. In a remarkable restorative act, the *Wake* undertakes the reforestation of Ireland by spreading the names of indigenous trees across the narrative.

In the end, the *Wake*'s deliberate formation of things quaint and antiquated connects this book (admittedly in a very surprising and circumlocutory manner) with the earlier work all the way back to *Chamber Music* and that volume's ambition to make something new by wilfully embracing the old. The 'language of memory' (*P* 233) features all over again as well, albeit that the efforts of remembering frequently vanish into nothing, personified by the Four Old Men trying to 'remembore' (*FW-R* 303.14; *FW* 384.35) the past. History may be boring, but it is also an action that requires effort, like boring through a mountain from both sides. The strenuous, frustrated probing (*FW-R* 369.32; *FW* 476.12) that Mamalujo undertake in Chapter III.3 appropriately stands for the Joycean oeuvre as a whole. Joyce never ceased to probe the past – his own and that of his country.

James Joyce and Cultural Genetics is thus as much concerned with Joyce's understanding of himself as a writer, how it involved and impacted his work, as it is with the evolution of his writing. As such, this book triangulates writer, work and the cultural conditions that created both in what is a substantial extension of traditional forms of genetic criticism. The biological metaphor that I have chosen is a suitable rubric for the investigations that follow. As a code, the genome is a set of DNA instructions that is contained with each living cell; it provides the information that an organism needs to develop and function. Brought to bear on a work of literature, the genome is not the key to unlock its secrets, but a way of bringing to the fore how the work was created and how its critical functions as an aesthetic and hermeneutic object developed. The genetic viewpoint provides the method; the archive – consisting of Joyce's books, his notes and drafts, and the letters – forms the material or archaeological basis for the analysis; the framework for that analysis is cultural memory. What holds the arguments together, however, is Joyce's own interest in how things came to pass. His preoccupation with points of origin and moments of transformation, with evolution and genealogical links change, ultimately points to what one might call his 'genetic' art.

1

The Celtic note: *Chamber Music*

Chamber Music is often relegated to the margins of Joyce's canon. The reason is obvious. The book is the work of a young poet whose simple, naive, direct expression appears anomalous when compared to the sophistication of the later 'modernist' prose. *Chamber Music* has its own integrity and aesthetic aims, however, and it is worth considering how the volume fits with the evolution of Joyce as a writer. Its genesis as well as the context against which it appeared can do much to help us reach a better understanding of the intrinsic and historical meaning of Joyce's earliest writing. My main purpose here is to take it out of the context of High Modernism, which it preceded by a good number of years, and insert it more properly in the time the poetry came into being – written between 1902 and 1906 and published in 1907 – and the places that had an impact on its production: Dublin and London. This aim immediately invites a consideration of the knotty question of influence, which is frequently considered but never satisfactorily answered. *Chamber Music* is full of echoes and allusions, but on closer inspection none of the echoes is very specific or tangible – not even those of the early Yeats.

The figure of Yeats nonetheless looms large in the production of *Chamber Music*, not only in the personal relationship between the younger man and the older poet but also in the aesthetic affinities between them. Some disentangling of facts is necessary. Joyce's biographers (not least Richard Ellmann) and critics have consistently depicted Joyce and Yeats as antinomies. I want to show, however, that this was not the case. In temperament and religious heritage, they were different, and no doubt also in politics and aesthetics, but in their views on the artist's role in reinvigorating the cultural life of the nation one can find a fair deal of agreement. Like Yeats, Joyce believed that art should not be subservient to politics. The difference between the two writers, however, was that Joyce's position was absolute, while Yeats was more supple in bringing art and politics together in a way that would best support the cultural project that became known as the 'Irish Revival'. Before his departure, Joyce was a willing participant in the movement's activities. Even after 1904, his interest in the Revival did not quite cease (his letters to his brother Stanislaus provide a running commentary on Revival activity), even though he began framing an alternative view of Irish cultural identity in essays like 'Ireland: Island of Saints and Sages' and 'Ireland at the Bar'. These alternative views of Irish nationalism were developed in *Ulysses* and culminated in *Finnegans Wake*, his most Irish book of all. But it is in *Chamber Music*, and in some of the ancillary materials that Joyce was gathering in an unpublished notebook around the time of its composition, that the origins of these views can be found. That notebook, the 'Early Commonplace Book' (NLI 36,639/2/A), will prove an important document in instigating a reassessment of the beginnings of Joyce's career as a writer. It is from this notebook that Herbert Gorman in the 1930s transcribed Joyce's famous quotations from Aristotle and Aquinas for his biography (1949, 135–8).[1] It also holds vital clues to Joyce's wider influences that are relevant for comprehending the making of *Chamber Music*, specifically its connection with Yeats's theories about speaking to the psaltery.

Chamber Music is probably the least 'Irish' work in the Joycean canon. But did Joyce see it that way too? What this chapter sets out to achieve is to look at the collection's production as well as its early reception in order to place *Chamber Music* within the development of Joyce's aesthetics and politics and to bring out how the volume was construed as decidedly, if not distinctly, 'Irish'. The publication history of *Chamber Music* and a number of early reviews certainly placed the volume in an Irish context. The argument, however, requires some careful revision of received opinion by looking at the historical and textual evidence in a new light. This revision, first of all, concerns Joyce's most vociferous statements about the Revival in 'The Day of the Rabblement' (1901), in which he castigated W.B. Yeats and Lady Gregory for their pandering to the philistines, and 'The Holy Office' (1904), where he resolutely turned his back on 'gold-embroidered Celtic fringes' (*PSW* 97). The critical paradigm of Joyce modernizing himself against the grain of a stunted Irish tradition is, as I will show, simply too neat. Second, the revision requires a consideration of the 'Irish Revival' not as an institution, but as broad group of artists and intellectuals whose ideas, ambitions and motivations diverge as much as they converge. Joyce's critics have tended to polarize Joyce's relationship with the Revival and with Yeats in particular. I contend that that relationship is richer

---

[1] Before its rediscovery, the notebook was known as the 'Paris-Pola Notebook' (Scholes and Kain 1965, 52–5, 80–91).

and more complex. In redressing this issue, this chapter delves into the making of *Chamber Music* and the circumstances that led to its publication and early reception. While Joyce as a man of a younger generation may have been on the fringes of the movement that Yeats and Gregory were seeking to build, he was not a total outsider either; rather, for a time at least, he was inclined to go along with them, the proud, scornful ending of 'The Holy Office' notwithstanding.[2]

Influences

A cursory review of *Chamber Music* criticism yields a substantial list of influences, echoes and allusions as to both period and persons: The Song of Solomon, Dante, Boccaccio, the Troubadours, the Elizabethans, the Jacobeans, Shakespeare, Ben Jonson, John Dowland, John Wilmot, Robert Herrick, Richard Lovelace, Francis Thompson, George Herbert, Henry Vaughan, the Romantics, Byron, Shelley, Blake, Thomas Moore, James Clarence Mangan, the symbolists, Verlaine, D.G. Rossetti, Tennyson, Matthew Arnold, Arthur Symons, Ernest Dowson, the Irish folk song, the Irish Revival, George Russell and W.B. Yeats. The sheer range of identifications makes clear that intertextuality in *Chamber Music* is a strange phenomenon indeed. Or are they not actually influences? Influence is, of course, notoriously difficult to measure. In the case of *Chamber Music*, the problem is exacerbated by the fact that its language makes frequent use of commonplaces. The phrase 'unquiet heart' with which poem XXIV ends (*PSW* 46), for instance, can be found in Shelley, Tennyson, Arnold and Yeats, as well as in a spate of minor poets like George Buchanan and Margaret Courtney. Less obvious examples are the present participle in 'All day I hear the noise of waters | Making moan' (*PSW* 46), which can be found in Chaucer's *The Knight's Tale* and *Troilus and Criseyde*, as well as in 'The Face against the Pane' by the nineteenth-century American poet T.B. Aldrich, a poem frequently included in popular anthologies and elocution guides. The screeching seabirds, moreover, echo Joyce's line 'Sad as the sea-bird is' from the same poem (*PSW* 46). None of these echoes is actually to be taken as influence. The point rather is that Joyce's phraseology and imagery are so generic that they do not belong to the vocabulary of any individual poet, but to a stock repertory of poetic diction.

---

[2] In later life, Joyce did avoid public association with the Revival. In August 1922, he asked Lady Gregory if she would kindly not include him in her forthcoming book on the Irish literary movement (*SL* 290).

Where many early commentators on *Chamber Music* seemed intent on noting influence, Ezra Pound bucked that trend and put Joyce's poetry in a category all its own: 'The wording is Elizabethan, the metres at times suggesting Herrick, but in no case have I been able to find a poem which is not in some way Joyce's own, even though he would seem, and that most markedly, to shun apparent originality' (Pound, quoted in Deming 2007, I, 168). Pound, clearly on the defensive here, was carving out a niche that in 1918 was also a belated justification for his inclusion of Joyce's verse, noteworthy for its 'profoundly emotional' quality and 'strength and fibrousness of sound', in *Des Imagistes* (1914) (quoted in Deming 2007, I, 168–9).³ Pound's disclaimer that Joyce was apparently shunning originality was not an attempt to obfuscate plagiarism; rather it says something about Joyce's diction. The issue is not that the verse is too coloured, but that, as one reviewer put it, it is 'colorless' (A.C.H. 1919, 100):

> In a single poem one sometimes finds several distinct threads of reminiscence which one may not be able to trace all at once, an occurrence which proves disturbing as failure to remember a name or a word. Of course for some people this does not detract from a poem – it seems rather to add a certain classic flavor to it; but unless this tendency is offset by something very positive of the author's own, it is, I think, likely to prove annoying.
>
> (A.C.H. 1919, 99)

The reaction is not unlike the discomfort of some readers regarding Joyce's use of pastiche in his later writings. Randy Malamud (1999, 96) carefully sums up the situation, however, when he states that 'the poetry presents copious (and fairly obvious) appropriations of traditions: conventionally recycled images of the most common symbol in the most common kind of poetry'.

Furthermore, there is another aspect that adds to the sense of tradition, but detracts from the notion that Joyce is vaguely appropriating poetic styles: the language in *Chamber Music* has a certain archaic quality, which, although sounding somewhat artificial, looks forward to the way Stephen thinks about the English tradition in *Stephen Hero* and *A Portrait*. While for the most part the poems are cast in simple language, there is a noticeable sprinkling of polysyllabic words that appear to be of Elizabethan origin. Words like 'disconsolate' (*PSW* 16), 'visitant' (*PSW* 16), 'welladay' (*PSW* 21) and 'plenilune' (*PSW* 24) have their first cited occurrence between the fifteenth and seventeenth century, according

---

³ Pound made the comment in 'Joyce', an essay published in *The Future* (May 1918) on the appearance of the American edition of *A Portrait of the Artist as Young Man*.

to the *OED*, and are found in the works of Edmund Spenser, Ben Jonson and their contemporaries; words like 'unzone' (*PSW* 23), 'enaisled' (*PSW* 32) 'unconsortable' (*PSW* 33), 'conjurable' (*PSW* 38) and 'raimented' (*PSW* 41) are all new derivations with an antiquarian ring to them. The language of the poems, therefore, is modulated towards a classical period in English literature.

This importation of an Elizabethan tone is no coincidence. Towards the middle of his life, Joyce confessed his discomfort with the English language: 'I cannot express myself in English without enclosing myself in a tradition' (Zweig 1964, 275). Enclosing himself in the English tradition was troublesome for him as an Irishman. The scene in *A Portrait* in which Stephen discusses the word 'tundish' with the dean of studies and the priest (*P* 188–9) and thinks about the phonological differences in the words '*home, Christ, ale, master*' as he pronounces them rather shows that the Irish have made the language of the colonizer their own and gave it their own distinct idiom. English is therefore not – or not just – a symbol of cultural dispossession effected under colonial rule. The argument about this linguistic appropriation has been made before, but it is relevant for the way Joyce, and his fictional counterpart, boldly turned to Elizabethan models.[4] To an extent, the hegemony of the English tradition was simply inevitable for Joyce, as it was for many of his contemporaries across the nationalist spectrum (Foster 1993, 305).[5] But he uses the Elizabethan model, not unlike Yeats, to turn against Irish-Ireland nativism. In an early essay from 1898 on Irish folk beliefs, Yeats characterizes the west of Ireland speech as 'the partly Elizabethan speech of Galway' (Yeats 2010, 234), whose divergence from 'standard' English preserves the inflections of English as it was first spoken in Ireland. For Joyce, this language is not just other and archaic; he recognizes it, despite being a cause of colonial disaffection, as an origin of Irish cultural identity. For Joyce's verse, the Elizabethan model became a tool to do things differently. The poetic conventions that he abstracted from it enabled him to manufacture a new, highly stylized form that goes counter to the popular Irish lyrical verse of the time.

In particular, *Chamber Music*'s polysyllabic words create an unusual cadence. Through alternating monosyllabic and polysyllabic words, Joyce generates a halting rhythm that mostly avoids the patterns of regular metre. As such, the verse stands out as special. On occasion, Joyce's lines stay close to a more conventional

---

[4] Linguistic appropriation, or 'contamination', is crucial, for instance, in Andrew Gibson's reading of 'Oxen of the Sun' (2002, 180–2).
[5] The altercation over whether Byron or Tennyson is the better poet in *A Portrait* indicates not only how present the English tradition was but also how it was part of the Catholic middle-class's cultural aspirations.

rhythm, as in 'I would in that sweet bosom be' (VI). Even though the strong, masculine rhymes can hardly be missed – they emphasize the lover's insistence, his almost frantic, anxious pleading for his love to be requited – the metre is on the whole in iambic tetrameter, as in Robert Herrick's 'A Meditation of his Mistress': 'You are a tulip seen to day, | But (Dearest) of so short a stay' (Herrick 1906, 78). Apart from metrical similarity, as Pound correctly noted, Herrick's poem also uses mostly masculine endings, and shares the phrase 'rude wind' with Joyce's poem. Joyce's metres, however, are more varied than his Elizabethan models. The way he plays with word length, he also plays with alternating line lengths and greatly varies the number of stresses in a line – sometimes two, sometimes four – making them more remarkable, playful and modern.

Where critics have seen similarities with Yeats's rhythms (see, for example, Hogan 1995, 53), it is not always clear whether they were primarily guided by rhythm, poetic diction, imagery or the general mood of the poem. Still, it is possible to detect points of contact. Probably the most widely accepted instance of a Yeatsian resonance can be heard in 'I hear an army charging', which contains obvious echoes in rhythm and imagery from 'Michael Robartes Bids his Beloved be at Peace', as well as some close verbal collocations between 'And the thunder of horses plunging, foam about their knees' (*PSW* 48) and 'The Horses of Disaster plunge in the heavy clay' (Yeats 1989a, 96). The two poems also culminate in an apostrophe – of the poet to the beloved and her eyes and heart in Yeats's poem, and of the poet to his own heart in Joyce's.[6] Thematically, the poems are also alike. Both depart from an auditory vision that vexes the speaker in his sleep, whose restlessness, if not downright despair, is caused by his desire for the absent lover.

Although striking, such correlations are not particularly meaningful or indicative of a close affinity. On closer inspection, the two poems are radically different in their symbolism and formal constitution. The metaphorical agony of Joyce's speaker – his anguish 'clanging upon the heart as upon an anvil' (*PSW* 48) – is caused by the heartache over his lost love. The trope derives from courtly love poetry, whereas the 'tumult' in Yeats's poem is at once more apocalyptic and symbolic (Yeats 1989a, 96). Tormented by restless love, Robartes attempts to ward off the horses ('Shadowy Horses', 'Horses of Disaster') by retreating into a mystical embrace with the lover.[7] Prosodically, too, the poems are very different,

---

[6] 'Michael Robartes Bids his Beloved be at Peace' is the original as Joyce encountered it in *The Wind among the Reeds* (1899). Yeats later removed Robartes' name and changed it to 'He'.

[7] The horses are either the horse-shaped Pucas, Fomorian divinities who transformed into mischievous spirits, or the horses of Mananaan MacLir, the sea god who reigned over the afterlife (see notes in Yeats 1989a, 514).

as is the rhyme scheme. Yeats's iambic hexameter with regular ABBA rhymes contrasts with Joyce's alternating five- and seven-foot half-rhymed lines.

I do not simply want to conclude from this that Joyce had no affinity with Yeats's poetry, for he clearly had, but it does not fall within the category of influence. That affinity lies elsewhere. It exists in Joyce's remarkable fascination with the confluences that Yeats forged between folklore and magic in his early poetry and prose. At various stages in his life, Joyce expressed admiration for Yeats's writing and he was able to recite from memory many of the poems from the early period, such as 'Down by the Salley Gardens', and some of the songs from *The Countess Kathleen* (1899), 'Impetuous Heart' and 'Who Goes with Fergus'. He also admired *The Celtic Twilight* (1893) and *The Tables of the Law and the Adoration of the Magi* (1897), calling the former his 'happiest book' in his review of Lady Gregory's *Poets and Dreamers* (1903), in which Yeats retold 'with such delicate scepticism' the same folk legends that Gregory had treated with such depressing 'senility' and lack of 'imaginative wholeness' (*OPCW* 74–5). One may wonder if it was the heterodox mysticism of the stories, which was met with disapproval by the Church and, consequently, the Irish reviewers, that attracted Joyce (see Yeats 1994, 71). Certainly, it is the directness of Yeats's prose and the simplicity of his lyrics – and the fact that they are songs – that explain Joyce's attraction. The simplicity of expression and depth of feeling is the element that brings together his penchant for the Elizabethan lyric and the Yeatsian 'song'. Without being imitative, *Chamber Music* seeks a new form for precisely the lyric genre of the song that retains that ambivalent status as poetry and lyric to be sung. That intention explains their 'slightness' and why Joyce wanted the poems to be set to music by 'someone that knows old English music such as I like' (*Letters* II, 219). As songs, however, the poems are not composed with any pre-existent melody in mind (Paterson 2012, 128). As such, they are poetry rather than song. Yet it will become clear to what extent their melodic structure is influenced by Yeats's notion of speaking to the psaltery.

Encounters

Before I deal with Joyce's interest in Yeats's theory of verse speaking, it is necessary first to reassess the relationship between the two writers and redress the widespread misconception that Joyce and Yeats are simply polar opposites. The differences in background and, to some degree, artistic aims are clear. That Yeats belonged to the Anglo-Irish Protestant Ascendancy, and thus possessed a different worldview, was a fact not lost on the Catholic Joyce. But his antipathy to Yeats's work and ideas has sometimes been exaggerated, as has been his alleged rejection of the Irish Revival, which leaves room, too, for revision.

According to Joyce's first biographer, Joyce always 'belonged completely to himself' (Gorman 1949, 281) and did not align himself with any factions or coteries. This image of the proud individualist was further propagated by Richard Ellmann who highlighted Joyce's egotism and staunch resistance to orthodoxy. The brand of criticism that resulted from it, celebrating Joyce as an urban – and urbane – author who looked towards the Continental literary traditions, concluded that Joyce had rejected all forms of narrow-minded conservativism. This included the Revival's devotion 'to an essential national identity', which he superseded with 'exile, alienation and dislocation'; instead, he forced an artistic disengagement from his nationalist contemporaries and fabricated a modern, enlightened nationalism (Nolan 1995, 23–4). Yeats, in this same logic, was cast as a poet who feared modernity and whose legacy of Irish cultural nationalism was 'constrictive' (Nolan 1995, 16; see Platt 1998, 10–13). The assessment that Joyce freed himself from parochialism and resisted the cultural binaries in which Yeats and the Revival were trapped seems critically attractive, but is not fully supported by events, nor by Joyce's early Irish reception. Although Joyce was at times outspokenly critical of the Revival, his opposition was ambivalent at best, while his personal relationship with Yeats remained far from unfriendly.

It is perhaps an obvious point to make, but the Revival was not – or not just – reactionary and inward-looking. As Len Platt (1998, 7) points out, Irish nationalism and Revivalism are two different things. It is incorrect to lump together the Literary Revival, the Gaelic League and the Irish cooperative movement as all being ideologically one and the same. No doubt the Revival was implicated in some of the more extreme forms of ethnic nationalism propagated by, among others, D.P. Moran and Daniel Corkery. At the same time, among its many voices was also a modern, cosmopolitan outlook that did not eschew European culture. Few were more explicit about this than Thomas Kettle (1910, viii), who wrote:

> If this generation has, for its task, the recovery of the old Ireland, it has, for its second, the discovery of the new Europe. Irelands await her Goethe – but in Ireland he must not be a pagan – who will one day arise to teach her that while a strong people has its own self for centre, it has the universe for circumference.

Kettle was not alone in his entreaty. Yeats too looked beyond Ireland to complement the development of a new, indigenous art; Yeats, too, had '"that northern phantom" Dr. Ibsen' in his purview (Yeats 2010, 437). Even *The Irish Homestead*, in advocating its brand of rural modernity, explained to its readers that a political economy of self-sufficiency did not necessarily stand for ideological insularity (O'Dea 2017, 497). On the whole, Dublin was, in John Eglinton's words, 'a centre of vigorous potentialities' (Scholes and Kain 1965, 198).

Joyce's voice was among these. While he spoke out against Ireland's insularity and parochialism, the Church's grip on cultural life, and the Revival's obsession with primitivism and peasantry, he did not stand apart from the broader aspirations of cultural nationalism that he shared with the Revival movement. Joyce's non-fiction writings, Kevin Barry (2000, xxviii) rightly observes, did not originate in an intellectual and critical vacuum, but meld with the lively contemporary debates about Irish national culture.[8] In particular, Joyce's ideas about nationalism had much in common with organs such as *Bealtaine*, edited by Yeats, and *Dana: An Irish Magazine of Independent Thought*, founded by John Eglinton and Fred Ryan, to which Joyce submitted his prose sketch 'A Portrait of the Artist'. Barry suggests that Joyce would not, in fact, have submitted it to *Dana* if he had not thought the magazine a suitable outlet.[9] The magazine was openly antagonistic to the idea of 'sentimental unity in Irish life' because it stunted the opinion of the individual; instead, it wanted to 'achieve through the sincere confessions of poets and the strenuous operation of thought the elemental freedom of the human mind' (Eglinton and Ryan 1904, 2). Eglinton's appearance in 'Cyclops' as 'Magee Mor Matthew' dressed in Celtic garb (*U* 9.817–23) is highly ironic in the light of his defence of a liberal, culturally diverse Irish nationalism; most likely this depiction was inspired by Joycean revenge for rejecting 'A Portrait of the Artist'. Eglinton allegedly turned down Joyce's sketch because it was 'incomprehensible' (Scholes and Kain 1965, 200). But this is surprising, given Eglinton's insistence on individualism and thought, two conditions that chime with Joyce's piece: 'the notion that in Ireland, a writer is to think, first and foremost, of interpreting the nationality of his country and not simply of the burden he has to deliver. The expression of nationality, literature cannot fail to be; and the richer, more varied and unexpected that expression the better' (Eglinton 1906, 43). A copy of *Bards and Saints*, in which Eglinton put forth this defence of intellectuality and the individual, was in Joyce's Trieste library. As an advocate of religious unity, Eglinton had perhaps misunderstood, read too hastily, the tone of Christian mysticism that colours Joyce's evocation of the

---

[8] What is more, the sources from which he obtained his information are still recognizable (Barry 2000, xxi).
[9] On Joyce's possible affinities with Eglinton and *Dana*, see also Scott (1975).

awakening of the artistic soul.[10] The reason was certainly not that the essay was too avant-garde for *Dana*'s readership.[11] The magazine did later accept one of Joyce's poems – 'My love is in a light attire' – which appeared in August 1904 under the title 'Song'.

Joyce's critical writing is also generally less directly damning of the Revival than is often thought. Joyce's review of Lady Gregory's 1903 *Poets and Dreamers* for the *Daily Express* is a frank condemnation of the book's treatment of Irish folklore. Joyce particularly objected to the fact that Lady Gregory had abandoned the legends of 'heroic youth' in favour of Irish folk tales narrated by dull, old peasants in a manner 'almost fabulous in its sorrow and senility'. His ire is directed at her dull picturesque representation, not at the mythology itself, nor at the poems of the Irish bard Raftery, and he finishes by comparing *Poets and Dreams* unfavourably to the 'delicate scepticism' in Yeats's 'happiest book', *The Celtic Twilight* (OCPW 74–5). Notwithstanding the severity of his criticism, he still intended, as he informed his mother from Paris not long after the review had been published, 'to write to Lady Gregory one of these days' (*Letters* II, 380) to clarify, it would appear, his stance. This suggests quite a different sentiment than Mulligan's rebuke in *Ulysses*: 'O you inquisitional drunken jewjesuit! She gets you a job on the paper and then you go and slate her drivel to Jaysus. Couldn't you do the Yeats touch' (*U* 9.1159–61).

'The Day of the Rabblement' (1901), too, is reasonably moderate in its appraisal of the Revival. The piece is frequently taken to be Joyce's fiercest anti-Revival piece, but this perception derives from a misunderstanding of the biographical evidence. Vociferous in his attack, Joyce is certainly indignant about the fact that the Irish Literary Theatre had embraced peasant drama as its subject to the exclusion of others, accusing the theatre's directors of pandering to popular taste. As an intervention in the debate on the remit of the national theatre in Ireland, Joyce makes a strong point for integrating the theatre in a wider European culture. However, what critics overlook is that, on the one hand, the necessity for a connection with European drama was also very much Yeats's position and that, on the other, Joyce was not fully au fait with the issues as they were unfolding. Ellmann (1982, 88) alleges that on learning that the Irish Literary Theatre was putting on only Irish plays for its next productions,

---

[10] Addressing religious sectarianism in Ireland, Eglinton was of the view that the division between Catholics and Protestants results from confusing religion with politics, and that both or neither are essentially Irish. Eglinton, like Joyce, was in fact quite heterodox in his views (Eglinton 1906, 24–6).

[11] According to Stanislaus Joyce, the 'Portrait' essay was rejected because of its sexual overtones; to Joyce because it was too much about himself (Ellmann 1982, 147). On *Dana*'s modern, anti-nativist editorial policy, see Latham (n.d.).

Joyce indignantly sat down to write his essay, the well-known gist of which is a complaint about a missed opportunity for Dublin and an accusation against the theatre's directors for pandering to popular taste. He did not give credit to the fact that Yeats had, on a number of previous occasions, likened the development of a national theatre to that in Scandinavia, where people, as he put it in 'The Irish Literary Theatre, 1900', 'understand that a right understanding of life and of destiny is more important than amusement' (Yeats 2007, 126). Still, as far as the theatre's aims, Yeats announced that, at least for now, all plays would be on Irish subjects, recognizing however that these plays would, in the first instance, appeal to the 'imaginative minority and not to the majority which is content with the theatre of commerce' (Yeats 2010, 437). Joyce disagreed with – or perhaps missed the point about – the Irish plays not being popular.[12] He regretted that the Irish Literary Theatre had failed to fulfil how it presented itself, proclaiming 'war against commercialism and vulgarity' as 'the champion of progress' (*OCPW* 50). But while he accused George Moore and Edward Martyn, who had been champions of Wagner and Ibsen, of selling out, he was more circumspect about Yeats, resorting to back-handed compliments. Where Moore and Martyn were lambasted as unoriginal, he regarded it 'unsafe' to say 'at present' whether Yeats 'has or has not genius'; he called his belief in fairies all but ridiculous, but at the same time praised *The Wind among the Reeds* as 'poetry of the highest order' and called 'The Adoration of the Magi' 'a story which one of the great Russians might have written' (*OPCW* 51).[13] But he scorned the poet's 'treacherous instinct of adaptability' (*OPCW* 51). No doubt Yeats and the other directors were 'shy of presenting Ibsen, Tolstoy or Hauptmaun [sic]' (*OCPW* 50), but they made a pragmatic choice. Yeats would, however, on and off suggest European plays (Foster 1998, 281).

To Yeats's mind, the real rabble were not the masses who wanted sentimental plays, but those who jumped on the bandwagon, putting politics and religion before art.[14] His view was that literature, as the 'the principal voice of the

---

[12] The Irish Literary Theatre's later incarnations, the Irish National Theatre Society and the Abbey Theatre, were never commercial ventures, but were reliant on Annie Horniman's sponsorship, their affluent (often Ascendancy) patrons and supplementary income from profitable American tours.

[13] Joyce's 'at present' might sound damning, but also guarded. While in 1901, Yeats's *Poems* had brought him some acclaim, and *The Countess Kathleen* and his work for the Irish Literary Theatre notoriety, he had not yet written any of the great work for which he is mostly remembered today.

[14] Tymoczko (1994, 17) notes that the art versus propaganda debate was far from Joyce's own at the time; at a time when literature was 'under extreme pressure to be a tool of political revolution', not everyone was of the opinion that it should. She also suggests that the 1903 production of Synge's *The Shadow of the Glen* by the Irish National Theatre Society was a deliberate step away from subjugating art to politics, effectively causing a split in the Irish dramatic movement.

conscience', has its own morality independent from the 'special moralities of clergymen and churches' (Yeats 1994, 119). Yeats wrote these words in the *Freeman's Journal* on 14 November 1901 in response to George Moore who the day before had advocated in the same paper for censorship in the Irish theatre. Bizarrely, he argued that 'intelligent censorship from the Church' would protect stage 'from the unintelligent and ignorant censorship of the public' (quoted in Yeats 1994, 118n). For Yeats, the idea smacked of the ecclesiastical censure that had plagued *The Countess Kathleen* in 1899. Moore had played some part in this, too, by trying to stir up the devoutly Catholic Edward Martyn (Foster 1998, 209).

Whatever the intent behind 'The Day of the Rabblement', its impact in Dublin was limited. A tiny print run – only 85 copies were produced – meant its readership was small, although its message may have spread by word of mouth. Joyce had made sure it was circulated to the newspapers, but the only notice appeared in *The United Irishman* (see *OCPW* 295n). According to Eglinton, 'nobody had a quarrel with [Dublin's] Dante' (Scholes and Kain 1965, 202). His contemporaries either forgave or ignored Joyce's outburst. So when Yeats first encountered Joyce in November 1902, he met him in good spirit as one who could be useful to the movement.

The account of that meeting is familiar. Ellmann (1982, 103) relates the circumstances of the encounter as one in which kindness was rebuffed with egotism. Before parting company with Yeats, Joyce asked how old he was; when Yeats told the younger man his age (although fudging it by a year), Joyce replied: 'I thought as much. I have met you too late. You are too old.' That the conversation probably did not happen the way Ellmann reports is not what matters most. Although it is not immediately apparent, Ellmann uses Yeats's rendition of the meeting, as the poet had remembered and recorded it sometime after the facts.[15] Ellmann (1967, 37, my italics), however, also circulated a second account of the meeting, whose origin is attributed to Dublin 'rumor' rather than Yeats, which this time quotes Joyce as saying: 'You are too old for me *to help you*.'[16] Whatever the truth, literary history was left with the idea that Joyce was settling a score

---

[15] One needs to follow a trail of footnotes, however, through several publications eventually to arrive at Ellmann's source. For the words quoted in *James Joyce*, Ellmann first cites his own *The Identity of Yeats* (1954, 89); that book in turn refers the reader to his 'Joyce and Yeats' published in *The Kenyon Review* from 1950; that article at last cites an unpublished essay by Yeats. Although Ellmann provides the full text (1950, 624–6), he does not give its source. Foster identifies it as an unpublished typescript called 'The Younger Generation' (1998, 276). Ellmann's *Kenyon Review* article, furthermore, quotes this version of the meeting as well as the version reprinted in *Eminent Domain* (1967, 37–8). See also Crowley (2015).

[16] Padraic Colum (1922, 52) published another version of the conversation in *The New York Times* in which Joyce reputedly replied: 'You are too old for me to influence you.'

with old Yeats and backward Dublin. Yet the portrayal of Joyce as incapable of deference seems unjustified. When the anecdote resurfaced in the obituaries after Joyce's death, Thomas McGreevy wrote to the *Times Literary Supplement* to point out that he had frequently heard the story from AE (George Russell), but had never believed him. When he had had occasion to ask Yeats and Joyce about it, they both denied it; Joyce reportedly added that he had had 'nothing but kindness' for the older poet when he was young (McGreevy 1941, 43). Yeats, for his part, never alluded to the arrogance that others seemed to find in Joyce. When Joyce spent the day with Yeats in London while en route to Paris in December 1902, Yeats was struck by the young man's affability; contrary to expectations, Joyce had not come knocking at his door with all his 'old Ibsenite fury' (Yeats 1994, 268). On his return to Dublin for Christmas, just a few weeks later, Joyce again spent the morning with Yeats, telling him he had decided to give up medicine for literature. On this occasion, Yeats played the Bloomian role, reporting later to Lady Gregory that Joyce had said some absurd things and that he had scolded him for it, but on the whole they had been on good terms with each other.

What transpires from Yeats's testimony is the importance he attached to his meeting with Joyce. Rather than indicating Joyce's brazenness, the line about being too old betrays Yeats's vain self-consciousness and his eagerness to bring this precocious, self-assured, twenty-year-old man into the fold of the Irish movement. Yeats, in fact, misled Joyce about his age, saying he was a year younger than he was. (He was 37.) He was keen to downplay any generational and temperamental differences between them.

What had led to the meeting is of equal interest: the letter of introduction that AE sent to Yeats in August 1902:

> I want you very much to meet a young fellow named Joyce whom I wrote to Lady Gregory about half jestingly. He is an extremely clever boy who belongs to your class more than to mine and more still to himself. But he has all the intellectual equipment, culture and education which all our other clever friends here lack. And I think writes amazingly well in prose though I believe he also writes verse and is engaged in writing a comedy which he expects will occupy him five years or thereabouts as he writes slowly. Moore who saw an article of this boy's says it is preposterously clever. Anyhow I think you would find this youth of 21 with his assurance and self-confidence rather interesting. He is I think certainly more promising than Magee.
>
> (Russell 1961, 43)[17]

---

[17] Denson transcribes 'clan', but see Foster (1998, 275).

The 'preposterously clever' article is likely his paper on 'James Clarence Mangan' published earlier in May in *St. Stephen's*, the Royal University's monthly magazine, whose defence of Mangan as a *poète maudit* who might one day become a national poet only if Ireland rejects all its sentimental, nationalist pieties (*OCPW* 130) went against the grain of Irish literary historians; Moore might have chuckled at Joyce's swipe at their 'hysterical nationalism' (*OCPW* 136). What this letter shows, though, is that AE wanted to recommend Joyce for the promise he showed as a writer – an indication that talent was more important to the literary movement they were trying to build than orthodoxy.

AE's suggestion that 'this clever boy' might belong to Yeats's 'class' sounds rather peculiar, although presumably he meant intellectual class, not social class or tribe. Yeats certainly had no qualms about acting on AE's recommendation. Yeats invited Joyce to dine with him, Lady Gregory and Yeats senior (*Letters I*, 15; Yeats 2000a, 242) at the Nassau hotel, 16-20 South Frederick Street, Dublin, where Yeats was staying on 2 or 3 November. The hotel, a neat and moderately priced 'Temperance and Family Hostelry' (Wakeman n.d., 417; see also Yeats 2000a, 386), functioned as an unofficial base of operations for the Revival. It had been Maud Gonne's preferred lodging since the 1880s; Yeats, too, habitually stayed there when on business from London. Although no account of the dinner exists, a lot of what Yeats had on his mind might have struck a chord with Joyce. His play, *Where there is Nothing*, published only a week or so before in the *United Irishman*, and the subject of a major row with Moore, had been heavily criticized by a Jesuit priest (Yeats 2000a, 244). Yeats's 'The Freedom of the Theatre', a defence of the new play, appeared in the same paper on 1 November. In this article, Yeats railed against the moral majority in Dublin, that 'zealous class who write and read the *Freeman's Journal*, and the *Independent* and the *Irish Times*' and who pronounce against the morality of certain plays (Yeats 2000b, 92). The artist for Yeats was not shackled by general opinion and he defended a theatre that was without everyday responsibility: 'Drama describes the adventures of men's souls among the thoughts that are most interesting to the dramatist, and, therefore, probably most interesting to his time' (Yeats 2000b, 93). It is hard to imagine that Yeats's position would not have resonated with his interlocutor.

Whatever the conversation, an invitation was extended either then or shortly thereafter for Joyce to attend another meeting at the Nassau hotel, which Padraic Colum, who was also present, referred to as 'one of Lady Gregory's evening parties' (Colum 1959, 10).[18] The meeting was in fact a celebratory

---

[18] According to Eglinton, Joyce had crashed the party and snubbed Lady Gregory 'with his air of half-timid effrontery' (quoted in Scholes and Kain 1965, 201).

gathering of the Irish National Dramatic Company. As Yeats and Gregory reported to John Quinn on the 8th, they had just 'had a busy fortnight' (Yeats 2000a, 344) with, as its highlight, the Samhain Festival at the Antient Concert Rooms (28 October to 1 November) showcasing plays by AE, James Cousins, P.T. MacGinley and Yeats himself (O'Ceallaigh Ritschel 2001, 12–13). At the meeting, the company discussed 'possible plays, possible productions' over tea or sherry (Sullivan 2008, 343). In an unpublished version of his memoir, Colum describes Joyce, and Oliver St. John Gogarty who was with him, as being rather 'aloof from the rest of this company' (see Sullivan 2008, 343). But so was Colum himself, apparently, who had been introduced to Yeats only a few months earlier. The purpose of the gathering was to attract new writers for the theatre; Colum, who had by then written a few plays that had not yet been staged, was to join the company's reading committee in February and his *The Saxon Shillin'* was put on for a run of three nights in May 1903. It might have been around this time (although the dating is not precise) that Lady Gregory asked Joyce whether he would like to 'write something for our little theatre' (quoted in Sullivan 2008, 343; O'Ceallaigh Ritschel 2001, 16).[19] Joyce's presence in the Nassau hotel shows him, to some extent, a willing participant in what Yeats wontedly referred to as 'our little movement'.

Affinities

In the wake of the celebration at the Nassau hotel, Joyce sent Yeats some of his poems. Yeats read them sympathetically:

> The work which you have actually done is very remarkable for a man of your age who has lived away from the vital intellectual centres. Your technique in verse is very much better than the technique of any young Dublin man I have met during my time. It might have been the work of a young man who had lived in an Oxford literary set.
>
> (Yeats 1994, 249)

But he also warned Joyce that he must allow himself time to mature. The praise is genuine, the criticism candid. That he remarked on the Oxonian quality of Joyce's

---

[19] A shorter account of the meeting at the Nassau hotel appears in Colum (1959, 10–12). It is also mentioned briefly in his *New York Times* article (1922, 52).

verse probably meant that Yeats found it a little studied and contrived. Joyce, of course, intentionally strove to write a kind of lyric with a specific rhetorical effect, but judging from what survives in the manuscripts, the early lyrics do not yet have the consistency, musicality or the range of voice in *Chamber Music*.

> Love that I can give you, lady
> Ah, that they haven't, lady
> Lady witchin', lady mine.
> O, you say that I torment you
> With my verses, lady mine
> Faith! The best I had I sent you,
> Don't be laughin', lady mine.
> I am foolish to be hopin'
> That you left your window open (*PSW* 77)

One month later, after Joyce sending him another short lyric, Yeats again emphasized that it was good. He found the poem 'charming' in its rhythm but (much like the example just quoted) 'a little thin' in subject matter and lacking the 'magical phrases' and 'passion' of the earlier poems. It was the work 'of a young man who is practising his instrument' (Yeats 1994, 282). His opinion of Joyce's verse would not alter: more than ten years later, when arranging a stipend for Joyce from the Royal Literary Fund, he praised, with equal measure, *Dubliners* and *Chamber Music*, and twice singled out 'I Hear an Army Charging' for its particular merit, calling it 'a tecnical [*sic*] & emotional masterpiece' (Yeats 2002, #2734).

The language that Yeats uses in his criticism of Joyce's poems reflects his wider thinking about art. He never put nationalism before literary value, but always hoped the two would work hand in hand. Although he wished that Irish poets would seek their subject matter in Irish folklore and myth, as he wrote in deepest Celtic Twilight mode, this was not just to find inspiration, but to discover 'new methods of expressing our selves' (Yeats 1986, 119). In poetry he searched for 'copious streams of beauty', as he wrote to Katharine Tynan, praising her along with the older William Allingham and Samuel Ferguson for having done 'the largest quantity of fine work' (Yeats 1986, 450–1). He was of the view that she and others like AE and Lionel Johnson stood out for their 'deliberate art' and their 'preoccupation with spiritual passions and memories' (Yeats 1989b, 108). Poetry is not driven by ideas, but by passion. And passion was for him a particularly Irish trait to be used in the struggle against dull, English rationalism and the deadening middle-class mind (see Foster 1998, 53). Joyce, too, when he was engrossed in *Stephen Hero* talked about 'individual passion as the motive power of everything – art and philosophy included' (*Letters* II, 81).

The affinity between Joyce and Yeats, in other words, has a reasonable grounding in their conceptions of art and artist. One of the reasons why literary history has misjudged that affinity is because its views on Joyce's aesthetics were filtered through Joyce's (and Stephen's) theory of the epiphany and its correlative in the philosophy of Thomas Aquinas – *integritas, consonantia* and *claritas*. The absence, however, of a tangible connection between Joyce's poetry – including the fictional poems Stephen produces in *A Portrait* and *Ulysses* – and his theory has often been noted. An aesthetic framework for *Chamber Music* is, in other words, as good as nonexistent. But we can reconstruct, if not a framework, at least a sphere of influence through the interest that Joyce shared with Yeats in the musical qualities of poetic rhythm, which, for both writers, were an essential component of their poetic style (see Longley 2015).

Unlike for most of the later work, no documentary evidence exists that reveals Joyce's composition methods for *Chamber Music* and the verse that preceded it. All extant manuscripts are fair copies with no trace of development. Joyce's fiction, however, provides a usable alternative when it accounts for the moment Stephen composes his vampire poem on Sandymount strand. The creation of Stephen's poem happens extemporaneously. The moment of inspiration is casual, almost imperceptible, much like Shelley's fading coal; the words come into his mind not fixed, but formless and protean: 'He comes, pale vampire, through storm his eyes, his bat sails bloodying the sea, mouth to her mouth's kiss' (*U* 3.397–8). The words of the poem, moreover, are undifferentiated from the rest of Stephen's interior monologue; they are wrapped up in Stephen's ruminations on the moon, sea and tide, on fertility, sleep and death. The reader barely recognizes they belong to an emerging poem, until he encounters them again complete, and revised, in 'Aeolus':

On swift sail flaming
From storm and south
He comes, pale vampire,
Mouth to my mouth. (*U* 7.522–5)

Nor does Stephen himself, until he suddenly realizes that his train of thought has given way to inspiration, and he knows he must stop the flow of words before they escape him: 'Here. Put a pin in that chap, will you?' (*U* 3.399). But he does not have any paper (having twice forgotten to take blank book request slips from the desk in the National Library) and so his mind quickly returns to the emergent poem, trying to compose the poem in his head, weighing off meaning and rhythm against each other: 'Mouth to her kiss. No. Must be two of em. Glue em well. Mouth to her mouth's kiss' (*U* 3.399–400). While he thinks this, the narrator's voice takes over and describes Stephen silently enunciating the poem to himself: 'His lips lipped and mouthed fleshless lips of air: mouth to her moomb. Oomb, allwombing tomb. His mouth moulded issuing breath, unspeeched: ooeeehah: roar of cataractic planets, globed, blazing, roaring wayawayawayawayaway' (*U* 3.401-3). This 'unspeeched', aural moulding of the sounds is again interrupted by the need for paper, at which point Stephen decides to tear off the bottom of Deasy's letter to the press and scribbles down the text using a rock for surface.

As Stephen finishes the writing ('ending' [*U* 3.408]), his interior monologue resumes, so it seems, and his mind turns to 'delta of Cassopiopeia', an allusion to Shakespeare seeing his own initial in the night sky when he walks home at night returning to Stratford from Ann Hathaway's cottage. The allusion to the constellation and the image of the stars shining bright in the darkness that precedes it is prompted by the question: 'Why not endless till the farthest star?' (*U* 3.409-10). But what prompts the question? The narrator's 'ending' just before it, obviously, but that is not a word in Stephen's mind, unless 'endless' and 'the farthest star' are part of the poem too. Which would make sense, for it links with the 'roar of cataractic planets' and the near-synonyms that suggest the flying 'away' of the planets through the universe. These too might be words belonging to the poem – perhaps not all literally, but as part of Joyce's associative 'mind-game', linking Stephen's cognition and the narrator's voice. Nonetheless, it seems an attractive proposition to argue that the composition of Stephen's poem did not end on the line 'mouth to her mouth's kiss'. For one, the genitive structure of the sentence, 'Endless, would it be mine, form of my form?' (*U* 3.414), echoes the poem's 'mouth to her mouth'; similarly, 'Our souls, shamewounded by our sins, cling to us yet more, a woman to her lover clinging, the more the more' (*U* 3. 421-3) continues Stephen's cognitive process of associative gestation, as he thinks up rhyme words that link back to the rapturous embrace of the vampire and his lover. If that is the case, why not see 'She trusts me, her hand gentle, the longlashed eyes' (*U* 3.424) as part of the genesis as well? Who is this but the woman in the poem? In other words, Stephen's poem as we encounter it in 'Aeolus' only gives us the first quatrain, whereas the poem's genesis – if not on paper, then at least in Stephen's mind – carried on much further, perhaps all the way to 'Touch me. Soft eyes. Soft soft soft hand. I am lonely here. O, touch me soon, now' (*U* 3. 433-6). At this point Stephen crams the paper and pencil back in his pocket.

While Stephen's process of creative cognition matches that of Edgar Allan Poe's in 'The Philosophy of Composition', his manner of voicelessly 'mouthing' his poem into existence is reminiscent of the way Yeats used to rhythmically intone his lines as he committed them to paper. Joyce is not likely to have known about Yeats's habit, but the process Joyce describes in 'Proteus' is one that is similar in many respects to aural writing practices of not only Yeats but also Wordsworth and other poets. What Joyce does allude to in 'Proteus' are Yeats's ideas about speaking verse. When Stephen's reflections shift from Berkeley's imponderables of the senses to reading, he wonders: 'Who ever anywhere will read these written words.' What Stephen has in mind is not silent reading per se, but recitation: 'Somewhere to someone in your flutiest voice' (*U* 3.414–16). The melodic voice of Stephen's imagined reader brings to mind Yeats's method of chanting. Joyce first experienced, and was impressed by, Yeats's method of recitation when he saw *The Countess Kathleen* on 8 May 1899 at the Antient Concert Rooms. For the performance, Yeats had added two songs to the play, 'Impetuous Heart' and 'Who Goes with Fergus', which were recited by Florence Farr and Anna Mathers accompanied on a small harp (Schuchard 2008, 35–6, 39).

In the years that followed, Yeats, with the help of the actress Florence Farr, expanded his experiment and trialled various instruments – the harp, the organ, the piano – for the best effect, but he had been consistently dissatisfied by the 'two competing tunes' that the instrument and the verse produced (Yeats 2007, 14). So they looked instead for an instrument that remained subservient to the verse (Schuchard 2008, 52–3). In February 1901, following an illustrated lecture at Clifford's Inn in Fleet Street on the 26th, Arnold Dolmetsch offered his assistance. He first tried a number of stringed instruments, before designing his famed psaltery, first one with twelve strings, one for each note in Farr's voice, before making one with twenty-six strings that covered the full range of her speaking voice. The instrument was made out of satinwood, with inlaid strips of ivory over the bars, fine steel and twisted brass for the strings, and carved in the body of the sound box was a Yeatsian rose (Schuchard 2008, 56).

On 15 May, also at Clifford's Inn, Yeats delivered the first of several lectures on 'Speaking to the Psaltery' that would lead to his famous essay in *Ideas of Good and Evil* (1903). William Archer, writing in the *Morning Leader*, summarized the main points as follows:

> First, that poetry ought to be recited in such a way as [to] throw into relief its metrical structure; and, second, that the musician ought not to be allowed to smother it, so to speak, in melody, perverting its natural phrasing and accent.

A third point was emphasised by Mr. Dolmetsch: namely that the system of 'speaking through music' (known in Germany as melodrame) led to horrible dissonances and was wholly inartistic.

(quoted in Schuchard 2008, 61)

The main point for Yeats was that the poem should be chanted, not sung, as this would better bring out the musical notes of the natural voice.[20] (For this reason, he did not like to work with professional singers, whom he felt tended to slip back into song.) Unlike singing, chanting involved the fixing of the pitch, but still allowed for sufficient variety in modulation, but the crux was that he believed that his way of chanting corresponded to the ancient method of the Greek chorus from which the Irish bards derived their singing. His main aim was to reintroduce the art of verse speaking in the theatre.

When precisely Joyce learned about Yeats's theories is not known. But it is likely that, at the time of their first meeting, he attended Yeats's 'Speaking to Musical Notes', with a demonstration by Farr accompanied on the psaltery, during the Samhain Festival in the Antient Concert Rooms in November 1902 (Schuchard 2008, 100, 102). Regardless, when Stephen Dedalus holds forth on the notion of there being a rhythmical gesture, 'an art of gesture' that does not express emphasis but rhythm (*SH* 184), Joyce shows an affinity with Yeats's theories. The older poet had liked the way Joyce had read his poems, recognizing that the young man shared with him certain rhythmical sensibilities (see Yeats 1994, 249n). About Joyce's manner of reading, Gogarty recalled how, when reciting Dowland's 'Weep no more, sad fountains', Joyce would 'caress the end line of the last stanza' (quoted in Scholes and Kain 1965, 215). Colum (1959, 22) remembered him as reading his own poems with 'deliberateness and precision' in a voice that was 'naturally beautiful' and 'that had been cultivated for singing'; the effect was 'more personal' than AE's and Yeats's chanting. Elsewhere, Colum speaks of Joyce singing his lyrics (1922, 52). C.P. Curran (1968, 41), finally, quite categorically stated that Joyce chanted his favourite Yeats' lyrics, 'Who Goes with Fergus' and 'Impetuous Heart', as well as 'Had I the Heavens' Embroidered Cloths', 'in the manner of Florence Farr'.[21] What is clear is that Joyce, like Yeats,

---

[20] Yeats had been pleased to learn about an experiment conducted by Thomas MacDonagh, who discovered that tone-deaf poets compose their song through chanting rather than through song. Yeats, famously tone-deaf, recognized his own method of composition in this (Schuchard 2008, 84–6).

[21] Stanislaus also remembers Joyce 'almost chanting' passages from *The Tables of the Law* (Joyce 2003, 215).

emphasized the lyric modulation of poetry, defining it (according to Colum) as 'the simple liberation of a rhythm' (1959, 23). As he has Stephen Daedalus proclaim, 'verse to be read according to its rhythm should be read according to the stresses' (*SH* 25).

Joyce, as is well known, contacted Arnold Dolmetsch in June 1904 to inquire about purchasing a lute, a whim that came to nothing. Dolmetsch, an instrument maker and authority on early music, replied that such an instrument would be difficult to play and also quite expensive, which was sufficient to put Joyce off. He also had the idea to hear a tour of the English performing old English songs (*Letters* I, 54). The idea of chanting poetry and 'old music such as I like' (*Letters* II, 219) intersected in Joyce's mind at a time when he was also working on *Chamber Music*. Joyce's reading at the time reveals he was exploring certain aspects of musical history. In the 'Early Commonplace Book' (NLI 36,639/2/A, f. 6r), the same notebook begun in 1903/4 in which he recorded his notes on Aristotle, he wrote down a short list with the names of two musical societies, the Percy Society and the Musical Antiquarian Society, as well as a number of books on musical history (see Crispi 2009; Witen 2018, 4–5). The aims of the Percy Society, active between 1840 and 1852, were the compilation and publication of early English poetry, ballads and songs and popular music from the Middle Ages, while the Musical Antiquarian Society, active between 1846 and 1848, promoted the rediscovery of work by English Elizabethan composers. The books Joyce refers to are Sir John Hawkins' *A General History of the Science and Practice of Music* (1776) and Charles Burney's *A General History of Music, from the Earliest Ages to the Present Period* (1776), two of the earliest, although quite distinct histories of music in English; and Henry Davey's *History of English Music* (1895). Also listed are John Wilbye, an English madrigal composer (1574–1638), whose *Works* had been published in two volumes by James Turle and G.W. Budd for the Musical Antiquarian Society in 1841 and 1846; and Edward F. Rimbault's *Bibliotheca Madrigaliana: A Bibliographical Account of the Musical and Poetical Works published in England during the Sixteenth and Seventeenth Centuries* (1847), whose purpose was to bring together an exhaustive list of publications from 'a period when "part-singing" was in its zenith' (Rimbault 1847, v).

Joyce's research on Rimbault is telling (he particularly cites pp. 11 and 28, where Rimbault lists *The First Set of English Madrigals* (1598) and *The Second Set of Madrigales* (1609) composed by John Wilbye. The madrigal is generally considered to be the earliest form of chamber music; in the monodic form, which is mainly Rimbault's subject, the singer was usually accompanied by the lute or the viol.[22] The influence of this interest on the development of Stephen is noticeable in *A Portrait*. When Stephen turns his attention away from the 'spectral words of Aristotle or Aquinas' to the 'dainty songs of the Elizabethans' whenever he is 'weary' of his search for definitions of 'the essence of beauty', he imagines himself standing 'in the vesture of a doubting monk' under a window listening to the 'grave and mocking music of lutenists' (*P* 176). The 'mocking' nature of the madrigal is not a characteristic of their lowliness, however; at once light-hearted and beautiful, the madrigal's playful harmonies and multiple voices may be unusual to classical taste, but require great skill in their execution (see Fellowes 1921, 144, 209).

Light-hearted and playful are a good way to describe the verse of *Chamber Music*. More immediately relevant, however, is the example of a madrigal-style lyric, not included in the volume, that references traditional music and has pastoral merriment for its theme:

> Come out to where the youth is met
> Under the moon, beside the sea,
> And leave your weapon and your net,
> Your loom and your embroidery.
> Bring back the pleasantness of days
> And crystal moonlight on the shore.
> In old times on the ivory floor.
> The weapons and the looms are mute
> And feet are hurrying by the sea.
> I hear the viol and the flute,
> The sackbut and the psaltery. (*PSW* 94)

It would not warrant us to assume that Joyce makes a direct allusion to Yeats's famous psaltery. Through the poem's pastoral theme, though, Joyce expresses his interest in reviving the traditional English song and the old instruments. Another poem (actually a free translation of Verlaine's '*Chanson d'automne*') touches similarly on the musical theme, although here the lulling sounds of the instruments metaphorically match the poet's state of mind:

> A voice that sings
> Like viol strings
> Through the wane

---

[22] Rimbault writes: 'I speak here of the *Madrigal* as a musical composition. The term equally applies to music and poetry' (1847, vii).

Of the pale year
Lulleth me here
With its strain. (*PSW* 74)

Catherine Flynn (2019, 26) notes that Joyce rewrote Verlaine's poem 'as an aesthetic vocation ... an artistic sensibility responding to a human call'. The effect that Joyce strives for is, in fact, not only to remove 'the speaker's identification with decomposing matter', but to write the Symbolist aesthetic out of the poem and replace it with something that sounds much more like Dowland.[23]

To Joyce, the old music was as important as Aristotle's aesthetics and Aquinas's writings on beauty. The 'Early Commonplace Book' provides plenty of evidence and rich pickings to support this view, for the notes on aesthetics that for a long time have only been available through Herbert Gorman's (1949) biography now appear alongside a substantial and varied set of other notes, sources and quotations.[24] Apart from the materials already mentioned, the notebook includes quotations from Ben Jonson, W.B. Yeats, Edmund Gosse (from 'Guenevere', a poem in *On Viol and Flute* [1873], which includes the lines, 'Gawain lounged in the hot gold air | Fingered a lute' [NLI 36,639/2/A, f. 5v),[25] and Thomas Percy's *Reliques of Ancient English Poetry*. Another page lists side by side books on aesthetics and Aristotle's poetics with books on ancient Greek and Arabic music (f. 9ᵛ); this list includes, complete with Bibliothèque national shelfmark 'Ya 8° 35-pièce', Martin Hartmann's *Metrum und Rhythmus: Die Entstehung der arabischen Versmasse* (1896). (Hartmann's book is a pioneering study on the origins of Arabic metre by one of the founders of Islamic studies in Germany.) Two pages earlier, Joyce had excerpted a passage from Hartmann's study consisting of a bar of music and two lines of an Arabic poem accompanied by two different scansions, labelled 'Rhythm of the Verse' and 'Rhythm of the Music' (f. 7v). The poem, identified as Marğūza Nr. 1 (Hartmann 1896, 10) is a modern Bedouin song from the Hadhramaut region on the southern Arabic coast. Without recourse to the source, Michelle Witen (2018, 85) correctly assessed that the notes fit with Yeats's theories about verse speaking, which promotes accentuation rather than elongation of the vowel. While Joyce merely

---

[23] Most strikingly, Verlaine's autumn's 'D'une langueur | monotone' (quoted in Flynn 2019, 24) becomes 'the wane | of the pale year | Lulleth me here | with its strain' (*PSW* 74).
[24] For details, see Crispi (2009), who reminds us that Gorman, who had access to this notebook, describes some of its contents. See, in particular, Gorman (1949, 89–90, 94–96).
[25] Crispi (2009) incorrectly identifies Gosse's collection as the 1890 edition published by Kegan Paul, Trench, Trübner & Co. 'Guenevere', however, appears in the 1873 edition published by Henry S. King & Co., which has different contents.

notes the rhythmical differences, the gist of Hartmann's argument is that Bedouin songs were metrically composed according to the '*rhythmischen Bewegung*' of natural speech patterns rather than melodic feeling (1896, 10).

Another significant page in the notebook is the one where Joyce places Jonson side by side with Aristotle; Jonson's song, beginning 'I was not wearier where I lay' (which Stephen quotes in *A Portrait* [P 176]), is followed by a string of quotations or paraphrases from Aristotle's *De Anima* (*On the Soul*).[26] Gorman (1949, 94) speculates that Joyce's reading of Ben Jonson alongside Aristotle was mostly part of an eccentric intellectual curiosity, and that he may have been attracted by the 'toughness' and 'Aristotelian exactness' of Jonson's characterization and motivation or by the lyrics 'strewed through the plays'. While this may be the case, it is also clear that Joyce was considering developing a lyrical-aesthetic theory in which rhythm is central. As he notes in the 'Early Commonplace Book': 'Rhythm seems to be the first or <necessary>formal relation of part to part in any whole or of a whole to its part or parts, or of any part to the whole of which it is a part … … … … Parts constitute a whole so far as they have a common end' (NLI 36,639/2/A, f.12v). Rhythm, in other words, is what ties a poem (but possibly also, when considered more abstractly, a drama or a novel) together and creates an aesthetic unity. However, as Joyce turned from poetry to prose, the dramatic elements of Aristotle's poetics became more crucial to him.

Traditions

For Joyce, the musicality of *Chamber Music* was thus more important than any purely 'literary' intent. The lyrical quality of the old music, and its rhythmical effect on Joyce's own poetry, was to him part of the verbal tradition of the well-tuned word, neither quite poetry nor song, but halfway in between – a tradition that also included the Irish ballad tradition and *come-all-you*.

One final question remains and that is to what tradition *Chamber Music* belongs. The fine balance Joyce strikes between originality and imitation is one of the volume's deliberate effects, and as such the volume fits well with plenty of contemporary poetry that was conscious of past literary traditions and strove to

---

[26] Joyce's source, as originally identified by Jacques Aubert, is J. Barthélemy-Saint-Hilaire's French translation of Aristotle's *De Anima: Psychologie d'Aristote: Traité de l'âme* (Paris: Librairie Philosophique Ladrange, 1846). See Crispi (2009).

engage with the past to reinvigorate modern poetry. But could *Chamber Music* also be called Irish?[27]

This looks like another matter altogether. With both Pound and Yeats as champions, Joyce's poetry was perhaps being pulled in two directions: one Imagist, the other lyrical. But in its material form *Chamber Music* is also sufficiently ambiguous: it is neither Irish, nor completely English. Thomas Kettle, reviewing the volume for the *Freeman's Journal*, noted the absence of any allusion to 'folklore, folk dialect, or even the national feeling' (quoted in Deming 2007, I, 37). Yet although the verse avoids any explicit Celtic motifs, its Irish origins were never far off. To all intents and purposes, Arthur Symons, who brokered publication with Elkin Mathews on Yeats's instigation, played down the Irish connection with the publisher. In his letter to Mathews dated 9 October 1906, he applauded *Chamber Music* as 'a book which cannot fail to attract notice from everyone capable of knowing poetry when he sees it', praising it as being 'of the most genuine lyric quality of any new work I have read for many years'; but he made sure to emphasize that, despite Yeats's support, Joyce was '*not* in the Celtic Movement' (Symons 1989, 183). He points this out to Mathews because he knew about 'The Day of the Rabblement', although evidently he had not read Joyce's piece first hand; he was simply surprised that Yeats admired Joyce.[28] However, Symons was projecting his own predilections. Having distanced himself from the predominantly 'Celtic' flavour of the Rhymers' Club, of which he had been a member in the late 1890s, he was now primarily interested in Early Modern writing. (He had just edited *A Pageant of Elizabethan Poetry* [1906].) Undoubtedly, he found Joyce's verse 'almost Elizabethan in their freshness' (Symons 1989, 183), more interesting than any Celtic Twilight echo could accomplish.[29] Nevertheless, it is, in itself, significant that he thought it germane to mention to the publisher that Joyce was not of the movement.

Over the years, Mathews had built up a reputation as a publisher supporting the Revival (now as well as in the days of his partner John Lane), not least for

---

[27] Among Joyce's critics, the question does not seem to arise. Only Garratt (1989, 84–5) hesitatingly places *Chamber Music* within the Irish Literary Movement.

[28] The letter reads more fully: 'He is *not* in the Celtic Movement, and though Yeats admits his ability he is rather against him because Joyce has attacked the movement. Oddly enough it is to him that Yeats refers in the prefatory to "The Tables of the Law" in that very series!' (Symons 1989, 183). Yeats's preface to *The Tables of the Law and the Adoration of the Magi*, published by Elkin Mathews (1904) in the Vigo Cabinet Series, mentions that he had met a young man in Dublin who liked his stories book more than anything else he had published.

[29] Symons' anonymous review of *Chamber Music* in *The Nation* repeated his disassociation of Joyce from the Revival: 'I advise everyone who cares for poetry to buy *Chamber Music*, by James Joyce a young Irishman who is in no Irish movement, literary or national, and has not even anything obviously Celtic in his manner' (Deming 2007, I, 38).

having issued Yeats's *The Wind among the Reeds* (1899) and Synge's *The Shadow of the Glen and Riders to the Sea* (1905). Playing on Mathews' double strength as a publisher of poetry and a publisher of Irish writing, Symons was therefore carefully plugging Joyce's book. While separating Joyce from the Revival, he was smart enough to mention his background and connection.[30] Mathews' Vigo Cabinet Series, to which Symons was recommending *Chamber Music*, was exactly right. Not only had Mathews cornered the market for cheap poetry books (the Vigo Cabinet Series retailed at one shilling) and attracted a lot of new poets (Nelson 1989, 31–5, 55–64), he was able to take advantage of the situation that there were few Dublin publishers. Synge's book as well as work by Tynan and Todhunter had appeared in the series.

Although it did not appear in the Vigo Cabinet Series, *Chamber Music* fitted in with Mathews' list because it matched the light lyrical mode of many of Mathews' other titles. Among these were several books that also explicitly referenced music: R.W. Dixon's *Songs and Odes* (1896), John Masefield's *Ballads* (1902), W.W. Gibson's *Urlyn the Harper, and Other Song* (1902), John Todhunter's *Sounds and Sweet Airs* (1905), and several others like it. The poetical qualities of Todhunter's book in particular are reminiscent of *Chamber Music*: 'These poems are not meant to be paraphrases in verse of the music that suggested them. They are merely a record of a listener's moods, phantasies inspired by the emotional spirit of each composition' (Todhunter 1905, 5). Joyce's poems were not paraphrases either; they were likewise inspired by moods and musical phantasies. When Symons reviewed Joyce's collection for *The Nation*, he noted that there was almost 'no substance at all in these songs', but found them 'full of ghostly old tunes ... played on an old instrument' (quoted in Deming 2007, I, 39).

Mathews understood the market for this genre very well and he did his best to highlight *Chamber Music*'s musical credentials. Proposing to publish the volume in the 'Pott 8vo' format, the smallest and perhaps daintiest of the octavo sizes (159 x 102mm), Mathews told Joyce: 'Pott 8vo. is a very pretty size. If you know the Golden Treasury series you will be able to judge the size at once' (quoted in Nelson 1989, 116). Mathews' plan for the design, however, not only implied a look but also its poetic ancestry; F.T. Palgrave's *The Golden Treasury of the Best Songs and Lyrical Poems in the English Language* (first published in 1861) might have been intended for a genteel Victorian audience, but the format subtly

---

[30] A week before contacting Mathews, Symons (1989, 182) had also written to Grant Richards, another London publisher with quite a few Irish authors on his books.

underscored the volume's lyrical qualities. As it happened, *Chamber Music* was issued in a slightly larger format, bound in green cloth boards with gilt lettering and priced at 1s 3d. Mathews, however, laid the musical connection on thick with an ornamental title page that depicted decorated pillars draped with musical scores and a drawing of (what Joyce called) an 'open pianner' (*Letters II* 219). (In actuality it is a clavichord.) Showing foresight and good business acumen, moreover, Mathews included a clause in his contract with Joyce stipulating that the musical rights would be split equally between author and publisher (Nelson 1989, 116).

When the volume went into production, Mathews placed an advance notice of *Chamber Music* in the *Book Monthly*; going against Symons, he related how the book had come to him, explicitly linking Joyce with Yeats (Nelson 1989, 118). No doubt his strategy was motivated by commerce as much as by affinity. As a message, though, it did not go entirely unnoticed. Padraic and Mary Colum (1959) write that the poems belonged more to 'a young man's musician's' world than they did to the imagination of a poet and their Elizabethan and Jacobean influence was unmistakable. But while the 'full-blooded gaiety' of the Elizabethan songs contrasts sharply with the 'mournfulness of Irish melodies', they felt it was impossible to say whether the poems were totally without a trace of Irish influence (Colum 1959, 83–4). A select number of poems also had a specifically Irish afterlife when during Joyce's lifetime they were included in various Irish anthologies.[31]

Expressions

Such afterlife is certainly due to the integrity of the poetry. The marginalization of *Chamber Music* in the Joycean canon is due to the dominant position of modernist poetics in literary historicism that sweeps away large swathes of early twentieth-century lyrical poetry in which tradition and modernity are not incommensurable. The simplicity of form, however, is not something that Joyce relinquished in his writing. The epiphanies most clearly form a transition

---

[31] Alfred Perceval Graves included 'Strings in the Earth and Air' in *The Book of Irish Poetry* (London: T. Fisher Unwin, n.d.) under the rubric 'Spiritual and Philosophical Poetry'. *The Dublin Book of Irish Verse, 1728–1909*, edited by John Cooke (Dublin: Hodges, Figgis & Co.; London: Henry Frowde, 1909) reprinted 'Strings in the Earth and Air', 'Bid adieu, adieu, adieu' and 'What counsel has the hooded moon'. 'At that Hour when all Things Have Repose' appeared in Katharine Tynan's popular *The Wild Harp: A Selection from Irish Poetry* (London: Sidgwick and Jackson, 1913), and also in *A Golden Treasury of Irish Verse*, edited by Lennox Robinson (London: Macmillan, 1925).

between the lyric ideals of *Chamber Music* and the symbolical effectiveness of the prose in *Dubliners* and *A Portrait of the Artist as a Young Man*, neither of which is devoid of lyricism. The emotional charge that lies at the basis of the epiphanies and the artist's need to capture the moment effectively in language remains the essential ingredient of Joyce's oeuvre, and comes to the fore again most explicitly in *Pomes Penyeach*. Going against his development towards ever more sophisticated forms of writing, Joyce's return to lyric form in the late 1920s has been seen as a contradiction, coming as it did when 'Work in Progress' was in full swing. (*Pomes Penyeach* gathered together poems that Joyce had written over many years, starting in 1913, and published in 1927.) But even underneath the sophistication of *Finnegans Wake* lies a form of simplicity.

That Joyce partially disowned his early poetry is not tantamount to a renunciation of its simplicity per se. When seeing *Chamber Music* through the press three or four years after its original inception, and after it had been turned down by at least three different publishers, he at once renounced and embraced the book. As he wrote to his brother Stanislaus in October 1906, he felt it was too much the work of his younger self:

> The reason that I dislike *Chamber Music* as a title is that it is too complacent. I should prefer a title which to a certain extent repudiated the book, without altogether disparaging it. ... I went through the entire book of verses mentally on receipt of Symons' letter and they nearly all seemed to me poor and trivial: some phrases and lines pleased me and no more.
>
> (*Letters* II, 182)

The verse, in other words, was a little thin. In February 1907, he wrote again to his brother: 'I don't like the book but wish it were published and be damned to it. However, it is a young man's book. I felt like that. It is not a book of love-verses at all, I perceive. But some of them are pretty enough to be put to music' (*Letters* II, 219). By this time, he may also have begun to see himself more as a prose writer than a poet. He was not so much repudiating old work, therefore, than reflecting on the making of his authorial self. In the same letter to Stanislaus, he wrote:

> I have certain ideas I would like to give form to: not as a doctrine but as the continuation of the expression of myself which I now see I began in *Chamber Music*. These ideas or instincts or intuitions or impulses may be purely personal. I have no wish to codify myself as anarchist or socialist or reactionary.
>
> (*Letters* II, 217).

When he wrote this, he was, of course, also enacting another form of self-repudiation in the creation of his mock-heroic double in *Stephen Hero*, the writing of which was more than half completed. Nonetheless, the desire to see his writing in print was greater than his aversion to the immature work.

What 'expression of himself' there is in *Chamber Music* perhaps remains a mystery; it seems difficult to match the idea that it was a 'young man's book' with what he said two years later about the female figure in his poems to Nora: that she was not created from experience, but from his reading, 'a girl fashioned into a curious grave beauty by the culture of generations before her' (*Letters* II, 237). Maybe he was trying to see himself as a Yeatsian poet. The expression of personality – or as Joyce had written about James Clarence Mangan, 'the presence of an imaginative personality reflecting the light of imaginative beauty' (*OCPW* 57) – was very much a Yeatsian notion for whom 'the nobleness of the Arts' lies in the 'perfection of personality' (Yeats 2007, 186). Nonetheless, the self-expression that he was foreboding in his letter to Stanislaus was likely also an exercise in self-discovery that would lead from autobiography to auto-creation – the formation of the smithy of his soul. *Stephen Hero*, said to be half-finished in March 1906, was now moving towards its turning point; on 8 September 1907 he told Stanislaus he was going to begin rewriting it as soon as he had finished 'The Dead'. In this novel, and its eventual reworking as *A Portrait of the Artist as a Young Man*, Joyce would fictionalize the coming-into-being of the aesthetic principles that sit at the heart of *Chamber Music*, placing the rhythm, music and language of the Elizabethan song alongside the epiphanic application of Aquinas's ideas on art and beauty.

2

Over the dark sea: *Exiles*

This chapter, like the previous one, also offers a biographical take. It tells the story of another aspect of Joyce's authorship: his belief that he could only be an Irish writer if he left the country of his birth. I hope to demonstrate that this belief did not appear overnight, but resulted from circumstances in Joyce's life and certain decisions he made as a result. In line with the genealogical argument of this book, I seek to uncover the evolution behind Joyce's self-fashioning as a writer in exile. This approach also requires a historicist slant, given Ireland's history with emigration. In essence a socioeconomic event, Ireland's confrontation with emigration is deeply embedded in the culture in terms of its presence in Irish writing as well as its oxymoronic manifestation in the nation's cultural identity where to be Irish becomes synonymous with leaving.

The preponderance of the image of the exiled writer in Joyce studies has, to a large extent, obscured Joyce's preoccupation with Irish emigration, which is present as a minor theme in all his writing. This chapter proposes a correction to this view by looking closely at Joyce's attitudes and behaviour towards exile and emigration against the backdrop of the larger cultural and historical conditions that shaped his views on the subject as they appear in his writing. 'Eveline' and 'A Little Cloud' from *Dubliners*, in particular, as well as comments in the Trieste lectures, reflect those views. But for the most, this chapter is concerned with how *Exiles* is as much a play about emigration as it is about artistic liberalism.

Exiles is usually considered a minor work within Joyce's canon, but despite being his only play written at a relatively early stage in his career, it actually takes up a pivotal position in his development as a writer. In certain ways, the play worked as a catalyst that helped him define his identity as an Irish writer. Quite literally, it was a thought experiment, a fictional working out of what it would mean if he were to return to settle permanently in Ireland. Insofar as the outcome of the experiment was a foregone conclusion, in the process he clarified the need for himself to live as an exile outside Ireland. In the voices that Richard

Rowan hears on Merrion Strand, symbolical of the personal and emotional burdens that he must endure, lies a foreboding of Stephen's 'silence, exile and cunning' (*P* 247). The play defines what exile is to be for Joyce – a withdrawal into the self – but it also lays bare the complexities of the politics of exile.

Given the conditions surrounding the history of emigration in Ireland, exile is a theme that many Irish writers have explored before and after Joyce. What gives this theme critical resonance, however, is the shifting semantic space between exile and emigration. The root causes of emigration before and after the Famine were without doubt economic necessity. But if this need was so great that it takes away agency and choice, the Irish emigrant's search for a better life on the other side of the Atlantic becomes something else entirely. Furthermore, colonial exploitation, landlord greed, and oppression created a strong sense of victimhood among emigrants who saw themselves being driven into involuntary exile.[1] This reimagination of a socioeconomic situation into a political condition was emotionally and ideologically charged. The 'romantic and mournful connotations' that departure elicited tapped into larger nationalist narratives of loss and suffering (Foster 1993, 301; Miller 1985, 247, 312). The Irish language, furthermore, did not have a word for emigration until the early twentieth century, *eisimirce*; the only word in the vocabulary was *deoraí*, 'exile' (Falc'her-Poyroux 2014, 167). Not only was going away usually permanent, a kind of symbolic death in a culture devoted to rootedness, the conditions of transit were so appalling that an escape from attrition could still result in death.

In 'Cyclops', the citizen remembers the peasants who were driven from the country in 'hordes': 'Twenty thousand of them died in the coffinships. But those that came to the land of the free remember the land of bondage' (*U* 12.1371–3). Remembering the motherland was a persistent trope in the popular imagination on exile inscribed in scores of ballads on the subject, as in 'The Emigrant': 'Oh, land of my forefathers, sea girded Erin! | My heart throbs aloud as thy hills disappear' (quoted in Litvack 1996, 75; see also Ward 2002, 21; Miller 1985, 103–5, 564). Thomas Moore's 'Tho' the Last Glimpse of Erin' is another example of particular significance for Joyce quoted in his 'Alphabetical Notebook' compiled in Trieste:

> Tho' the last glimpse of Erin with sorrow I see
> Yet wherever thou art shall seem Erin to me;
> In exile thy bosom shall still be my home,
> And thine eyes make my climate wherever we roam. (Moore 1856, 148)

---

[1] The discourse around involuntary exile was particularly strong from the 1880s onwards (Miller 1985, 427–9).

Joyce noted down the second line from the first strophe under the heading 'Nora' (Cornell 25-36; *JJA* 7:144). The 'note of sadness' and the lines filled with 'pathos and guilt' in these ballads had a more heroic counterpart in the nationalist ballads about the Flight of the Earls and the Wild Geese, which 'provided heroic models of dignity in defeat' that were emblematic of the hope for 'recovery, return and restitution' (Litvack 1996, 4). Joyce employs the heroic models as such in *Finnegans Wake* (e.g. *FW-R* 057.02; *FW* 071.04). Patrick Ward (2002, 10–11) has commented on the 'feelings of nostalgia' that pervade constructions of, and literary writing on, emigration. The 'whole linguistic and affective domain of "exile"' is incorporated into a process of mystification that 'establishes and reinforces the simplistic sentiments, postures and vocabulary' employed in the literature of exile. This mystification manifests itself even if the conditions of 'exile' are economic. The idea that Ireland had rejected the emigrant was a common trope (Hackett 1918, 178).

Although Joyce outgrows the guileless sentimentality of his early poetry, nostalgia is a constituent aspect of his writing. If exile is a force that drives his creativity, as is commonly believed, it is the migrant's backward glance, the looking towards home and past, that motivates this nostalgia. The view of Ireland – and that of Dublin in particular – in his writing is a place re-created from memory (as well as from secondary sources, for that matter, such as *Thom's Directory* and other printed materials). He wrote about home from a distance, without actually living through the experience of a country and a city in transformation. We know how well he kept himself abreast of Dublin affairs (an attitude typical of many migrants) by voraciously reading the newspapers and relentlessly questioning informants like his Aunt Josephine Murray or the numerous compatriots who came to see him in Paris for information about Dublin, but the changes effected by the prospects of Home Rule, the Easter Rising and the War of Independence and Civil War made the Dublin Joyce had known very much a thing of the past. Consequently, his perspective on Irish culture and politics is tinted through distance in time and space. When we compare *Dubliners* to *Ulysses*, it seems that as Joyce grew older and more mature as a writer, his representation of Dublin became more hyper-real, through the scrupulous accumulation of countless details, but the city he represented in his book was not the one that actually existed in 1922. The exigencies of change meant that Joyce's Dublin was inexorably nostalgic: a memorial to the city he had experienced before he left it for the Continent.

This chapter, therefore, will read Joyce's 'self-exile' against the discourses of migration that pervade Irish culture and writing and that, as I argue, form an important subtext to *Exiles*. For this, it is again important to unravel how Joyce fashioned his own exilic identity. The notion that he was driven out of Ireland only came to feature in his biography when he was firmly settled in Austria and felt the need to defend his departure so that it becomes part of his artistic ambition (Lowe-Evans 1989, 36). Is it possible, therefore, to think of Joyce's decision to live on the Continent as motivated by economic circumstances rather than dissatisfaction with a nation in paralysis? Did he grow increasingly disaffected with the country of his youth only when he began to work through in his art that intellectually, politically and morally Ireland was holding itself back? Between *Stephen Hero* and *A Portrait* there is a noticeable evolution that shows the making of the self-exile. Throughout *Stephen Hero*, Joyce's alter ego struggles with the 'Irish ineffectualness' (*SH* 66) of the nationalist movement, which is doomed to provincialism if it does not embrace modernity. The danger is, as Joyce put it in his notes, that the country would lapse into becoming a second-rate nation within Europe: 'Ireland – an afterthought of Europe' (NLI 36,639, 2/A, f. 17v).² The only position possible seems that of a proud egotism, the artist who stands 'self-doomed, unafraid, | Unfellowed, friendless and alone' (*PSW* 99), as the 'Holy Office' has it. It is only later in *A Portrait* when Joyce pushes this egotism to its logical limit that he makes 'silence, exile and cunning' (*P* 247) a condition for a new art worthy of expressing the racial conscience.

The accepted critical view is that Joyce left to escape the vestiges of provincialism, emancipating himself from service to two masters (the Church and the British Empire), to embrace a cosmopolitan, European culture. The political economy of Joyce's exile, however, is more complex and deserves further scrutiny. The migrant characters depicted in his writing are prompted mostly by the desire to seek a better life for themselves. In *Dubliners*, Joyce explores the vicissitudes of and the contradictions inherent within Irish emigration at a personal and social level. He showed himself in tune with the Irish experience of emigration and how it affected, reinforced and, in some

---

² In *Stephen Hero*, the phrase is simultaneously more specific and problematic: 'While the multitude of preachers assured them [the Irish] that high honours were on the way and encouraged them ever to hope. The last should be first, according to the Christian sentiment, and whosoever humbled himself, exalted and in reward for several centuries of obscure fidelity the Pope's Holiness had presented a tardy cardinal to an island which was for him, perhaps, only the afterthought of Europe' (*SH* 53). The cardinal in question is Cardinal Paul Cullen, appointed as primate of Ireland in 1866 by Pius IX. Cullen was an Ultramontane who, in forcing the Irish Church to conform to Rome, launched the devotional revolution, supported an absolutist, anti-intellectual approach to Church dogma, and tightened the Church's grip on every aspect of Irish life (see Van Mierlo 2017, 85 and Downes 2002, 42–7). This is the anti-modern Church that refused to support Parnell and against which Joyce rebelled.

ways, disturbed the emigrants' sense of Irishness. The dominant trope that sees the emigrant 'trapped in a state of permanent yearning nostalgia' is one that he questions in favour of the migrant's state of in-betweenness: uprooted from the homeland to which he remains unalienably and emotionally attached, the emigrant is nonetheless ineluctably altered by his new life in the adopted land (Foster 1989, 288). Elsewhere in his writing, in the Trieste lectures and *Ulysses*, Joyce shows himself astutely aware of the political implications of emigration: the continuing problem, on the one hand, of a population that was depleting itself – something of an embarrassment to the nationalists – in a political climate that, on the other, was reliant on the solidarity and financial support of the Irish diaspora – the 'sea-divided Gael', in the citizen's words (*U* 12.1189) – in the struggle for emancipation.

In *Exiles* many of these factors come to a head. As a biographical fantasy in which Joyce imaginatively probes what might happen if he returned home, the play upholds the aesthetics of egotism and the impossibility of the artist to live in Ireland (Benstock 1985, 73; Fargnoli and Gillespie 2016, 8). But within its fabric Joyce also gives meaning to the multifarious notion of Irish exile. A play about return migration, Joyce stages the conflict between home and elsewhere: the return migrant might believe himself unchanged, yet he discovers how the experiences abroad have affected him.

The self-made exile

Early in his career, Joyce made some bold statements about how Ireland had driven him out. His biographers and critics have mostly taken his words at face value. For Richard Ellmann (1982, 110 and 54), 'departure from his country was a strategy of combat' and exile was a 'condition' for his art. But there is a different side to the story of Joyce's self-exile, one that is more complex and nuanced. In his famous letter to Lady Gregory (of all people), Joyce announces categorically: 'I seem to have been driven out of my country here as a misbeliever.' But besides numerous grandiose statements of an overly confident and rather entitled young man, the letter also contains a more down-to-earth reason for leaving: he wants to study medicine, but cannot afford the fees, and he is passed over by the Royal University for financial support. They declined, he maintained, to offer him paid tutorials or invigilation, although they had offered it to others 'who were stuck in the exams I passed' (*Letters* I, 53). Pecuniary circumstances, therefore, were a big factor in his decision to find teaching abroad.

The idea that Joyce was driven out is part of a myth that he constructed himself. The rancorous lines in 'Gas from a Burner' (1912) about 'This lovely land that always sent | Her writers and artists to banishment' (*PSW* 103) sounds very much like the ultimate parting shot. It was fired following the debacle that was the non-publication of *Dubliners* after the protracted battle with the publishers over unprintable words and passages. Joyce wrote the poem on the way back to Trieste after an unsuccessful meeting in Dublin with George Roberts of Maunsel & Co. It would be his last visit home. Not long afterwards, in November 1913, he started compiling notes in preparation for *Exiles*. Joyce's claim that he left Ireland friendless may be, as Barbara Freitag puts it, 'disingenuous' (1997, 75). That certainly was not the case when he left for Paris in 1902. Yeats had introduced him to various newspapermen in London and Lady Gregory had provided introductions to John Millington Synge and Maude Gonne, who were both in Paris at the time (see *Letters* I, 15, 19 and II, 18). Joyce, however, cared more about the money he could earn from reviewing than about making friends among the Irish nationalists (see *Letters* II, 26–7). Nor was it the case now. Although it is rarely seen as such, AE's invitation to write stories for *The Irish Homestead* was an important break for a young, unpublished author on the verge of moving abroad. Among the Dublin literati, people were looking out for him in the way they could.

The young Joyce, however, had a knack for antagonizing people. Without doubt his disposition to rebel against convention is an important ingredient in the development of his exilic identity, as he wrote in a letter to Nora in August 1904: 'My mind rejects the whole present social order and Christianity – home, the recognised virtues, class of life, and religious doctrines' (*Letters* I, 48). This 'struggle against convention', as he explained to Stanislaus a year later, did not stem from a simple urge to protest against convention, but for his desire 'of living in conformity with my moral nature' (*Letters* II, 99). Of course, Joyce put similar thoughts in Richard Rowan's mouth who, almost as soon as he sets foot on the stage, is full of resentment about his 'struggle' with the conflict between love and freedom, with Beatrice's 'pride and scorn' for him (and the pride and scorn of others), and with his mother who on her deathbed, 'fortified by the rites of holy church', had not forgiven him (*E* 31, 32, 36). The freedom that Richard writes about in his book, and by which he wants to live so ardently, suggests from the off that a life in Ireland might well be impossible. In his letter to Stanislaus, Joyce went on to say that 'there are some people in Ireland who would call my moral nature oblique', but setting aside 'Irish opinion', he wishes 'not be judged by 12 burghers taken at haphazard, judging under the dictation of a hidebound bureaucrat, in accordance with the evidence of policeman but by some jury composed partly of those of my own class and of my own age presided over by a judge who had solemnly forsworn all English legal methods' (*Letters* II, 99–100). From the vagaries in the language and the self-aggrandizing rhetoric (there is always a sense that Joyce needed to impress his brother), one might infer that the 'Irish opinion' against which Joyce defends himself is something of a fabrication. It comes close on the heels of another letter, dated 28 February 1905, nearly five months after he had left Ireland, in which Joyce for the first time identifies himself as an exile:

> I have come to accept my present situation as a voluntary exile – is it not so? This seems to me important both because I am likely to generate out of it a sufficiently personal future to satisfy Curran's heart and also because it supplies me with the note on which I propose to bring my novel to a close.
> (*Letters* II, 83-84)

The tentativeness in expression is striking, as if he had only just realized himself. Like other Irish writers, he seems to be, in Freitag's phrase, 'making a fetish of exile' (1997, 72). Furthermore, the projection about how *Stephen Hero*, on which he had been working steadily since 1903, was to end makes it apparent that Joyce was thinking through his condition from the point of view of his art. During this period, he also began his campaign to persuade Stanislaus to join him in Trieste.

In the months before Joyce's departure in October 1904 (and in the months preceding his first stint in Paris in 1902), there was no explicit mention of exile; instead, he is preoccupied with practical arrangements, which include, first and foremost, securing a teaching position. With his mind set on going to Paris, he approached the Midland Scholastic Agency in Lincolnshire, which was able to secure him a job in a Berlitz School on the Continent (*Letters* I, 54). Checking the agency's credentials with the Berlitz School in London, however, he learnt that Berlitz might be able to get him a position in France (*Letters* I, 55). A week later, the situation had changed. He writes to Nora that he has accepted a job on her behalf in London. He regrets that the English capital would be their starting point, but he hopes he might be sent on directly to Paris. At least it was better than Amsterdam. By the first week of October, though, the Midland Scholastic Agency sent him instructions to go to Zurich. The upshot is that at first Joyce was not intending to relocate very far from home in his 'exile'. The circumstances of his departure provide room to speculate about his reasons for leaving. His resistance to conform to Irish social expectations was no doubt an important factor. Yet it is likely that he was also motivated by economic factors

(Lowe-Evans 1989, 3, 32). With social fluidity stunted and the socioeconomic gap between Protestants and Catholics widening, professional opportunities for the Catholic middle class were limited in turn-of-the-century Ireland (Miller 1985, 432). Joyce's personal circumstances, moreover, made a bad situation worse. Owing to his father's social downfall, he had little to go on in terms of financial support or social connections, except to look at emigration as a way of bettering himself. His friend C.P. Curran, who at the time was working for the Accountant General's Office of the Four Courts, certainly believed as much:

> Joyce left Dublin in 1904 not as an Aristides driven out by his fellow-citizens but 'self doomed and unafraid'. He was primarily a victim of economics, his departure the inevitable outcome of his circumstances – in the heel of the reel Shem the Penman out of a job would sit and write. To write he had to escape from the situation created by his father.
>
> (Curran 1968, 73)

Joyce's final months in Dublin were characterized by making ends meet by borrowing money from his friends.

The apparent speed with which Joyce effected his departure is striking, as if it happened on impulse. The precise moment of his decision is not marked in the biographical record. But a letter to Nora dated 29 August 1904 shows him restless. In it he rejects the present order of Catholic life and virtue, virulently accuses his father of ruining the family, and confesses, albeit jokingly, to fickleness in his character. He writes her that on three separate times he had started studying medicine, once law, and once music, and that only 'a week ago I was arranging to go away as a travelling actor' (*Letters* II, 48). Just after mid-September, after his failed stay at the Sandycove Martello Tower and the publication of 'Eveline' in *The Irish Homestead*, he is inquiring with the Midland Scholastic Agency in Lincolnshire and the Berlitz School of Languages in London about securing a teaching position on the Continent. On 8 October, he and Nora boarded the ferry at Kingstown intending to go to Zurich.

Joyce's emigration narratives

Whatever the exact circumstances of Joyce's leaving, the reimagining of that leaving finds its parallel in the numerous Irish emigrants who left the country for the far corners of the globe. Regardless of the trauma of 'our missing twenty millions of Irish', the 'lost tribes' (*U* 12.1240–1) wiped out by starvation and the exodus that followed the Famine, emigration in Irish culture was often accepted as a fact of life. The origins for this attitude lie in the period before the Famine. Despite sporadic waves of emigration dating back to the beginning of the eighteenth century, the population in the pre-Famine years had increased nearly fourfold (Miller 1985, 30, 35, 137). This increase created the myth that Ireland was overcrowded and led (mainly British) analysts to believe that emigration was the only means of bringing the population back to sustainable levels according to the available food resources, even if, by mid-century, approximately 1 million Irish had left the country (Miller 1985, 35, 193, 245; Lowe-Evans 1989, 1). The Famine would only fuel the Malthusian argument. Even when the worst was over, the idea that Ireland was overpopulated remained strong, even in Ireland itself. One of the major factors that sustained this belief was private gain and money. Government subsidies and aid schemes to settle in the colonies made emigration attractive; emigration was a means to prevent the breaking up of farm smallholdings into increasingly smaller parts under partible inheritance; there were also the businesses that profited from ticket sales and job brokerage, while families back home benefitted from the small sums of money they received from sons and daughters making a better living abroad (see Foster 1989, 284–5; Miller 1985, 357).[3]

Although no longer faced with a stark choice between starvation and emigration, poor socioeconomic conditions – the result of deindustrialization and the practice of rundale farming, in which small plots of land were jointly cultivated by multiple tenants – provided little opportunity and, consequently, the flow of emigration continued steadily in the late nineteenth and early twentieth century (Foster 1993, 284).[4] As the citizen in 'Cyclops' recognizes, the wanton destruction of Irish trade – potteries, textiles (wool, lace and tweed), tanneries – by the British was disastrous for the economy (*U* 12.1241–55). Add

---

[3] As Miller (1990, 100) further observes: 'the source of this dilemma was that most Catholic leaders, bourgeois products of an increasingly capitalist society, had little or no inclination to take the really radical measures necessary to restructure that society and so halt emigration. These men had risen to the top of an Irish Catholic society whose very shape and stability depended to a large degree on emigration's continuance; indeed, their very affluence and authority derived from existing socioeconomic structures and institutions which could not flourish or perhaps even survive if emigration ceased. As a result, with very few exceptions such as Michael Davitt and James Connolly, once they had achieved national prominence no post-famine political leaders advocated, much less implemented, measures sufficient to stop emigration.'

[4] Although the direct cause of the Famine was the potato blight in 1846 and again in 1847, the underlying causes were economic too. For decades, Irish farmers had been forced to compete in the export market with beef, grain, oats and other cereals against a background of depression and falling prices, leaving little land for the cultivation of food. The overreliance on the potato – a staple food that was easy to grow – left the country vulnerable when the crops failed (Miller 1985, 29, 53, 290–10, 221; Davis 2000, 21; see also Lowe-Evans 1989, 16–18).

to this the phenomenon of 'chain migration', when those who had already been lured to America encouraged family members back home to come out as well, and the reasons why emigration was normalized are clear (Miller 1985, 357).

It was not until the establishment of the Free State that the tide turned against the idea that Ireland was overpopulated. The argument for Irish self-sufficiency, which for some decades had been the backbone of the argument for Home Rule, was now adopted in the new anti-emigration rhetoric. In 1922 *The Leader*, the nationalalist paper known for its 'Buy Irish' campaign, complained that emigration was draining the country's population: 'Ireland has need of all her sons. And Ireland is, or could be, a land of milk and honey to an extent probably much beyond what Australia is' (*The Leader*, 21 October 1922, 260). Only economic welfare at home could solve the employment problem. In its advertising, *The Leader* encouraged its readers to buy only products made in Ireland to bolster Irish industry and support the fledgling state's economy and it sought to bolster Irish industries in its advertisements: 'Why Work is Scarce | Buy from this list and help to provide work in Ireland' (14 October 1922, 237). The paper was deeply aware, moreover, that the unrest caused by the Civil War did little to stem emigration and sharply criticized the 'armed and destructive revolt against our Saorstat', denouncing the conflict as 'the main cause of abnormal unemployment in Ireland' (28 October 1922, 269).

> Emigration: what is before many of the young people, in Ireland, in these days of destruction rather than construction, but emigration? Many of the young will tend to emigrate if there are any countries that will accept them. You may attempt to stop emigration, but if the would-be emigrants have no work they must in one way or another be a charge on the country. Blowing up bridges and holding up industrial and business activities impel emigration.
>
> (*The Leader*, 8–15 July 1922, 486)

According to *The Leader*, peace and a stable economy would do much more to prevent emigration than any government measure. But no matter how much they regretted people voting with their feet, they 'could hardly blame the ordinary man who has no particular duty or obligation compelling him to live in Ireland packing up and going out of it' (2 September 1922, 78). In the fledgling Free State, emigration remained something of an embarrassment for the government (Foster 1989, 305).

In his writing, Joyce responded to the conditions that underlie the problem of emigration in Ireland. In *Ulysses*, emigration is woven into the social fabric of the novel; apart from stirring the citizen's ire, it is a frequent topic of conversation. Before appearing as one of the newspapers' headlines in 'Eumaeus', the 'Emigration swindle' case is alluded to once by J.J. O'Molloy (*U* 7.383) and once by Joe Hynes (*U* 12.1084).⁵ The drove of cattle that blocks the funeral cortège in 'Hades' prompts Mr Power to observe lackadaisically that they are 'Emigrants' (*U* 6.389). His remark resonates far, however, for it brings to mind English colonial trading practices that were believed to have caused, or at least exacerbated, the Famine, and were continuing to this day, which leads Bloom to think: 'Roastbeef for old England. They buy up all the juicy ones' (*U* 6.393–4). Not surprisingly, *Finnegans Wake*, a book named after a song that has its origins in the Irish diaspora, makes frequent reference to emigration too. The *Wake*'s perambulatory narratives constantly evoke that double, or paradoxical, sense of 'Hither-on-Thither Erin' (*FW-R* 351.16; *FW* 452.27–8) in which emigration is part of Irish identity. Moreover, in calling Ireland 'this country of exile' (*FW-R* 78.4; *FW* 98.4), Joyce indicates how exile and emigration exist as one in the Irish imaginary. Shem is pointedly called 'an Irish emigrant the wrong way out' (*FW-R* 29–30; *FW* 190.35) because as the internal exile he does not leave.

But long before this, Joyce made the cultural significance of Irish emigration a central concern in 'Ireland: Island of Saints and Sages', the lecture he delivered at the Università Popolare in Trieste on 27 April 1907. In this wide-ranging lecture, Joyce quickly turns from celebrating Ireland as a centre of learning in medieval times to its current state as a country economically and politically stifled from the after-effects of colonial misrule and the influence of the Church. Ironically, though, the manner in which medieval Ireland put its stamp on the world of learning – and the spreading of Christianity – is due not only to bishops like Saint Finnian (470–549), nicknamed the 'tutor' of Irish saints, whose monastery at Clontarf is said to have offered teaching to some 3,000 monks from across Europe, but also to a host of holy men, from Saint Mansuetus of Toul (d. 375), the first Irish saint, to Sedulius Scottus (*fl.* 840–860), who left Ireland for the Continent to preach, establish churches and monasteries, and participate in Church politics. In contrast to Ireland's contribution to cultural development in medieval Europe, contemporary Ireland may look like a cultural backwater. Joyce, however, categorically rejects the notion that the country had become culturally retrograde; 'in spite of the obstacles', he said, Irish culture

---

⁵ The story featured on 17 June 1904 in the *Freeman's Journal* and *The Irish Times*. Headlined respectively: 'Bogus Emigration Agent. | Case in the Police Court' and 'Pretended Emigration Agent', the papers gave the account of a Dublin man named James Wought who had defrauded three individuals from Leeds, Benjamin Zaretsky, Harry Crown and Jacob Cohen, after presenting himself as a representative of the Canadian Emigration Society.

still 'contributes to English art and thought'. Nonetheless, he also blames the 'economic and intellectual conditions' that 'do not permit the individual to develop'. Paradoxically, it is only 'outside of Ireland' where the 'Irishman … knows how to make his worth felt' (*OCPW* 123).

Despite mixing in his own feelings about Irish paralysis, Joyce shows himself in tune with his country's complicated attitudes towards emigration, accepting of the idea that emigration is both natural and necessary.[6] He snarls that 'no self-respecting person wants to stay in Ireland', but would rather 'run from it, as if from a country that had been subjected to a visitation by an angry Jove' (*OCPW* 123). At the same time, he furnishes his audience with the chilling statistics of a country whose population was decimated: '5,000,000 emigrants' had gone to America since 1850 and an additional 40,000 who continue to leave annually (*OPCW* 124). (Statistics like these were, in Joyce's time, frequently cited in the Irish press [Lowe-Evans 1989, 39].) Like the citizen, though, he holds out the hope that the 16 million Irish in the United States, a 'rich, powerful and industrious colony', might one day be instrumental in 'the Irish dream of resurgence' (*OPCW* 124). The expectation that ordinary emigrants are imagined as modern-day Wild Geese who might one day return to the fledgling, independent nation is a commonplace in Irish nationalist discourse. The image of the Wild Geese and the calling back of 'those exiles' is central to Yeats's 'September 1913' as well as to scores of other texts. The 'elegiac idealisation' of 'exilic heroes' rhetorically served the 'hopes and dreams', a 'penumbra of projected wishes that mingled, refracted and distorted according to the needs of the moment' (Ward 2002, 50). If not active return, the financial contribution that Irish-Americans made to the nationalist cause, and particularly the importance of those contributions to the War of Independence, was significant (see Fox 2019).

Insofar as Joyce looks through the lens of paralysis at the Irish condition, life for many of his Dubliners has very little in store in terms of self-improvement. It is no coincidence that Bob Doran in 'The Boarding House' contemplates for a brief moment flying 'away to another country' (*D* 67) to escape his predicament; not acting upon his impulse, he will finish up a pathetic drunk in Barney Kiernan's pub in *Ulysses*. In spite of their personal and pecuniary difficulties, Joyce's Dubliners do not vote with their feet. Neither Bob Doran nor Little Chandler, Lenehan, Corley, Farrington or Maria in 'Clay' – characters

---

[6] In his annotation of this passage, Kevin Barry quotes from D.P. Moran's *Philosophy of Irish Ireland*, an unlikely ally for Joyce, that is similar in sentiment: 'The Irishman of modern times has succeeded in every land but his own. For at home is the only place he cannot make up his mind … he will not be English or Irish' (quoted in 'Explanatory Notes', *OCPW* 320).

who are far from upwardly mobile – follow the emigration trail abroad. It is not just a complacent attitude towards their fortune, however, that prevents Joyce's protagonists from leaving. Rather, as Joyce stages the matter in 'Eveline', the story of an impressionable young woman who relinquishes the opportunity for a better life elsewhere, the bond with home is not easily broken. Eveline literally holds on to home when she clutches the quay railings instead of boarding the boat that would put her en route to an unpredictable adventure overseas.

It is easy to dismiss Eveline as one of the 'onimpudent stayers' (*FW-R* 364.15; *FW* 469.24) derided in *Finnegans Wake*. Yet Eveline's case is more than an instance of unremitting paralysis. In his story Joyce portrays with great precision 'the psychological conflict of a young Dubliner on the verge of leaving' (Lowe-Evans 1989, 45) who does not take her decision to go abroad lightly. Eveline is already aware of the 'here' and 'elsewhere' that delineate the emigrant experience even before she had met Frank. The photograph in the family living room of a friend of her father's, a priest who has moved to Australia, is there as a marker of emigration. Although an insignificant detail, the photo possesses a strong emotional value. It acts as a reminder of what it means to see friends and family leave, a loss Eveline does not want to inflict again on her father.

Such confrontation with 'here' and 'elsewhere', with leaving and staying behind, was very much a staple ingredient of the emigrant narrative. It is inscribed ideologically in a type of story that appeared regularly in *The Irish Homestead* whose plot, according to Katherine Mullin (2003, 59), typically featured a protagonist lured away from home in (rural) Ireland only to wind up by the story's end in a condition of greater misery, living friendless and disappointed in a foreign country that often failed to live up to its 'promises of material gain'. In an unused but striking note for his play *Exiles*, Joyce, too, registered the sense of being left behind:

> It is the quay of Galway harbour on a bright morning. The emigrant ship is going away and Emily, her [Bertha's] dark friend, stands on deck going out to America. They kiss and cry bitterly. But she believes that some day her friend will come back as she promises. She cries for the pain of separation and for the dangers of the sea that threaten the girl who is going away … Homesickness and regret for dead girlish day are again strongly marked … The note of regret is ever present and finds utterance at last in the tears which fill her eyes as she sees her friend go. A departure. A friend, her own youth, going away … And she too, like the dark lover who sleeps in Rahoon, is going away from her … over the dark sea which is distance, the extinction of interest and death.
>
> (Buffalo III.A-32-6; *JJA* 11:32–6)

This strongly emotional sequence, riddled with echoes from the entire Joycean canon and Joyce's biography, again underscores how spiritual exile is interwoven with the patterns of Irish emigration and the multitudes that travelled 'over the dark sea' to an uncertain life elsewhere. It captures the underlying factor of nostalgia and worse, which Miller finds at the heart of the emigrant experience. The rootedness in 'archaic customs and landmarks' and 'particular locales now thousands of miles behind them' causing social, cultural as well as psychological conflicts was a factor that enhanced the emigrant's sense of banishment (Miller 1985, 259 and 240). Joyce, furthermore, underscores the traumatic link between 'distance' on the one hand and 'extinction' and 'death' on the other. Despite all hope for return, emigration was, for most, permanent.

The emigrant returns

Whatever gains Joyce was expecting from leaving Ireland, the reality of life abroad offered him something different. He thoroughly disliked his new environment, first in Pola and later in Trieste, suffering from something 'worse than the solitude of the intellect' (*Letters* II, 80; see also *Letters* I, 57). He was not prepared for the estrangement from familiar living and the process of adaptation that emigration involves: 'to migrate is to enter another's narrative' (O'Sullivan 1997, 3). Emigration is never just about moving elsewhere, as Edward Said (2001, 177) argues; geographical relocation is also 'first and foremost movement in a socio-economic, ethnic and cultural sense'. Describing the emotional and politic effects of expatriation, Said (2001, 177) highlights the 'perilous territory of not-belonging' and the 'discontinuous state of being' of the migrant who is 'cut off from their roots, their land, their past'. This state of separation can create a reactionary impulse in the migrant whose private emotions and collective sentiments about national identity start to coalesce. While life in the host country may feel alien, the migrant discovers a new form of comfort in nationalism. As is reflected in his writing, once on the Continent, Joyce no doubt began to think more systematically, deeply and analytically about what Ireland and Irish nationalism meant. But his early experiences also marked a turning point in how he adopted his exilic persona. In doing so, he conformed, perhaps unwittingly, to an essential, but paradoxical condition of Irish identity.

Joyce's exile may look peremptory. His desire to turn his back on his native cultural environment cannot be easily discountenanced (even if our understanding of it is also coloured by the fiction). Nonetheless, his positioning of himself as an exile came more gradually and was influenced by circumstances. Life in Pola, where he ended up after a series of frustrating logistical mishaps (no teaching proved to be available at the Berlitz School in Zurich), was a disappointment. Trieste at first was difficult too. He confessed to bouts of homesickness: 'I should very much like to eat a slice of boiled leg of mutton with turnips and carrots' (*Letters* II, 98). But eventually he settled in. Still, while he accepted that '"home" was now more of a reality in Trieste than in his native city', he remained preoccupied with the possibility of returning to Dublin – whether in actual fact (considering a professorship in Italian at the National University proffered him by his former classmate Thomas Kettle in 1909) or in his imagination. Joyce's narratives of return – 'A Little Cloud' and *Exiles* – deal with the inevitable consequence of Said's 'not-belonging'. The Irish migrant once again enters 'another's narrative' (O'Sullivan 1997, 3) when he finds on returning home that his experiences abroad have inalienably changed him.

'A Little Cloud' thematizes the differences between life at home and abroad through the eyes of Little Chandler who feels the desire to escape the drab routine of his existence, but lacks the courage to do so. When he meets an old friend, Ignatius Gallaher, on a visit back to Dublin, Chandler can barely contain his jealousy. Gallaher has done well for himself on the London press; he is a man of the world, the stereotypical, overconfident *arriviste* or 'mick on the make' (Foster 1993, 282) encountered so often in Irish narratives, who obviously has money in his pocket and means to show it to that native population he has left behind. The critic and novelist Francis Hackett, who emigrated in 1901, paints an image of the 'way-wise' 'Returned American' who comes back home feeling superior for what he has accomplished and looks down on the ramshackle, subservient state of his family and friends, considering them 'old fashioned and behind the times' (Hackett 1918, 309–11):

> He sees no reason for self-effacement. He longs to assert himself against all the powers to which his childhood had been enslaved. He grows loud, aggressive, crude. He jingles his sovereigns and cocks a belligerent hat. He swears more than is good for him, and doesn't give a damn who knows it. Somethings tells him he is out of joint with the world he knew. He criticizes, to set himself right.
> (Hackett 1918, 310–11)

The image may be a type, but it is that of Gallaher through and through. As is the resentment that the indigenous Irish feel towards all this bravado: he has become 'too good for them'. The gap that exists between leads to 'words that should be spoken are left unspoken, and both take refuge in idle, rasping talk' (Hackett 1918, 311).

Little Chandler, despite admiring his friend's success and the boldness with which he talks about licentiousness in the Continental metropolitan cities, quickly grows wary of his friend's pretensions. He notices Gallaher's 'new gaudy manner' and garish dress – his 'vivid orange tie' – and realizes that 'there was something vulgar in his friend' (*D* 77). Gallaher's bravado feels threatening, upsetting 'the equipoise of his sensitive nature', highlighting his own shortcomings, especially as Gallaher 'was his inferior in birth and education' (*D* 80). 'A Little Cloud' portrays Dublin as a backwater, but the ironies cut two ways. More so than the homely Eveline, Little Chandler is the epitome of Dublin paralysis. But Gallaher is a blustering windbag, who, having shaken off his 'shabby and necessitous guise' (*D* 71), has come home to flaunt his success. Overwhelmed by his friend's attitude, Little Chandler keenly feels that 'Gallaher was only patronising him by his friendliness just as he was patronising Ireland by his visit' (*D* 80). In his portrayal of Gallaher, Joyce heaps a fair amount of criticism on the return migrant, notwithstanding that Gallaher is the type of self-made man whom Joyce praises in 'Ireland: Island of Saints and Sages' for knowing very well 'how to make his worth felt' once he shakes free of the country that was holding him back (*OCPW* 123). Gallaher's assertiveness, nonetheless, resolutely shades into arrogance.

Exiles expresses similar feelings of alienation. In response to the theme of the play – the tension between, on the one hand, a liberal modernity and free union of body and soul and, on the other, the realities of convention, human relationships, pride and jealousy – critics have readily understood *Exiles* as a drama about inner exile. Richard Rowan's desire to live with complete spiritual and moral freedom, which he so freely grants but equally freely thwarts, is an ideal that he is unable to realize; as events unfold – his secret assignation with Beatrice, Robert's with Bertha, and Beatrice's and Bertha's rejection of both – he becomes aware that his ethics are unworkable and the only way out is to retreat into an exile of the self (Benstock 1984, 377; Fargnoli and Gillespie 2016, 11). The play's dialogue largely furnishes the critical vocabulary for this interpretation, when, like Stephen in *A Portrait*, the artist expresses dissatisfaction with the nation's spiritual life, seeking the experience of life elsewhere.

In *Exiles*, the experience of life always comes at a price, not least for the women in the play who cannot partake in the freedoms that the men take for themselves. (The magnanimity in Richard's words, 'I have allowed you complete liberty – and allow you it still' [*E* 85], is largely void for Bertha who has to live with the whispers behind her back about Archie, their son born out of wedlock.)[7]

---

[7] As the notes to the play have it, Joyce intended Richard to have a misogynist strain: 'Richard must not appear as a champion of woman's rights' (Buffalo III.A-29; *JJA* 11: 29).

Hence, for Bertha, exile was not an easy state to endure. Rome for her was not a heroic flight from the fetters of convention; instead, she felt isolated in a foreign environment, often waiting long hours for Richard to come home: 'and then I used to think of Ireland and about ourselves' (*E* 175). Especially in the notes, Joyce represents Bertha as a vehicle of cultural stasis and the bonds of family through her emigrant's yearning for the homeland: 'Rome is the strange world and strange life to which Richard brings her. Rahoon her people. She weeps over Rahoon. Too, over him whom her love has killed, the dark boy whom, as the earth, she embraces in death and disintegration' (Buffalo III.A-19; *JJA* 11:19). The dead childhood lover Michael Bodkin, who also features in 'The Dead' as Michael Furey and as the nameless 'dark lover' in 'She Weeps over Rahoon' from *Pomes Penyeach*, is a Joycean symbol of guilt, expressing the sway that the past, almost unalterable 'then as now' (*PSW* 54), holds over the present.[8] In the context of Joyce's play, however, it is an ambivalent emblem of the ties that must, but cannot be, broken.

As a condition, exile is not just a part of the psychological fabric of Joyce's play; it has quite a bit of political traction in the way the play examines its effects. Robert Hand serves as its mouthpiece and it is through his eyes and his words that Joyce develops the play's highly ambivalent position on exile, not least because his attitudes are at times rather pompous and difficult to take seriously. His exact views cannot easily be pinned down: while he publicly defends Richard's move to Italy and his return to Ireland, privately he condemns him and, at the end of the play, rather petulantly announces his own departure.

The article that Robert writes for the newspaper announcing Richard's return is a masterful piece of opportunist spin. As a public defence of his friend's previous departure and return, it is telling as much for what it actually says as for what it glosses over. He asks Richard not to contradict 'any rumours' he 'may hear concerning what happened' (*E* 62) because his intended audience is the university committee who, on the grounds of Richard's morality, may need convincing that Richard is the best candidate for the chair in romance literature. (Robert has also arranged an invitation for dinner, 'strictly private, of course' [*E* 67], with the vice-chancellor, no doubt so he can get to know Richard first-hand.) Nine years earlier Robert himself had censured Richard's plan to leave with 'a young girl not exactly your equal' as 'impulsive' and a 'folly' (*E* 61–2): he

---

[8] 'She Weeps over Rahoon', composed in 1913, is roughly contemporaneous with the compilation of the *Exiles* notes.

expected that Richard was burning all his bridges. Now he mounts a defence against Richard's betrayal of having left Ireland in its hour of 'need':

> *A Distinguished Irishman* ... Not the least vital of the problems which confront our country is the problem of her attitude towards those of her children who, having left her in her hour of need, have been called back to her now on the eve of her longawaited victory, to her whom in loneliness and exile they have at last learned to love. In exile, we have said, but here we must distinguish. There is an economic and there is a spiritual exile. There are those who left her to seek the bread by which men live and there are others, nay, her most favoured children, who left her to seek in other lands that food of the spirit by which a nation of human beings is sustained in life. Those who recall the intellectual life of Dublin of a decade since will have many memories of Mr Rowan. Something of that fierce indignation which lacerated the heart ...
>
> (E 155–6)

Robert's article reads like a blueprint of Joyce's cosmopolitanism, a deprecation of Irish provincialism in favour of the worldliness of Continental culture and morals; he also sets aside as inconsequential the emigrant who seeks to improve his condition abroad. Taken at face value, the article is not of a kind one is likely to encounter in the contemporary nationalist press. One might wonder even if it would not, in fact, have adversely affected Richard's chances for the chair. In his notes to the play, Joyce wrote that 'a nation exacts a penance from those who dared to leave her payable on their return' (Buffalo III.A-6; *JJA* 11:6). As such, bearing in mind also Molly Ivors' reaction in 'The Dead' to Gabriel Conroy's preference for Continental cycling holidays, Robert's article forms part of the fictional experiment that Joyce set up with *Exiles* to gauge what the consequences of a possible return would be for him. But looking beyond the confines of extreme nationalist discourse, one also finds a more liberal position, one that accepts exile as 'a liberation and an education too' (Foster 1989, 301).

Robert's apology thus carefully manoeuvres between artistic freedom and public sentiment. The reader may imagine that Robert's 'fierce indignation' is not unlike that found in 'The Day of the Rabblement'. Defending spiritual exile is not entirely self-evident in a country trying to rebuild a native culture that believes in the natural bond between the land and its people. Precisely because of this Robert distinguishes between the economic and the spiritual exile. The fact that the two are imbricated in Irish culture – the economic migrant is suffering spiritual exile – prompts him to redefine spiritual exile as an enrichment, not of abandonment. The language he uses therefore is the nationalist language on emigration. In a double ploy, he alludes, on the one hand, to the anti-emigration rhetoric, which condemns emigration as a betrayal ('the hour of need') of the country's efforts to become politically and economically self-sufficient, and, on the other hand, to the nationalist discourses of redemption, in which the Irish abroad, and returning emigrants, make a contribution to the nationalist cause, fulfilling (in a sense) the citizen's expectation that the Irish diaspora ('We have our greater Ireland beyond the sea' [*U* 12.1364]) will be a powerful force in overthrowing the British. As Andrew Gibson (2013) has demonstrated, with the phrase 'on the eve of a longawaited victory', Robert links Richard's return to an important political moment in the history of Ireland's struggle for emancipation: the reintroduction of the Home Rule Bill on 11 April 1912 in the House of Commons, a Bill long in the making and several times postponed (and eventually deferred indefinitely on 30 July 1914).[9]

The core of Robert's argument is that the artist abroad does not compromise his cultural identity, but is there on a mission to gather 'the food of the spirit by which a nation of human beings is sustained in life' (*E* 156). This is not about importing foreign influences that are incompatible with homegrown ideas, but represents a liberal attitude about self-improvement, which is important to the nation's cultural self-realization. Robert's position is not unique; George Moore (1925, I, 375), no doubt tongue in cheek, said: 'Those who have lived too long in the same place become melancholy, AE. Let him emigrate.' That the world of the Ancient Gael was dead and gone was, for Moore (1925, I, 375), an inevitable consequence of modernity; it had 'died at the beginning of the nineteenth century' and therefore he believed that to gain a genuine artistic or political perspective on Ireland, one must go abroad: 'Far more would it be to say that an Irishman must fly from Ireland if he would be himself. Englishmen, Scotchmen, Jews, do well in Ireland – Irishmen never; even the patriot has to leave Ireland to get a hearing. We must leave Ireland; and I did well to listen in Montmartre' (1925, I, 5). Oscar Wilde, too, was of the view that exposure to the art of other countries was essential to the development of a modern Irish culture (Kiberd 1996, 2).[10] Ultimately, Robert argues that, for the artist, exile is not a question

---

[9] The action of the play takes place in June 1912. Gibson (2013, 210) comments that 'the summer of 1912 was ... a momentous period in Irish history'. See his chapter on *Exiles* (pp. 209–34) for a rich, historicist reading of the play.

[10] In his 'Mangan' essay, Joyce argues that to create national art, Ireland would need to free itself from Britain and the Catholic Church; the art the new Ireland would produce would 'be either indigenous or purely foreign' (*OCPW* 130). Joyce's position is not unique, but matches the terms of the widespread debate among Revival intellectuals over nationalism *versus* cosmopolitanism (Kiberd 1996, 155–65).

of dislocation, as it was for Ireland's economic emigrants, but a temporary relocation in search of new materials to stimulate the nation's spiritual growth. For Robert, Richard will bring Continental culture home in order to create the new Ireland: 'If Ireland is to become a new Ireland she must first become European. And that is what you are here for, Richard' (*E* 68). Possibly, Robert is echoing Thomas Kettle, Joyce's friend who was trying to get him the lectureship in Italian, who wrote that for Ireland to 'become deeply Irish, she must become European' (1910, ix).

Critics have often gone as far as to argue that Joyce could not have written his great books if he had stayed in Ireland. Be that as it may, his emigration precipitated a backward look that gave him his subject matter: a nostalgia for the Dublin he had left behind.[11] In its ambivalence, however, *Exiles* does not necessarily portray exile in the idealistic manner that Robert conceives it. As I have shown, Bertha's experience of the Rowans' Italian adventure was not positive at all. Richard's was the opposite. Unlike Stephen's stint in Paris, Richard does not return disappointed. As far as we can tell from the play and its preparatory notes, Richard did well for himself in Italy. Again, unlike Stephen, who went abroad looking for opportunities as a medical student and an artist, what brings Richard back to Ireland is a domestic affair, his father's will, but also the chance to win a position at the university. He leaves his exile unfinished, so to speak, because the lectureship can provide him with a platform to voice his ideas on the shaping of modern Irish culture. However, confronted by the political economies of Dublin's bourgeois society exacting a penance of conformity, none of this will come to pass. On the one hand, his return is a middle-class dream. In the end, the material comfort of suburban Dublin and Robert's smug notions that smoking cigars and drinking black coffee is what Europeanizes him (*E* 68) leave Richard feeling deflated. In a self-deprecatory tone, he dismisses Robert's extolling of him as a great artist by pointing out that only thirty-seven copies of his book had been sold (*E* 61).

But, most importantly, it is his philosophy of unfettered living that proves impossible when his emotional relationships with the people he loves fall apart because of sexual and political betrayals (Benstock 1985, 75). Love is the word that Richard does not want to know; his dismay over discovering that Bertha's affair with Robert is based on love leads to a confrontation with Robert at his cottage in Ranelagh in which Richard speaks with derision: 'Explain to me what is the word

---

[11] 'Like many migrants in the decade since, Joyce performed in Central Europe his own research and field work, his own reverse anthropology, while perpetually fretting that the homeland he had abandoned was about to disappear' (Kiberd 1996, 326–7).

you longed and never dared to say to her' (*E* 95). The problematic word is *love*. In 'Scylla and Charybdis', Stephen, too, thinks of it as the 'love that dare not speak its name' (*U* 9.659). While the Wildean overtones are obvious, Stephen thinks of the phrase in the context of husbands and their shrewish wives, mistresses and daughters (Xanthippe, Elizabeth I, Nell Gwyn, the women in Tennyson's *The Princess*) and, specifically, William Davenant of Oxford's mother who allegedly gave birth to Shakespeare's illegitimate son. The parallel with Richard and Archie is perhaps not lost. That the sexual betrayal in *Exiles* is less about jealousy than about undermining Richard's pride in his system of belief is bad enough in itself; the fact that the secret assignation between Robert and Bertha, orchestrated to coincide with Richard's dinner appointment with the vice-chancellor, makes the betrayal political, for it was Robert who had set up the appointment as the final move in his scheme to bring Richard back to Ireland, not to create a new Ireland, but so he could woo Bertha. Towards the end of the play, the action almost literally grinds to halt when Richard, out for a walk after writing for the greater part of the night, his mind unsettled, hears the voices of demons on the strand. Richard's allusion to *The Tempest*, 'The isle is full of noises' (*E* 154), suggests that the penance which Ireland exacts is the nightmare of history. But the demons' voices include the voices of Bertha and Robert; Richard's spiritual crisis is also very much caused by the moral conflict in the present.

In his planning notes for *Exiles*, Joyce had foreseen that 'at the end either Robert or Richard must go into exile', foreshadowing that personal conflict would affect the spiritual rejuvenation of the nation that had brought Richard home: 'Perhaps the new Ireland cannot contain both' (Buffalo III.A-41-2; *JJA* 11:41–2). But Robert's place of exile, in a final ironic gesture, is Surrey, where he is going to stay with his cousin Jack Justice (*E* 169). One does not particularly associate the English Home Counties of the early twentieth century with spiritual emancipation and resisting convention, which makes Robert perhaps a bit of a shoneen. Prompted by a bitter disagreement with his friend and unrequited love, his departure has little to do with politics, art or necessity, but everything to do with spite. Whereas Richard had fled an old Ireland, Robert flees the new.

The shortest route to Paris is via Mullingar

That Joyce steered the action of his play towards ineluctable bitter disappointment is also evident from the notes he compiled where the key themes are doubt, inaction, inevitability and incertitude. The notes were written almost as a separate treatise on the problem of moral freedom and its inherent limitations, contradictions, undesirable consequences and obstacles. The notes position Richard and Robert as diametrically opposed to one another. Richard's belief system is represented as a conduit through which humanity advances itself, only to be held back 'by the type which Robert stands for' (Buffalo III.A-21; *JJA* 11:21). Richard's 'spiritual revolt' must do battle with 'Robert's decrepit prudence' (Buffalo III.A-10–11; *JJA* 11:10–11). In this opposition, it is also possible to recognize the confrontation between the self-assertive modern worldview of the returning migrant with the parochial experiences of the native, alongside which sit evocations of Bertha's homesickness and yearning for tradition. The notes, however, exist epigenetically as an exploration of the characters' motivations and beliefs that goes well beyond the play's action.[12] Yet, as such, the notes deepen the sense of crisis that pervades the play in which the return from 'spiritual exile' precipitates a spiritual crisis. This goes to the heart of how, biographically, *Exiles* works as a thought experiment: Joyce imagining that his return to Ireland was meant to fail.

By comparison, when Joyce fictionalized exile again, he redefined the spiritual crisis as an awaking. In *Stephen Hero*, abandoned several years before *Exiles* was written, Stephen, tellingly, is concerned too with 'love and freedom' (*SH* 202), but he does not get mired in its inconsistencies. He aspires rather to a 'spiritual renewal' (*SH* 192) through art – something we might assume that Richard Rowan was trying, but failing, to achieve in his writing. Interestingly, Stephen's awakening comes in aural epiphany, as he hears voices that call to him: 'nations. They were held out to say: We are alone – come: and the voices said with them: We are your people: and the air grew thick with their company as they called to him, their kinsman, *making ready to go*, shaking the wings of their exultant and terrible youth' (*SH* 237, my italics). This bit of incomplete text, from a fragment that survives in the *Stephen Hero* manuscript, cannot be interpreted satisfactorily, but the gist is obviously the Daedalian flight. Joyce, though, appears to place the flight within a context of nationhood. Ironically, the passage is followed by a long description of Stephen's visit to Mullingar, in the Irish midlands, where he goes to stay with his godfather, Mr Fulham, who is contributing financially to his university education. The visit is, on the whole, anti-climactic and somewhat tawdry, although it gives Stephen occasion to sneer

---

[12] Joyce was conscious of this when he noted that the 'dialogue notes' he had prepared were too 'diffuse'; his solution was to let the action follow the characters' expression rather than the notes' ideational explorations: 'it is not necessary to bind them to the expressions in the notes' (Buffalo III.A-58; *JJA* 11:53).

at religion and nationalist pieties. When Joyce returned to the abandoned novel, revising it as *A Portrait*, he dramatically wrote across this part of the manuscript the words 'Departure for Paris' (*SH* 237; Yale MS; *JJA* 8:1). Joyce had abandoned *Stephen Hero* before he could narrate the moment Stephen decides to leave Ireland. The famous phrase from *A Portrait*, 'The shortest way to Tara was *via* Holyhead' (*P* 250), finds its origin in this part of the *Stephen Hero* manuscript. The coalescing of a vision of flight and the journey to the parochial centre of Ireland gave rise to a new project, which is the subject of the next chapter: Joyce's search for a new understanding of nationalism. Stephen's geographical riddle, though, expresses a paradoxical truth that to be Irish is equivalent to going away. It is an idea that was already strongly present in the cultural discourses around exile and emigration in Ireland, but also one that *A Portrait* helped to enshrine further.

3

Spiritual manifestations and genetic psychohistories: *Epiphanies, Stephen Hero* and *A Portrait of the Artist*

As the critical discourse around migration and exile makes apparent, identity and nationhood are not necessarily coterminous. The paradox that to be Irish is to leave Ireland entails that identity is an individual experience only loosely connected with the nation as a geopolitical entity. To counter the temporal value of the nation state, nationalism creates an ineluctable connection between race and place. Such a notion of an immemorial, immutable past was very much present among late nineteenth-century and early twentieth-century Irish historians and intellectuals. In his writing, Joyce questioned such essentialist views of nationalism, yet he never ceased to be a nationalist (Gibson 2002, 113).

Critics have extensively explored Joyce's attitudes towards nationalism, doing so mostly from a liberal agenda, which represents Joyce as exposing, deconstructing, ironizing and rising above the essentialist discourses of racy of the soil nationalism. This view has its limitations in that it eradicates differences among the historical players – made up of competing factions with varied and variable opinions – and downplays imprecisions and contradictions in ideological positions and how these are reflected in the public debate. This includes Joyce himself who is portrayed by critics as acting *against* his time by offering a radical critique of every form of political, racial, sexual or gender-based essentialism. As I explained in Chapter 1, this attitude comes to the fore in Joyce's reaction to the purported essentialism of the Irish Revival and Yeats's cultural nationalism in particular (Platt 1998, 26, 30; Castle 2001, 174, 197). That Joyce might be *of* his time, holding opinions similar to those of the zealot Mr Deasy and the rabidly racist citizen, was for a long time not considered within the dominantly liberal strain of Joyce criticism (Nolan 1995, 93, 96; Gibson 2002, 107–8, 124–5).

This chapter, as well as the next, will look into these historical intricacies while unravelling some of Joyce's stances on nationalism within the context of their time. I will set out how his views have evolved in the transition from *Stephen Hero* to *A Portrait* (and to *Ulysses* in Chapter 4). I will do so by analysing how Joyce mediates history in these works. Nationalism is an act that reconciles the past with the present; therefore, the manner in which cultural agents in the present negotiate, interpret and transform the past determines the form and tenor of nationalism. In other words, what we are dealing with is cultural memory. In line with the double helix of this book, I approach these issues from a genetic angle. This approach involves mining Joyce's early notebooks for relevant materials that illuminate the question of identity; in many cases, the notes and sources in question specifically relate to the development of Stephen's mind and experiences across the three books.

The trajectory by which this happens is the result of a gradual process that is not necessarily linear. Driven by various internal and external stimuli, the creative process is (for the lack of a better word) interactive. Therefore, the integrity of this process needs to be understood in the light of wider considerations that are present in the writing – matters of aesthetics, style, narrative, ideology and so on. Consequently, the nature of Joyce's notetaking in itself must be subject to reconsideration. My contention is that Joyce's notetaking, in early life and his later career, is not reducible to just one mechanical function: the collection of ideas or useful verbiage that, at suitable moments, are transferred to the text. Rather, as a culturally defined practice, the notetaking is integral to Joyce's creative framework. As such, an understanding of the 'poetics' of notetaking needs to take on board Joyce's preoccupation with aesthetics in his writing prior to *A Portrait* before we can fully explore the origins of the question of identity in his notes.

Epiphanies: the psychohistory of notetaking

The reasons why Joyce eventually abandoned *Stephen Hero* in 1908 are invariably attributed to failure. Hugh Kenner (1974) believes that the 'mythopoeic process' by which Joyce had sought to transform the 'memories of his earlier self' into art was lacking in control. The book had no centre or form because 'it was neither a novel, nor an autobiography, nor a spiritual or social meditation'. It is certainly the case that *Stephen Hero* was getting very long and perhaps looked unfinishable. For Kenner (1974, 31), Joyce's failure stems from the fact that the novel was not 'modernist' enough, citing the book's realism as a reason: *Stephen Hero* is merely 'documentation from the past, transcribed from the Dublin notebooks', by which he probably means the epiphanies manuscript (Buffalo I.A). Kenner's assessment matches the view articulated by other critics that *Stephen Hero* was what Stephen himself would have written at the end of *Ulysses* (see Saunders 2010, 315). But this says more about the critics' taste than about Joyce's intentions: it was a way to exorcise the early novel from the true Joycean canon.

The fact of the matter is that *Stephen Hero* was becoming unwieldy: the manuscript was running to over 900 pages by the time Joyce had completed 25 chapters (of a projected 63) (*SL* 56). With such length, the inability to create narrative tension becomes real. Like the novel, life-writing needs an arc with a beginning, middle and end. But in *Stephen Hero*, that arc is not drawn sharply enough. As a result, the deliberate abrasiveness in Stephen's attitudes (is there anything to which he does not object?) begins to grind after a while. Furthermore, as Virginia Woolf (2002, 79) noted on the difference between life-writing and fiction, Joyce's portrait of Stephen provides an account of what happened to him, but says little about how he experiences the events that happen to him. The transformation of soliloquy into internal drama that took place in rewriting *Stephen Hero* as *A Portrait* substitutes the social perspective for the psychological, discussions for meditations, external reporting for internal struggle (Levin 1960, 48). It also signalled a crucial change of pace in Joyce's prose, adapting a more economic style that also effected a greater fluidity and ambivalence in both Stephen's aesthetic theory and his attitude towards the Irish nationalist movement. Stephen is made into an artist-thinker, hesitantly discovering and deliberating his ideas rather than dogmatically imparting them, as he did in the earlier version. As *Ulysses* has it, he is not a teacher, but 'a learner rather' (*U* 2.403). But whereas it is fair to say that *A Portrait* was an improvement in form, this should not leave us blind to what Joyce was attempting to do in *Stephen Hero*. Nor should it mean that Joyce's discarding of 'naturalism' (a label that at best describes Joyce's form in only the most general terms anyway) involved his rejection of realism. Observation was – and was to remain – a crucial ingredient in his oeuvre.

Joyce's observational art originates in three places – the epiphanies, *Dubliners* and *Stephen Hero* – that are chronologically and genealogically related. The epiphanies come first: an initial series of fifteen was completed by early March 1903. On his birthday in 1904, Joyce began work on *Stephen Hero*, using the essay 'A Portrait of the Artist', composed in January, as a starting point. In July of that year, he wrote 'The Sisters', the first of three stories that he sent to *The Irish Homestead*; seven other stories – 'Eveline', 'After the Race', 'Clay', 'A Painful Case', 'The Boarding House', 'Counterparts' and 'Ivy Day in the Committee

Room' – were completed by the summer of 1905, when he stopped working on *Stephen Hero*. The last-but-one chapter that he produced, Chapter XXV, sets out Stephen's definition of the epiphany.

As Robert Scholes (1992, 64) notes, Stephen's definition of epiphany combines two opposing aspects: one springs from an external stimulus, 'the vulgarity of speech or of gesture'; the other from an internal impulse, 'a memorable phase of the mind itself' (*SH* 211). (In case it needs noting, 'vulgarity' should be understood here in its etymological sense of *ordinary* or *vernacular*.) The presence of this external and internal impulse suggests that the epiphany works in two different aesthetic modes. The first is realistic or strictly 'observational'. The root of this mode is found in the aesthetic notes from the 'Early Commonplace Book' where Joyce discusses 'The act of apprehension' and defines beauty as 'a quality of something *seen*' (NLI 36,639/2/A, f.17r and f.3v, my italics; see O'Rourke 2011, 208–10). The second mode is romantic in the sense that the epiphany springs from the imagination, with the added proviso that the internal impulse must be 'memorable', that is, both *noteworthy* and *easy to remember*.[1]

The epiphany's emotional force stems from its trivial and ephemeral nature; precisely because of its 'delicate and evanescent' nature, it is the artist's task to 'record these moments' (*SH* 211). While to all intents and purposes Stephen defined a new genre, the mere recording of these moments is not sufficient in itself: 'For Stephen art was neither a copy nor an imitation of nature: the artistic process was a natural process' (*SH* 171). In thus defining art as genetic, he does not believe in art that is not transformative. Aesthetic beauty does not reside intrinsically within the work of art, but emerges in the process of making the work of art: 'to talk about the perfection of one's art' entails talking about 'a veritably sublime process of one's nature which had a right to examination and open discussion' (*SH* 171). Art must be both personal and memorable. That said, Stephen leaves in the middle whether the spiritual manifestation comes before perception or whether observation engenders the spiritual manifestation. Nor does he say whether the 'spiritual manifestation' is itself such a 'sublime process' or whether it is yet in need of this process.

What purpose, then, does observing and recording serve? For Joyce observation is what sparks the artistic temperament. When crossing Grattan Bridge, Little Chandler in 'A Little Cloud' notices by way of a quasi-epiphany the

---

[1] Because of the importance of memory, this aspect of the epiphany is thus different from William Wordsworth's famous statement that poetry originates from 'emotion recollected in tranquility' (1965, 460). Whereas for Wordsworth the memory of an emotion leads to poetry, for Joyce the emotion of an experience leads to memory.

'stunted houses' along the 'lower quays' that 'seemed to him a band of tramps, huddled together along the river-banks' (*D* 73), but he later expresses his frustration over his inability to articulate that 'sensation of a few hours before': if only 'he could get back into that mood' (*D* 84). By comparison, the senseless words of 'every mean shop legend' (*P* 178) that Stephen thinks of in his English lecture give way to a rhythmical improvisation, the onset of a poem. Stephen's abilities are similar to those of his creator. From sometimes quite rudimentary materials, recorded in his notebooks, he was able to create impressions, moods, situations, character traits and entire narratives. Joyce adopted the practice of collecting and storing notes for the writing of *Dubliners* and continued with it all the way through *Finnegans Wake*. Although these notes may appear as random verbiage, their importance to the creative process cannot be underestimated, not least because they are more than just words and phrases. They also possess, to put it so, an epiphanic ring.

Grasping the significance of this practice helps us understand why Joyce undid his epiphanies to use them as verbal material in *Dubliners*, *A Portrait* and *Ulysses*. Why were these moments of heightened perception transformed back into mundane scenes? One possible explanation is that Joyce at some stage simply 're-read' the epiphanies 'as compositional materials for the novels' (Natali 2011, 8). Genetically as well as aesthetically, however, more is at stake.[2] Scholes (1992, 68, 64) contends that the epiphanies are not really a key to Joyce's aesthetics, but rather that they are materials 'in their raw and inartistic state' that belong to a 'process of aesthetic apprehension' different from 'artistic creation'.

There is no doubt that Joyce intended the epiphanies as independent artistic creation. In a letter of 8 February 1903 from Paris to his brother, he mentions for the first time that he is working on 'Epiphany' (*Letters* II, 28), the manuscript of which he had lent to AE. Not much more is said, so it is difficult to guess what state the work is in, although the use of the singular is conspicuous. Is this a work whose form and structure resembles that of *Giacomo Joyce*? Some weeks later he updates Stanislaus on progress, alluding now to the familiar aesthetic fragments: 'I have written fifteen epiphanies – of which twelve are insertions and three additions' (*Letters* II, 35). Joyce's use of 'insertions' and 'additions' indicates

---

[2] Elsewhere, Natali (2008a and 2011, 12) finds that the epiphanies lose their 'evanescence' in the course of reuse in a manner that matches Joyce's creative practice. Defying the simplistic notion that revision is always expansive and progressively improving the text, she argues that in creating *A Portrait* out of *Stephen Hero*, Joyce applied a dual process of 'textual increase and decrease', expansion and condensation.

that the epiphanies did not spring 'whole' from Joyce's mind but resulted from a process of gestation.

The epiphanies nevertheless possess a clear note-like quality that is not unlike Joyce's other notes.[3] Not only does the genesis of the epiphanies bear this out but also not all epiphanies contain that element of momentary revelation. Epiphany 25, for instance, is a straightforward prose fragment:

> The quick light shower is over but tarries, a cluster of diamonds, among the shrubs of the quadrangle where an exhalation arises from the black earth. In the colonnade are the girls, an April company. They are leaving shelter, with many a doubting glance, with the prattle of trim boots and the pretty rescue of petticoats, under umbrellas, a light armoury, upheld at cunning angles. They are returning to the convent – demure corridors and simple dormitories, a white rosary of hours – having heard the fair promises of Spring, that well-graced ambassador …
>
> Amid a flat rain-swept country stands a high plain building, with windows that filter the obscure daylight. Three hundred boys, noisy and hungry, sit at long tables eating beef fringed with green fat and vegetables that are still rank of the earth.
>
> (Cornell 17.61–2; JJA 7:67–8)

The 'Early Commonplace Book' (NLI 36,639/2/A), moreover, contains a page of notes that look like preparatory materials for further epiphanies. Although this notebook contains notes for, among others, *Dubliners* and *Stephen Hero*, its purpose is non-specific. Work on *Stephen Hero* had not started yet. Joyce was reading J.M. Synge's *Riders to the Sea* and he compiled his 'Esthetic notes' (see *Letters* II, 35).[4] The notebook's contents, however, consist in the main of quotations from a wide variety of poets and writers (see Chapter 1), hence the name given to it by Luca Crispi (2009). Although the elaborate notes on Aristotle, which are the notebook's core, are exogenetic material for his autobiographical novel, their nature suggests that Joyce was, in the first instance, working through an aesthetic philosophy in its own right. Amid these materials appears the following group of notes:

Beauty is so difficult
I once saw a bleeding Christ (W Yeats)/Beardsley

---

[3] MacDuff (2020, 189) analyses some of the *loci* where Joyce recycled his epiphanies in his later work. An appendix (2020, 233–5) lists all known instances. He also observes the note-like quality of Joyce's epiphanies, comparing it to Hayman's epiphanoids.
[4] The 'Early Commonplace Book' was previously known as the 'Paris' and 'Pola' notebooks from scribal copies made by Herbert Gorman (Scholes and Kain 1965 52, 80; Crispi 2009).

Old Murray and Dante
'Miss Esposito I never saw a rose but I think of you'
'I got the highest marks in Mathematics of any man that ever went in'
'Ah Paris! What's Paris? The theatre, the cafés, les petites femmes des boulevards'
~~Ladies['] bonnets, High Mass at Pro-Cathedral~~
Signs of Zodiac: Earth & living being
'The English have their music-hall songs but we have the melodies'.
Moments of spiritual life
"That queer thing—genius—
'Synge's play is Greek, said Yeats &c'
'With all his eccentricities he remains a dear fellow'
Epiphanies:
Lalor & Alice: The Boy in Dalkey; One servant
~~Dr Doherty and the Holy City~~
Trained by Owner—Mr Casey? (NLI 36,639/2/A, f. 17v)

The entries are similar to a second set of notes in the 'Early Commonplace Book' under the heading 'Stephen Hero' (f. 18r). In style and subject, however, the above notes possess a quality that is reminiscent of the epiphanies. Because their scope is wider, more eclectic than the other *Stephen Hero* notes, they may even be onsets for new ones.[5] 'Lalor & Alice', 'The Boy in Dalkey' and 'One servant' sound like titles for epiphanies, while the entries in inverted commas indicate snippets of conversation, the hallmark of the epiphanic mode, or suggest a biographical origin, which is again characteristic of the epiphanies. Furthermore, in the Paris entry and the entry on the eccentric fellow, Robert Scholes and Richard Kain (1965, 84–5) hear the voice of George Moore; Joyce ventriloquizing the speech mannerisms of his friends is another aspect of the epiphanies. Other phrases, not least 'that queer thing, genius', which found its way into *Ulysses* (*U* 9.303), have a ring of the clever *bon mot*, which again we find in several epiphanies.

Besides offering further evidence of the proximity between notetaking and the exogenetic potential of the epiphanies, the notes also provide an interesting polygenetic connection. In January 1903, as Joyce was stopping over in London, C. Lewis Hind, editor of *The Academy and Literature*, had asked whether Joyce wanted to contribute 'moments of his spiritual life' (Gorman 1949, 85) to his

---

[5] As a shorthand, 'Gradual irreligiousness (Epiphany of Thornton)' (Buffalo II.A-16; *JJA* 7:86) also sounds like the notes I am discussing here; found among the brief notes for the chronology of *Stephen Hero*, it presumably refers to a lost epiphany that Joyce was planning on reusing (see Natali 2008b, 63–4). Thornton was a neighbour of the Joyces when they lived in North Richmond Street, Dublin (Ellmann 1982, 43).

magazine. This was the same week Yeats shared with him the Beardsley anecdote about the bleeding Christ and, presumably, his view on Synge's play.[6] Nothing by Joyce's hand was ever printed in *The Academy*, but it is tantalizing to speculate that Hind's request was for epiphanies; it came just weeks before we know for sure that Joyce was writing epiphanies.

Preparing himself for *Stephen Hero*, however, Joyce was clustering events from his own past. The notes correspond to at least three different phases of his life. Coming first chronologically are family acquaintances from his childhood around 1884–92: Old Murray, most likely an earlier name for Uncle Charles, is a character based on Joyce's great uncle William O'Donnell; Mrs 'Dante' Hearn Conway, the Joyce's governess in 1887, is the fictional Mrs. Riordan; and Mr Casey is based on John Kelly, a friend of John Stanislaus Joyce who had lodged with the Joyces for about eight years when they lived in Rathmines, Bray and Blackrock. The second period relates to 1902 and/or 1903 and includes his stay in Paris and visits with Yeats in London. The third corresponds to events from 1904: on 15 June he met Vera and Bianca Esposito, the daughters of the Italian musician Michele Esposito, at the house of James and Gretta Cousins in Ballsbridge. Vera was involved with the Irish Literary Theatre, which held its rehearsals at Camden Hall at which Joyce was regular visitor. It was after one of these rehearsals, on 20 June, that Vera and her mother stumbled over a drunken, incapacitated Joyce (Ellmann 1982, 160–1). The incident did not affect their relationship, though, for on 8 July Joyce visited the Espositos at their Sandymount house (see *Letters* II, 43).[7] The mention, finally, of Dr Doherty, later renamed Malachi 'Buck' Mulligan, also likely refers to an event from 1904. Although one entry is crossed through, neither this nor any of the others appear in the surviving portion of *Stephen Hero* or *A Portrait*.

Nonetheless, we can speak here of a polygenetic relationship at the conceptual level. Instead of a single line of development, we have a crossover between observations that are epiphanic and those that are recollections from life. This

---

[6] Yeats (1999, 252–3) writes: 'Presently, Beardsley came to me and said, "Yeats, I am going to surprise you much. I think your friend is right. All my life I have been fascinated by the spiritual life – when a child I saw a vision of a Bleeding Christ over the mantelpiece – but after all, to do one's work when there are other things one wants to do so much more is a kind of religion."' Since Yeats did not use the anecdote until *The Trembling of the Veil*, published in 1922, Joyce likely heard the story directly from Yeats. In the same letter in which Joyce announced he had written fifteen epiphanies, he remarks, not without a note of jealousy, that Arthur Symons and Yeats admired *Riders to the Sea* very much: 'Yeats told me it was quite Greek: and I suppose Synge will be boomed now by the Irish Theatre' (*Letters* II, 35).

[7] On the basis of Joyce's mentioning that 'Colm [sic] ought to propose to his roselike Esposito' in a letter from 1906, Ellmann concludes that the phrase, 'Miss Esposito I never saw a rose but I think of you,' is 'evidently' Padraic Colum's (*Letters* II, 150).

crossover is characteristic of Joyce's notetaking practices throughout his creative career. More than storehouses of random verbiage, the notebooks record memorable phrases, moments of life – or history – and interesting slices of narrative whose rhetorical potential drove Joyce's creative engine. Scholes (1992, 141) perceptively links Joyce's abandonment of the 'epiphanies' manuscript to his habit of keeping notebooks, suggesting a continuation in practice, and to the elimination of epiphany from Stephen's theory in *A Portrait* in favour of an aesthetic theory based on Aristotle and Aquinas. What happened is not quite so linear. Drawing on his notes in the 'Early Commonplace Book', Joyce had put the Scholastics already in *Stephen Hero*, but Joyce folded into his revision of that theory in *Portrait* elements from the earlier concept of epiphany.

In *Stephen Hero*, 'radiance', one of the 'three things requisite for beauty' alongside 'wholeness' and 'symmetry', exists in the apprehension of the object as the mind lifts the object 'away from everything else' (*SH* 212–13). In this process, there are three stages of awareness:

> First we recognise that the object is *one* integral thing, then we recognise that it is an organised composite structure, a *thing* in fact: finally, when the relation of the parts is exquisite, when the parts are adjusted to the special point, we recognise that it is *that* thing which it is. Its soul, its whatness, leaps to us from the vestment of its appearance. The soul of the commonest object, the structure of which is so adjusted, seems to us radiant.
>
> (*SH* 213)

It is in this final realization that the ordinary object, or (one might assume) the vulgar moment, 'achieves its epiphany' (*SH* 213). The moment of revelation is that 'radiance' and 'whatness' – *claritas* and *quidditas* – are one and the same. At this stage, Stephen still pretty much adheres to the classical theory of aesthetics that sees beauty as an objective quality present in the object. As an articulation of creativity, however, he goes against the grain of the commonplace view of inspiration. In *A Portrait*, Joyce further revises Stephen's classical, idealist view on an aesthetics into a more dynamic theory of creative energy:

> I thought he might mean that *claritas* is the artistic discovery and representation of the divine purpose in anything or a force of generalisation which would make the esthetic image a universal one, make it outshine its proper conditions. But that is literary talk ... The radiance of which he speaks is the scholastic *quidditas*, the *whatness* of a thing. This supreme quality is felt by the artist when the esthetic image is first conceived in his imagination. The mind in that mysterious instant Shelley likened beautifully to a fading coal. The instant wherein that

supreme quality of beauty, the clear radiance of the esthetic image, is apprehend luminously by the mind which has been arrested by its wholeness and fascinated by its harmony is the luminous stasis of esthetic pleasure, a spiritual state very like to the cardiac condition which the Italian physiologist Luigi Galvani, using a phrase almost as beautiful as Shelley's, called the enchantment of the heart.

(*P* 213)

This turning away from classicism – which also involves a turning away from the theogenetic view where inspiration comes from above – to an aesthetic of creative inspiration is significant in Stephen's development. One might name this form of inspiration (to borrow a biological term) 'ontogenetic'. Akin to the development of individual organisms from fertilization to adult life, Stephen's creative ontogenetics suggests the cognitive process that takes place in the mind before a poem is 'mouthed' (*U* 3.401) into existence orally or manufactured on paper. In Stephen's new view, the mind is no longer just perceiving the object; it actively transforms the ordinary object into a beautiful image. Note the shift in word use here from *object* to *image*, from something external to a creative moment that induces the 'spiritual state'.[8]

The quotation from Galvani, an Italian physician and biologist who discovered animal electricity in 1780, is not coincidental. From its place within Stephen's new aesthetic theory, Galvani's phrase, 'enchantment of the heart', becomes part of Stephen's (and Joyce's) diction through its echo of the refrain in the villanelle: '*Tell no more of enchanted days*' (*P* 223). Although the passage in *A Portrait* in which Joyce describes the poem's composition as Stephen wakes up in the morning uses traditional imagery of inspiration, the associative coalescing of images that occur to him strongly suggests an ontogenetic process. Stephen finds himself in a languid state, his mind 'waking slowly to a tremulous morning knowledge, a morning inspiration' and becoming awash with 'faint sweet music' as if a 'spirit filled him': 'The instant of inspiration seemed now to be reflected from all sides at once from a multitude of cloudy circumstance' (*P* 217). While in contradistinction to Stephen's theory, what we get, as free indirect discourse,

---

[8] In Sam Slote's Heidegerian take, *claritas* is 'ontological unconcealment or revelation': 'the apprehension of the thing *as* the thing that it *is* … is the apprehension of the object presencing itself as itself'. Although in Stephen's theory the object becomes clear as 'image' rather than as thing, the power of the imagination is transformative rather than metaphysical; it does not involve the 'irruption of some abstract, idealised form' (Slote 2010, 16). When restating the argument in *Joyce's Nietzschean Ethics*, Slote (2013, 25) adds that the 'presencing' of the object is, first, an ongoing action rather than a '*fait accompli*' and, second, it is 'occasioned, or more precisely fulfilled, through a sensory, that is, aesthetic apprehension'.

are Stephen's whirligig of impressions of the moment of inspiration. Underneath this is Galvani's phrase, which has been resonating in Stephen's memory from the moment he used it in conversation with Lynch the day before: 'An enchantment of the heart! The night had been enchanted. In a dream or vision he had known the ecstasy of seraphic life. Was it an instant of enchantment only or long hours and days and years and ages?' (*P* 217).

Stephen's aesthetic theory is, in the end, a genetic theory about the creative mind in action that is not unlike that of T.S. Eliot who in 'Tradition and the Individual Talent' compares the mind of the poet to a catalyst in a chemical reaction. While the mind remains inert, it nonetheless causes the transformation of emotion into art (Eliot 2014, 109). It shares, moreover, several traits with eighteenth-century associationism, which substantially influenced the Romantic poets. Emerging as a reaction against idealism in classical criticism, associationism has an empirical bent. Concerned not with the abstract and ideal, but with observations of particulars, it strives to create a synthetic unity through coalescence of ideas and feelings (Bate 1961, 118–19). Stephen's theories thus also help to elucidate Joyce's notetaking practices, highlighting both the transformative potential of the notes and the epiphanies' dual role as creative output and exogenetic material. As Denis Donoghue (1986, 92) remarks about the Galvani quotation, the beauty of a phrase sometimes depends upon its removal from its context (see also Gifford 1982, 11).[9]

The 'Alphabetical Notebook' as nicely polished looking-glass

If Joyce's art is observational, its naturalistic impulse is not restricted to transforming observation into description. Despite the many fine, imagistic phrases in his writing, observation also has a personal and moral motivation. This is indicated by Joyce's famous exhortations about the necessity of the artist to reprove his culture by holding up his 'nicely polished looking-glass' to his

---

[9] Using the noun *incantesimo*, Galvani describes the momentary cessation of the heart when a needle is inserted in the spinal cord of a frog (Gifford 1982, 254 and 'Explanatory Notes' in *P* 536). The 'enchantment of the heart' is, literally, an aesthetic arrest. Joyce's interest in mechanical factors that stimulate the creative mind is apparent from his notes for the passage in *Portrait* from the 'Alphabetical Notebook'. He notes down Galvani's phrase first under the heading 'Esthetic' and then contrasts lower order 'stimuli which produce a reflex action of the nerves', such as those produced by pornography and the cinema, with inspiration proper. 'The instant of inspiration' is characterized as 'a spark so brief as to be invisible' (Cornell 25-13; *JJA* 7: 121). Galvani's influence shows here more readily than *Portrait* does.

people and faithfully presenting 'whatever he has seen and heard' (*Letters* I, 64 and II, 134). Simultaneously calling for engagement and disengagement, this seemingly contradictory statement proves why cultural memory is a fruitful way of understanding Joyce's work, for Joyce shows history and culture not as an external narrative but rather 'as something felt and remembered' (Garratt 2014, 34). The relationship with Irish history and culture is for Joyce a matter of both private and public concern. Looking at how Joyce imagined Ireland is therefore also an opportunity to show how the evolution from *Stephen Hero* to *A Portrait* and into *Ulysses* stands in relief genetically as well as culturally.

In *Stephen Hero*, Joyce created a portrait of a young would-be artist uncompromising in every aspect of his thinking. He is scathing about art, culture, the university, the Church and so on:

> He spurned from before him a world of the higher culture in which there was neither scholarship nor art nor dignity of man – a world of trivial intrigues and trivial triumphs. Above all he spurned from before him the company of [the] decrepit youth – and he swore an oath that never would they establish with him a compact of fraud.
>
> (*SH* 38)

Even his own brother is not spared. Stephen disdainfully accuses Maurice of imitating his ideas when he finds his brother's imagination wanting (*SH* 36). The artist as ultimate egotist – it should come as no surprise – keeps himself aloof from all things political, yet he positions himself as the arch-critic of public affairs. Neither nationalism, nor institutional authority, have legitimacy: 'I care nothing for these principles of nationalism, said Stephen. I have enough bodily liberty ... My own mind ... is more interesting to me than the entire country' (*SH* 246).

Like Stephen, Joyce rejected the pieties of the nationalist movement, but unlike his alter ego his own youthful anti-patriotism did not descend into a wholesale disavowal of Irish culture and history (see Valente 2004, 74). Joyce's depiction of a nation in paralysis stems from a belief in a golden age, an ideal past, a *before time* (quite important to *Finnegans Wake*), when everything was as it should be. Parnell's loss of power and subsequent death was a turning point that took away Ireland's future hopes for independence. Joyce's perception of these events was influenced in no small part by his father's politics. The frustration over the Church's abandoning of Parnell, although based on a simplification of historical events (Fairhall 1993, 126–42), casts its shadow over Joyce's fiction, not least the Christmas dinner scene in *A Portrait*. Historians, however, have rightly decried the reality of a country in paralysis in the period after 1890 (Foster, 1989, 431).[10] If anything, political nostalgia for a long lost political leadership was a trope in Irish public life. The high regard with which Burke and Grattan were held in the early twentieth century, and in Joyce's fiction, is the clearest instance of this. Half ironically, half endearingly, Joyce evokes the Sheehy house in Donnybrook where 'the atmosphere' was one of 'liberal patriotism and orthodox study' (*SH* 43) in a passage that links Grattan to Parnell. Joyce's own 'study' was not 'orthodox' in the sense that he was not, unlike many of the nationalists of his time, interested in learning the Irish language or steeping himself in Celtic mythology. Yet he was, as we will see in this chapter and the next, exploring Irish history, culture and economics in great detail. The exploratory work that he was doing for *Stephen Hero* and *A Portrait* relates to framing Stephen's vision of his country; the results are recorded in a notebook known as the 'Alphabetical Notebook' (Cornell 25).

The 'Alphabetical Notebook' (compiled in 1909 and possibly later [*JJA* 7:xxix–xxx]) is an exogenetic link that contains material preparing for the rewriting of *Stephen Hero* as *A Portrait*; a link that extends also to the early chapters of *Ulysses* (Lassman 2008, 306, 319–20).[11] The notes are arranged under alphabetical headings: 'Byrne (John Francis)', 'Cosgrave (Vincent)', 'Clancy (George Stephen)', Casey (Joseph)', 'Calvacanti [*sic*] (Guido)', 'Dedalus (Stephen)', 'Devin', 'Esthetic', 'England', 'Gogarty (Oliver Saint John)', 'Gordon (Michael)', 'Giorgino', 'Henry (Father William)', 'Healy (Michael)', 'Ireland', 'Jesus', 'Ibsen', 'Jesuits', 'Lust', 'Mother', 'McCluskey', 'Nora', 'Pappie', 'Prezioso (Roberto)', 'Poppie', 'Roucati (Venanzio)', 'Rogers (Marcellus)', 'Skeffington (Francis Joseph Christopher)', 'Sordino (Conte Francesco)', 'Shelley (Percy Bysshe)', 'Uncle William (O'Connell), and 'Walshe (Louis)'. The distinctly biographical impetus indicates that Joyce was not departing from his original ambition in *Stephen Hero* to use his own life as a moral emblem in the resistance to dogmatic patriotism. Nonetheless, the notes also reveal a new direction. The names included, some of whom, like Prezioso, were recent acquaintances from Trieste, would suggest that Joyce was thinking about expanding *A Portrait*'s timeframe beyond his

---

[10] This is not to say that contemporary commentators did not share a sense of stagnation. Writing in 1904, Horace Plunkett attributed 'the paralysis of our activities in the past' to the perennial 'weakness of character' (165). More often than not, however, this notion was pushed aside as nonsense, finding blame with the long history of English exploitation instead (Hackett 1914, 8–10). Indeed, the cooperative movement in the early decades of the twentieth century, spearheaded by Plunkett himself and the subject of *Ireland in the New Century*, was a sure sign of proactive socioeconomic and political enterprise.

[11] This conceptual unity in the notebook also lends credibility to the argument that, genetically, the Stephen narrative in *Ulysses* was at first intended for *A Portrait* (see Rose and O'Hanlon 1993, xi–xii, xiv–xx). Transcriptions of the 'Alphabetical Notebook' (formerly known as the Trieste Notebook) are found in Scholes and Kain (1965, 92–105).

departure from Ireland. At the same time, the notetaking appears planned and controlled. Especially the style of the entries – pithy, condensed observations and ideas that are not unlike some of the earlier epiphanies – suggests that Joyce was working out a new mode of expression.[12] The notebook, in other words, forms an intermediate stage in the revision in which Joyce takes the events from *Stephen Hero*, but reconceptualizes the fabric, the characters and some of his themes to give them sharper definition. In the course of doing so, he also refines his attitudes about Ireland and the Irish.

The first noteworthy aspect of the 'Alphabetical Notebook' is its interest in identity through language and voice. As Seamus Heaney (1980, 160) observes, Stephen is 'hyperconscious of words as physical sensations' and in his notebook Joyce fleshes out the speech of some of his protagonists. The first entry of this kind deals with J.F. Byrne's accent: 'His speech has neither the rare phrases of Elizabethan English nor the quaintly turned versions of Irish idioms which I have heard with Clancy. I hear in its drawl an echo of the Dublin quays, given back by the decaying seaport from which he comes, and in its energy an echo of the flat emphasis of Wicklow pulpits' (Cornell 25-1; *JJA* 7: 109). Accent is an important social marker as well as a marker of authenticity. In *A Portrait* Stephen frequently judges his interlocutors by their accent, not least the provincial Davin, whom Joyce furnishes more reservedly with a 'simple accent' (*P* 182). Byrne's 'drawl', however, is neither as old and noble as Elizabethan English, nor as low as the rural Irish brogue. Joyce hears in it, rather, a mongrelization that reflects Byrne's lower middle-class upbringing. Byrne's father was a farmer in Wicklow who, after losing his farm in a fire in the mid-1870s, moved to Dublin to open a dairy and general food shop in East Essex Street (parallel to Wellington Quay), a busy commercial area, where Byrne was born (*Dictionary of Irish Biography*, s.v. 'Byrne, John Francis'). In *A Portrait*, Byrne's fictional counterpart, the often moody but clever Cranly, is Stephen's most sympathetic listener. Using a slightly modified version of the note, Joyce writes that 'Cranly's speech, unlike that of Davin, had neither rare phrases of Elizabethan English nor quaintly turned versions of Irish idioms. Its drawl was an echo of the quays of Dublin given back by a bleak decaying seaport, its energy an echo of the sacred eloquence of Dublin given back flatly by a Wicklow pulpit' (*P* 195). The 'eloquence' of Davin's 'Irish idiom' reflects Stephen's – and Joyce's – opinion that Hiberno-English preserves within it the authenticity of Elizabethan English and the history of

---

[12] It is relevant to note, though, that the 'Alphabetical Notebook' is not a 'first-order notebook' (Crispi 2011); the regular handwriting suggests the notes were prepared elsewhere and fair copied in the document.

English colonialism. Cranly's accent by comparison does not contain any of the idiom's authentic vigour: his speech is coarse, tinged by the bleakness of commercial enterprise, economic decline and the commonplaces of Catholic oratory. Compare this also to what Stephen thinks of the 'captain' (a nameless acquaintance of Cranly's in the National Library) who has 'a genteel accent, low and moist, marred by errors' (P 228) and we recognize that language is a social marker within the Dublin microcosm and is strongly linked to genealogy. One's voice is determined by where one comes from.

Although the notes in the 'Alphabetical Notebook' touching on cultural identity all but form a consistent pattern, they do give the impression that Joyce was exploring how to make *A Portrait* less caustic in its portrayal of Irish nationalism. Where in *Stephen Hero*, Madden (as Davin was originally called) is a regular at the meetings of the 'very stout black-bearded citizen' Michael Cusack who could always be heard 'criticising, denouncing and scoffing' (SH 61), in *A Portrait* Davin 'had sat at the feet of Michael Cusack, the Gael' (P 180), an event first recorded under 'Clancy (George Stephen)' on whom Madden/Davin was based in the 'Alphabetical Notebook' (Cornell 25-4; JJA 7:112). Despite associating Davin with the pre-historic, pre-Celtic era of the Firbolg, *A Portrait* is more nuanced about his politics. Gone in the revision is the open attack on Cusack's 'separatist centre' whose 'irreconcilable temper' pursued their brand of atavistic nationalism (SH 61); it is substituted with a memory of Davin's rooms and a warmer feeling of fascination with his friend who is so utterly different in mind and being. Stephen still looks down on his Davin's 'rude Firbolg mind', his 'delight in rude bodily skill' and his 'rude imagination' fed by the artless Irish legends of his nurse (P 180, 181). Yet he is 'won over to sympathy by' Davin's 'simple accent' with its 'quaint turn of old English speech' (P 182, 180). The lingering presence of Elizabethan inflections in Davin's Hiberno-English meshes with 'the verses and cadences' (P 180) of the poems that Stephen recites for his companion. Given Stephen's fascination with Elizabethan and Jacobean lyrics, we can take it that the poems he recites are similar to those that intrigued Joyce when he was working on *Chamber Music*. Despite Stephen's supercilious rejection of his friend's attitudes and beliefs, his relationship with Davin is more plausible and symbiotic than that with Madden in *Stephen Hero*. The passage, moreover, is deeply ambiguous as to Stephen's own position. On the one hand, Davin represents a cultural experience he does not understand; his bigotry, which entails a categorical dismissal of anything 'by way of English culture' and complete ignorance of international culture, is for Stephen part of the 'hidden ways of Irish life' (P 181). On the other hand, Stephen's inquisitiveness, his mind 'eager of speculation', suggests another hidden aspect of Irish life that he wants to uncover. Behind this sentiment lies the desire to create the conscience of the race. For Joyce, it marks his preoccupation with alternative takes on the genealogy of Irish history and identity that will shape *Ulysses* and *Finnegans Wake* as Revivalist works.

Another poet on Stephen's mind, and another accent, mentioned in the 'Alphabetical Notebook' is Percy Bysshe Shelley: 'He spoke his ecstatic verses with an English accent' (Cornell 25-46; *JJA* 7:154). Of this 'cryptic statement', Timothy Webb (1982, 32–3) writes that 'in view of what Joyce has to say about the English temperament elsewhere', the note 'seems like a contradiction in terms, a surprising genetic mutation'.[13] The English temperament notwithstanding, the note, although not used anywhere, suggests an interesting development in Joyce's thinking about Shelley. Joyce's interest in Shelley, unlike as Webb notes that of Yeats, did not lie in the visionary aspects of Shelley's poetry but in its lyrical, rhythmical qualities (1982, 33). As such, Joyce's note offers a useful revision of the discussion about *Prometheus Unbound* between Stephen, Cranly and Glynn on the porch of the National Library. The young men ponder the aptness of the verb *illumine* in the lines 'I will watch from dawn to gloom | The lake-reflected sun illume | The yellow bees in the ivy bloom' (*SH* 129) spoken by the Fourth Spirit. Cranly's literal-minded reading ('Illume – it's just the word, d'ye know, for autumn, deep gold colour') is no match for Stephen's observant mind. The watcher in Shelley's poem is the visionary poet that the Spirit evokes.[14] And so Stephen instead thinks about the spiritual sense *illume*, which according to the *OED* signifies the original meaning of the verb, and its unusual use in its context: 'A spiritual interpretation of landscape if very rare'. The Shelley passage may not strike one as spiritual, but in truth it does not 'strike your eye or your sense of colour' either (*SH* 129). Cranly's crude joke that 'yellow bees' are called 'red-arsed bees' in Wicklow interrupts the discussion, leaving it open to doubt whether Joyce was 'unimpressed' by Shelley's 'symbolic language' and 'the political and intellectual content' of *Prometheus Unbound* (Webb 1982, 33).

---

[13] Although the evidence is not particularly strong, the note possibly alludes to Shelley's *Address to the Irish People* and the incongruity of the nineteen-year-old poet rallying for Catholic emancipation to a bewildered Dublin audience in February 1812. Far from visionary, Shelley's speech was a repertory of patronizing, hollow rhetoric: 'The certain degree of civil and religious liberty which the usage of the English Constitution allows, is such as the worst of you men are entitled to, although you have it not; but that liberty which we may one day hope for, wisdom and virtue can alone give you a right to enjoy' (Shelley 1890, 10). Speaking for an hour in his shrill English voice, he did not endear himself to his middle-class audience of Catholic shopkeepers (Campbell 1988, 125).

[14] Shelley (1977, 157) actually wrote: '*He* will watch from dawn to gloom'. Joyce's misquotation of the pronoun makes it less clear that the Spirit is the watcher.

As Webb also notes, Joyce did compare 'the inspired songs of Shelley' favourably to the 'rhythms of extraordinary and unstudied beauty' that he found in the work of James Clarence Mangan (*OCPW* 128–9). (The 'ecstatic Shelley' thus certainly includes his lyrical poems.) The incongruousness of speaking 'ecstatic verses with an English accent' is not unlike the 'old phrases' from 'Dowland and Byrd and Nash' (*P* 233). While Stephen admires the cadences of these Early Modern song writers, they are 'sweet' only like the 'disinterred sweetness' of the 'figseeds' that Cranly extracts from his teeth; their 'language of memory' calls to mind also a grotesque vision of the licentiousness of James I's London: 'the cesspool of the court of a slobbering Stuart' and 'poxfouled wenches of the taverns' in Covent Garden (*P* 233). Stephen is careful not to idealize the purity of the Early Modern lyricists. It may be that the irrepressible associations called up by their words result in 'an epiphany of revulsion' (Campbell 2012, 55); however, it is also possible, as is the case in *Stephen Hero*, that Stephen takes delight in their dubious morality and deliberately performs them at the McCann house in order to shock his audience (*SH* 43).

The pursuit of immorality is a driving force for Stephen. At the end of Chapter II of *A Portrait*, Stephen deliberately seeks out the iniquitous sections of town to animate his soul before visiting a prostitute for the first time. But beyond the importance of sexual experience to the artist, Joyce is also thinking about the political economy of sexuality for Ireland's development as a mature nation (Brown 1985, 126; Lowe-Evans 1899, 48). One of the aspects that Stephen lambasts in *Stephen Hero* is chastity, the 'one virtue', according to Madden, for which the Irish are known 'all the world over'. Like Little Chandler in 'A Little Cloud', Stephen recognizes that his countrymen have a natural repulsion for vice, but that is 'because they can do it by hand' (*SH* 55). The sexual innuendo is clearly intended to put off Madden. Yet Joyce believed that political emancipation went hand in hand with sexual liberation, as when he noted the following in the 'Alphabetical Notebook' under the heading 'Ireland': 'One effect of the resurgence of the Irish nation would be the entry in the field of Europe of the Irish artists and thinkers, a being without sexual education' (Cornell 25-25; *JJA* 7:133). Joyce, it seems, was still thinking about how to live 'in conformity with my moral nature', as he had written to Stanislaus in 1905; although, equally, his rejection of the Irish 'duty' to pay 'one's debts' – literally and figuratively – is based somewhat naively on his perception that European culture is liberal and progressive (*Letters* II, 99–100). Dwelling further on the subject, Joyce told his brother in November 1906 (when he had abandoned *Stephen Hero* but had not yet begun its revision as *A Portrait*) that sex was going to be 'inter alia' an important theme in his novel as part of the artist's soul-searching and a reflection of his own disdain for nationalist Ireland's obsession with 'pure men and pure women and spiritual love' occasioned by some 'lying drivel' that Sinn Féin had published on the subject of venereal disease (*Letters* II, 191–2; see Mullin 2003, 12–13). In addition to all this, Joyce's directive for the artist to be a sexual being assumes an even bolder form when he writes, under 'Dedalus (Stephen)': 'He hoped that by sinning whole-heartedly his race might come in him to the knowledge of herself' (Cornell 25-8; *JJA* 7:116). A far cry from Robert Hand's Europeanizing cigars, or Gallaher's great pleasure domes of Paris and London, the note, although it remains unused, gives an entirely new meaning to the famous phrase about forging the uncreated conscience of his race.[15] In *A Portrait*, sexual transgression is an instrument on the road to Stephen's '*Non serviam!* in *Ulysses* (*U* 15.4228), a proclamation not accidentally made in a brothel: 'Beside the savage desire within him to realise the enormities which he brooded nothing was sacred' (*P* 98–9). Joyce renders Stephen's personal trajectory, 'his own soul going forth to experience, unfolding itself sin by sin' (*P* 103), into a prerequisite for making a modern nation of Ireland.[16]

That Joyce had the intention of making his novel *about* Ireland is apparent from three pages of notes, the longest entry in the 'Alphabetical Notebook', under the heading 'Ireland'. Included here are some of Stephen's *bon mots* that ended up in *Ulysses*: 'The sow that eats her young', 'Irish art is the cracked looking-glass of a servant', 'The shortest way from Cape of Good Hope to Cape Horn is to sail away from it. The shortest route to Tara is via Holyhead', and 'The Irish are washed by the Gulf Stream' (Cornell 25-6; *JJA* 7:133–4; see *P* 203, *U* 1.146, *P* 250 and *U* 1.477). A minor theme is Joyce's perception of the backward nature of Ireland: 'The Irish provinces not England and her tradition stand between me and Edward VII' (Cornell 25-6; *JJA* 7:134). Irish provincialism is a greater force than British imperialism in hampering the artist's free expression. In this case, the culprit is Maunsel & Co. In a recent spat with the publisher over an insult to the king in 'Ivy Day in the Committee Room', Joyce was at a loss as to why

---

[15] One of the tragic consequences of Joyce's position here is the way Joyce's women often become the victim of his moral principles; his work is replete with male characters who attempt to force sexual freedom on their female companions: Frank in 'Eveline', Mr. Duffy, Gabriel Conroy, Leopold Bloom (in the case of Martha Clifford) and Shaun the Post. Most explicit of all, Richard Rowan's endeavour in *Exiles* to force Bertha to make her own 'sexual and emotional choices' is not, as Richard Brown contends, 'the cause of a wider kind of emancipation' (1985, 95), but one of the great cruelties perpetrated in the play.

[16] While Joyce's stance on sexuality puts the pieties of much Revivalist writing into relief (a point argued by Mullin 2003), his ideas find their precedent in George Moore's *The Untilled Field* (1903). The priest in 'A Letter to Rome', for instance, petitions the pope for the abolition of celibacy, for allowing the clergy to marry would resolve the depopulation of Ireland.

an Irish publisher should object (*Letters* II, 292). For Joyce, however, at the root of this conservatism lies the Irish aversion to disturb the status quo: 'The first maxim in Irish morals is: omertà (the Sicilian law of silence)' (Cornell 25-25; *JJA* 7:133). This moral silence is surely ironic, given that the Mafia's code of honour was based on not speaking up, not giving up one's own. It contradicts what Joyce thought was the Irish penchant for betrayal.

These *bon mots*, furthermore, signal more than an ironic regard for Ireland, especially when we look at them in context. Apart from their obvious aphoristic quality, the notes under 'Ireland' comment on the state of the nation, but with a clear sense of its historical trajectory. Ireland's fate over the past 800 years has left the country depleted and dispirited: 'Her state is like that of France after the Napoleonic wars or Egypt after the slaughter of the first-born' (Cornell 25-25; *JJA* 7:133). Colonialism has left its impact on the arts: 'Irish wit follows in the footsteps of King James the Second who struck off base money for Ireland which the hoofs of cattle have tramped into her soil' (Cornell 25-6; *JJA* 7:134). As this Irish bull suggests, Irish wit, the hallmark of the quick repartee and the sharpness of the Irish mind, is now as debased as the coins that James II had minted to fund his campaign against William of Orange. Struck in base metal, James II's currency was to be redeemable for silver and gold money upon his victory over the Williamites, but his defeat at the Boyne rendered the coins worthless. In 'Nestor' we encounter a small display of Stuart coins in Mr Deasy's office (*U* 2.201), a character who stands in no relationship at all to Irish wit. Joyce, however, found inspiration in the incongruity of the Irish bull, especially the kind that turned the table on an unsuspecting interlocutor (Gibson 2002, 6-7); in Trieste he had a copy of H.P. Kelly's *Irish Bulls and Puns: 500 Gems of Irish Wit and Humour* (1906).

The effects of British rule are also still felt in daily life: 'The curfew is still a nightly fear in her starving villages' (Cornell 25-26; *JJA* 7:134). When used in *A Portrait*, this phrase becomes slightly less direct. The use of the past tense – 'the curfew was still' (*P* 181) – indicates a 'residual terror' (Gibbons 2001, 144) as the memory of the curfews – an instrument of the British to keep the peace in rural districts for much of Ireland's past – continues to resonate. In his note, Joyce suggests that in early twentieth-century Ireland, the nightmare of history is less a 'terror of soul' (*P* 181) than it is still an actual fear present in the social consciousness. We are reminded perhaps of the young Stephen's confused feelings towards the peasants of Clane, as he imagines how pleasant it would be to spend the night in one of the cottages 'before the fire of smoking turf', but the thought of the road and the trees in the darkness make him afraid (*P* 18).

When it comes to the idea of armed resistance, Joyce is reluctant to embrace violence. But noting Ireland's 'rebellions are servile wars' (Cornell 25-26; *JJA* 7:134), he points to the ineffectualness and futility of the Irish uprisings against the Britain's greater power. (The Servile Wars in the second and first century BC were a series of uprisings of the Roman slaves who were brutally beaten.) The phrase, furthermore, had currency among Ascendancy commentators in the nineteenth century who used it to deprecate the manifestation of agrarian unrest (see O'Connor Morris 1901, 29, 156; see also Hackett 1918, 335–6).

To say that Ireland's belatedness in the arts is due to the country's provincial morality is to recognize the impact of the Church: 'Its learning is in the hands of the monks and their clerks and its art in the hands of blacklegs who still serve those ideas which their fellow artists in Europe have rebelled against' (Cornell 25-25; *JJA* 7:133). Nonetheless, the learning produced by Irish monks is worthy of attention, albeit with a degree of qualification:

> Duns Scotus has won a poorer fame than S. Fiacre, whose legend sown in French soil, has grown up in a harvest of hackney-cabs.
> If he and Columbanus the fiery whose fingertips God illumined, and Frigedius Viator can see as far as earth from their creepy-stools in heaven they know that Aquinas, the lucid sensual Latin, has won the day.
> (Cornell 25-27; *JJA* 7:135)

The note is reprised twice, first in 'Ireland: Island of Saints and Sages' (*OCPW* 111) and then in *Ulysses* (*U* 3.192–4). Its meaning in the notebook pertains to the status that the Irish saints have in the national consciousness. And it is thus that Joyce introduces them in his lecture: to note the long tradition of Irish influence on learning and on the development of the Catholic world in Europe. Saint Columbanus, whom the *Catholic Encyclopedia* describes as 'impetuous and even head-strong' in his pursuit of God's cause (s.v. 'St. Columbanus'), became one of the most prolific saints in establishing monasteries on the Continent, most notably the abbeys at Luxeuil, Saint Gall and Bobbio; as such, he is believed to be 'the first to express a sense of pan-European collectivity' in his writing (O'Hara 2018, 14). His life was noted, too, for his conflict with the French bishops over the observance of Easter – he clung to the old, Irish method of calculating the date of the feast day – and for preferring the Irish form of tonsure. He also embroiled himself with the politics of the Frankish court. Saint Fiacre was also Irish by birth, but moved to France in 682 where he was given land by Saint Faro, the Bishop of Meaux, at Breuil in recognition of the kindness the bishop and his family had received from Columbanus. There he established a hermitage, with a vegetable and herb garden, and built a hospice for travellers. His tenuous association with Paris hackney cabs is due to the fact that the first hackneys around 1650 plied their trade from the Hôtel Saint Fiacre in the rue Saint-Martin.

For Joyce, this connection with the public commercial sphere makes the fame that Saint Fiacre enjoys of a lesser order than that of John Duns Scotus, the thirteenth-century Franciscan theologian and philosopher known for his commentary on Aristotle's *Metaphysics* and his fervent defence of the Immaculate Conception.[17] (He is credited with inventing the doctrine.) Scotus's reputation was not without controversy, however. Because of his relentless criticism, and the fact that he only produced commentaries on the work of others without developing a coherent system of thought of his own, he was perceived to be 'better at tearing down than at building up' (*Catholic Encyclopedia*, s.v. 'Bl. John Duns Scotus'); some of his writing also came close to heresy. Along with Scotus being expelled from the University of Paris in 1304, these incidents provide ironic (albeit probably unintentional) parallels with Stephen. The connection with Stephen is borne out, though, by a later note for *Finnegans Wake*, 'Aquinas v Scotus | SP v D' (VI.B.14.048), which appears in the context of other notes about the settlement of Irish saints on the Continent. Frigedius Viator, finally, is an amalgamation of Saint Fridianus (or Frigidanus) (560–88), the son of the Ulster King Ultonius, who became Bishop of Lucca, and Saint Fridolinus (d. 498), also the son of an Irish king, whose received his agnomen Viator because of his extensive travels across France and Germany, where he founded several churches and monasteries.

As I said, Joyce sets out in his note to contrast the Irish zeal in the apostolic mission with true philosophic learning, but he does not wholly decry the importance of the saints' achievement. Much of the literature on the subject from the late nineteenth and early twentieth century that Joyce was familiar with (see Chapter 4) was patriotic in nature and frequently highlighted the national character of the Irish Church, which took pride in resisting the influence of Rome. Joyce reflects this in another note under 'Ireland', 'The cable of Catholicism that links Ireland to Latin Europe is eaten by two seas', which at once expresses the connection between Irish Catholicism and the Continent and the idea that, in his own time, there are lingering differences between Irish Catholic culture and the Church of Rome (Van Mierlo 2017, 18–19). When Stephen in 'Proteus' casts himself as 'missionary to Europe after fiery Columbanus' (*U* 3.192), he ironically heralds the end of the great Irish tradition of exporting learning. Not only do we know that his Parisian ambitions to study medicine and become a poet had come to nothing, his image of Fiacre and Scotus sitting 'on their creepystools

---

[17] Although of Scottish descent, Scotus is often claimed as Irish.

in heaven' is a grotesque inversion of learning; drunk, spilling their beer, they mockingly cough-cum-applaud the world below: 'loudlatinglaughing: *Euge! Euge!*' (*U* 3.193–4). (Latin 'euge' means *well done, bravo!*) With this antithesis to Aquinas's 'lucid sensual Latin' (Cornell 25-27; *JJA* 7:135), has Stephen's apostolate for 'applied Aquinas' (*SH* 77) come prematurely to an end?

One final note under 'Ireland' seems different from the others: 'There is hope for her: in 500 years the coal supply of England will run out' (Cornell 25-27; *JJA* 7:135). Obliquely referred to in 'Eumaeus' (*U* 16.989), the note alludes to the concern, repeatedly voiced by the British elite throughout the nineteenth century, about the finite nature of national coal supplies, which early in the century was estimated as lasting only 500 years; the need to import coal would have a detrimental impact on British industry and its economic position in the world. At the turn of the century, coalmining in Ireland could not compete with imports from the richer seams in Britain, yet it possessed significant coal fields in Kilkenny and Tyrone, with twenty-four mines generating about 125,000 tons annually (Coyne 1902, 17; Keenan 2006, 134). By 1910 the issue had disappeared; the continued discoveries of new arteries and improvements in deep mining meant that coal production had arrived at its peak. But while Joyce's note may be anachronistic, it points to debates about economic self-sufficiency that, according to Irish nationalists, was imperative to Ireland if it was to gain independence from London. If Irish coal could penetrate the British market, it would help to turn the tide against the 'degeneration of economic tissue' that had eroded the nation since the Act of Union (Kettle 1910, 150).

Regardless of the precise context, the note is something of an anomaly in the 'Alphabetical Notebook'; with the notes on Irish saints in Europe, it looks beyond the central concerns in *Stephen Hero* and *A Portrait of the Artist*, and even *Dubliners*. Where Joyce had sought to give expression to his personal experience of Ireland and Irish nationalism, we see an early sign of his preoccupation with the political economies of the Irish nation and with a new sense of historical particularity that would characterize *Ulysses* (Gibson 2002, 123). More than anything else, *Ulysses* was to be a book of local colour, and this required a new approach in collecting notes and materials to that which Joyce had employed in idea-driven notebooks such as the 'Alphabetical Notebook'.[18] The 'Subject Notebook', the oldest extant notebook for *Ulysses*, which is the subject of Chapter 4, possesses such an aim.

[18] The later transference of notes from the 'Alphabetical Notebook' to the *Ulysses* notesheets confirms the conceptual importance of its contents. Of the entries that I quoted that were copied to the notesheets, along with other notes, are: 'Catholic cable eaten by 2 seas' and 'mill. years E no coal' ('Eumaeus' 5: 21–2; Herring 1972, 394).

4

Creating the conscience: *Ulysses*

In the Library chapter, Stephen listens, wryly perhaps, to John Eglinton who declares that, according to George Sigerson, 'our national epic remains to be written' and that George Moore 'is the man for it' (*U* 9.309-10). This is not strictly what George Sigerson (1904, vii) had said though; rather, he argued that European literature did not remain unaffected by the presence of the 'Irish spirit'. Without Irish influence, there would be no fairies in Shakespeare; no rhyme in medieval Germanic poetry; and the Irish landscape would not have left its imprint on the *Nibelungenlied*, *Tristan and Isolde* and Spenser's *Faerie Queene*. In more ways than one, this influence was due to the great tradition of scholars who spread Irish knowledge and culture abroad, a tradition that continued when the 'descendants of those who had taught Europe for three centuries … were driven from their hospitable land by famine' (xii). Ireland, therefore, must continue to 'live by the energy of intellect' and produce new literature worthy of taking its place among the 'nations of the earth' (Sigerson 1904, xii–xiii). Taken at face value, however, Sigerson overlooks the writing produced in Ireland in the last century, the implication being, as Stephen certainly takes it, that the work produced by the early Revival was too inconsequential to represent Ireland in world literature (Tymoczko 1994, 55). There was no lack of contenders, however. Samuel Ferguson's long poem *Congal* from 1872, for instance, was noted for its 'epic aim' (Yeats 1989b, 106). Neither was there a lack of ambition. In 1904, Yeats was collaborating with George Moore on *Diarmuid and Grania*, which they intended to fill that void, but it never saw the light of day.

It is something of a commonplace in Joyce criticism that *Ulysses* was the first Irish work to qualify as a national epic. Although it would take several decades for its reputation as such to be cemented, the book's early reception unambiguously points to its importance as an *Irish* work. Mary Colum wrote in her 1922 review that it was 'one of the most racial books ever written, and one of the most Catholic books ever written'; no one not deeply familiar with the 'heroism, tragedy, folly and anger of Irish nationalism' would ever truly understand it.[1] In her autobiography, Colum (1947, 386) stated that, because of the book's unparalleled detail, Irish readers would see it as a 'national masterpiece'. Yeats thought it had 'our Irish cruelty & also our kind of strength ... A cruel playful mind like a great soft tiger cat'; 'some passages have great beauty, lyric beauty, even in the fashion of my generation' (*CL Intelex* #4085, 4152). Above all, he believed that *Ulysses* was the answer to the Irish Revival's call for a new form of writing to emerge in Ireland.

Yeats repeated this call in 1923 on the back of his reading of Joyce's new book. In 'The Irish Dramatic Movement', he considered that Ireland was about 'to create a new form' of writing that would complement the kind of work that the Abbey Theatre had produced; *Ulysses*, he said, 'a strange Irish novel' that had been published the other day, 'certainly' represented such a 'new form' (Yeats 2000b, 161).[2] Ten years later he contemplated using Joyce's novel as a starting for his essay 'Ireland, 1921–1931', an essay that celebrated a new dawn in art and literature at the birth of a new nation, the Irish Free State (*CL Intelex* #5564). As the piece took shape, however, Yeats focused not on the new, but on the old in what became a panegyric on the Anglo-Irish eighteenth century – Berkeley, Swift and the books that his ancestors had read – to express his disgust at the betrayal of the Protestant bishops who were trying to outmanoeuvre the Cosgrave government in 1931, which would have kept the Irish courts subordinate to the Privy Council (Yeats 2000b, 232–3). One might say that he got sidetracked by current events. What he had in mind at first, though, was Joyce's audacity, his strength of contrariness, which Yeats had already referred to obliquely some years earlier in 'The Need for Audacity of Thought' (1926), a piece in which he rebuked the 'Irish Religious Press' for their unnecessary attacks on Lennox Robinson (Yeats 2000b, 201).

Joyce without doubt had wilfully made his book contrary to the reigning pieties of the day. Because of this polarity, *Ulysses* does not, in the end, contain a vision for the new Ireland. Many of Joyce's critics find revelation in the language of *Ulysses* whose discursive practices disrupt the binaries of national, colonial and ecclesiastical power. It is the case that through 'the dramatization of verbal inventiveness, invective and parody as aggressive responses to colonial power'

---

[1] Colum's review, 'The Confessions of James Joyce', was first printed in *The Freeman*, 19 July 1922; http://marycolum.com/articles/confessions-of-james-joyce.
[2] Yeats recycled the title 'The Irish Dramatic Movement' a number of times. This version is the one published as 'A Letter to the Students of a Californian School' in William George Fitzgerald's *The Voice of Ireland* (1923), marking the creation of the Irish Free State.

(Nolan 1995, 120) *Ulysses* undermines power. The central presence of parody and pastiche in the book comes from a deliberate 'strategy of adulteration' (Gibson 2002, 178). But Joyce, shunning abstract idealizations, does not rebuild what his critique breaks down. Nonetheless, he wanted to frame his book as an Irish work. When Random House was preparing a circular to advertise the first American edition with images of locations mentioned in the book, Joyce wanted accurate photos by an Irish photographer, T.W. Pugh (Gibbons 2015, 190–1). What is clear, however, is that in *Ulysses* Joyce moved beyond his early position vis-à-vis Ireland. His initial bitterness towards the country of his birth, fictionalized in the early writing, dissipates into a more sustained exploration of Irish nationhood.

Ulysses is thus concerned with identity in a manner both substantial and ephemeral, from the citizen's exhortations in Barney Kiernan's pub to Bloom's poem, never written, on *'If Brian Boru could but come back and see old Dublin now'* (*U* 17.419). This new exploratory mode was not so much the result of a predetermined plan, but a continuation of how the artist sees Ireland. As the autobiographical interest receded, Joyce brought Ireland's political and cultural diversity, already explored in *Dubliners*, back to the fore. Although not always depicted sympathetically, the presence of Protestant characters in Joyce's fiction is a sign of this, as is Bloom's mixed Jewish-Protestant-Catholic heritage. The diversity is further supplemented by the perspective implied in the novel's 'historical' setting. Set in 1904, *Ulysses* mixes hyper-reality with a form of idealism as it looks back to a Dublin that, at the time of publication, had already changed perceptibly from the city that Joyce had left. Certain anachronisms notwithstanding, it nostalgically creates a snapshot of a city suspended in a time lapse (see Gibbons 2015, 197–8).

The choice of date was perhaps fortuitous. Predating the Easter Rising and the War of Independence and Civil War, it created a 'prefall paradise peace' (*FW-R* 24.13; *FW* 35.15) condition by which Joyce avoided any direct mention of these cataclysmic events. Behind its commemoration of a personal event, however, the date Joyce and Nora went out lovemaking for the first time, lies a political intent that allowed him to become a 'compulsive historian' (Spoo 1994, 4). He put as much history and reality into his book to record the memory of, and construct a monument to, his culture. Critics have bought into the idea of *Ulysses* as an 'undeveloped possibility' (Gibson 2002, 40). Luke Gibbons (2015, 197–8) has demonstrated that for certain early Irish readers the novel brought back Dublin 'from the wreckage of dreams' as they came to terms with the 'psychological abrasions' of war and lost ideals. *Ulysses*, in that respect, is what is called a 'formative text' in memory studies, an expression of a cultural group's self-image (Erll 2011, 34). The appreciation for the past is present throughout the novel, for instance in Ned Lambert's admiration for the Rev. Hugh C. Love who, he says, is 'well into history, faith' (*U* 10.439). Equally, the past also poignantly intrudes on the present. Deasy's 'I remember the Famine' (*U* 2.269) should give pause to consider how collective memory emerges and evolves (see O'Callaghan 2014, 105–6). Nevertheless, the characters in *Ulysses* are so specifically tied to their own time and memory that, barring bourgeois fantasies about the new 'Bloomusalem', the book offers no definite vision for the future.

Ulysses is sometimes explicitly read as an anti-Revival novel (Platt 1998; Gibson 2002). On the face of it, this may well be the case. The novel's urban modernity is a 'revivalist anti-world' (Platt 1998, 189). As noted before, such readings rest on a reductive understanding of the Revival as a unitary movement, which it clearly was not. Still, because the novel is concerned not with what is essentially, but self-evidently Irish, *Ulysses*, more than any of Joyce's previous works, engages with the particulars of Ireland's past and present (Gibson 2002, 8, 13–14, 18).[3] In eliciting these particulars, Joyce genealogically probes Ireland's image of itself and its cultural roots. Critically, therefore, a historicist approach to the novel is profitably complemented by an exploration of cultural memory in that *Ulysses* does not just represent the past; it dramatizes its characters' engagement with the past, how they remember and experience it. Memory is rooted in experience, involving not only the recollection of what happened and when it happened but also the recollection of what that experience was like. This is what Sven Bernecker (n.d., 3) calls 'experiential memory', that is, memories formed 'by acquaintance' with 'people, places, things, events, and situations'. This type of 'lived' experience (Erll 2011, 31) is in fact what makes *Ulysses* so rich and unique. The thousands of notes in Joyce's notebooks and notesheets are the foundations from which he so meticulously built the personal and interpersonal experiences of his characters.

Likewise, the extent to which the Irish Revival is a cultural memory project is adumbrated in *Ulysses* and elsewhere in Joyce's work. From the middle of the nineteenth century, members of the Revival engaged in nation-building

---

[3] Gibson's point that Joyce used 'historical particularities' to counter 'Revival historiography' (2002, 123) assumes that all Revivalists were generalists, which they were not. *The Irish Homestead*'s concerns with creating a robust, self-sustaining agrarian economy are a case in point, as are T.M. Kettle's arguments for fiscal autonomy, without which Home Rule would be meaningless, in *Home Rule Finance: An Experiment in Justice* (1911). Joyce had a copy of Kettle's pamphlet in his Trieste library.

as it participated in historiographical research, ethnography, the editing of its textual sources, and the education of the people through establishing libraries, publishing, public lectures, journalism and, of course, the theatre. The results of these efforts had a deep influence on the nation's self-perception, but they also left their traces in Joyce's consciousness, as well as in his personal library and notebooks. As I suggested in Chapter 3, the notes' function as a psychohistory, an exogenetic exploration of mind and nation, remains crucial to the creative process. Of all the preparatory materials for *Ulysses*, there is one notebook that stands out. The 'Subject Notebook' (NLI 36,639/3), the first extant notebook specifically compiled for *Ulysses* at a significant moment in the novel's composition, is directly concerned with probing the artistic mind in relation to the culture it inhabits. As it happens, this notebook, whose discussion complements that of the 'Alphabetical Notebook' in Chapter 3, also sits on the cusp of the first important turning point in the composition of *Ulysses*. Not only is it the earliest document to survive in the composition history, it bears witness to the changes the novel was undergoing from an inchoate proto-book to a work in progress with a more precise sense of direction.

Notes for the spirit of a nation

Ulysses was begun in 1915, but during the early stages of writing the shape of the book was far from fixed. He had informed his brother that he had begun a new novel on 16 June 1915, projecting a total of twenty-two chapters, with the Telemachia comprising four chapters, Ulysses' wanderings fifteen and his homecoming another three; but so far he had actually written only one (*SL* 209). By October 1916, he had 'about finished the first part' and 'written out part of the middle and end' (*Letters* II, 387), but the novel had not yet found a definite form. By the summer of 1917, the situation had not improved much. In a letter to Ezra Pound from 24 July, he wrote: 'As regards *Ulysses* I write and think and write and think all day and part of the night. It goes on as it has been going these five or six years. But the ingredients will not fuse until they have reached a certain temperature' (*L-Corr* #68393). The writing during those first years had obviously not progressed very well. But the prospect of serialization in *The Egoist* and *The Little Review* provided Joyce with a new sense of purpose. The writing now progressed steadily. By May 1918 he had delivered 'Telemachus' through to 'Hades' to *The Little Review*. But also slowly. On 18 May 1918, he told Harriet Shaw Weaver that he had spent about 200 hours on 'Proteus' alone; the chapter had remained for 'a long time in the second draft'. Moreover, 'just how much of the book [was] really written' remained 'impossible to say' (*Letters* I, 113).

Elements needing to fuse as they sit in each other's proximity is a recurrent image in Joyce's correspondence about his writing. Notetaking was to play an important part in this process of welding the elements together. With *Ulysses*, Joyce's notetaking practices shifted to a higher gear. The collecting, organizing, rearranging and mining of notes became a sustained process, resulting in large quantities of verbal material that are recorded and stored in scores of notebooks and notesheets. Much of this material consists of words and phrases, often relevant for their tone, that could be slotted into the text when needed. As a result, Joyce's method of composition also changed. Where he had previously written his stories and novels in a largely 'traditional' manner, proceeding from beginning to end with little need for extensive revision and recasting, with *Ulysses* he adopted a laborious accretive 'revise-and-expand' approach. Chapters would start from one or more rudimentary vignettes that would slowly grow into fuller narratives, while he mined his notes for the verbal and cultural minutiae that he had previously collected. The method was not entirely new, for he had employed it already in the writing of *Dubliners*, drawing on notes from the 'Early Commonplace Book'. But it was to be his preferred method.

What *Ulysses* looked like in those early years remains tantalizingly elusive, because no archival documents survive from that time. The 'Subject Notebook', begun in October 1917 and used almost immediately in the earliest extant draft for 'Proteus' (V.A.3), is the first document that gives us any insight into the novel's early development.[4] As drafting began afresh, he also consolidated what he already had. Like the 'Alphabetical Notebook', the contents of the 'Subject Notebook' reflect the state of *Ulysses* as it had existed up till then. One of the interesting findings is just how much of *Ulysses* had been mapped out at this stage; we find material that conceptually prefigures chapters that were not composed until much later.[5]

Also the way the 'Subject Notebook' is organized is similar to its predecessor. The notes are stored under various topical headings: 'Simon', 'Leopold', 'Books',

---

[4] The 'Proteus' draft and 'Subject Notebook' were written in the same type 'Modello C | Quaderno' notebook. The two were purchased together when Joyce was holidaying in Locarno (Spielberg and Crispi 2010).

[5] The 'Subject Notebook' contains notes for chapters not drafted until 1919 and 1920 that must have already existed in embryonic form or as an idea. Some examples are 'wishes to write on barmaid's blank face' (NLI 36,639/3, f. 2r; *U* 11.1086–7); 'Come where the boose is cheaper (6 pm)' (f. 17v), prefiguring a late-afternoon pub scene; and the Tyrone street address of Mrs. Mack and Mrs. Cohen (f. 12r: *U* 15.1285–7) and other entries for a brothel scene, such as 'whore tells his fortune' (f. 2r; *U* 15.3698–9).

'Recipes', '???', 'Gulls', 'Stephen', 'Theosophy', 'Choses vue', 'Irish', 'Jews', 'Blind', 'Art', 'Names & Places', 'Jesus', 'Homer', 'Rhetoric', 'Oxen', 'Weininger' and 'Words'. While some of these headings are immediately familiar to readers, as a whole the subjects do not indicate a skeleton key to *Ulysses*. Their interest is topical rather than conceptual. The notes themselves were clearly intended to shape the everyday events of Bloomsday as well as the social interactions of the novel's characters. Despite the fact that the notes only connect occasionally with specific chapters, they clearly build on an already existing text.[6] The specificity of the material under 'Recipes', 'Gulls', 'Oxen' (not yet a reference to the chapter) and 'Choses vue' (containing aspects of Dublin social life that Bloom observes on 16 June) suggests that Bloomsday had already been fleshed out in considerable detail. Yet, as a whole, the 'Subject Notebook' betrays a speculative intent that indicates a turning point in the writing, if not a new departure.

The 'Subject Notebook' opens up a new understanding of how *Ulysses* was germinating as a quintessentially Irish novel. The question of identity, which hitherto in Joyce's writing was mainly anchored in Stephen's experiences, re-emerged in *Ulysses* in a broader spectrum. Ireland and to be Irish were no longer something to run from as from 'an angry Jove' (*OCPW* 123); instead, the novel's deep engagement with memory and history introduced a new form of cultural nationalism that reflected the diversity of opinion and recognized different shades within the nationalist discourse. This includes the voices of the Irish Revival that earlier he had appeared to reject. The exploratory intent that lies beneath the materials in the notebook is apparent from the notes gathered under 'Books', 'Theosophy' and 'Weininger' in particular. While the entries under 'Books' suggest a deliberate plan on Joyce's part to read up on Irish history and politics among other subjects, the notes under the other two headings venture into new ideational territory, casting light on how Joyce was modulating Stephen's battle with identity and selfhood.

As such, the 'Subject Notebook' is a rich source for the development of Stephen as a character. The handful of notes under 'Stephen' mostly gives us incidental detail about his day, but they also hint at notions of selfhood and aesthetics. Without directly referencing Stephen's theory that Shakespeare's tragedies have a biographical grounding, the idea that the 'artist remakes little plays out of incidents' (NLI 36,639/3, f. 6r) gives expression to a central concern in Stephen's – and Joyce's – art. The biographical impetus, and observation from

---

[6] It can be said that therefore the 'Subject Notebook' contains the memory of *Ulysses* as it existed prior to 1918.

life, drives creativity. The artist's experiences, and his memories of the past, furnish the material for his art. Just like 'painter paints himself unwittingly (cf. old masters put the face in the crowd)', an entry under 'Art' that found its way into 'Scylla and Charybdis' (NLI 36,639/3, f. 11r; *U* 9.921–3), the artist 'sees faces of those known in youth on | strip of tapestry (10 a[m])' (NLI 36,639/3, f. 6r). The time, 10am, suggests that these ideas belong to 'Hades'. Adapted for 'Proteus' as 'the oval equine faces, Temple, Buck Mulligan, Foxy Campbell, Lanternjaws' (*U* 3.111–12), the note also connects with Stephens's almost obsessive preoccupation with memory in that chapter (Garratt 2014, 33–4). A considerable part of Stephen's interior monologue consists of recollections from his own past. The tone of these recollections, however, is often despondent, indicating something of his own personal nightmare. At the same time, Stephen is aware that memory can play tricks and that, as he realizes in the failed history lesson from 'Nestor', the fabling of 'the daughters of memory' cannot always be relied upon (*U* 2.7–8).

The 'Subject Notebook' also contains matter that enriches the fabric of Stephen's thought. In *Ulysses*, Stephen attempts to redefine his problematic relationship with history in philosophical and spiritual terms; where in 'Proteus' he does this on a personal level, in 'Scylla and Charybdis' he switches to the public life of the artist. The 'Subject Notebook' supplies important philosophical sources for these two aspects. The first is a compilation of notes on 'Theosophy' collected from different journal articles. The second, under the heading 'Weininger', is an extensive index in German taken from Otto Weininger's *Über die letzten Dinge* (1904). Finally, the notebook also contains a cluster of notes under 'Irish', which, with some elements under 'Books', point to a mature perspective on the subject of Irish nationalism in *Ulysses*. None of these notes converge in a single key to understanding the development of *Ulysses*, but they are part of the novel's microstructure and thus intersect with its political and cultural concerns.

Theosophy

Going by the text of *Ulysses*, critics tend to understand Joyce's interest in theosophy negatively as an opportunity for ridicule; two passages – one in 'Scylla and Charybdis' (*U* 9.279–86) and one in 'Circe' (*U* 15.2267–76) – unmistakably poke fun at the theosophical movement and AE's mystical affinities in particular. Yet the young Joyce was genuinely interested in hermeticism and the occult, which left its mark on the 'Portrait of the Artist' essay (Aubert 1991, #11). According to Joyce's brother Stanislaus, this was an early interest, dating from the time after his mother's death, but one he soon abandoned (Joyce 1950, 11–12; see also Joyce 2003, 131). However, as the 'Subject Notebook' and Joyce's personal library indicate, Joyce's preoccupation with theosophy lasted until the writing of *Ulysses*.[7] As an aspect of the novel's genesis, the question is what function it held for Joyce. Stuart Gilbert suggests that the akashic records, a spiritual archive of all past and future human actions, thoughts and experiences containing 'all that ever anywhere whereever was' (*U* 7.883; Gilbert 1961, 128; see also Gibbons 2015, 124), were of interest to Joyce. Stephen's allusion in 'Aeolus' to the akashic records occurs in connection with Daniel O'Connell's 'words' spoken 'to the four winds' at a public meeting in the Hill of Tara in 1843 (*U* 7.81–2'; Gifford and Seidman 1988, 150). Rhetoric, history and cultural memory come together here, but even if the words and political sentiments are transient, their spiritual force left its imprint.

In the fictional world of *Ulysses*, Stephen also has engrossed himself in hermeticism since his return from Paris. The exchange in the Library chapter, in which AE defends art as 'ideas, formless spiritual essences' (*U* 9.49) against Stephen's pseudohistoricist reading of Shakespeare (calling them 'Clergyman's discussions of the historicity of Jesus' [*U* 9.47]), elicits the following stream of random thoughts:

> Formless spiritual. Father, Word and Holy Breath. Allfather, the heavenly man. Hiesos Kristos, magician of the beautiful, the Logos who suffers in us at every moment. This verily is that. I am the fire upon the altar. I am the sacrificial butter.
>
> Dunlop, Judge, the noblest Roman of them all, A. E., Arval, the Name Ineffable, in heaven hight, K. H., their master, whose identity is no secret to adepts. Brothers of the great white lodge always watching to see if they can help. The Christ with the bridesister, moisture of light, born of an ensouled virgin, repentant sophia, departed to the plane of buddhi. The life esoteric is not for ordinary person. O. P. must work off bad karma first. Mrs Cooper Oakley once glimpsed our very illustrious sister H. P. B's elemental.
>
> (*U* 9.61–71)

---

[7] Gilbert also has it that Joyce was 'conversant' with theosophical literature but 'shied off the subject' (1961, vii–viii). But his interest was more sustained, judging by the fact that he advised Gilbert to read A.P. Sinnett and the presence in his library of books by Annie Besant, W.T. Horton, Henry S. Olcott and Yogi Ramacharaka, among others. The most recent title in the library is a copy of *The Occult Review* from July 1923 (Terrinoni 2007, 6).

This prolific recitation of gnostic elements, esoteric lore and gossip from the Order of the Golden Dawn is almost too detailed and exhaustive to be mockery. Stephen certainly shows himself knowledgeable about the mystical interpretations of Christ's life as well as about the doings of Madame H.P. Blavatsky and her circle.[8] The passage is composed from the 'Theosophy' notes, wholly unironic in their own right, in the 'Subject Notebook':

> ᵇit is | the Logos who suffers at any momentᵇ ... ʳChrist's bride sister the moistening | of light, born of virgin, repentant Sophia. Christ blendedʳ with Sophia descender on Jesus ʳGod of Karmic law | wanted to kill Christ so Christ etc departed to the incorruptible | eonʳ ... ʳthe master K.H. (TS)ʳ ... ʳHPB kept a pet elemental.
>
> (NLI 36,639/3, f. 7r)

Joyce extracted his notes from several articles in theosophist publications. The first is by G.R.S. Mead, 'A Study in Christian Gnosticism', published in *The Theosophical Review*, December 1908; the second, in the same issue, 'The Secret of Jesus', is also by Mead. The third, 'Advice from a Master', a letter 'by the Master K. H. to a member of the T. S.', comes from *The Theosophist*, May 1910. The fourth, 'In the Twilight' by Annie Besant, appeared in the same issue (see JJDA, 'UN1 (NLI 3): The Subject Notebook', www.jjda.ie/main/JJDA/U/FF/unbs/un1all.htm). Are we to presume, anachronistically, that Stephen read the same material? Most likely not. But one can take the shared interest in Joyce and Stephen in the gnostic elements in particular as a sign of their attraction to heterodoxy.

Slightly further on in the chapter, in a section also derived from the 'Theosophy' notes, Stephen thinks about the hocus-pocus that happened at AE's Thursday night meetings of the Hermetic Society in Dawson Street.

> Yogibogeybox in Dawson chambers. Isis Unveiled. Their Pali book we tried to pawn. Crosslegged under an umbrel undershoot he thrones an Aztec logos, functioning on astral levels, their oversoul, mahamahatma. The faithful hermetists await the light, ripe for chelaship, ringroundabout him. Louis H. Victory. T. Caulfield Irwin. Lotus ladies tend them i'the eyes, their pineal glands aglow. Filled with his god he thrones, Buddh under plantain. Gulfer of souls, engulfer. Hesouls, shesouls, shoals of souls. Engulfed with wailing creecries, whirled, whirling, they bewail.
>
> (*U* 9.279–86)

---

[8] The belief that Joyce was 'an avowed sceptic' seems a simplification of his engagement with theosophy (Mullin 2003, 132).

The tone is now more back-handed, but the level of his acquaintance with hermetic discourse is still impressive. This should come as no surprise in a chapter whose symbols in the Linati schema include 'Scholasticism and Mysticism'. On the one hand, Stephen's knowledge of hermeticism – and gnosticism in particular – fits in with his fascination with dogma, heresy and how the early Christian Church differed from the Roman (see Van Mierlo 2017, 16). But it also connects with a spiritual side in Stephen that is not often commented upon; the 'Theosophy' notes, for instance, also include a quotation from *Centuries of Meditations* (1908) by Thomas Traherne, the seventeenth-century poet and theologian: 'fields of orient and immortal wheat | standing from ever lasting to ever lasting (Traherne)' (NLI 36,639, f. 7v). The quotation finds its way into 'Proteus', where Stephen contemplates the Kabbalistic 'Adam Kadmon', the primordial man (*U* 3.42–4). Related too is the epiphany as a 'spiritual manifestation', which, Stephen fantasizes, might 'in a few thousand years' be read in the manner of a 'mahamanvantara' (*U* 3.143–4), another borrowing from the 'Theosophy' notes.[9]

What it also shows, on the other hand, is that Stephen does not completely stand outside the circle of mystical men who link with the Irish Revival. The 1917 notes suggest that hermeticism, and other spiritual influences like it, were folded into Stephen's aesthetic theories, which ironically he treats like Christian theology (see Lernout 2010, 117, 119, 129–30). In the early 'Portrait of the Artist' essay, Joyce had set out his plans to 'reunite the children of the spirit, jealous and long-divided', invoking the heterodoxies of Joachim Abbas, Giordano Bruno, Michael Sendivogius, Emanuel Swedenborg and St John of the Cross against the 'natural pieties' of social convention, race, motherhood and the Church. In this, the 'rhythms of phrase and period, the symbols of word and allusion' – another manifestation of Joyce's interest in language, voice and rhythm discussed in Chapter 3 – are 'paramount things'; and it is out of their 'marvellous life, wherein he had annihilated and rebuilt experience' that came his purpose to pursue a path of spiritual unification.[10] As a treatise on art and life, however, the early essay did not steer Joyce univocally towards AE's position that art consists of 'formless spiritual essences'; rather, repeating the dualism in the epiphany theory, it leads him back to a materialism rooted in experience.

---

[9] Joyce took the entry from another article in *The Theosophist* of September 1910 by G.E. Sutcliffe titled 'Scientific Notes' (see *JJDA*, 'UN1 (NLI 3): The Subject Notebook', www.jjda.ie/main/JJDA/U/FF/unbs/un1all.htm). A third passage deriving from the 'Theosophy' notes is the ghostly sighting of Paddy Dignam 'etheric double' in 'Cyclops' (*U* 12.338–44). All passages are discussed in detail by Mullin (2003, 122–3, 128–9).

[10] In much the same vein, Joyce admires Bruno for bringing rationalism, mysticism, theism and pantheism into play with each other in his philosophy (*OCPW* 93).

Life informs art and aesthetics: 'Sceptically, cynically, mystically, he had sought for an absolute satisfaction and now little by little he began to be conscious of the beauty of mortal conditions' (Scholes and Kain 1965, 63–4, 65). The 'beauty of mortal conditions' are the material conditions of life. Still, Joyce's language undeniably retains elements of a mystical language that leans, specifically, towards Yeats, himself a devotee of Joachim Abbas and Swedenborg (Ellmann 1982, 146).[11] *Ulysses* too maintains the possibility that Stephen was seriously probing theosophical questions. The story is circulating in Dublin that one time Stephen visited AE in the early hours of the morning to 'ask him about planes of consciousness'. In 'Aeolus', J.J. O'Molloy asks Stephen: 'What do you think really of that hermetic crowd?' He wants to know whether Magennis was right that Stephen was pulling AE's leg (*U* 7.786–7). Stephen does not answer.

Weininger

Also important for Stephen's genetic development is the second cluster of reading notes from Weininger's *Über die letzten Dinge* (*On Last Things*) (1904). These notes take us away from Irish matters, but, like theosophy and mysticism, Weininger provided Joyce with a heterodox, anti-empirical (and often problematic) view on matters relating to biology, psychology, philosophy and ethics. *Über die letzten Dinge* extends Weininger's earlier thought in the more famous *Geschlecht und Charakter* (*Sex and Character*) (1903), which has been cited by Joyce critics as the inspiration for Bloom as the 'new womanly man' (*U* 15.1798–9) (see Ellmann 1982, 463; Brown 1985, 97–107), into a philosophy of negation.[12] In the earlier book, Weininger had argued for a psychogenetic understanding of gender. His premise is that the genders are not biologically absolute; each human being has masculine and feminine traits, but where in normal human beings one of the genders dominates, a more heterogeneous split results in an imbalance. His androgynist theory, in other words, serves mostly as a pretext for developing a treatise about the weakness of women, their incapacity for logical thought and so on. By casting Jews as the feminine race, this denigration of women is fundamentally racist as well.

---

[11] The remainder of the phrase, 'to reunite the children of the spirit, jealous and long-divided, to reunite them against fraud and principality' (Scholes and Kain 1965, 64), also suggests the infighting among the factions within the Order of the Golden Dawn.
[12] Marilyn Reizbaum (1995, 207–8) notes, however, that there is no direct evidence for Joyce's reading of *Geschlecht und Charakter*.

A posthumous volume containing essays and aphorisms, *Über die letzten Dinge* does not, by comparison, present a coherent philosophy; its manuscript was left incomplete in 1903 when its author died by his own hand. Although Weininger probably never intended the book to have one central thesis, its idiosyncratic, diverging contents stemmed from a desire to look for unity in self, nature and race/nation. As a treatise on the dualistic relationship between subject (individual) and object (world), the book touches on much he had already examined in *Geschlecht und Charakter*:

> The investigation has yielded a harvest rich in its bearing on the fundamental problems of logic and their relations to the axioms of thought, on the theory of aesthetics, of love, and of the beautiful and the good, and on problems such as individuality and morality and their relations, on the phenomena of genius, the craving for immortality and Hebraism.
>
> (Weininger 1912, xii)

The description almost sounds like a blueprint for much of what preoccupies Stephen in *Ulysses*. Taking up the same concerns, *Über die letzten Dinge* is, as a reflection on the psychology of emotional states, concerned with egotistical power and the need (if not the right) of the individual to transgress against morality that is passed off as a masculine 'condition of self-awareness': '[man] has no object outside himself' (Sass 2001, 114; Weininger 1912, 162). Moreover, both artistic genius (a 'queer thing' after all [*U* 9.303]) and evil originate from the same inner drive to transgress, but they manifest themselves differently (Weininger 1912, 109). In *Über die letzten Dinge*, Weininger understands this need as culminating in the destructive actions of the murderer. The psychological and biological capacity to commit murder, a capacity that places human beings above animals, was also a theme explored in *Geschlecht und Charakter*. Murder, together with friendship, loneliness and so on, is for Weininger an 'eminently psychological' problem overlooked by psychologists (1912, 83). Looked at it this way, the annihilation of life becomes the inevitable outcome of all aspirations, including love; the 'sexual union ... is allied to murder' because procreation, as the necessary means for self-preservation, 'robs' man and woman 'of their consciousness to give life to the child' (1912, 248). Not surprisingly, the Jew lacks the capacity for murder and violent crime; this incapacity stems not from moral objection, but from his weakness: 'He is rather non-moral, neither very good nor very bad' (Weininger 1912, 309).

That Joyce was interested in Weininger's psychology of murder is apparent from one of the entries in the 'Subject Notebook': 'Mord ist die Tat des schwächsten

Menschen' (NLI 36,639/3, f.15r). In the section of *Über die letzten Dinge* on 'Tierpsychologie' ('animal psychology'; a very Bloomian topic), Weininger develops a dual notion of the criminal's psychology. The transgression that the murderer commits by taking away a life does not stem from a rational or intentional desire to kill, in that he resembles animals, specifically the dog, which is the symbol of the criminal (Weininger 1904, 115; 2001, 98). Ruled by fatalism, the criminal is predestined to repeat the original sin; he therefore does not judge, nor attaches value to anything, including the idea of *free will* itself, which the criminal cannot conceive of. To have a will is to possess a sense of hope and future; it is what makes us human (1904, 117; 2001, 91). But the criminal finds all of this – freedom, morality, innocence, saintliness, wisdom, perfection, remorse, hope and so on (1904, 119; 2001, 101) – repellent. Disconnected from the world around him, he lacks all awareness even of the presence of space and time and descends to the level of the animal (1904, 106, 117; 2001, 91, 99–100).

One can imagine that some of these ideas fed into 'Circe' when Stephen, reeling from drink, unaware of his surroundings, delivers his final renunciation: '*Nothung!*' (*U* 15.1242). This renunciation – the ultimate rejection of language, religion, nation – is but symbolic, however; apart from a broken chandelier in the brothel, the gesture leaves little impact until Stephen walks off into the night after leaving Bloom's house a few hours later. For Weininger's criminal, by contrast, the drive to destroy all forms of existence, which signify to him the freedom that he hates, is inevitable and all-encompassing. Murder is thus an act of last resort, taking the Nietzschean sense of negation, which must lead to destruction, to its ultimate outcome: 'Der Mord is das letzte, was der Verbrecher tun kann, sein letztes Mittel, sich als Verbrecher zu behaupten.' But herein also lies its paradox. For the impulse to kill comes out of the desperation to refute existence. The murderer is the victim of his own weakness: 'Der Mord is die Tat des *schwächsten* Menschen' (1904, 120; 2001, 102).

One may wonder what attracted Joyce in Weininger's work. Weininger's anti-Semitism and misogyny seem far removed from his own attitudes. Perhaps he overlooked this less palatable side in favour of Weininger's brutal critique of social convention. It is crucial to remember that, at the time, Weininger was not an obscure, racist crank, but an intellectual whose influence on other intellectuals, although cut short by his early death, was significant (not least on Ludwig Wittgenstein, but also Italo Svevo, Dora Marsden, D.H. Lawrence and Gertrude Stein). Weininger is credited with criticizing from within the 'aestheticist subjectivism and irrationalism' of Viennese modernism, taking apart its 'romanticism of nerves' and its 'sentimental scurrility' (Janik 2001, ix–x). Whether Joyce saw him this way is another matter. To all intents and purposes, he skipped the most rounded piece in the volume, 'Peer Gynt und Ibsen', in which Weininger addresses 'the question of how there can be moral relations between the sexes' (Janik 2001, x). It might be that, as Joyce had already dealt with precisely this question in *Exiles*, the essay offered him no creative opportunities. The microcosm of *Ulysses* – neither in the form in which it already existed, nor in its later development – left much space for grand moral structures. Yet avoiding Weininger's less palatable ideas, Joyce was likely attracted by his 'deconstruction' of the egotistical sublime; for Weininger, contrary to Giambattista Vico's genealogical conception of world history, society progresses not through the efforts of the group but through the will of the strong individual who is able to act unconventionally and selfishly. Joyce undoubtedly read Weininger with the development of Stephen in mind, whose struggles with the inner conflict between individual and nation remain at the forefront. While individual freedom is a necessary condition for the artist, art that does not participate, in whatever form, in the development of a nation remains potentially sterile.

One of the difficulties with the Weininger notes, despite being crossed out indicating usage, is that identifying with certainty the specific instances where Joyce might have used them in *Ulysses* is not easily done. Nonetheless, we can observe, as Joyce is working Weininger's ideas, that several of the notes possess a conceptual value that matches (sometimes explicitly) the themes and motifs of *Ulysses*: 'Er kehrt zum Vater wenn er die Erbsünde verneint' fits the father–son relationship of Bloom and Stephen; 'Die Geburt is eine Feigheit' suggests 'Oxen of the Sun'; 'Personen die in einem Raum beisammen sind bilden eine Gemeinschaft gegen Neu-Eintretende' matches the situation in Barney Kiernan's pub; 'Mit vieren beginnt die Mengenpsychologie (Library)' obviously pertains to 'Scylla and Charybdis'; and 'Unetisch ist es die Vergangenheit zu ändern' might link with Stephen's fear of history's 'back kick' (NLI 36,639/3, f.15r). But none of these notes can be traced directly to the text. It is likely that the notes were transferred elsewhere, as happened among others with 'Der Mensch schämt sich des Mundinneren (Boylan)'. Taken from a passage where Weininger talks about the shame that stems from the morphological and psychological association of the mouth with the anus and genitalia (Weininger 1904, 76; 2001, 65–6), this note was copied to the 'Eumaeus' notesheets (5:16; Herring 1972, 393), where it remained uncancelled.

Judging from the nature of the notes, however, Joyce was clearly taken with Weininger's predilection for paradoxes, which made him a fitting source for his modelling of the new, disillusioned Stephen in *Ulysses*. Weininger, therefore, supplied Joyce with a kind of philosophy for Stephen's development that was different from his normal scholastic fare. In essence, and despite the fragmentation of his own work, Weininger sought to make sense of the human condition's search for truth and knowledge:

> Grundzug alles Menschlichen: Suchen nach Realität ... Was der Mensch erlebt, sind jeweilig abgehobene Teile aus einer unendlichen, zeitlichen, räumlichen, stofflichen, farbigen, klingenden Mannigfaltigkeit. Darum sind zunächst zweierlei Dinge möglich: Er sucht die Realität im Ganzen, in der Totalität des Alls und seinem unendlichen Zusammenhang; oder ihm wird zur Realität jedes einzelne, sozusagen punktuelle Element des Weltganzen.
>
> (Weininger 1904, 65; 2001, 55–6)

Although this passage is not filtered through the 'Subject Notebook', it does, to some extent, inform Stephen's confrontation with the world around him. Much of Weininger's language in the passage above seems to echo in Stephen's interior monologue: 'coloured signs', 'Sounds solid', 'Am I walking into eternity along Sandymount strand?' (*U* 3.4, 18, 19–20). This last question especially pertains to Weininger's inquiry as to whether we discover the totality of the world in its infinitely variable coherence or whether we experience reality in each individual particle. In a nutshell, this is also Stephen's theory of the epiphany and how it grapples with perception and sense-data. Owing to the ineluctable modalities of the visible and audible, reality is there to be perceived and 'read' – 'Signatures of all things I am here to read' (*U* 3.2). The phrase is itself from Jacob Boehme's *De Signatura Rerum* (1621), which posits that the signs of God's existence are everywhere present and visible in the objects that he created (see Gifford and Seidman 1989, 44; *Joyce Project* n.d., http://m.joyceproject.com/notes/030020signatures.html). Joyce, however, mixes Boehme's mysticism – along with Aristotle's theories of vision and Berkeley's views on perception and sense-data – with the materialism of Weininger. *Über die letzten Dinge* uses psychology to redress metaphysical questions. In that regard, Stephen might be aware that Weininger indirectly denies the relevance of Boehme's signature. While Boehme holds that faith, not knowledge, is the key to recognizing the signatures, for Weininger faith directs one to timelessness (1904, 105; 2001, 91).

While these echoes need not be solid, of greater interest is the fact that the modalities of the visible and audible – the sense-data that stimulate epiphanic creations – interrelate with space and time. The words '*Nacheinander*' and '*Nebeneindander*' that Stephen repeats (*U* 3.13,15, 17) are taken verbatim from *Über die letzten Dinge* via the 'Subject Notebook': 'Der Raum ist also eine Projektion des Ich (aus dem Reich der Freiheit ins Reich der Notwendigkeit). Er enthält im nebeneinander, was nur im zeitlichen Nacheinander erlebt werden kann. Der Raum ist symbolisch für das vollendete, die Zeit für das sich wollende Ich' (Weininger 1904, 107; 2001, 92; see NLI 36,639/3, f. 15r).[13] Although inextricably linked, space and time are not equal aspects. Because Weininger associates time with the self's capacity for volition ('das sich wollende Ich'), time is primary. Space is a projection of the ego; it stands for completeness, realized by the self, and is therefore material and secondary. Yet while paradoxically the self holds within itself the dialectical unity of all dimensions and contradictions, the multidimensionality (or simultaneity) of space can only be experienced temporally through movement.

One can see, perhaps, why in later years Joyce was miffed about Wyndham Lewis's attacks on him as a time writer. Insofar as he shows an affinity with Weininger's philosophy, he finds in *Über die letzten Dinge* confirmation for a psychogeographical experience of history and the connection between past and place also shared by Stephen in 'Proteus'. When Stephen considers, strolling with eyes closed, that he is 'walking through it [space] howsomever', he is aware of the existential aspect of Weininger's argument for movement as both embodied and volitional. Stephen takes from this that motion is the essence of the self: 'I am, a stride at a time' (*U* 3.11). This is an allusion to *Ambulo ergo sum*, Pierre Gassendi's response to Descartes on the inseparability of body and mind. But there is more. Weininger (1904, 107; 2001, 92) associates the will with a 'mental movement', showing its capacity to create. What all this means for Stephen is that walking – and counting his steps, 'Five, six: the *Nacheinander*' (*U* 3.12) is rhythmical: 'Rhythm begins, you see' (*U* 3.23), and rhythm, a sonic sequence that moves aurally through space and time, is what engenders poetry. Where in *Stephen Hero* Joyce highlighted the genetic nature of the artistic process, in 'Proteus' he gives further credence to the idea that poetry is not 'creation from nothing' (*U* 3.35).

Stephen's aesthetic theories, from the epiphany to his exposition on Shakespeare, lend particular strength to the importance of the self and identity.

---

[13] For a long time, the critical consensus held that Gotthold Ephraim Lessing's *Laocoön* was Joyce's source (Gifford and Seidman 1989, 45), despite the fact that the word 'nacheinander' does not actually feature in Lessing's writing. Because Lessing does use 'aufeinander', Fritz Senn (1965, 135) speculated that Joyce may have used a summary or textbook that rendered 'aufeinander' as 'nacheinander'. Accepted orthodoxy notwithstanding, the *Laocoön* as a source never completely rang true. Lessing's unfavourable comparison of time belonging to the domain of poetry versus space belonging to the plastic arts is not the subject of Stephen's ruminations. Stephen does, however, invoke Lessing in 'Circe': 'Moment before the next Lessing says' (*U* 15.3609).

Among others this is why questions about Irish identity are so much more deeply woven into the fabric of *Ulysses* than in the earlier works as Joyce becomes more concerned with the historical roots of that identity. More on that in a moment. For now, Stephen shows himself more historically aware in *Ulysses*. In *A Portrait*, and to a lesser extent *Stephen Hero*, Stephen is already conscious of the cultural differences that set him apart from the dean of studies in terms of language: 'How different are the words *home, Christ, ale, master*, on his lips and on mine! I cannot speak or write these words without unrest of spirit. His language, so familiar and so foreign, will always be for me an acquired speech' (*P* 189). But in *Ulysses* his historical consciousness deepens. We find an indication of this in 'Nestor', where Mr Deasy's poor grasp of the historical facts and his misjudging of Stephen's historical awareness ('You fenians forget some things' [*U* 2.272]) contrasts sharply with Stephen's powers of recollection, which are 'sharp and active' (Garratt 2014, 31; see also Spoo 1994, 96–7). It is no coincidence that in the Linati schema, History is the art of 'Nestor'.

Yet, for Stephen, history is very much a matter of personal experience (Garratt 2014, 29) that loosely connects with the importance that Weininger puts on self-exploration and self-awareness: '*Das Leben ist eine Art Reise durch den Raum des inneren Ich*, eine Reise vom engsten Binnenlande freilich zur umfassendsten, freiesten Überschau des Alls' (1904, 108). The point that Weininger is adumbrating is that the entire universe is reflected or contained within the ego ('Ich') because of its capability to possess within itself 'the unity of all contradictions'; hence, this is the prime reason as to why space is a projection of the ego (Weininger 1904, 107). For Stephen, then, the nightmare of history demands an internal resolution. This is why Joyce's use of the verb 'awake' is significant for its connotations: to *awaken* is to become conscious of a new state, to reach new awareness. Akin to what Pierre Nora (1989, 16) calls the 'psychologization of memory', what Stephen remembers is, in a sense, 'memory itself'. Stephen, therefore, is not simply looking to *escape*, as most critics argue, the nightmare of history – which is to stand outside time equivalent to the end of all history – but to come to terms with the fact that the Irish are conditioned to remember the oppressive legacy of eight centuries of foreign domination.[14] 'What's left us then?', Stephen asks (*U* 2.10), if we are without history and without the trauma that accompanies our memory of the past. Memory and

---

[14] Gibson notes that the paradox of resisting colonialism, resisting the effects of history, meant continuing within history. According to him, Joyce 'demonstrates that those of his characters who are caught up in *ressentiment* are also still in thrall, subordinate to power in the very intensity of their reaction to it' (2002, 18).

trauma, Weininger would argue, are necessary for the human condition. For Irish selfhood, too, memory is a condition without which the Irish could not exist. This is an aspect, as Joyce observes elsewhere in his notes, that the Irish have in common with the Jewish race: 'Jews & Irish remember past' ('Cyclops' 1: 53; Herring 1972, 82; see Gibson 2002, 54).

Über die letzten Dinge contains several statements that relate to Stephen's desire for self-awakening: fear can only be subdued by the consciousness of one's self-worth (Weininger 1904, 145) and 'the present is the one thing over which a person has power; whoever feels free in it will use it, like the sadist; whoever feels that he suffers in it, because it is not real for him, seeks to awaken it to eternity' (1904, 69). The second provides context for Joyce's note, 'Der Masochist muss erst die Ewigkeit fragen [ob er sich töten dürfe, müsse] (Selbstmort)' (NLI 36,639/3, f.15r), which derives from the same passage in the source (Weininger 1904, 69). Joyce also notes that 'Bewußtsein ist nur durch Gegensatz möglich' (1904, 75). Self-realization, which is achieved through self-knowledge, is possible only when a person acts against his destiny, that is, his destiny to obey God. But what he notes and uses is a trivial idea about canine melancholy: 'Das Auge des Hundes ruft underwiderstehlich den Eindruck hervor, daß der Hund etwas *verloren* habe: es spricht aus ihm (wie übrigens aus dem ganzen Wesen des Hundes) eine gewissen rätselhafte Beziehung zur *Vergangenheit*. Was er verloren hat, ist das Ich, der Eigenwert, die Freiheit' (Weininger 1904, 121–2). In Weininger's peculiar philosophy, the dog is the ultimate symbol for the criminal instinct, because more than any other animal, the dog is a despondent, morbid creature that is aware of its own worthlessness – which is why people are afraid of it (1904, 115, 123). Joyce imbued the dog that comes trotting along the strand in 'Proteus' with these qualities. His aimless rooting in the sand for 'something lost in a past life' represents a futile search for something he does not know he has lost (*U* 3.333). Joyce later explained to Budgen, 'he is the mummer among beasts—the Protean animal', to which Budgen coyly responds:

> 'Weininger says something about the imitative nature of the dog in his *Über den letzten Dingen* [sic]', I remembered. 'He does?' said Joyce. 'This one mimics the other animals while Stephen is watching him. Listen.' [Joyce then reads the passage from 'Proteus'] 'There he is', said Joyce. 'Panther: all animals.' 'I don't know a better word-picture of a dog', I said. 'English and Irish, we are all dog-lovers. But when we write about dogs or paint them we sentimentalize them. Landseer'.
>
> 'This certainly wasn't done by a dog-lover', said Joyce. 'I don't like them. I am afraid of them'.
>
> (Budgen 1972, 53–4)

Reading for an Irish nation

The dog-fearing Joyce may be a convenient mythology, but Weininger's wayward view of the dog provides unexpected connections between Stephen's spiritualism on the one hand and his anxiety about the nightmare of history on the other. Directed at Stephen, the notes under 'Theosophy' and 'Weininger' in the 'Subject Notebook' show two routes for artistic self-realization. The third major component of the notebook takes a different tack: the entries under 'Books' more readily point to Irish and political subject matter. Until *A Portrait*, Joyce had treated most forms of Irish nationalism dubiously; the national pieties and narrow-minded orthodoxies of the Gaelic League and Irish Ireland movement found little favour. Only Parnellism represented a form of moderate nationalism (Foster 1993, 62) that was palatable to the middle-class Dedalus/Joyce family because it offered the right, hope and mechanisms for political self-determination without the usual nationalist rhetorical bluster. Home Rule was a political ambition for a disenfranchised people. In *Ulysses*, Joyce's attitude towards nationalism became less openly strident, while his treatment of his Irish subject matter grew richer, more subtle and politically more powerful. This change in sensibility was in no small part due to the 'Subject Notebook' and the programme of reading that he undertook in preparation for the writing.

The entries that Joyce gathered under 'Books' are of interest for a variety of reasons: its length, scope and topical interest. Reading lists are a common feature in Joyce's notebooks, but this list stands out because it is the second longest of all, surpassed only by the list in the 'Early Commonplace Book'. Coincidentally, that list is the most 'Irish' of all: on two densely packed pages, with entries arranged in two columns, Joyce records no less than 162 authors and titles. Under the heading 'Verse', he gives most of the major Irish poets and ballad writers from the nineteenth century; under 'Biography & History', a wide selection of historical writings; under 'Fiction', writers of stories and fiction from the eighteenth to the twentieth century; under 'Speeches', the names of some of Ireland's most famous political orators (NLI 36,639/2/A, ff. 8v-9r). Elsewhere in the same notebook, Joyce copied a shorter list of 'Verse', 'Drama', 'Old Literature' and 'Modern Literature' written in Irish, translated or adapted from Irish (f. 15v), as well as writing that deals with old Irish history and myth. A very short third list under 'Books' contains mainly titles on art, music and drama, as well as Alice Stopford Green's popular *Irish Nationality* (1911) (f.22r). These lists are Joyce's most extensive indication of his interest in Revivalist culture. What Joyce's purpose was with the list is not clear. Was it an ambitious reading programme? Did he intend a teaching course? Was it research for an article? Whatever the answer, he did see fit to copy the entries wholesale from an article on stocking a rural library with good Irish writing in *The United Irishman* (Callanan 2010).

The 'Books' list in the 'Subject Notebook' is similarly problematic. Its contents are much more eclectic: it lists titles in German and English on art and culture, philosophy and mathematics, as well as, in reverse chronological order, English fiction, poetry and drama.[15] Nor does it have an obvious source. Directly relevant for my discussion, however, are the six titles on Irish history:[16]

> *The Irish National Invincibles and their Times* by Patrick J.P. Tynan (London: Chatham and Co., 1896).
> *The Geographical Distribution of Irish Ability* by D.J. O'Donoghue (Dublin: O'Donoghue & Co., 1906).
> *Twenty-Five Years in the Secret Service: The Recollections of a Spy* by Major Henri Le Caron (pseud. of Thomas Miller Beach) (London: W. Heinemann, 1892).
> *Ireland, 1798-1898*, by William O'Connor Morris (London: A.D. Innes, 1898).
> *Two Centuries of Irish History, 1691-1870: Being a Series of Papers*, edited by R. Barry O'Brien, 2nd edn (London: Kegan Paul, Trench, Trübner, 1907).
> *A History of our Own Times: From the Accession of Queen Victoria to the General Election of 1880*, 7 vols, by Justin McCarthy (London: Chatto and Windus, 1907).[17]

The Irish National Invincibles and their Times gives an extensive, first-hand account of the Phoenix Park murders. The book contains an overabundance of detail, but its rambling narrative and, as Luke Gibbons (2015, 216, 218–19) notes, 'overblown fustian' style are too self-conscious: under 'pretext of candor' the narrative is 'as much an exercise in obfuscation as revelation'; as such, the book bears a resemblance to half-spoken messages about the events in 'Eumaeus' (see also Fairhall 1993, 27–9). D.J. O'Donoghue (1866–1917) was a bookseller, bibliographer, author of, among others, biographies of William Carleton, Robert Emmett and James Clarence Mangan, and a founding member of the London Irish Literary Society. Another peculiar book of facts, *The Geographical Distribution* uses statistics and indices to prove that Ireland has more per capita geniuses than England; nonetheless, it is an important book that provides a bibliographical and historiographic foundation for the Irish Revival. Henri Le Caron's (1841–94) memoir is a buccaneering tale of an English spy who infiltrated a faction of the

---

[15] For a speculative analysis of the English canon list, see Van Mierlo (2016).
[16] Except for O'Donoghue, Joyce took these titles from the bibliography to the article on 'Fenians' in the *Encyclopaedia Britannica* (*EB* X, 256). None of the books is present in the personal library.
[17] Except for *A History of our Times*, Joyce did not cite specific editions. I refer to the most recently published, and thus the edition he most likely had access to.

Fenian Brotherhood in the US who, instead of supporting rebellion in the home country, wanted to attack British army barracks in Canada. Posing as a Frenchman, Le Caron passed on information to the British government, which led to, among other things, the failed invasion of 1870. Joyce took some notes about this event and Le Caron's role in it among his 'Irish' notes: 'Le Caron (Eng spy) inspects | Irish repub. troops in America " distributed 15000 stand [sic] of arms for | invasion of Canada, dispersed by 1st volley' (NLI 36,639/3, f. 8v). The notes did not come from Le Caron's book, but from the article on 'Fenians' in the *Encyclopaedia Britannica*:

> Le Caron (q.v.), who, while acting as a secret agent for the English government, held the position of 'inspector-general of the Irish Republican Army', asserts that he 'distributed fifteen thousand stands of arms and almost three million rounds of ammunition in the care of the many trusted men stationed between Ogdensburg and St Albans', in preparation for the intended raid. It took place in April 1870, and proved a failure not less rapid or complete than the attempt of 1866. The Fenians under O'Neill's command crossed the Canadian frontier near Franklin, Vt., but were dispersed by a single volley from Canadian volunteers; while O'Neill himself was promptly arrested by the United States authorities acting under the orders of President Grant.
>
> (*EB* X, 255)

Le Caron's identity was revealed when he was called as a witness before the Parnell Commission in 1888/9.

William O'Connor Morris (1824–1904) was a county court judge, historian and landowner, whose liberal ideas on land tenure influenced the Land Act of 1870. His *Ireland, 1798–1898*, although a standard textbook, is noteworthy for its opposition to Home Rule. Yet his treatment is even-handed. Of the 1798 Rebellion he writes, for instance, that both the United Irishmen and Orangemen, as well as the Irish Parliament, were at fault, and the situation was such, ineluctably leading to the Act of Union, that an uprising was unavoidable. R. Barry O'Brien (1864–1918), by contrast, was a Home Rule advocate and staunch supporter of Parnell; his two-volume biography 'codified' what became known as 'the Parnell myth', built around his stoic resolve in the face of opposition and persecution, his 'pose of calculated indifference', which heavily influenced Joyce's appreciation of the man (Fairhall 1993, 128; Gibson 2002, 5). *Two Centuries of Irish History* was a series of essays that O'Brien edited together with James Bryce in 1888, which were, in effect, intended to gain political support for Home Rule; in fact, the essays were, in part, Gladstone's own idea (Sheehy 2010, 129). Although framed as a dispassionate piece of liberal historiography produced by academics from both sides of the Irish channel, the volume put forward as an underlying truth the historical legitimacy for rejecting direct British rule (Sheehy 2010, 131–2).[18] Justin McCarthy (1830–1912), like O'Brien a member of the London Irish Literary Society, was a journalist, novelist, historian and politician, who led the majority faction of the Irish Parliamentary Party after Parnell's fall, becoming the party's chairman in 1890. His *History of our Own Times*, originally published in 1879/80, was immensely popular. Joyce, however, mistakenly gives the name of the author as 'J. Huntley McCarthy'; James Huntly McCarthy was Justin McCarthy's son who wrote an *Outline of Irish History, from the Earliest Times to the Present Day* (New York: John W. Lovell Company, 1883).

Whether these books left any trace in the text of *Ulysses* or in the archive needs further exploration, but the titles are indicative of Joyce's reading strategies. The basic purpose is to read and collect salient historical information that could be put to use. The specific and varied nature of the books listed, however, suggests that the reading was intended to inform the various nationalist interventions in *Ulysses*. Aside from straightforward Irish historiography, therefore, the list includes more peculiar historical narratives of the kind that would become part of the 'Cyclops' chapter.

The set of 'Irish' notes in the 'Subject Notebook' betray a similar duality in the material that takes in, on the one hand, the peculiarities of Irish history and, on the other, the socioeconomic effects of British rule. These notes, first of all, show an interest in Celtic mythology. With likely irony, Joyce observes, for instance, that the Irish have a rich vocabulary despite reading very little. He alludes here to the rich folkloric traditions, including accounts of the exploits of Finn McCool and his warriors, which, until the nineteenth century, to the delight of Yeats and Lady Gregory, only circulated orally and in manuscript (Gregory 1970, 357). A single German quotation, taken from a brief article by Julius Pokorny, called 'Perlen der irischen Literatur' ('Pearls of Irish Literature') (see Ó Dochartaigh 2004), likewise references Celtic myth:

> In keiner anderen alten Literatur, außer der keltischen, finden wir dieses einfachen Entzücken an der Natur, ungetrübt un unbeeinflußt ... die Allbelebung der Natur, sondern auch durch das Fehlen jeglicher Moral, jedes beherrsschenden Sittengesetzes charakterisiert wird. Der keltische dichter kennt nur persönliches recht und unrecht, aber keine Nemesis, kein drohendes Sittengesetz, das über dem menschen schwebt, – daher auch keine unmoral, keine sünde.*
>
> * Der irischen heidnische religion kennt keine Hölle.
>
> (Pokorny 1917, 343)

---

[18] Sheehy (2010) gives a full account of the publication history. The second edition, which Joyce cites, differs from the first.

This pre-Christian, pre-fall world, which returns in *Finnegans Wake*, is a world in which guilt does not exist; the Fenian and Ossianic cycles are replete with stories of simple reparation – the exacting of 'blood money' or 'satisfaction' when an injustice was done (Gregory 1970, 44, 126) – that comes to a head, specifically, in the dialogues between Oisin and Saint Patrick in which Oisin, although a convert, persists in his archaic beliefs.

The quotation becomes, anachronistically, part of *Ulysses* when Haines, over coffee and scones, cites Pokorny from the as-yet unpublished article: 'He can find no trace of hell in ancient Irish myth, Haines said, amid the cheerful cups. The moral idea seems lacking, the sense of destiny of retribution' (*U* 10.1082-4). In the context of the 'Subject Notebook', it is perhaps impossible not to notice the echo of the Weiningerian criminal destined to blast all moral cowardice out of the water, especially as there seems to be a momentary conflation of Pokorny and Stephen: 'Rather strange he should have just that fixed idea. Does he write anything for your movement?' Haines asks. To which Mulligan replies: 'He is going to write something in ten years' (*U* 10.1084-5, 1089-90). As it happens, Pokorny was very much in touch with 'the movement'. A Celtophile who later succeeded Kuno Meyer to the Chair of Celtic Philology at Berlin, Pokorny had made regular visits to Dublin in the 1910s where he came to know Richard Best, Douglas Hyde and Eoin MacNeill (see Ó Dochartaigh 2004, 826). His contributions on Irish history and politics to the *Irische Blätter* (*Irish Leaves*), the newspaper of the Deutsch-Irische Gesellschaft (German-Irish Society), were outspokenly pro-Irish. Both paper and society were committed to promoting Irish interests against a common enemy. Noting the establishment of the society, the *Freeman's Journal* quoted extensively, but without any editorial comment, from the paper's inaugural issue of 29 October 1917, which contained Pokorny's article: 'It will see that the voice of the Irish nation, which has been oppressed and sucked dry by England, again finds expression, and generally in every way to further the progressive development of the Emerald Isle in the interest of the German as well as the Irish people.' If the hope to see Ireland stand among the fellow nations was not sufficient to pique Joyce's interest, Pokorny's reputation and the attention the *Irische Blätter* was receiving in Ireland makes it apparent that Joyce's discovery was not entirely serendipitous.

From the same article in the *Encyclopaedia Britannica* that furnished Joyce with the list of books and the information about Le Caron, he took some short notes on the 1867 Clerkenwell Prison explosion mentioned in 'Proteus', one of the most infamous attacks perpetrated on British soil by the Irish Republican Brotherhood (known as 'Fenians'). Arrested for attempting to buy arms for the Fenians, Richard Burke was awaiting trial in Clerkenwell, when a band of comrades seeking to free him blew up the prison wall, killing twelve bystanders and wounding about 120 others. Michael Barrett was the only one of six men convicted of the atrocity and condemned to death. The notes are interesting in the manner they differ from their use. Recast as a memory, Kevin Egan appears to have told Stephen in Paris that he had been involved in the bombing for love: 'Lover, for her love he prowled with colonel Richard Burke, tanist of his sept, under the walls of Clerkenwell and, crouching, saw a flame of vengeance hurl them upward in the fog. Shattered glass and toppling masonry' (*U* 3.246–9). Joseph Casey, Egan's real-life counterpart, was not exactly 'prowling' under the prison walls; he was one of the gun runners arrested with Burke and inside the prison who had joined the Brotherhood for the love of his country. Casey, though, was acquitted and settled in Paris where he lived in exile, 'Loveless, landless, wifeless' (*U* 3.253).

The notes, by contrast, record an event with which Joyce was already familiar; he had written about it in 'Fenianism: The Last Fenian', his 1907 article for the Triestine daily *Il Piccolo della sera* on the death of John O'Leary. What is crucial, however, are not just the historical facts, but their political outcome, which makes the nature of their transformation in *Ulysses* all the more striking, for the *Encyclopaedia* notes that the Clerkenwell atrocity directly influenced Gladstone in his decision to disestablish the Church of Ireland in 1869 'as a concession to Irish disaffection' (*EB* X, 255). What may have caught Joyce's attention, as Brian Fox observes (2019, 25), is just how close the *Encyclopaedia*'s view is to Joyce's in its suggestion that 'history full supports' the claim that England never made any concessions except 'unwillingly, at bayonet-point, as the saying goes' (*OCPW* 138). Although a political anomaly in the history of Anglo-Irish relations, the view that Clerkenwell had achieved this was already a historiographical commonplace. What interested Joyce, rather, for his new book, as well as in his *Il Piccolo* article, was the diversity of the political landscape. As he put it in his article, the 'so-called physical force party' was at odds with both 'the English parties' and the 'Nationalist parliamentarians' (*OCPW* 138). Joyce is not apt to sentimentalize the string of failures that characterize violent uprising in Ireland – unlike Yeats who enshrined O'Leary's death as the end of an era: 'Romantic Ireland's dead and gone, | It's with O'Leary in the grave' (Yeats 1989a, 210). Nor does he yearn for its future fulfilment. Joyce was, after all, remarkably silent on Easter 1916. Yet *Ulysses* commemorates the Irish rebellions because they are written into the collective memory.

Joyce's 'Fenianism' is illuminating for the 'Subject Notebook', however, for its unexpected angle. Unlike the 'ridiculous rebellion' of 1798 or the fervency of the Young Irelanders, he thought of Fenianism as a 'well-organized movement' (*OCPW* 138 and 139). Its unexpected demise, then, is attributed, predictably, to betrayal, but also to unforeseen historical occurrences that seemingly happen in the background: 'a population decreasing with mathematical regularity year by year, in an uninterrupted flow to the United States or Europe of Irish people who found the economic and intellectual conditions of their country intolerable' (*OCPW* 139). Under 'Irish' he recorded an echo of this: 'Malthus in I. Food decreases | in arithm progress, population in geom. progression' (NLI 36,639/3, f. 8v). And almost as if he was re-reading his own piece in which he had lamented how 'the country had allowed itself to be exploited by England' (*OCPW* 140), the notes turn to this very question:

> Cattle trade less good
> than agriculture? ʳrobs country of raw stuffs (bones & hoofs for
> combs) hides for shoes, tanners, fallow, bones etc for manure
> Slaughtered meat trade better. 6/7 of whole crop of I.ʳ
> goes to feed oxen. ʳDeepen beds of Barrow and Shannonʳ.
> Century ago ʳB. Parl advised drainage of marsh ½
> million acres: it increasesʳ. Internal rlwy rates higher
> than Brit. forwarding rates ʳWool, textile & potteries. Killed. Danish
> butter in Limerick!! Elizabeth Westbrook making Claddagh
> shawl in DMCʳ(NLI 36,639/3, f. 8v)

The source for this index remains elusive, but its scope and intent are clear: an attack on British liberal trade policy that had negatively affected the Irish economy since the Famine – what Francis Hackett (1918, 168) called 'the wickedness of dealing with Irish disadvantage in the spirit of laissez-faire'. The Irish cattle trade, in all appearances doing well, was second in value only to the linen trade; the number of animals exported rose fourfold in the period between the Famine and the First World War. Agriculture, however, remained underdeveloped, despite efforts for improvement by the cooperative movement, created in 1889, and the establishment, after proposals made by Horace Plunkett, of the Department of Agriculture and Technical Instruction in 1899. The major reasons were the large number of small, unprofitable holdings, a lack of investment, and the wet soil, suitable for grazing, but not for tillage; pasture yielded four times more than cereal anyway (Keenan 2006, 40–4). The question in Joyce's source, therefore, does not relate to the economic value of farming, as such, but sets up an analysis of the drawbacks of raising cattle for export. Because production in Ireland focused on the export market, a greater range of goods had to be imported; as cattle were shipped live to Liverpool, this included many animal byproducts used in the making of combs, shoes, leather and even fertilizer. Slaughtering the cattle at home and shipping the meat would have a clear benefit.

The dredging and deepening of the Barrow and the Shannon rivers had been debated since at least the 1830s. One objective was improving navigation, but equally important was the protection and reclamation of surrounding marsh lands so they could be used for pasture (Coyne 1902, 32). In 1835, the British government had ordered a survey of the River Shannon with a view to improving navigation and arterial drainage (Collison Black 1960, 183). A Royal Commission set up by Lord Castletown in 1886 noted that annually 45,640 acres of arable land were subject to damage from flooding on the Upper Barrow alone. The *Leinster Leader* newspaper, which quoted this statistic, complained in 1916 that despite repeated notices of urgency, especially in times of wartime pressures on food production, nothing had been done: 'it is absolutely necessary that those swamps, breeding-grounds of disease, should be done away with' (*Leinster Leader* 1916). The British government perpetually dragged its feet over the high cost.

The comparatively high rates for railway freight in Ireland were another bone of contention at the turn of the century. Because Ireland was not an industrialized nation, and with the transportation of bulk goods mostly absent (especially minerals and coal, which were in scarce supply), rail freight to be profitable charged higher rates than it did in Britain. In 1900, the difference of the average rate per ton was as much as 37 per cent. Yet it also seems that because competition from canals was less severe in Ireland, the railway companies could keep prices up (Coyne 1902, 80, 95, 98; Gribbon 2012, 314; Keenan 2006, 97). As a result, by 1918 there were cries to nationalize the railways, not just to curb profiteering but also to support the stagnation and decline of Irish production, of which, according to a report from the 1910 Vice-Regal Commission on Irish Railways, 'the woollen trade, and the textile and pottery industries, furnish conspicuous examples' (quoted in Hackett 1918, 389). It was in fact the Vice-Regal Commission that lambasted the imbalance in the rates by which internal and export transit rates were higher than the import transit rates. Cheaper railway rates would create better conditions for export, mitigate competition from British imports, and create jobs (Hackett 1918, 169, 172).

The complaint that Irish manufacturing was not supported, and that the Irish market was flooded with cheaper goods produced in Britain and elsewhere, was widespread (Hackett 1918, 390). In *Ireland: A Study in Nationalism*, an essay contemporary to Joyce's notes, Francis Hackett (1918, 164) argued fiercely that Home Rule was so much more than 'patriotic passion'; its 'underlying realities' were 'fiscal autonomy', the ability to set economic policy. Furthermore, Hackett (1918, 166) was quick to point out that the decay in industry was not just due to emigration; in particular, the disappearance of the woollen, textiles and potteries industries was a sensitive point, for these were also ancient industries.[19] The manufacturing of woollens dates back to at least the eighth century; while of more recent origin, the Belleek Pottery, established in 1857, produced porcelain that could rival that of Staffordshire in quality but not in output and economic efficiency.

Butter making, too, was very much an indigenous product, and a topic much debated in Parliament around 1910. The butter trade suffered badly when, in 1884, following a free trade agreement, the British and Irish markets were flooded with butter produced in Denmark (Keenan 2006, 46), an issue that Joyce would pick up again in *Finnegans Wake* (see Geheber 2016). Irish producers responded by setting up cooperative creameries to pool production and centralize processing, and adopting new technological methods, including increased mechanization; as a result, output increased from 900 tonnes in 1892 to over 9,070 tonnes in 1904. Of these creameries, Cleeve's, which operated out of Limerick, Cork, Tipperary and Waterford, was the biggest, but these cooperatives pushed out smaller creameries using traditional methods (Bielenberg 2009, 74–5). In the first decade of the twentieth century, only about one-sixth of butter imported by Britain came from Ireland, pointing to continuing competition from abroad (Hackett 1918, 166); however, the real point of contention is the fact that foreign butter is found in an area that produced so much itself.

A lesson that textiles manufacturers learnt from the creameries is that combining efforts and resources can work in other sectors as well. This led, for example, to the establishment of the 'Co-operative Embroidery and Needlework Society' in Dalkey in 1895 (Coyne 1902, 440). Possibly this is the context of 'Elizabeth Westbrook making Claddagh | shawl in DMC'. The suggestion is that the claddagh, or Galway, shawl, the traditional heavy woollen shawl

---

[19] Coyne (1902, 400–1) reports, however, that the woollen industry showed signs of recuperation, as the number of power looms in operation and the export of Irish tweed, particularly, had increased (see also Keenan 2006, 126).

with a wide patterned border, made by DMC, an eighteenth-century French weaving company that became a European brand, might indicate an interesting progressive 'fusion' of heritage and international textiles trade. But the ironies are probably too great, not least because the Galway shawl was made in Paisley, Scotland, not in the Galway woollen industry, which promoted traditional skills and patterns, and the use of native materials (McMahon 2008, 146).

The industries notes cluster finds its way into two distinctly individual passages in *Ulysses*, one is the private consideration of transporting cattle across the city in 'Hades', the other is the citizen's diatribe against colonialism:

> Thursday of course. Tomorrow is killing day. Springers. Cuffe sold them about twentyseven quid each. For Liverpool probably. Roast beef for old England. They buy up all the juicy ones. And then the fifth quarter is lost: all that raw stuff, hide, hair, horns. Comes to a big thing in a year. Dead meat trade. Byproducts of the slaughterhouses for tanneries, soap, margarine.
>
> (*U* 6.392–7)

> *Raimeis*, says the citizen. There's no-one as blind as the fellow that won't see, if you know what that means. Where are our missing twenty millions of Irish should be here today instead of four, our lost tribes? And our potteries and textiles, the finest in the whole world! And our wool that was sold in Rome in the time of Juvenal and our flax and our damask from the looms of Antrim and our Limerick lace, our tanneries and our white flint glass down there by Ballybough and our Huguenot poplin that we have since Jacquard de Lyon and our woven silk and our Foxford tweeds and ivory raised point from the Carmelite convent in New Ross, nothing like it in the whole wide world! Where are the Greek merchants that came through the pillars of Hercules, the Gibraltar now grabbed by the foe of mankind, with gold and Tyrian purple to sell in Wexford at the fair of Carmen? Read Tacitus and Ptolemy, even Giraldus Cambrensis. Wine, peltries, Connemara marble, silver from Tipperary, second to none, our far-famed horses even today, the Irish hobbies, with king Philip of Spain offering to pay customs duties for the right to fish in our waters. What do the yellowjohns of Anglia owe us for our ruined trade and our ruined hearths? And the beds of the Barrow and Shannon they won't deepen with millions of acres of marsh and bog to make us all die of consumption.
>
> (*U* 12.1239–57)

Bloom's thoughts are prompted by the drove of cattle that blocks the funeral cortège on its way to Glasnevin cemetery. The point worth noting is that he is not, in fact, without knowledge of the meat trade, since he had worked for about a year at Cuffe's and Sons, of the Dublin Cattle Market on the North Circular Road. Although his idea that the corporation should run a tramline to the quays may border on the ridiculous, it shows that he is not only concerned with the economic aspects of the meat trade but also has concerns for its humanitarian or ecological impact. The number of animals that died or suffered injuries while in transit was considerable; shifting to the dead meat trade by slaughtering in Dublin would prevent this, while having the advantage of retaining animal byproducts for the home market. What is striking about the elements in the citizen's argument is that they are a significant expansion on the original notes; he mentions not just the native industries but emphasizes their long, classical origins. The establishment of such 'parallels' is, of course, a conceit of *Ulysses* as a whole, but, in effect, it also makes the outlook quite cosmopolitan, showing how Ireland was firmly connected to the most important ancient and medieval trade routes.

The political sentiment that lies behind these notes was not something incidental, but was present in nationalist debates about economic self-sufficiency at the time.[20] The Gaelic League, for example, in addition to campaigning for the preservation of the Irish language, spoke out in support of native industries (McMahon 2008, 188), while the pages of *The Irish Homestead* and *The Leader* continuously made the argument that political independence was not possible without economic independence. Typical for the period is a work like Francis Hackett's *Ireland: A Study in Nationalism*, addressed to an Irish-American readership, which rehearses all the points implied in Joyce's notes. When the arguments are made explicit in *Ulysses*, what becomes apparent is the extent to which Bloom and the citizen share the underlying justification. This is not to make an apology for the citizen's reactionary nationalism. Rather, what is important here is that the economic argument was made across the political spectrum.

The notes, furthermore, also reflect Joyce's own position on the socioeconomic conditions in Ireland expounded in his lectures and articles produced in Trieste (Nolan 1995, 99). In 'Ireland: Island of Saints and Sages', he made the point that 'Ireland is poor because English laws destroyed the industries of the country, notably the woollen one' (*OCPW* 119), and that the devastating effects brought on by British liberal policies continued to drive emigration. In 'Fenianism', he

---

[20] According to Gibson (2002, 236), *Ulysses* makes hay of the fact that 'the talk of Ireland's natural resources and the need for industrial renewal was commonly vague'. Joyce's notes make clear that this was not so.

mounts what can be construed as praise for Sinn Féin's efforts to bolster the Irish economy:

> They boycott English goods ... They are attempting to develop the industry of the whole country and, rather than fork out one and a quarter million each year to maintain the eighty deputies in the English parliament, they want to institute a consular service in the principal world ports with the aim of merchandising industry, without the intervention of England. From many points of view, this latest form of Fenianism may be the most formidable.
>
> (*OCPW* 140)

Joyce's comments are a gloss on Sinn Féin policy, a comprehensive programme of socioeconomic reform that covered everything from education to banking, as announced in 1905 by Arthur Griffith. Remarkable for its non-partisan take on socioeconomic progress, the programme would, however, prove too ambitious and impractical: when Easter 1916 put an end to Sinn Féin's passive resistance, very little had been achieved in terms of the plan's ambitions (Hackett 1918, 326–9; see also Foster 1993, 88). Joyce's stance on the policy, however, shows that as a political economist and a nationalist, he was an idealist rather than a realist. The fact that he planted a rumour in *Ulysses* that 'it was Bloom gave the ideas for Sinn Fein to Griffith to put in his paper' (*U* 12.1574–5) – ideas that Griffith propounded in *The Irish Homestead* between January and July 1904 – is indicative of the sort of politics *Ulysses* represents.

All the notes discussed in this chapter date from early in the genesis of *Ulysses*. They are important for understanding how Joyce developed the cultural spectrum of *Ulysses*. This happened directly through his reading in Irish political economy, but also, indirectly, refracted through the growth of Stephen's mind after his return from Paris. Whether as a consequence of disillusion or not, the major change in Stephen's evolution is the realization that history has made him, which drives him to understand the processes of memory and identity making. The notes are not *Ulysses*, however, and one should be wary not to overdetermine their meaning. Nevertheless, and especially within a cultural genetics project, notetaking is a forward-looking act. On the one hand, Joyce's notes reflect an intention (or intentions) that feed into the composition process. On the other, the notetaking also reverberates and builds on what is already written. When dealing with the cultural genetics of *Finnegans Wake*, this dialectic becomes even more complex and polyvalent. But as the emphasis seemingly shifts away from creating the conscience of the Irish race, Joyce moves further into exploring, and weaving together, the tapestry of Irish history as he creates a Revival of his own invention.

5

Sketching histories: *Finnegans Wake*

More than in any of Joyce's early works, Irish history takes centre stage in *Finnegans Wake*. If *Ulysses* presented the past as contested territory, he nonetheless put his own perspective into it. As I have shown in Chapter 4, *Ulysses* reprises Joyce's view on economic nationalism that he had developed during his Trieste period. To say that in *Finnegans Wake* the past is contested too is an understatement. For one, so much history is thrown in together, almost to create a vast compendium of historical incidents, great and small, that, at first glance, have little rhyme or reason other than the simple fact that they happened at some point in time in Ireland, Britain or elsewhere in the world. The sum total of this historical bric-a-brac is nevertheless meant to become a universal history that slowly unfolds itself (*FW-R* 146.39; *FW* 186.1) within a loosely structured framework made up from the philosophies of history of Vico, Michelet, Quinet and, to a lesser extent, Hegel.[1] Yet Joyce advised Colum not to make 'overmuch' of the Vichian cycles because it was only a 'trellis' upon which to hang his material (1959, 123). The result is a history in which the past is ever present, giving the impression that past events are flatlined in a perennial form of simultaneity (see Fordham 2007, 55–6). Yet the *Wake* does not extirpate the past's pastness. The book incorporates all kinds of historical materials, but it also notably focuses on a number of specific moments from Irish history: the Anglo-Norman invasion, the eighteenth century and (although Joyce did not live through the events first-hand) the advent of the Irish Free State.

I will elaborate on some of those moments in Chapter 6. Of particular concern for this chapter, rather, is a third aspect: the *Wake*'s concern with historiography, the narrating of history, and the quest for origins. Probing the origins of Earwicker's name, the phrase 'concerning the genesis' (*FW-R* 24.2; *FW* 30.2) is

---

[1] Joyce did not, as far as we know, encounter Quinet first hand, but through Léon Metchnikoff's *La Civilisation et les fleuves historiques* (1889) (Landuyt and Lernout 1995).

emblematic of the book as a whole. The *Wake* is obsessed with figuring out how things happened, but humorously fails to do so at every turn in the narrative, creating an anti-history mired in confusion caused by fruitless speculation and the compounding of double negatives: 'the unfacts, did we possess them, are too imprecisely few to warrant our certitude' (*FW-R* 46.16–17: *FW* 57.16–17). That facts are hard to come by is certainly the gist of the passage; however, taken literally, the statement is true: 'unfacts' cannot provide 'certitude'. In an ironic twist, the professor analysing ALP's letter disappears down the rabbit hole conjecturing what the 'unfacts' – the lies – might reveal.

From a genetic perspective, the *Wake*'s own origins are, by comparison, uncommonly real and specific. As is well known, Joyce started writing what would become *Finnegans Wake* on 10 March 1923:

> Yesterday I wrote two pages – the first I have written since the final *Yes* of *Ulysses*. Having found a pen, with some difficulty I copied them out in a large handwriting on a double sheet of foolscap so that I could read them. *Il lupe perde il pelo ma non il vizio*, the Italians say. The wolf may lose his skin but not his vice or the leopard cannot change his spots.
>
> (*Letters* I, 202)

That we know the precise moment when composition began seems appropriate for a book obsessed with origins. But this is historical serendipity. In part it stems from the circumstances in which the writing emerged. Almost all of Joyce's previous works were begun in an atmosphere of relative uncertainty as to whether they would find an audience. The last time this happened was with *Ulysses*, but as soon as serial publication was guaranteed, he proceeded in a quite methodical manner with composition until the book was completed. In writing *Ulysses*, he had perfected the habit of drafting, revising and expanding. This habit would stand him in good stead with *Finnegans Wake*. The wolf did not lose his vice.

Joyce was almost obsessive in his writing habits, which also included the taking, sorting through and using of notes. No doubt the elaborate, laborious way in which he wrote helped him to overcome the material difficulties that lay along the way. The *Wake*'s coming into being was often far from straightforward. Not only was there his rapidly deteriorating eyesight, often Joyce could not quite see the way ahead with the work. The direction of 'Work in Progress' repeatedly changed, while at moments Joyce worried how the different parts of the book would fuse together (see *Letters* I, 205). 'Work in Progress' was to undergo several twists and turns that clearly deviated from whatever intention or plan Joyce may have had in mind. This process began with the so-called 'early sketches' about Roderick O'Connor, Saint Kevin, Tristan and Isolde, Mamalujo, Saint Patrick and Humphrey Chimpden Earwicker.

For some time now, the complete composition history of *Finnegans Wake* has been carefully researched and plotted out.[2] Nevertheless, the origins of *Finnegans Wake* remain open to further scrutiny. Two earlier, but contrasting treatments of the *Wake*'s origins have laid important groundwork, but each has its limitations. With his 'nodal structure', David Hayman (1990) provides a useful framework for a developmental understanding of Joyce's composition process. The idea of a nodal structure is a genetic extension of Clive Hart's approach in *Structure and Motif* (1962), which addresses the *Wake*'s make-up outside the familiar cyclical patterns and correspondences. Hayman demonstrates how the 'Tristan and Isolde' sketch served as a structural basis around which Joyce wove some of the *Wake*'s other narratives. In a way, he treats the sketches as the genetic code of the *Wake*; even though Joyce set them aside, they continued to influence composition. The notebooks, meanwhile, provide similar embryonic concepts in the epiphanoids, 'highly charged personal observations' (Hayman 1990, 93), from which again the writing flows. Danis Rose (1995, 21n, 2013), by contrast, believes that the sketches do not belong to the genesis of *Finnegans Wake* at all, but were intended for a different work entitled *Finn's Hotel*. Instead of setting the sketches aside so they could germinate, Joyce abandoned them, when suddenly the writing of the Earwicker sketch took on a life of its own. In 1938 he remembered their existence and spliced them into his text. The argument that Earwicker was a turning point is certainly persuasive. The invention of a character in a piece of historiographic metafiction offered a creative opportunity that moved the writing away from the historical set pieces that he had produced so far. More problematic is the notion that the sketches were sufficiently finished and coherent to call them a 'projected history of Ireland' as a work in its own right (Rose and O'Hanlon 2018), particularly because they include segments written after the 'Earwicker' sketch had already been extended to at least three sequels that became Chapters 2–5 of Book I. The relevance of Joyce's notes for the sketches, furthermore, if adumbrated in Rose's theory at all, is merely as fodder for the text.

What is needed, in other words, is a reorientation of the earliest stages in the composition of 'Work in Progress'. Recognizing that Joyce himself may not have

---

[2] The most comprehensive, and most accurately dated, account is Crispi and Slote (2007). In terms of dating and arrangement of drafts, the *James Joyce Digital Archive* (Joyce 2018) supplements the Garland *James Joyce Archive* (Joyce 1977–1978).

been clear about where his writing would take him, I will offer interpretations of each of the sketches individually (something that has not been done before) to articulate their scope and direction in aesthetic and political terms. The historical intent of the sketches is apparent, but what kind of history are they? Joyce allegedly told Harriet Shaw Weaver that he planned to write a history of the world (Ellmann 1982, 536–7).[3] This may well have been the case. However, the Irish focus in the sketches, as well as the majority of the early notebooks, certainly points to a more particular focus: a history rooted in the Irish experience that, despite being 'fantasized, ahistorical, and comic' (Fordham 2007, 3), could function as a Revivalist project. That experience, furthermore, was that of Joyce's 'tribe', making a central theme of the Catholic Ireland that he grew up in and that he had tried so hard to resist. Catholic Ireland in the *Wake* is the Ireland of 'all saints of incorruption of an holy nation' (*FW-R* 50.12–13; *FW* 62.18–19).[4]

Roderick O'Connor

The two pages of writing that Joyce produced on 10 March is a piece of historiographic metafiction that captures the final days of Roderick O'Connor, the last High King of Ireland.[5] The grotesque sketch is completely imaginary; it does not relate any of the historical circumstances that accompanied the end of O'Connor's reign, but as a historical narrative it represents Joyce's most direct answer to the Irish Revival.[6]

O'Connor, the King of Connaught, was inaugurated High King in Dublin in 1167. Romanticizing O'Connor as the last High King of Ireland, historians placed his reign at the end of a long unbroken tradition of High Kings. By the twelfth century, however, the High Kingship system, intended to maintain a balance of power between the Irish kings, had for some time been in a precarious state as a result of the internecine conflict between the Irish provinces. O'Connor

---

[3] Ellmann (1982) dates Joyce's remark to summer 1922, when he saw Weaver in London. When 'Work in Progress' was properly under way, Joyce worked in more universal and world history. Notebook VI.B.1, compiled in February/March 1924, provides the first evidence for this.
[4] For an extensive treatment of Joyce's Catholic cultures in *Finnegans Wake*, see Van Mierlo (2017).
[5] On 11 March, Joyce reported to Weaver that two days ago he had written and copied out 'two pages' of a new book; on 19 July he sent her a second fair copy with the request to type it out (*Letters* I, 202–3). As this second fair copy is the earliest version of the sketch that reached a 'contingent state of completion' (Bushell 2009, 73, 79), this is mainly the one I use for my analysis. For further details on the composition, see Deppman (1995).
[6] For the dating of the early sketches, I follow the *James Joyce Digital Archive* (Joyce 2018), which revises the original dating in the *James Joyce Archive* (Joyce 1977–1978).

rose to power only after defeating Muirchertach Mac Lochlainn, the previous High King; he then forced his rivals into submission after deposing Dermot MacMurrough, King of Leinster. But O'Connor's brief period of stability came to an end when MacMurrough sought help from Henry II. Anglo-Norman mercenaries landed at Bannow Bay, Co. Wexford in 1169, joined forces with MacMurrough's army and quickly occupied Leinster and surrounding areas. He was confronted by O'Connor and his allies, which resulted in an agreement: in return for the Leinster throne, MacMurrough declared fealty to O'Connor. But the arrival of Strongbow with a much stronger force in 1170 changed all this. The Anglo-Normans launched a devastating campaign, conquering much of the midlands and burning the abbeys of Clonard and Kells. O'Connor was able at first to drive them back, but failed to recapture Dublin; while he laid siege to the city, Strongbow carried out a surprise attack on O'Connor's camp at Carrick, resulting in the Irish defeat. In 1175, O'Connor signed the Treaty of Windsor with Henry II, granting him as King of Connaught the right to rule Ireland as Henry's vassal, except for Leinster, Meath, Dublin, Waterford and surrounding areas, which fell under direct Anglo-Norman rule. O'Connor was subsequently unable to control the lesser barons and he abdicated in 1183. The Treaty of Windsor, which was signed in the presence of the bishops of Winchester and Ely and Laurence O'Toole, Archbishop of Dublin, was seen as the first manifestation of the Church interfering in Irish politics. In 1155, Henry had sought to legitimize the invasion of Ireland first by obtaining the bull *Laudabiliter* from Adrian IV, the English pope; the bull asked for the reformation of the Church in Ireland to bring it in line with Roman ecclesiastical practice. The Synod of Cashell in 1172, called together by Henry, finalized this process.

None of these historical events are in Joyce's sketch, aside from the mention of Art MacMurrough Kavanagh, O'Connor's alleged predecessor who is 'now of parts unknown'. But this is a case of anachronous history or the fortuitous mistake of an inebriated chronicler who confuses Dermot MacMurrough, who died in 1171, with his later descendant who was King of Leinster until his death in 1417. From a nationalist perspective, Art MacMurrough Kavanagh seems the more formidable leader, for he spent much of his reign rebelling with considerable success against the Anglo-Norman settlers, whereas Dermot was a treacherous figure who, history has it, betrayed Ireland for a woman: 'The adulteress and her paramour brough the Saxon robbers here' (*U* 12.1157–8). The purpose of the sketch is commemorative: it looks back to the past, before the moment of historical transition when the Anglo-Norman colonists ended Irish self-governance, to a celebration of O'Connor's ascension to the High Kingship, 'the anniversary of his 1st coming' (47480-267; *JJA* 55:446a).

The precise genetic route to Roderick eludes us. Certainly there is no direct indication in VI.B.10, the notebook that he began compiling in late October 1922, that Joyce would turn to Ireland's legendary past as his subject.[7] Apart from a handful of notes (mentioning the Carman fair, an ancient Irish festival; Muirchertach of the Leather Cloaks, the tenth-century King of Ailech who campaigned against the Danes; a tour Brian Boru made around Ireland; and Mac Murrough Kavanagh, who was King of Leinster in the fourteenth century), VI.B.10 contains little engagement with the Irish past. Instead, this notebook is a ragbag of words, phrases and random titbits that are not, however, completely without direction. Joyce was particularly focused on the trivial and the everyday, showing a fascination for what was modern, fashionable and gossipy, as he read and took notes from articles and advertorials on film stars and fashion, including a column from *The Daily Mail* written by Dorothy Richardson, decrying the 'ankle-gazers' who advocate for the return of the long skirt (30 November 1922, VI.B.10.54). This preoccupation with the everyday and the culturally trivial – always slightly weird and askew – would have its influence on the direction that some of the sketches would take.

VI.B.10, however, contains one very relevant contemporary theme: the Civil War. Joyce's notes seemingly avoid the openly political, but they are far from 'tangential' (Crispi 2010, 58), insofar as they gather some of the atrocities that were a daily occurrence. Among the events that Joyce noted are a raid by National troops on Oddfellows Hall, Upper Abbey Street (VI.B.10.25), an act of terrorism at Liffey Junction Station, sending an engine at full speed down the line to the North Wall (VI.B.10.31); ambushes on the Meath-Kildare border and in Collinstown, where Free State troops discovered a weapons dump, listing the type of firearms used (VI.B.10.49); an account of protestations in the Dail from across the political spectrum condemning the government's recent spate of reprisal executions (VI.B.10.67); a report on a military tribunal in Co. Kerry, which resulted in the death sentence of one man for attacking Free State troops in Trallee and the incarceration of several others, including one Sheila Harnett

---

[7] Presumably, Joyce's exploration of history happened in a lost notebook that chronologically follows VI.B.10. Designated VI.X.1, it likely contained notes for the development of the first of Joyce's sketches, 'Roderick O'Connor' (Rose 1995, 25, 46). The notebook after this, VI.B.3, consists almost entirely of historical notes, including some conceptually significant sources, such as J.M. Flood's *Ireland: Its Saints and Scholars* (1917) and Benedict Fitzpatrick's *Ireland and the Making of Britain* (1921). For a speculative account as to how Joyce arrived at Roderick O'Connor as the subject for his first sketch, see Henkes (2011).

(VI.B.10.97; *FW-R* 139.11–12; *FW* 176.03); as well as several other attacks on the railways, one at Sligo (VI.B.10.102), one at Mountpleasant, north of Dundalk (VI.B.10.103), and one near Enniscorthy, in which the driver and fireman were killed (VI.B.10.118). While these notes, all from *The Irish Times*, capture the impact of the Civil War on public life, highlighting that both sides in the conflict were culpable of the destruction of life and property, Joyce also took notes from *The Leader*, which, as a pro-treaty publication, was staunchly critical of the war. Joyce turned to the op-ed pieces in 'Current Topics' and the satirical 'Our Ladies' Letter'. In the latter, a supposedly ordinary person reflects sardonically on the events of the day, producing comments like: 'Things are quiet in Dublin – if you'd call it quiet not to be shot' (*The Leader*, 28 October 1922, quoted in VI.B.10.19). However, most of the articles that Joyce noted are almost all about the conflict's impact on daily life: the increase in prices, the disruption of the railways, public drunkenness. One in particular expresses the sense of waste: 'Many young men who had done good work in the past wished to settle down after the Truce or the signing of the Treaty' but who were prevented from doing so because of the fighting (*The Leader*, 11 November 1922, quoted in VI.B.10.29). The treaty had finally offered an opportunity for a prosperous Ireland that could finally govern itself, but that opportunity was being wasted. The writer went on to complain that the government was out of touch and that it did not do enough to assist patriotic businesses: 'A good deal of the work performed at home has been handed to un-Irish and anti-Irish firms, whilst firms with any tinge of Irish-Ireland management have been ignored' (11 November 1922, quoted in VI.B.10.29).[8]

To claim that Joyce's notes on the Civil War are a preamble for 'Roderick O'Connor', whose historical antecedent suffered usurpation from a discontented rival, or for any of the other sketches is too deterministic. Nonetheless, the Civil War belongs to the historical conditions that framed Joyce's new writing. An addition to the 'Roderick' sketch makes this evident: 'Art MacMurrough Kavanagh ^now of parts unknown^ ^God guard his generous soul^' (47480-267; *JJA* 44:446a). The origin on which the addition is based is particularly interesting: 'God guard his generous | soul | Mick Collins' (VI.B.10.29). Joyce took it from that same 11 November article in *The Leader* that celebrated Collins' achievement: 'Michael Collins (God guard his generous soul) assisted some of

---

[8] In *Finnegans Wake*, Joyce turns his note 'Irish tinge' (VI.B.10.29) into the 'Lucan tinge' (*FW-R* 368.6; *FW* 474.7) of Shaun's hair, alluding to the village west of Dublin that was the seat of the Jacobite Sarsfield family and that became a spa town in the eighteenth century much frequented by the well to do.

these men' (quoted in VI.B.10.29). If the humour that pervades much of VI.B.10 presents an image of a modern world at odds with itself, it also shows Joyce coming to terms with the radical transformation that Ireland is undergoing in this period. Although life in Paris was quite removed from what was happening at home, he cannot but have been struck by the impasse in Ireland's politics and the nightmare of history repeating itself. Is it a coincidence that at this precise moment he turns to imagining an 'end-of-time' narrative?

The narrative of 'Roderick O'Connor' treats a crucial moment of transition in Irish history when the era of the Irish High Kings ended and the period of Anglo-Norman domination began. Ostensibly the tale of a last great annual feast, the sketch introduces Roderick as the 'last paramount chief', a title suggesting a distinctly Irish pedigree, at the moment just before his reign ends. This 'last supper' may be an allusion to the last-ever Tailteann Games in 1168, at least insofar as the date matches Roderick's age; born around 1116, Roderick is said to be fifty-four or fifty-five years old in the sketch. This is not a random choice, for not only had the Irish Free State taken the decision in 1922 to revive the games, the social and political intent of the original games was important to Joyce. The annual event was different from the heroic and mythological meetings at Tara; the games were part ritual – funeral games to honour the dead – and part administrative – an annual proclamation of the laws so that everyone might remember them. The disappearance of the Tailteann, which coincided with the arrival of Anglo-Norman culture and the termination of the Brehon Laws, thus comes to symbolize historical transition itself.

Joyce appropriately highlights the celebratory nature of the festivities, but this is where the reverential part of the sketch ends. The narrative turns the celebrations into a topsy-turvy 'barbecue beanfeast' (47480-270; JJA 55:446c). The scene is very much the morning after the night before with the debris of drunken debauchery lying around the room. Roderick, like a pathetic Nero watching his kingdom go under, drinks the dregs from the abandoned bottles after everyone else has gone home.

The language that Joyce uses is well adapted for the chaos at the party. He wrote the sketch in a new idiom that makes some use of portmanteau words: 'last preelectric king', 'footback', 'switchbackward road', 'notmuchers', 'maltknights and beerchurls', 'replenquished drinking utensils', 'slygrogging suburbanites', 'chateaubottled Guinness's' (47480-270; JJA 55:446c). Strikingly, these portmanteaus cluster in the final lines of the sketch. For the most part, however, Joyce reprises the style of gigantism from 'Cyclops', including stage Irish expressions ('arrah bedamnbut', 'sorra'), mixed with a few other ingredients familiar from *Ulysses*: the non-sequiturs from 'Eumaeus' and 'Penelope', including the almost total absence of punctuation creating something like stream of consciousness; and the verbal deconstructions of 'Sirens' ('I've a terrible errible lot by todo today todo toderribleday') (47480-270; JJA 55:446c). In addition, Joyce puts in a good number of archaic words that hark back to Stephen's fascination with the hybridity of language, such as 'whilom' in 'whilom joky old top', meaning *former* or *late* (first attested in this sense in the mid-sixteenth century according to the *OED*). In the phrase 'heeltapping through the winespilth', *heeltap* is slang for the leftovers of a drink. Finally, Joyce introduces stock elements that will return in the other sketches and other parts of *Finnegans Wake*: Mamalujo's Anglo-Irish expletive 'arrah' and their catch-phrase 'poor old', and the washerwomen's 'wait till I tell you'.

With this language and setting, Joyce creates a version of the Celtic past that is starkly at odds with the romanticized retellings of Irish mythology of the Irish Revival. (Although Joyce's prose, or his notes, do not elicit any specific target, his distaste in particular for Lady Gregory's writings does come to mind.) The Roderick O'Connor of Joyce's sketch, furthermore, openly denigrates the noble origins of the Celtic race: 'the unimportant Parthalonians with the mouldy Firbolgs and the Tuatha de Danaan googs and the rest of the notmuchers that he didn't care the royal spit out of his ostensible mouth about' (47480-270; JJA 55:446c, simplified). Roderick's disparagement of the mythological races that inhabited ancient Ireland is a direct reneging of his own ancestry and hence a rejection of history. But while Roderick refuses to go down the 'switchbackward road', rejecting his own genealogy and the cultural obsession with a long, lost glory, he knows he has no future either. Instead, 'overwhelmed … with black ruin', his mind turns to the leftovers and, wallowing in his misery, he sings 'to himself through his old tears'. Nostalgia makes way for maudlin sentiment and self-pity: 'heart of Midleinster' (47480-270; *JJA* 55:446c) is no more.

The echo of Sir Walter Scott's 1818 novel, *The Heart of Mid-Lothian*, reverberates in different ways. There is Scott's own romanticized brand of Scottish nationalism; the fact that the novel opens with a bloody skirmish over England's new tax levy on malt; and the presence of the Jacobite threat. (James II's defeat at the Battle of the Boyne heralded a new phase in Irish colonialism, some five centuries after the Anglo-Norman invasion at which O'Connor lost his throne.) The allusion, however, first and foremost, fits an important property of Joyce's sketch and *Finnegans Wake* as it would become: the fluidity, or permeability, of history. The narrator, as I indicated earlier, proves himself a rather poor historian, confusing Dermot MacMurrough with Art MacMurrough Kavanagh. (Appropriately, on the first typescript, Joyce added instances of the Mamalujo-like narrative 'us' [Hayman 2007, 295]). The mode and voice of his narration is that of a barfly who regales his hearers with a long-winded tale from the Irish past in an irreverent, hyperbolic manner. The festivities are described as a 'barbecue beanfeast', O'Connor's seat is a 'grand old pile', his liegemen/ancestors are 'notmuchers' (47480-270; *JJA* 55:446c). As the narrator babbles on, he laces his story with interjections and non-sequiturs. His version of history is highly idiosyncratic to say the least. Importantly, we do not know on what authority he relates the history of Roderick's last night. Was he an eyewitness? Nonetheless, we can assume it contains more fiction than fact.

In that sense, again, rather than being a direct attack on Revivalist writing, the sketch stages how folklore, mythology and cultural memory are created. People tell stories all the time, and attribute value and veracity to them that reflect wider norms and beliefs; when these stories are repeated, they attract new elements in the popular imagination and contribute to the creation of the nation's collective memory. This agglutinative effect of storytelling – the 'reusable texts, images, and rituals' of any given culture or society (Assmann 1995, 132) – sits right at the heart of *Finnegans Wake*, whose narratives, like a game of Chinese whispers, take on a life of their own, perform their mutations away from where they originated, and become increasingly unreliable. Although Joyce would bring this type of narration to fruition in the retellings of Earwicker's biography in Chapter I.2, he planted the seeds for this process of agglutination in the 'Roderick O'Connor' sketch whose history is retold and distorted by a drunk in the pub. The sketch's subject matter, the era of the High Kings, puts it squarely in Revival territory, in particular Lady Gregory's early writings in *Gods and Fighting Men: The Story of the Tuatha de Danaan and of the Fianna of Ireland* (1903). But while Joyce takes distance from the vague boundary between history and myth that can be found in much Revivalist writing, he writes history back into myth and creates his own version of a Revival narrative. As an end-of-history narrative, 'Roderick O'Connor' is not stuck in an idealized version of Ireland's past; instead, it repudiates the idea of a stable, culture-defining origin in favour of the instability and incoherence that comes with historical transformation. Ultimately, tracing the genealogy of these transformations provides a richer, less purified model of the past.

Saint Kevin

In *Finnegans* Wake, Joyce would play these conflicting notions of history off against one another, creating a fictional universe in which they are always at once idealized and crumbling, Edenic and dear dirty Dublin. The early sketches that followed 'Roderick O'Connor', however, start from a different position. On the one hand, he created a direct temporal overlap between past and present, which I will discuss later. On the other, he was looking to modify the traditional Revivalist model in Celtic origins in search for other cultural authenticities. In his second sketch, Joyce turned to his country's Catholic roots, creating the weirdest kind of hagiography. 'Saint Kevin' reimagines the historical acts of the saint who settled as a hermit in the woods around Glendalough after allegedly fleeing the advances of a young woman. That Joyce turned to Saint Kevin, rather than to the patron saints of Ireland, Saints Patrick, Columba and Brigid, might seem peculiar. He would turn to Saint Patrick soon enough.[9] For now, Saint Kevin, representing Irish asceticism and an example of vernacular devotion, furnished a mindset rather than a national emblem.

Within a week of drafting 'Roderick O'Connor', Joyce dictated the first draft of the Saint Kevin sketch to Nora:

> St kevin [sic] born on the Island of Ireland in the Irish ocean goes to lough Glendalough to live on an Island in the lake and as there is a pond on the Island and a little island in the pond [?] h[oly] K[evin] builds his hut on the islet and then most holy K scoops out the floor to a dept [sic] of one foot after which venerable K goes to the brink of the pond and fills his tub with water which he emptys [sic] time after time into a cavity of his hut thereby forming a pool having done which he blessed K half fills the tub very blessed sets it in the middle of the pool, blessed K[,] pulls up his frock and St Kevin seats himself in the tub and doctor Kevin meditates with burning zeal the sacrament of baptism or regeneration by water.
>
> (VI.B.3.42–5, simplified)

This short, absurd vignette in plain and simple language is richly suggestive of children's writing, Irish topography, hagiographical discourse and mysticism. Its abstract landscape poses a marked difference to that of contemporary hagiography. Writing in the picturesque tradition, John Canon O'Hanlon in the *Lives of the Saints*, a book Joyce was soon to read, describes Glendalough as 'that singularly romantic valley, lying embosomed in the midst of lofty and precipitous mountains'. Connecting landscape with religious devotion, he adds: 'The whole valley has that appearance of monastic retirement and religious awe, which have peculiarly fitted it, as a retreat for holiness and learning, from the earliest Christian ages' (O'Hanlon n.d., 38). The nested circles in Joyce's sketch,

---

[9] Joyce in fact first turned to Saint Columcille and Saint Columbanus, who he encountered in Flood's *Ireland: Its Saints and Scholars*, but did not find creative use for the materials he had collected (Deane 2001a, 5). The Kevin and Saint Patrick sketches were written about ten days apart.

consisting of islands within islands and bodies of water surrounded by other bodies of water, transform this landscape into a geometrical figure. This figure resembles the decorative patterns, a symbol of eternity, commonly found on carved objects and in burial tombs of Christian and pre-Christian Ireland as well as in the landscape itself.

Joyce's portrayal of Kevin as half-saint, half-mystic is an exercise (so to speak) in fluidity. According to his hagiography, Saint Kevin was in the habit of praying while standing in the lake at Glendalough where the historical Kevin had retired as a hermit (O'Hanlon n.d. 48). Joyce transforming the landscape into an abstract geometrical shape is typical of the *Wake*'s later topographical distortions that fold the Irish landscape into a global one (see Hart 1962, 111–12). The depiction of Kevin in his 'hiptubbath' meditating on the sacrament of baptism is, however, not just a ludicrous caricature, but serves as a comment on the quintessential place of baptism in the Church. Kevin bathing himself suggests the etymological origin of baptism, which comes from the Greek word *bapto* or *baptizo*, meaning to wash or immerse (*CE*, s.v. Baptism).[10] What is crucial, though, is that baptism is the first, and most important, of the sacraments because it is (as the Roman Catechism describes it) 'the sacrament of the regeneration by water in the word'. Baptism symbolizes 'the door of the spiritual life' by which Catholics are made members of the Church.

By the time Joyce had completed two more rounds of revision, the short vignette had gained a lot of new 'ecclesiological' and 'liturgiological' vocabulary (VI.B.25.154). But it had also become more universally Irish. The text gained an allusion to Thomas Moore ('amiddle of meeting waters of river Slaney and river Liffey'), a mock-Irish topography ('the circumfluent watercourses of Ishgagrania and Ishgadectera') (47488-25-26; *JJA* 63:38c-d), as well as an invocation of Yeats's 'Lake Isle of Innisfree'. The new topography further abstracted the actual landscape. The Celticized twin lakes whose names translate as Grania's water and Dectera's water, named after Finn McCool's betrothed and Cuchulain's mother, were originally simply '5 watercourses' (47488-25; *JJA* 63:38a-b), referencing the five rivers that flow through the Glendalough valley. So too Kevin's 'island in the lake' (VI.B.3.42) first became 'an isle in the lake' (47488-24; *JJA* 63:38a) and then 'its supreme lake isle' (47488-25; *JJA* 63:38c). And Saint Kevin's Cell, first a 'hut' (VI.B.3.443), became a 'beehivehut' (47488-24; *JJA*63:38a) and

---

[10] The *OED* gives 'Greek βαπτίζειν "to immerse, bathe, wash, drench" as derived from "βάπτειν to dip, plunge, bathe"' (s.v. baptize).

subsequently a 'honeybeehivehut' (47488-25; *JJA* 63:38c).[11] Of course – and this makes the Yeatsian connection likely – Glendalough does not have a lake island; Saint Kevin's Cell and Saint Kevin's Bed were located above the cliffs on the southern side of the Upper Lake.

The account of Kevin's bath was extended into a second vignette. This new vignette was written on the back of the second draft of the main sketch, but was never developed beyond its initial outline. Its set-up is crucial for the direction Joyce was taking in reimagining the Irish past. The extension casts Kevin 'as an infant' called 'Kevineen' who 'delighted himself by playing with the sponge on tubbing night' (47484-24v; *JJA* 63:38b). Although this reprises Kevin's bath, what follows is more significant:

> As a growing boy under the influence of holy religion which had been instilled into him across his grandmother's knee he grew more & more pious and abstracted like the time God knows he sat down on the plate of mutton broth.
>
> He simply had no time for girls and often used to say to his dear mother & dear sisters that his dearest mother & his dear sisters were good enough for him. At the age of six months he wrote a prize essay on kindness to fishes.
>
> (47484-24v; *JJA* 63:38b, simplified)

Kevin's growing piety is a hagiographical trope. Canon O'Hanlon writes of Saint Kevin's childhood that his parents, who saw in their son 'many indications of sanctity', placed him in the care of three local elders, Eogoin, Lochan and Enna, who lived in a nearby cell, to supervise his religious instruction; Kevin 'prosecuted his studies with the greatest diligence' (O'Hanlon n.d., 35). In Joyce's vignette, sanctity is made ordinary as it is made to reflect the religious devotion expected of every good boy or girl in Ireland. With an ironic twist, Joyce overlays this fervour with the language from the Bywaters trial, the sensational murder case that dominated the newspapers in the winter of 1922. The murder was a crime of passion. Frederick Bywaters, who was a lodger with the Thompsons in their house in Ilford, London, had become Edith Thompson's lover, until Edith's husband Percy discovered the affair and threw Bywaters out. The relationship did not end, however. One night, Bywaters waited near their house for the couple to return home and stabbed Percy Thompson to death. The lovers both maintained that Edith had not been aware of Bywaters' motivations, but their love letters produced at the trial revealed that they had frequently talked about eliminating

---

[11] The supposition is that Kevin's Cell was similar in structure to the beehive-shaped stone dwellings found at other monastic sites and that themselves were derived from the round native dwellings (see VI.B.3.115 and Flood 1917, 115).

the husband. The simple language Joyce uses in the Kevin sketch derives almost entirely from one of the many tabloid articles seeking to exculpate the murderer. 'My Boy's Life: By His Mother' in the *Daily Sketch* portrays Frederick Bywaters as a simple boy who was not interested in girls ('It was only last year that we knew of his friendship with Mrs. Thompson, and, as far as I know, she was the first woman outside his family circle he ever cared for') and who gained a first prize for writing an essay the theme of 'Kindness to Dumb Animals' (VI.B.10.073-074). Exploiting the discursive conventions of different media, Joyce constructs a tale of exemplary or emblematic innocence that meshes the pieties of the modern popular press with those of devotional hagiography. The vignette presents Saint Kevin *sub specie temporis nostri*.

Saint Patrick

The Saint Patrick sketch, begun in late March 1923 but not fair copied until July, continues Joyce's preoccupation with the national saints. But where 'Saint Kevin' retains vestiges of hagiography, the new sketch deals less with Patrick than with the 'archdruid' Berkeley. That Joyce's literary re-creation of Ireland's Christian origins should include Ireland's patron saint seems self-evident. But Saint Patrick is an ambivalent figure for Joyce, and throughout much of 'Work in Progress' he studies Patrick's life and legacy from all the different angles that scholarship and commentators offer him. This includes speculative and deliberately wayward accounts, such as that of the Rev. John Roche Ardill's *St. Patrick, A.D. 180* (1931), who claims against the grain that Patrick lived in the second instead of the fifth century (VI.B.45.81-2). The first twelve to eighteen months of 'Work in Progress' were the period in which Joyce actively sought to understand the origins of Patrick's existence. Notebook VI.B.14, compiled between August and November 1924, is the high point of this activity, containing notes from no less than seven sources. The reasons why Joyce was interested in Patrick are historical and political. Patrick did not bring Catholicism to Ireland as is popularly believed; Palladius' mission in AD 431-2 had already brought the faith to certain corners of the country (Bury 1905, 14, 54-8). Rather, as Palladius' successor, Patrick brought the spiritual power of the Church to Ireland (Bury 1905, 65-6). He stands on the divide between pagan and Christian Ireland.

This transformation is present in the mythic imagination of the Ossianic poems. The conversation between Patrick and Ossian, who lived two centuries prior, as retold, for example, by Lady Gregory in *Gods and Fighting Men* (1904), is one that expresses a regret for the disappearance of the old world order (see Morris 1908, 159–63). Patrick's sparring with, and defeat of, the Irish bards prompted Joyce to say that his sketch was about 'the conversion of S. Patrick by Ireland' (*Letters* III, 79), insofar as it presents Patrick, not as the usurper, but as having absorbed the culture he sought to supplant. On the one hand, this was part of his conversion strategy, using, for example, the shamrock to explain the Trinity. On the other, it places the comments about cultural continuity between pagan and Christian beliefs in a different light; these continuities are less historical accidents than the consequence of the intruder to some extent integrating with the host culture.[12] Time and again in *Finnegans Wake*, as elsewhere in his writing, Joyce dwells on cultural contamination as an inevitable factor when two cultures meet.

In Lady Gregory's version of the dialogue between Ossian and Saint Patrick, Ossian relates how his wife Niamh was worried that, wanting to return to Ireland to visit Finn again, he might not make it back to the Land of the Young. To dissuade him, she said that he would find Ireland much changed: 'you will not see Finn and his people, for there is not now in the whole of Ireland but a Father of Orders and armies of saints.' Saint Patrick, stalwart but compassionate, responds: 'Go on with your story … and you will get the same good treatment from me you got from Finn, for the sound of your voice is pleasing me' (Gregory 1970, 339). This is not quite the conversion of Patrick by Ireland, but close. Joyce's sketch mimics the dialogue with Ossian (as well as Saint Patrick's contest with the Druid Luchat Mael near Tara) but replaces him with the philosopher Bishop Berkeley.

In both its original and completed form, the sketch is perhaps more allegorical than historical. Saint Patrick is a chimaera, refracted through someone else's vision: 'Bigseer, refrects the pretty padre' (*FW-R* 479.3; *FW* 612.16). More so than with Saint Kevin, Joyce elicits the genesis of hagiography by which the life of a historical figure is transformed into a hagiographical trope; the events of the life are dramatized, and overlain with miracles, for the purpose of spiritual edification. In the case of Patrick, Bury argues, the creation of a 'hero saint' went hand in hand with Patrick's Hibernicization and the creation of a national icon (1905, 205).[13] Joyce's sketch, therefore, also refracts the changes that Patrick

---

[12] As Joyce could have read in Bury's *Life of St. Patrick and his Place in History* (1905), the most complete authority on the subject, the medieval lives of Saint Patrick may have modelled specific incidents in the saint's life, not least the events at Slane and Tara, on Irish legend (Bury 1905, 266–7).

[13] To be clear, Bury places the beginning of this Hibernicization in the early Irish Acts, from the sixth century, which predate the Latin lives (see 1905, 266–8). But the process is also relevant in the development of Patrick as the patron saint of Ireland.

effected in Ireland. The defeat of the druids after lighting of the fires at Slane on Easter eve to provoke King Leary is a key moment in Patrick's mission. It was the night of the Beltaine festival at Tara; custom dictated that no fires could be lit until the ritual fire was kindled at Tara. When seeing Patrick's fire, the king's druids predicted that, unless Patrick's fire was extinguished, it would 'never be quenched; and the kindler of it will overcome us all' (Bury, 104). In his sketch Joyce underscores Patrick's inertia to the druid's magic, as Berkeley attempts to explain 'the colourful world of joss' to 'silent whiterobed Patrick'. But does Berkeley manage to convince the saint? The pre-Christian worldview is of course 'joss', that is, of an idolatrous nature. More significantly, the Celtic world is not colourful at all, but only refracts a ubiquitous, nationalist green (Deane 2001a, 6). King Leary's 'fiery locks' and 'sixcoloured' turn into the colour of every drab vegetable or herb imaginable: 'boiled spinach', 'curly cabbage', 'laurel leaves', 'thyme and parsley', 'olive lentil' and 'a brew of senecassia' (47488-99r; JJA 63:146a). The leaves and pods of the senna cassia are said to have laxative properties. Prefiguring Shaun's painting the town green (*FW-R* 319.34; *FW* 411.24), the pervasiveness of green – the colour that does not even show in Berkeley's rainbow – is the only colour that light is 'unable to absorbere' (47488-99r; JJA 63:146c). In one fell swoop, Joyce denounces both Irish mythology and Irish nationalism. This places Saint Patrick in a totally ambivalent light, too, because his iconography was completely absorbed into the nationalist sentiment.

Tristan and Isolde

Joyce's tackling of the Tristan and Isolde legend follows a similar logic to that of the 'Saint Kevin' sketch. Renarrating the well-known legend was again a deliberate attempt to rethink the Revival's traditional canon with a story set in the Celtic fringe. Joyce seized the opportunity to transform the courtly romance into that of a modern flapper and a rugby player. Of all the sketches, 'Tristan and Isolde' is the one that most explicitly offers an alternative to Revivalist mythology. Looking back at his Celtic Twilight period, Yeats ruminated about his early determination to write about Irish subject matter:

> I could not endure, however, an international art, picking stories and symbols where it pleased. Might I not ... create some new *Prometheus Unbound*; Patrick or Columcille, Oisin or Finn, in Prometheus' stead; and, instead of Caucasus, Cro-Patrick or Ben Bulben? Have not all races had their first unity from a mythology that marries them to rock and hill?
>
> (Yeats 1999, 166–7)

Joyce simultaneously did and did not do what Yeats proposed. As a topographic narrative, *Finnegans Wake* is, of course, married to rock and hill – or rock and river for that matter – while Finn MacCool is its preternatural hero. For 'Tristan and Isolde', he took his cue – or confirmation – from the first of a two-part essay by T. Sturge Moore in *The Criterion* (1922/1923). Prompted by the question as to why certain stories, like that of Tristan and Isolde, lend themselves to reworking by other authors, while others, like Hamlet's, do not, Sturge Moore discussed a number of modern adaptations of the famous legend by Laurence Binyon, Tennyson, Wagner, Michael Field, Swinburne, Matthew Arnold, Debussy and Gordon Bottomley. Joyce noted down the names of the writers in Notebook VI.B.10 (15), but does not appear to have made any further use of them.

The composition of the 'Tristan and Isolde' sketch in July and August was a lot more convoluted than that of the earlier sketches. Creatively, the summer of 1923 was quite a productive period for Joyce, going back and forth between drafting his new sketch and revising the earlier ones. His treatment of Tristan and Isolde comprises several discrete parts: the first describes the declaration of love and the first kiss; the second extends the first part to the love scene itself (the section of the narrative that was incorporated into Book IV of *Finnegans Wake*); the third is a short fragment in which Isolde reflects on her love for Tristan (and which immediately follows a version of Mamalujo's song of the seabirds); the fourth, mirror 'Kevineen', is also an abandoned side-piece that deals with Isolde's growing up.[14]

The two parts that relate Tristan and Isolde's lovemaking are, like the addition to 'Saint Kevin', a reworking of the original legend *sub specie tempori nostris*. In terms of the characterization, there are few differences; in the first part, the pair are more ordinary lovesick individuals, while the second part stresses their heroic nature, with Isolde eventually becoming, in the third fair copy, a 'modern old ancient Irish princess' (47481-98; *JJA* 56:16–17). The language in the two parts is cast is an amalgam of discourses, or a 'persiflage' (NLI 41,818, f.1), that includes the language of popular romance ('felt him sweeter than cherry or plum … than the hawthorn valley' [f. 4v]), advertising ('sweeter than … candykisses or Lipton's fruitcake' [f. 4v]), mythology ('Hero of ten scrums, carrier of the ovum', that is, rugby ball [f. 4v]), medicine ('daily potions of extract of willow bark', 'with feverish pallor' [f.1r]), scholasticism ('Why this strangulation,

---

[14] The order in which the parts were written, and indeed the order of their narrative sequence, is not clear. The arrangement given by Rose and O'Hanlon appears somewhat arbitrary (Joyce 2018, http://jjda.ie/main/JJDA/F/FF/fdra/fhda.htm).

this yearning for a <u>bonum arduum</u> as distinguished from a <u>bonum simpliciter</u>?' [f.1r]), vulgarity ('Can that sobstuff' [f. 1r], 'you bloody bitch' [47480-267v; *JJA* 56:6–7], 'he had shut his duckhouse' [47481-94; *JJA* 56:2–3]), poetry – of all kinds ('innocent as the undriven snow', 'the sidereal host' [NLI 41,818, f.1v]; 'the twittingly twinkling' [47480-267v; *JJA* 56:6–7]), science ('uranographically' [f. 267v]), Hiberno-English ('girleen' [f. 267v]), the novel ('Hearing his name called before many minutes had passed he most sagaciously ceased to walk about and turned, his look now charged with purpose' [f. 267v], fashion ('in her quite charming oceanblue brocade with iris petal of sleeves' [47481-94; *JJA* 56:2–3]), esoterism ('I oculise my most inmost Ego most vaguely sense the deprofundity of multimathematical immaterialities whereby in the pancosmic urge the Allimmanence of that which Is Itself exteriorates on this here our plane in disunited solid liquid and gaseous bodies in pearlwhite passionpanting intuitions of reunited selfhood in the higherdimensional Selflessness' [f.94r]), and so forth.

This last quotation is itself significant, for in it Tristan gives expression to, or puts into vision, the mystical union between himself and Isolde. (The underlying note, 'occult (oculist)' [VI.B.3.078], plays on the double sense of 'vision' obfuscating the etymological difference between Latin *oculus*, 'eye' and *occultus*, 'secret'.) Through this vision, and by lathering his narrative with multiple types of lovers' discourse – congruous and incongruous – Joyce hones in on, and subverts, the essence of the original legend: Tristan and Isolde are the archetypal lovers. But it is only because they accidentally drink a love potion that they fall for each other; the original romance is therefore also about forbidden love, the subject of Joyce's own *Exiles*. (It is no coincidence that in the *Scribbledehobble* notebook Joyce stored many of his T&I notes under the 'Exiles' heading [VI.A. 271, 301–2]).

Joyce's modern adaptation of *Tristan and Isolde* is crudely sexual, mimicking the sexual liberation in the modern novel. Aptly, first of all, in the Young Isolde vignette, Isolde reads *Harry Coverdale's Courtship, And All That Came Of It*, by the English writer Frank E. Smedley (1855), who wrote entertaining, melodramatic novels about sports and adventure (VI.B.10.007). Published in 1855 by the aptly named publisher Virtue, Hall and Virtue, and allegedly a favourite of Joyce's father (Gorman 1949, 16), *Harry Coverdale's Courtship* is a story about a society cad, tall and good-looking, who loves the good life, but is cajoled into marrying a young woman, Alice. An unhappy power struggle ensues in a narrative full of intrigue that circles around the question of 'the maintenance of the proper authority, rule, and governance of the wife, over that legal and clerical fiction, her lord and master' (Smedley 1855, 339). A publisher's advertisement on p. 146 in *The Athenaeum* on 2 February 1856 describes the plot as 'showing how this misguided young man fell from the ways of good fellowship and (in) sobriety; how for his sins he was condemned to Matrimony; together with a detailed account of his sufferings in that state of bondage'. Second, and no less misogynistic, was the American O. Henry, whose collection of stories *The Four Million* (1916) furnished Joyce with a raft of notes on life on the margins of modern New York (VI.B.3.102–21). Joyce clearly read Henry's short stories with Tristan and Isolde in mind; an unused note, 'Man follows Is' (VI.B.3.121) comes from 'The Brief Début of Tildy', a story about a 'dumpy, plain-faced' waitress with 'hay-colored hair' who 'had never had an admirer' and her friend and rival, the 'beautiful, lively, gracious' Aileen 'who was learned in persiflage', or banter (Henry 1916, 249). 'Persiflage' (VI.B.3.120) is the word that Joyce borrows for Tristan's declaration of love in broken French (NLI 41,818, f.1r). Tildy is jealous of Aileen who, receiving plenty of male attention, tells her she was followed home by a man: 'Tildy listened to the adventure with breathless admiration. No man had ever tried to follow her. She was safe abroad at any hour of the twenty-four. What bliss it must have been to have had a man follow one and black one's eye for love!' (251). So when, one day, one of the customers, a Mr Seeders, grabs Tildy by the waist and kisses her 'loudly and impudently', she is over the moon that now she too is a 'man-charmer' (252), but to her disappointment Seeders returns and apologizes for his rudeness. Tildy is heartbroken, but Aileen comforts her, saying that he is not worth her sorrows: 'He ain't anything of a gentleman or he wouldn't ever of apologised' (Henry 1916, 256).

Henry's depiction of frank sexuality served Joyce to pervert the romance of Tristan and Isolde. On the one hand, Tristan is described as 'an inborn gentlemen with a gift of blushing' who, when discovering that 'a lady ... happened to have a libido', will offer her a piece of cheese (NLI 41,818, f. 1v). The lovemaking is coy and flirtatious. On the other hand, coyness gives way to unbridled passion and raw sexuality. Tristan, the tall, 'handsome ... rugger and soccer champion' (47481-94; *JJA* 56:002–003), is an ideal of Irish manhood, the athlete as Celtic hero (in the manner that painter Seán Keating would depict him in *The Tipperary Hurler* of 1928) with unrestrained virility. The lovers' kiss, described in the lingo of sports commentary, sounds in fact quite rapey: 'quick as greased lightning the Breton champion drove the advanced messenger of love with one virile tonguethrust past the double line of ivoryclad forwards fullback rightjingbangshot into the goal of her gullet' (47480-267v; *JJA* 56:006–007). And what, the narrator asks, does Isolde care about 'tiresome of King Mark'? 'Not as much as a pinch of henshit' (47481-94; *JJA* 56:002–003). The crudeness that Joyce interjects into this otherwise sweetly tale undoes not only the original legend but also the idealized view of womanhood found in nationalist discourse. This is apparent from Isolde's request for Tristan to recite some poetry, a safe drawing-room occupation: 'She murmorously asked for some but not too much of the best national poetry quotations' (47481-94; *JJA* 56:2–3). What Tristan recites is, ironically, a line from *Childe Harold's Pilgrimage* (1812/18) by Lord Byron, a poet whom Stephen's classmates, according to the beliefs of their class and culture, dismiss as 'a heretic and immoral' (*P* 81).

Of the additional drafts, the part dealing with Isolde as a girl or young woman is the most interesting. It introduces the young Isolde as being from a well-to-do background and consists mainly of a list of her virtues in the form of a pilgrim's progress: 'For her prudence', 'For her learning', 'For her charm', 'For her health', 'For her domestic economy', 'For her piety', 'For her pity' and 'For her charity' (NLI 41,818, f. 2r-v). The charitable act she committed was to give her petticoat to 'a beggar girl in the park' on a 'sneezing cold' day. This beggar, in a way Isolde's double, turns out to be Saint Dympna, a beautiful Irish princess who, to avoid the sexual advances of her pagan father, fled to Belgium, but to no avail; he catches up with her in Geel, then a small hamlet, and takes her life. The hagiographical subtext, together with Isolde's modern piety and prudence and charm, connects with Saint Kevin.[15] Isolde's prudence and charm, though, are complemented by her saucy nature. Like Gerty McDowell in *Ulysses*, she is a worldly girl interested in fashion and conscious of her sexuality: 'she knew how to stagemanage her legs in nude stockings under a straight as possible skirt in the several positions of goodytwoshoes, aunty Nance, stepladder, green peas, stella cometa[,] love me little, funny toast, lovers lever, love me long' (NLI 41,818, f.2r, simplified).[16] Presumably because the vignette is only a fragment, the main character is not identified as Isolde. But in developing her features, Joyce heavily drew on his notes from Notebook VI.B.3 that are tagged 'Is' and 'I', for example, 'Position of I's legs' (40), 'Is cleans flue | with blazing | Irish Catholics' (48), 'Is had pity for | poor old devil in | asbestos shirt in | [cooling]room in | hell' (85), 'Is gave her | jupon to beggar' (132). Joyce's decision to have the young Isolde burn *The Irish Times* instead of copies of *The Irish Catholic* (an anti-Parnellite paper) to

---

[15] Kevin, incidentally, is mentioned at the very bottom of the page in an incomplete sentence: 'Only sometimes it was how she would be studying something like the day God knows she sat down in the plate of soup (Kevin' (NLI 41,818, f.2v). The parenthetical phrase is incomplete; it ran across onto another page that is no longer extant.

[16] Most of the sketch is abandoned, but Joyce would reprise Isolde's leg for Issy when describing her siglum as a girl lifting her leg to tie her shoelaces (VI.B.8.145).

clear the chimney flue reveals, with deliberate intent, her political allegiance: important to Joyce's vision of a new Revival, it suggests the Catholic middle classes aspiring to positions of power once held by Protestants.

Domestic economy, furthermore, makes way for political collusion when (in an aside unconnected with the narrative but associated with the 'for her pity' segment) the vignette introduces Isolde as a barmaid serving drinks to Irish outlaws and revolutionaries: 'And flahoolagh bless her pretty face she had shaken cocktails, no lie, for pistoleers gunmen parabellumites munitioners from every barony in Ireland' (NLI 41,818, f.2v, simplified). The ordnance terms mentioned all come from Notebook VI.B.10: 'pistoleers' (73), 'parabellum (rev)' (49), and 'munitioneers' (112). Although the passage could imply any insurrectionary activity, from the Whiteboys to the Easter Rising, one of the notes in particular, taken from an article in *The Irish Times*, suggests a Civil War context: '[Free State] Troops from Monasterevan and Portarlington … discovered a "dump", making the following captures: … 1 Parabellum revolver' (28 Nov. 1922, quoted in VI.B.10.049). The Parabellum was a German semi-automatic pistol much used by the Irish Republican Army, the name deriving from the Latin motto *si vis pacem, para bellum* (If you want peace, prepare for war) (*OED*, s.v. Parabellum). The short passage speaks to the violence that punctuates Ireland's past and looks forward to a *Wakean* preoccupation with internecine strife. Towards the end of the vignette, Isolde morphs into a larger-than-life figure with her own mythology:

> On another occasion there was a pestilence caused by a certain dragon who said it would go on for ever unless she took off all her clothes and walked from Cape Clear to Mizzen head [word missing] Ireland her left hand to the sea. So she did this but she had herself painted green all over her body as far as mother nature allowed. And when her Pop they heard the moaning of the shies like the harbour bar telling she was off the weakness of death fell on everybody & everybody pulled down all the blinds in Ireland. The dragon there and then got a grip on the big clean ideals & converted and entered a convent nunnery.
>
> (NLI 41,818, f. 2v, simplified)

A parody of Irish fairytales, this narrative is a strange allegory of another sexual predator who realizes his sin and converts to Christianity; it also a version of *Cathleen ni Houlihan* who sacrifices herself for Ireland but morphed here into a female Brian Boru.[17] The narrative mode is that of 'Cyclops', with added

---

[17] Joyce's note, 'Brian marches round I — | his left hand to the sea | — (LB)' (VI.B.10.053), remembers Brian Boru's tour around the Northern O'Neill in 1006 after consolidating his power.

hyperbole and deliberate error. Cape Clear Island and Mizen Head, both on the Cork coast, count as Ireland's southernmost locations, only 13.5 miles apart as the crow flies and, of course, not walkable.

Of all the early sketches, the 'Tristan and Isolde' vignettes are the most wide-ranging in terms of scope and narrative matter. Certainly, when compared with 'Saint Kevin', 'Tristan and Isolde' is more directly a retelling of the original legend. Joyce's ambitions, however, in creating a modern version of the tragic love affair go beyond those of the earlier sketches. While they connect with the Irish past – historical and legendary – the vignettes also deal more explicitly with, and attack, social mores in modern Catholic Ireland. Isolde's (un)walk around Ireland, finally, is another engagement with Irish topography in a manner that is, incidentally, very recognizably *Wakean*.

Mamalujo

'Mamalujo' is the first of the sketches to link directly with one of the other sketches. That link, moreover, is furnished by topography. The 'well-mannered waves' (47481-94; *JJA* 56:2–3) that surround Tristan and Isolde's barque not only become 'the Four Waves of Erin' (NLI 41,818, f.3r), the new sketch opens with the seabirds flying overhead singing their song for 'Mister Mark' after 'they heard of the kiss of Tristan and Isolde' (NLI 41,818, f.3r):

> — Three caws for Mister Mark
> Sure he hasnt got much of a bark
> And sure any he has is all beside the mark.
> Wreneagle Highflighty wouldn't it be a sky of a lark
> To see that old busard whooping around in his shirt in the dark
> And he hunting about for his speckled trousers in Palmerston park.
> O moulty Mark
> Youre the rummest old rooster ever crawled out of a Noah's ark
> And you think you're the cock of the walk.
> Fowls up! Tristan's a spry young spark
> That'll tread her and wed her and bed her and red her
> Without even winking the tale of a feather
> And that's how that chap's going to make his money and mark. (NLI 41,818, f.3r, simplified)

This song about the cuckolding of King Mark was later affixed to a fair copy of 'Tristan and Isolde'. Here the 'Four Waves of Erin' also hear the song, as the traditional four seas surrounding Ireland bear witness.

'Mamalujo' was written in two stages between August and September 1923. Mamalujo are a collective character engaged in (re)collecting rather than, strictly speaking, recording history. They are memorialists in the double sense of the word, recalling and celebrating 'significant' events, building a collective memory (even if, ironically, the events they do remember are confused, inaccurate and trivial). The sketch's earliest iteration (in a manuscript in Nora's hand to which Joyce added a handful of revisions) already contains the essential ingredients: remembering the past, the power and failures of memory, historiographical authority, and the Four's transgendered identity. They first appear as 'Four eminently respectable old gentlemen', but Joyce changes them to 'heladies' (NLI 41,818, f.3r), as well as the 'Four Waves of Erin' that 'would cling tentacularly' to the sides of all the ships at the North Wall, Holyhead and the Isle of Man (NLI 41,818, f.4r). In the Joycean canon, two of these three locations are associated with exile and emigration; the third with the pan-Celtic fringe. What is also at stake is the geographical displacement of the Three Tonns or Waves from Irish legend: the Wave of Tuath at the mouth of the Bann in Derry; the Wave of Rory in Dundrum Bay, Co. Down; and the Wave of Cleena in Glandore Harbour, Co. Cork.[18] Only at the second stage are the Four identified as Matt Gregory, Marcus Lyons, Luke Tarpey and Johnny MacDougal; their names obviously suggest the Four Evangelists, but also the Four Masters, the seventeenth-century annalists Michael O'Clery, Peregrine O'Clery, Fearfasa O'Mulconry and Peregrine O'Duignan. The addition of 'master' in the phrase 'the four master waves of Erin' (474781-2; *JJA* 56:26) makes the reference clearer. In this expanded version, the Four have become active witnesses, voyeuristically straining to hear Tristan and Isolde's kiss ('listening to all the kissening' [474781-2; *JJA* 56:26]). But as their senses are confused (they listen with their mouths and eyes as well as their ears) and their faculties of recollection taxed, they turn into unreliable witnesses, mixing memory with boredom. In this draft, Joyce revises every instance of the verb *remember* to 'remembore'.

---

[18] Legend has it that during a storm the sea roars especially hard in these locations, which heralded the death of a king (Joyce 1910, I, 195).

'Mamalujo', therefore, extends the unreliable historian from 'Roderick O'Connor' into a narrative conceit that will become central to *Finnegans Wake*. No event in the *Wake* – historical or otherwise – ever has a stable foundation; as universal historiographical principles, confusion and doubt reign supreme. A historical relativist, Joyce recognized the subjective nature of historical narrative, a position that he shared with the new forms of historiography that were emerging at the time; the origin of this new historicism lies, of course, with Friedrich Nietzsche, but other commentators contemporary to Joyce were adopting similar positions. Perhaps the watery presence in the early sketches – Saint Kevin's bath, Isolde's walking by the sea, and Mamalujo as the Four Waves – is no coincidence. The first 'Mamalujo' vignette offers, literally, a fluid account of history as it anachronistically blends events from different periods. These events are:

> the capture of Sir Arthur Casement in the year ~~432~~ 1132 Coronation of Brian by the Danes at Clonmacnois the drowning of Pharaoh F Phitzharris in the (proleptically) red sea[.] The drowning of poor Mat Keane of Dunlearery [*sic*] the scattering of the flemish armada off the coasts of Galway and Longford, the landing of St Patrick at Tara in the year 1798, the dispersal of the French fleet under General Boche in the year 2002.
>
> (NLI 41,818, f.3r-v, simplified)

The significance of these historical 'unfacts' is that they all, except two, somehow involve events on the Irish coast. Roger Casement (not Arthur) was arrested on 21 April 1916, three days before the Easter Rising, shortly after arriving at Banna Strand, Co. Kerry; he had come back from Germany, where he had hoped to secure an arms deal for the Irish Volunteers. He was convicted of treason and executed in August; none of the arms had made it to Ireland. The year 432 was the year Saint Patrick returned to Ireland, landing in Leinster at the mouth of the River Vartry, to begin his mission of converting Ireland. From thence, according to one tradition, he travelled to Meath (Bury 1905, 89) where, at the Hill of Slane, he lit the Easter fire in defiance of the High King at Tara. Joyce's revision of 432 to 1132 probably stems from a desire to dissociate Brian Boru's coronation from any actual historical event. By this accident, Joyce created the key moment in the *Wake*'s desire to chronicle history, yet, ironically, in the annals of Ireland, 1132 is of no particular historical significance. Brian Boru, who died at the Battle of Contarf in 1014, succeeded his brother as King of Thomond in 976 and, after a long struggle subjugating the other kingdoms, became High King in 1002 (although his supremacy was not accepted until

1011). Having eliminated all regional and lesser kings, Brian styled himself *Imperatur Scottorum*, claiming political rather than, like the old High Kings, symbolical power to rule over the whole of Ireland. The sketch foregrounds the genealogical hybridity of the Irish past by having Boru crowned by the Danes at Clonmacnoise. Historically, of course, this did not happen, but it fits Joyce's view that, despite Boru's victory over the Danes at Clontarf, they were not ousted but assimilated with the Irish (*OCPW* 113). The monastery at Clonmacnoise is significant because it was the traditional burial place of the High Kings. Next in Mamalujo's chronicle appears the alliteratively named Pharaoh Phitzharris (or Fitzharris), which yokes together Moses's drowning of the Egyptians in the Red Sea and James 'Skin-the-Goat' Fitzharris, who drove a decoy getaway cab after the Phoenix Park murders. Matthew F. Kane died off Dun Laoghaire when he suffered a heart attack while swimming on 10 July 1904 (Kane 2013).[19] Where the Flemish Armada is concerned, strictly speaking, there wasn't one. According to the *Annals of the Four Masters* (n.d.), the Anglo-Normans landed in Leinster in 1169 with a 'fleet of the Flemings', but this arrival is mixed up with the landing of the Spanish Armada in various locations between Galway and Donegal, after it had been deflected by the British in 1588; the aim had been to invade England with an army of Flemish soldiers. Longford, like Tara, is, of course, landlocked. During the failed rebellion of 1798, the long-awaited French troops, under the command of Humbert, landed in Co. Mayo near Killala; Tara Hill, however, was the location where the United Irishmen had suffered a major defeat some four months earlier. Finally, at risk of spelling out the obvious, the term *Boche* was a pejorative term used by the French to designate the Germans in the First World War.

In the second draft, Joyce reworks some of the events, changing the detail and in some cases essence, as simple anachronism gives way to mythologizing. Brian Boru's coronation is performed by 'his grace bishop James H J. P. Bishop Senior' (47481-2v; *JJA* 56:29). Pharaoh F. Fitzharris became just 'Pharaoh'. Matthew F. Kane is renamed 'Martin Cunningham out of the castle', using Kane's fictional counterpart from *Ulysses*, while coalescing Dublin Bay with the Red Sea of Moses: Cunningham 'drowned off Dunleary in the red sea'. Likewise, the scattering of the Flemish Armada 'off the coast of Cunningham and Saint Patrick & St Kevin & Lapoleon our first marents' involves coastal places being transformed into some strange type of maternal/maritime genealogy (47481-3r; *JJA* 56:30). The year 1132 is now the year the French fleet under general Boche landed in Ireland.

---

[19] In *Ulysses*, Kane's drowning is backdated to around 6 June (*U* 1.674–75).

Mamalujo's chronicle of history is not just incorrect, it is imprecise, a condition underscored by the fact that all the events share only a few parameters. There is the similarity of dress between bishop Bishop, general Boche and Mamalujo themselves: a grey or tall 'shovel hat' (VI.A.981), a type of wide-brimmed hat with upturned sides often worn by Anglican clergy. More importantly, all the events either involve 'landing' or 'drowning', which, amplifying the mythic importance of the Three/Four Waves, points to the significance of the sea in Ireland's history. On the one hand, the sea is, as in J.M. Synge's *Riders to the Sea* (1904), a source of danger even as Irish fishermen rely on it for their livelihood. On the other hand, landings by sea were a gateway into Ireland for invaders (the Anglo-Normans, the Danes) and revolutionaries alike (arms were expected to be delivered by sea by the French in 1798 and the Germans in 1916).

Drownings and landings, in other words, symbolize transitional moments that are important to Joyce's conception of history in the early sketches and *Finnegans Wake*. Significant therefore is Mamalujo's recasting of Tristan and Isolde's kiss as a cataclysmic moment. In the earlier sketch, the Four Waves 'heard the detonation of the osculation (cataclysmic cataglottism) which with ostentation (osculum cum basio necnon c̶u̶m̶ suavioque) Tristan to Isolde gave' (NLI 41,818, 4r, simplified). 'Cataglottism', deriving from the Greek καταγλώττισμα, 'lascivious kiss' (*OED*), is a rare term for French kiss.[20] The parenthesis defends Tristan's rightful violent, erotic intentions; the pig Latin translates roughly as 'a hand kiss is not a kiss'. In the original legend, the kiss has irreparable repercussions; it is a token of the couple's illicit love and a symbol of the tragedy that ensues, leading to Tristan's death. More generally, one cannot but be reminded of how in Irish history, from the time of Dermot MacMurrough to Parnell, the love of a woman had dire consequences for the course of Irish history. The shock wave (so to speak) that the kiss produces prompts the Four Waves to sing 'in glee of grief of loneliness but with bardic license' their 'wavechant', an Irish 'planxty'.[21]

---

[20] The origin of Joyce's term is *Sexual Selection in Man*, volume 5 of Havelock Ellis's *Studies in the Psychology of Sex* (1905). Among a short cluster of notes in *Scribbledehobble* appears 'cataglottism (dovekiss)' (VI.A.851), which comes from: 'It is always the most sensitive parts of the body which seek to give or to receive caresses. Many animals rub or lick each other ... The kiss is not only an expression of feeling; it is a means of provoking it. Cataglottism is by no means confined to pigeons. The tonic value of cutaneous stimulation is indeed a commonly accepted idea' (Ellis 1905, 5–6). Other notes in the same cluster that come from Ellis are: 'ergograph', 'peduncle' and 'rhinencephalon' (VI.A.851).

[21] Probably of eighteenth-century origin, the planxty is 'a lively tune in triplets for harp, fiddle, flute, etc' (*OED*).

A birdless heaven, seadusk and one star,
low in the west
And thou, poor heart, loves image, faint and far,
Rememberest

——

Her seacold eyes and her soft foamwhite brown
And fragrant hair,
Falling as through the silence falleth now
Dusk from the air.

——

A why wilt thou
A why wilt thou remember these,
A why,
Poor heart, repine,
If the dear love she yielded with a sigh
Was never thine! (NLI 41,818, f4r-v, simplified)

The song at once foreshadows ALP's demise as she flows out into the Irish Sea at the end of *Finnegans Wake* and echoes some of the melancholy love verse from *Chamber Music*. Ostensibly a song about lost or unrequited love, the 'wavechant' has a distinct fatalistic ring. The lyric admonishes the 'poor heart' to remember, but when love is aweary (to bring in the 28th poem from Joyce's first collection) is love worth remembering? After the song, the text in the manuscript continues with one of the proto-drafts of Tristan and Isolde with which this early Mamalujo sketch forms a hybrid narrative.

Concerning the genesis

As histories, the early sketches do not show any obvious signs as to how they would have worked together. For sure, there are connections and similarities: the modernizing of ancient narratives, the integration of Tristan and Isolde with Mamalujo, the concern with childhood origins. But these connections are fairly loose and tenuous, and barely substantiate the idea that the sketches constitute a work in their own right (Rose 2013). In this context it is important to remember that they are fragments. Some achieved a more advanced state of completion than others, but they are fragments nonetheless. That said, we can imagine that Joyce would have developed the sketches further, forged them together, perhaps even written new ones, had the creation 'Earwicker' not brought about a turning point in the composition. (Does the sudden appearance of Napoleon in 'Mamalujo', as one of the 'first marents' besides Saints Patrick and Kevin [47484-3r; *JJA 56:30*], suggest a sketch on the Battle of Waterloo?)

By the same token, the early sketches are not *Finnegans Wake*. Again, to be sure, the sketches' themes, devices and political and aesthetic intents linger on the *Wake*. But despite these connections, despite even the increasing use of portmanteau words, their status as the kernel for *Finnegans Wake* is both tenuous and tantamount to overdetermining their meaning. They are decidedly *for* a new work that may or may not have had *Finn's Hotel* as a working title, but were set aside as this work took a new shape with the invention of its first fictional character, Humphrey Chimpden Earwicker.[22] Earwicker seems totally at odds with himself and the world, especially in comparison with the protagonists of the sketches. However, this is the attraction of his character. As a local, 'trusty' vassal, 'good duke Humphrey' of Lucalizod, he is an underling, 'forgetful of all but his fealty' (47472-97r; *JJA* 45:2), but also a person of ridicule and radical otherness. In the encounter with the royal hunting party on the high road while digging up his garden, he is mocked by the king for being 'a turnpiker who is also an earwicker' (47472-97r; *JJA* 45:2). Like the characters in *Ulysses*, history happens to Earwicker passively and subjectively. The workings of cultural memory are therefore crucial to the Earwicker sketch. Fittingly, the narrative assumes the form of a genealogy, which in the first draft fixes on establishing the 'origin genesis' of Earwicker's 'agnomen': how he became Earwicker and 'Here Comes Everything Everybody' instead of his 'actual' name Harold or Humphrey Coxon (47472-97r; *JJA* 45:2). Setting aside other theories in favour of the anecdote of the royal encounter, the sketch traces the permutations of Earwicker's identity, following hearsay and gossip, ending with the accusation that the man exposed himself to two maidservants in the park. In the chapter's later iterations, the narrative follows the game of Chinese whispers through its different steps, culminating in 'The Ballad of Persse O'Reilly', which, appropriate for the ballad genre, tells the events of what befell Earwicker in a way that is several stages removed from the (un)truth.

The transition away from historical narrative represented in the Earwicker sketch is also discernible in Joyce's *Finnegans Wake* notebooks. When 'Work in Progress' was still inchoate, Joyce's notebooks have fairly specific thematic

---

[22] Rose and O'Hanlon's (1989) suggestion that for a long time *Finn's Hotel* was Joyce's secret title for 'Work in Progress' is both speculative and tantalizing. If anything, they have convincingly shown that the establishment in Nassau Street where Nora Barnacle worked in 1904 is embedded in the *Wake*'s imaginary and stands for one of the symbolical components of the F siglum.

concerns. This would change as the book grew, but (generalizing to some degree) we recognize that the early notebooks are distinctive in terms of their content. As I argued at the start of this chapter, the first notebook, VI.B.10, was concerned with modern life, not unlike the world of *Ulysses*, in a manner that is often frivolous. The next notebook, VI.B.3, shifts towards history, with especial interest in hagiography. One of Joyce's sources that is significant here is J.M. Flood's *Ireland: Its Saints and Scholars*, published in 1917 by the Talbot Press, which played an important role in the Irish Revival.[23] Flood propagated the opinion, rehearsed by Joyce in his similarly titled Trieste lecture, that Irish learning had rescued European civilization from the new barbarism of the Goths and the Vandals (Flood 1917, 1–2, 6). With chapters on Saint Columcille and Saint Columbanus, alongside Saint Patrick, the book served Joyce well. Not that he needed Flood for the information. Flood, finally, also sings the praises of Irish archaeology and the ecclesiastical treasure discovered in the bog: the Ardagh Chalice, the Tara Brooch and the Cross of Cong, among others, which Joyce resorts to when drafting the Hen's Chapter I.5 (VI.B.2.011).

Joyce's reading of Flood coincides with the drafting of 'Roderick O'Connor', meaning that the source played a significant part in the conceptualization of the later sketches. Yet he only made use of a relatively small number of notes from VI.B.3; even to revisions of the earliest drafts, the notebook contributed fairly little. A source like Flood, for instance, did not have just one purpose. While books like these furnished Joyce with 'verbiage' or peculiar detail, they are also relevant for the cultural values they elicit in the sense understood by Herr (1986). 'Intended for popular use', Flood's work celebrated the splendour of Ireland's Christian heritage characterized by 'that strange mixture of fervour and austerity, of independence and respect for traditions, of simplicity and strong sensibility, of imagination held under sway and yet impetuous' (1917, v, 57). Portrayals like these of an important 'period in our national history' (1917, viii) were not well represented in other mainstream Revivalist work like that of the Abbey Theatre.

By the time he started filling VI.B.2 in late August 1923, Joyce was still doing historical and hagiographical research, among others in his reading of Margaret

---

[23] The Talbot Press was a new imprint, established in 1917, by The Educational Company of Ireland, which was extending its list from schoolbooks to general publishing. The imprint was instrumental in disseminating the work of Revival writers, cultivating 'an influential range' of Irish contacts worldwide, but it also ventured into the lucrative market of books on religious subjects. Books on Church history, and the lives of the saints in particular, formed a new trend in Irish publishing, stemming from 'the intense interest in national identity' (Allen and Brown 2011, 74–5; McCarthy 2011, 248).

Maitland's *Life and Legends of St. Martin of Tours* (1908). Joyce's preoccupation with this Gallic holy man had been prefigured in a small way in the 'Young Isolde' sketch; Isolde donating her petticoat to the beggar girl, who turns out to be Saint Dympna, is clearly inspired by Saint Martin who cut his cloak in half to help a freezing beggar. But in this case it is Saint Martin's historical connection with Saint Patrick that is important. Having escaped to Gaul from his captivity in Ireland, Patrick received religious instruction from Martin (Bury 1905, 274–5). However, by this point in the writing – working on the 'Earwicker' sketch – Joyce had moved beyond the initial hagiographical interest; his notes on Saint Martin remained unused.[24]

It is no coincidence, though, that Earwicker's exposure in the park happened during 'an abnormal S. Martin's summer' (47472-97^v; *JJA* 45:3). Although the sketches did not develop beyond the initial stage of their composition, their influence on 'Work in Progress' is noticeable. With the exception of Roderick O'Connor, all the historiographical characters that Joyce invented are present in the text. Chapter III.3 in particular, a colloquy between Mamalujo and Shaun, reprises them most explicitly, including a direct appropriation of the language of the 'Mamalujo' sketch in the first draft of the chapter's opening. Besides these intratextual reprisals, however, the sketches, as historical narratives, conceptualize and help us understand the vision of history that Joyce would go on to construct in *Finnegans Wake*. This is the subject of Chapter 6, in which I turn to how the sketches found their place in the book.

A cast of historical characters

The pseudo-chronicle in Chapter I.1 is the work of 'our herodotary Mammon Lujius' (*FW-R* 11.9; *FW* 13.20), our first encounter in *Finnegans Wake* with the Four Historians. The characters from other sketches are also strewn across the first chapter: Tristan (*FW-R* 3.4; *FW* 3.4); Isolde (*FW-R* 11.14; *FW* 13.26); Saint Patrick, called by his British name (*FW-R* 11.16, *FW* 13.28); and Kevin as a child (*FW-R* 21.26-28; *FW* 27.5-7). Their presence, like much else in this chapter, foreshadows their presence later in the book.[25] So what then happened with the

---

[24] Henkes (2014a, 2014b) is, however, of the view that the Saint Martin notes, together with the notes on Saint Patrick taken from William Bullen Morris's *The Life of Saint Patrick, Apostle of Ireland* (1908) and one or more unidentified sources on Saint Kevin, resulted from a plan to expand and fuse the early sketches.

[25] Composed in 1926, after the bulk of Book I, Chapter I.1 was constructed as a prelude to the rest of the book (Lernout 2007, 49).

genetic material that Joyce produced during those first months of 1923? As is well documented, Joyce revised and stitched his early historical sketches into *Finnegans Wake* during a late stage of the composition. After Joyce had written the final sketch about Earwicker, a fictional character in a historical setting, he set aside the other sketches to develop the narrative of HCE instead. The sketches developed polygenetically, first by way of the notebooks, then both as passing allusions and thematic or narrative clusters in the drafts.[26] Their presence in the fabric of 'Work in Progress' steadily grew until their cast of historical characters occupied a place alongside the Earwicker family.[27]

Returning in 1938 to the original sketches, Joyce applied a modicum of revision and spliced them into 'Work in Progress'. These revisions, however, do not really affect their meaning; they retain their value as historical skits retold for modern times, offering an alternative take on the Revival's vision of the past. But while they were slotted in wholesale, Joyce obviously considered their position within the whole structure. The 'Roderick O'Connor' sketch, first of all, as narrated by the inebriated historian, finds its place, appropriately, in Chapter II.3, the scene in the pub. The chapter's main conceit is genealogy, symbolized through the siglum F, which stands for the pub but also for the Earwicker family line, and prefigures in the obvious link between genealogy and genesis in the opening sentence: 'It may not or maybe a no concern of the Guinnesses but' (*FW-R* 238.1; *FW* 309.1). As the *Wake*'s most sustained exploration of origins, the chapter places the 'birth of an otion' (*FW-R* 238.11; *FW* 309.12) to the moment of the racial amalgamation of 'Hiberio-Miletians and Argloe-Noremen' (*FW-R* 238.10; *FW* 309.11). Not surprisingly, the conversation in the pub turns to history. Mamalujo make their appearance (*FW-R* 284.7–13; *FW* 367.8–14) while the customers recall an instance of gun running (*FW-R* 284.18.3–36; *FW* 367.20–368.6) like those of the 1798 Rebellion and the Easter Rising when Irish revolutionaries sought to obtain arms from abroad. Because 'Roderick O'Connor' marks the passages from one historical era to the next, Irish to colonial, Joyce

---

[26] My understanding of this proliferation is similar to, but less deterministic than, Hayman's 'nodal systems' (1990, 37). Often without significant alteration, Joyce reprised or expanded on ideas or materials from the original sketches in his notes as if to remind himself about reusing them. In VI.B.2, for example, he noted: 'Kevin prays in water | 50 times' (VI.B.2.9), echoing Kevin's prayers in the tub. The note's source, incidentally, also indicates Joyce's flexibility in appropriating the ideas. The note is based on William Bullen Morris' *Life of Saint Patrick*, a passage in which Morris describes Patrick's nightly prayer ritual. He notes, furthermore, that the saint's austerities were a model for later Irish monks (Morris 1908, 251–2).

[27] Isolde evolved into Issy; Kevin, Patrick, Tristan and Mamalujo developed into separate characters and, with exception of Kevin, assumed sigla of their own.

added the sketch to the end of the chapter as a final 'wind up' (*FW-R* 294.10; *FW* 380.8) before the pub closes. In 1923, Joyce had figured that the 'Roderick' sketch would come towards the end of the book (BL 57347-17ʳ). Its position in II.3 reinforces the sketch's original intent. Closing time in the pub is a winding up of history ('at the end of this age' [*FW-R* 294.3-4; *FW* 380.1]) with a last tale told by 'Keyhoe, Danelly and Pykemhyme' relating what happened to the 'Mocked Majesty in the Malincurred Mansion' (*FW-R* 294.3–7; *FW* 379.36–380.5). But like so many accounts in the *Wake*, the tale is based on hearsay (although we do learn the genealogy of its origin).

Integrated in Book IV, the 'Saint Kevin' and 'Saint Patrick' sketches came to function as opposing versions of the Church's role in Ireland's present. Book IV's opening announces by way of a radio message the arrival of a new dawn and the new *Sandhya*, a twilight period of 1,728,000 years according to *Isis Unveiled* (see FWEET). This announcement anticipates, among others, the coming of Saint Kevin himself as he descends from heaven surrounded by twenty-nine female saints whose names all refer to Dublin churches (*FW-R* 469.27–33; *FW* 601.21–8). An exalted reprisal of Shaun's arrival and departure in Chapter III.1, Kevin's meditation on 'the primal sacrament of baptism or the regeneration of all man by affusion of water' (*FW-R* 473.16–17; *FW* 606.10–11) is also a revelation of, as I said previously, what it means to be Catholic. The revelation is quite dubious, however, in that it ends in a sexualized romp in Chapelizod's idyllic environs: 'It is their segnall for old Champelysied to seek the shades of his retirement and for young Chappielassies to tear a round and tease their partners lovesoftfun at Finnegan's Wake' (*FW-R* 474.11–12; *FW* 607.14–16). The scene is Edenic, but it also involves a call to turn one's back on history. Significantly, the answer to 'the first last rittlerattle of the anniverse' is 'a. Watch!' (*FW-R* 474.7–8; *FW* 607.11–12), that is, a warning to be watchful for what would happen on Shaun's Watch.

The return of Shaun, the *Wake*'s most devious and 'protonotorious' character (*FW-R* 472.3; *FW* 604.32–3), heralds a retrenchment into the conservative Catholicism of de Valera's Free State. Kevin's sanctity and his contemplation of baptism as 'the primal sacrament' becomes synonymous with the centrality of Catholic piety; as the 'primace of the Gaulls', he is 'mitrogenerand in the free state on the air' (that is, self-generating or generating mitres or bishops), and 'blow[ing] a Gael warning' (*FW-R* 472.5; *FW* 604.22–4) (see Van Mierlo 2017, 125–6). By becoming primate, Saint Kevin rivals Saint Patrick as national saint. With baptism being the spiritual bedrock of the Church, Kevin emblematizes piety and devotion, which is more relevant to the hegemony and continuity of sacerdotal power of the contemporary Church in Ireland than Saint Patrick's accomplishments in converting pagan Ireland. This is a Joycean inversion of the Irish identity myth. It is not the coming of Christianity, but the dogmatic and popular adherence to Catholicism that is deeply embedded in the national spirit.[28]

This reading allows us to understand the 'Saint Patrick' sketch as another revelation and another reversal of a foundation myth. To integrate the sketch, Joyce created a segue from the Blanchardstown races ('Rhythm and Colour at Park Meeting. Two draws. Three ties. | And here are the details' [47488-93; JJA 63:157, simplified]) before adding the introductory word 'Tunc' (47488-107^v; JJA 63:174). Deriving from the line 'Tunc crucifixerant xpi cum eo duos latrones' ('Then there were crucified with him two thieves' [Matthew 27.38]) in *The Book of Kells*, the word is a minor motif in the *Wake*. As a marker of something that took place in the past, it introduces the Patrick sketch as a voice or revelation from the past. Crucially, though, Joyce had intended the original sketch to describe the 'conversion of S. Patrick by Ireland' (*Letters* III, 79). The sketch re-enacts the transition to Christianity that follows the defeat of the pagan High King Leary: 'Exuber High Oberking Leary very dead' (*FW-R* 478.31–2; *FW* 612.3–4). Patrick's suppression of the power of the High Kings is not simply a case of historical discontinuity, however; it involves both a usurpation and an amalgamation. Patrick's vision is of Leary in his green 'holmgrewnworsteds costume' (*FW-R* 478.28; *FW* 611.35), but it is also his own transformation into Leary. Patrick 'augumentationed himself' (*FW-R* 478.24; *FW* 611.31), that is, he projects himself into and thereby neutralizes Leary, in effect assuming his costume, stature and symbolic power over Ireland.

Expanding the original sketch, Joyce adds another twist in which he has the narrator speculate on contemporary Ireland and the future of a distinctly Irish Church: 'for beingtime monkblinkers timebeinged completamentarily murkblankered in their neutrolysis between the possible viriditude of the sager and the probable eruberuption of the saint' (*FW-R* 479.7–9; *FW* 612.21–4). We can paraphrase this as: for the time being, the monks/Christian converts were unclear as to what happened and they do not know whether this amalgamation/decomposition represents the 'greening' of Ireland (*Lat.* 'viridis') or the

---

[28] When appearing as a pair in Chapter II.4, Saint Patrick, the 'anabaptist', and Saint Kevin the 'lacustrian', or 'lakedweller', share the commonality of baptism and water (*FW-R* 301.13–14; *FW* 388.14), underlining once again the importance of baptism to the preceptual unity of the Church. Early Irish conversion narratives existed to inculcate precisely this foundational principle that baptism symbolized a submission to the ecumenical authority of the Church (Bury 1905, 370).

'reddening' (*Lat.* 'ruber') of the Church. This case of historical doubt as to the effects of Patrick's arrival creates two opposite forces: Irish nationalism *v.* the 'Cullenization' (in Father Prout's phrase) of the Church. The allusion to cardinal red is a reference to the growing alliance between the Irish Church and Rome that had taken place during the devotional revolution under Cardinal Cullen (see Van Mierlo 2017, 84–6). This is the same Irish Church that, in Joyce's eyes, took its stand in favour of conservative morality when it abandoned Parnell.

'Mamalujo' and 'Tristan and Isolde' were given a chapter all of their own. Although it is the shortest in *Finnegans Wake*, the conjoining of the Mamalujo and Tristan materials as a standalone chapter is significant. Genetically, the sketches were related, in that Mamalujo as a character was conceived within an extension to 'Tristan and Isolde' (the so-called 'Four Waves' sketch, NLI 41,818, f. 3-4), until Joyce soon after enlarged Mamalujo into a separate sketch (which in 1924 he published as a 'side-piece' in the *Transatlantic Review*). In 1938, Joyce fused the two narratives together again, this time by folding 'Tristan and Isolde' into the 'Mamalujo' narrative (Slote 2004/6, 21, 24–5, 29; Deppman 2007, 309–11). Joyce then placed the chapter at the end of Book II, where it comes after the farewell that finished Chapter II.3. The ship that sails out of the Liffey estuary, and offers the prospect of return ('As who has come returns' [*FW-R* 296.8; *FW* 382.28]) thus links with Mamalujo's ship in the opening of II.4. Not insignificantly, their ship barely makes any progress because the winds have dropped. Chapter II.4 reads like an interlude rather than a return. This return will come in Book III, as Shaun rolls down the river in his barrel, 'travelling backwards in the night through the events already narrated' (*Letters* I, 214). Furthermore, Chapter II.4 stands apart from the rest of the *Wake* in that, extraordinarily, its contents do not touch at all on the Earwicker drama re-enacted on nearly every other page of the book. Rather, it is a kind of allegory of origins or a poetics of history and memory in which Mamalujo engage in a project of cultural memory, while Tristan and Isolde represent an ur-narrative from which all other narratives unfold. Both demonstrate that storytelling is at the heart of history. Given how important Mamalujo are for the *Wake*'s genealogical art, these aspects warrant separate treatment.

6

Bringing the dear prehistoric scenes all back again: *Finnegans Wake*

If Chapter 5 showed how history became part of the *Wake*'s DNA, the purpose of this chapter is to explore how the *Wake*'s vision of the past developed. From the proto-*Wake* sketches to the vast repository of notes, the genetic material that Joyce compiled, used, adapted, transformed and politicized remains central to this investigation. I am interested in how history and memory are, as they were in *Portrait* and *Ulysses*, loaded concepts. Although ostensibly anti- or post-Revival, *Finnegans Wake* is, to all intents and purposes, Joyce's most Revivalist work. Of course, its political aesthetics are different from the work produced by Lady Gregory, Douglas Hyde and Yeats, who held that legend, folklore and rural and Irish-Gaelic culture were the key to an authentic representation of Ireland. Nonetheless, the *Wake* is Joyce's most extensive probing of the 'hidden ways of Irish life' (*P* 181). As such, the *Wake* is driven by the same forces that motivated the Revival's cultural nationalism, in that it looks to define, represent or – at least – capture the national past.[1]

As I suggested in Chapter 5, the early historical sketches were developed specifically as a Revivalist project that offered a different perspective from that found in the Irish Revival. This was a project that was more historicist than mythological, but also decidedly Catholic and sardonic. In its finished state, the *Wake* did not stray beyond Joyce's original ambition. Although the book's overabundance considerably complicated its point of departure, the act of displacing, distorting and disrupting the historical narrative is as much present in the early sketches as it is in the finished work. As such, *Finnegans Wake* is certainly no ordinary history of Ireland, although it mentions all, or most, of the significant moments from the Irish past.

---

[1] The *Wake* also shares many of the same mythical and historical reference points with the Revival, see Geheber (2015).

Its historiographical purport comes from its desire for origins, ascertaining how events came to pass, but each time failing to do so precisely. Although there is no shortage of sources, accounts of the past are vague and contradict one another because the sources are unreliable and cannot be trusted; the narratives of their own origin, where they come from and what they are, are equally marred by suspicion. The *Wake* certainly makes a mockery of 'scientific' historiography. At the same time, the book also enacts the genesis of cultural memory, the coming-into-being of stories that, whether true or not, become part of the collective imagination. The most obvious example is the story of how Earwicker got his name and how that story was transmitted through time until it became 'The Ballad of Persse O'Reilly'. Orality is the *Wakean* mode par excellence.

As the book developed, it adopted the trappings of a universal history.[2] Vico's *New Science* appeared early in 1923 and returned intermittently in the following years (see Braslasu and Henkes 2019a, 2019b, 2019c). But particularly from 1929 onwards, Joyce appeared intent on putting a more esoteric spin on his book. Besides some early incidental notes, the Egyptian *Book of the Dead* made its entry in 'Work in Progress' that year (Rose 1982, 1). In 1932, he read Emanuel Swedenborg's *The Angelic Wisdom* as well as George Torbridge's biography of the man (Deane 2001b, 16–18). In addition, Joyce also turned to contemporary sources such as Dora Marsden's *The Definition of the Godhead* (1928) and W.B. Yeats's *A Vision* (1937) not long after their original publication (*Letters* I, 277; Rose and O'Hanlon 1979). Universal history may well be, as Slote (2013, 130–1) argues, something of a red herring, in that it implies a single, unifying principle that explains all of human history, a principle that the *Wake*'s 'parapolylogic' (*FW-R* 368.04; *FW* 474.5) does not allow. (Its logic is not only multiple, *poly*, but also *para*, parallel but separate to logic and, consequently, always missing the point.) From this it is not difficult to see that Joyce was drawn to these philosophies as systems rather than something he believed in. Nonetheless, fundamental to many of these systems is the cyclicality of history, whose commonplace expression that history repeats itself is elemental in Joyce's book.

It crops up in the very first *Wake* notebook in a note that links Wolfe Tone's prison suicide in 1798 with Erskine Childers' execution on a trumped-up charge in 1922: 'cycles of hist W. Tone Childers' (VI.B.10.40). His early explorations in universal history, however, reveal a fascination with the human element of

---

[2] For Halbwachs (1980, 83), universal history is the outcome of a natural tendency to look for greater unity in historical fact: 'detail added to detail will form a whole that can in turn be added to other wholes'.

history. Vico, who built his universal history on a genealogical exploration of cultural practices around myth and jurisprudence, provided him with this material basis. A short set of notes in V.B.1 that mentions the names Herder, Theodor Mommsen, Vico and Thucydides betrays an interest in historiography and the development of historical thought. Among these is a note, 'Herder believed in Ossian' (VI.B.1.174), which alludes to Herder's fascination with Macpherson's poem; active in the German folklore revival of the nineteenth century, he judged that the ancient traditions of song and dance were still alive among the people and therefore that Macpherson's poem, constructed from folkloric sources, was authentic (Kristmannsson 2015, #5). This coalescing of ancient epic and folklore finds its parallel in another note: 'Myth man & symbol | Vico' (VI.B.1.174). In Vico's philosophy, mythology treats man as both actual and symbolic. Myths, as symbolic systems, originate from cultural practices and experience; over time, a process of agglutination takes place by which these experiences become abstract, producing a 'meaningful framework' by which cultures understand their interaction with their surroundings.[3] Clifford Geertz (1973, 250) calls this process 'the genic helix' of cultural development.

In his own way, Joyce responded creatively to this process of cultural genetics throughout VI.B.1. He looks at it specifically through the lens of geography and rivers. This notebook is important for the notes that he took from Léon Metchnikoff's *La Civilisation et les grands fleuves historiques* (*Civilization and the Great Historical Rivers*) (1889), a book that is entirely concerned with the relevance of rivers for history and their influence on the origins of human civilizations. Metchnikoff famously furnished him with the Quinet sentence, which has a significant place in *Finnegans Wake* because it points to an element of constancy within the perpetual flux. As a study in human geography, however, its influence on the *Wake* goes far deeper. Tracing the influence of rivers and geography on the development of human civilizations, Metchnikoff is layered onto the *Wake*'s own desire for origins and its genealogical preoccupation with sources. Furthermore, Joyce's reading of Metchnikoff finds its counterpart in a second series of notes taken from the *Encyclopaedia Britannica* on 'River Engineering', 'Geography' and, specifically, the 'Physical Geography' of Ireland (VI.B.1.179). The impetus behind these notes is unquestionably the writing

---

[3] As a precursor of Herder, and the Revivalist defenders of folkloric authenticity, Vico (1948, 19) held that the ancient 'poets spoke in poetic characters' who 'are found to have been true fables or stories, and their allegories are discovered to contain meanings not analogical but univocal, not philosophical but historical, of the people of Greece of those times'. See also his classification of Hermes Trismegistus, Orpheus and Homer as 'poetic characters' symbolizing the people of their age (1948, 36, 40, 289; see also 119ff.).

of the Anna Livia chapter, begun in February 1924. But the notes also show a clear interest in landscape as a symbolic entity so important in Irish culture. Universal history, in other words, does not come into *Finnegans Wake*, for its general affect – the key to unlocking the 'ekumene = habitable O' (VI.B.1.179) – is threaded through the material foundations of the flotsam and jetsam (a river term) of culture and history.[4] The debris of everyday life – important to Joyce from the epiphanies to the early notes for 'Work in Progress' in VI.B.10 – is the stuff of archaeology, genealogy, human geography and cultural genetics. In that sense, one can turn Finn Fordham's argument that Joyce is 'unravelling universals' (2007) by showing their impossibility also on its head; by knotting together all particulars, he is creating a new universal in which the whole is larger than the sum of its parts. (At least, this may be one implication of Joyce's ambition to see the discrete elements in the composition of his book fusing together.) Furthermore, Joyce famously used Vico's *New Science* as a 'trellis' against which he spelt the fragments of past and present. On the one hand, he adopted the cycles of history to support the progressive/regressive principle of the *Wake*'s narratives: the ebb and flow, coming and going, leaving and return that is epitomized in Shaun's peripatetic behaviour ('/\ zigzag v spiral/ʳcorsi ricorsi Vico' [VI.B.1.29]) and reflected in the contrapuntal structure that, at least in the early stages of 'Work in Progress', pitted Book I against Book III. On the other hand, his notes on Vico tellingly deal with the specifics of myth, history and legal history – in short, human customs – from which the universal laws of history are derived. The resulting 'collideorscape' (*FW-R* 114.24; *FW* 143.28) is a 'chaosmos of Alle' (*FW-R* 94.7; *FW* 118 118.21), chaotic and all-encompassing at the same time. Whether it is also a way out of the nightmare of history is a different matter altogether, for it is never quite clear whether the *Wake* offers any redemption (Fordham 2007, 5). Whenever 'history [comes] near its end' (VI.B.1.174), a phrase inserted in a late revision of 'Mamalujo', it starts again; there is always another memory, another story to repeat (*FW-R* 308-9-10; *FW* 397.8-9).

The plethora of historical, cultural, legendary and everyday matter that Joyce gathered in his notebooks and put into the *Wake* goes hand in hand with Joyce's continued interest in the hybridity of Irish identity, which this chapter

---

[4] The article on 'Geography' in the *Encyclopaedia Britannica* notes that while Aristotle, the father of scientific geography, was positing the earth as 'spherical, practical geographers were steadily directed towards ascertaining the outline and configuration of the *oikumene*, or habitable world, the only portion of the terrestrial surface known to the ancients and to the medieval peoples' (*EB* XI, 620).

will elucidate. The thrust of the *Wake* is its '"long view" view of history', which, as Emer Nolan (1995, 146) contends, 'has so often been ascribed to the so-called "Irish historical imagination"'. *Finnegans Wake* is the exposition of that imagination, calling forth the memory and desire to bring 'the dear prehistoric scenes all back again' (*FW-R* 298.40–299.1; *FW* 385.19). The desire to make the past present registers on many levels. First of all, it is the obverse of the nightmare of history in which the past is traumatically ever present. In the *Wake* Joyce complements the nightmare of history with the idea of a lost golden age, not unlike that envisioned by Revivalist writers. The recovering of lost histories, the discovery of origins and the creation of genealogical connections are central to the *Wake*'s narrative economy, even if those restorative actions usually flounder. The palaeographical analysis of the Letter in Chapter I.5 is one obvious example in which a superabundance of evidence fails to produce any meaningful result. Another is the attempt to find the truth behind HCE's sin in the park, which unravels into a historiographical rabbit hole involving an ever-widening investigation into the Irish (and global) past.

Where global history is concerned, and Joyce's ambition to create it, notebook VI.B.1 is also significant in that it contains a lengthy set of notes from H.G. Wells's popular *A Short History of the World* (1922), which tells 'the story of our world' (Wells 1922, 1) from the earth's origins to the political aftermath of the Great War; the most recent event included is the Genoa Conference, held in April/May 1922, which sought (but failed) to redress the post-war economic crisis. Joyce, however, only read the chapters from 'The Beginnings of Life' to 'Primitive Neolithic Civilizations', showing his interest in the early developments of animal and human life. What he notes are periods in the earth's natural development: 'Azoic (½ E[arth]'s life) | paleozoic | 1,600 mill yrs' (VI.B.1.170; Wells 1922, 10); 'Azoic 1400 Mill | Paleozic | Mesozoic 200 mill | ʳCainozoicʳ 80,000' (VI.B.1.172; Wells 1922, 26; *FW-R* 80.26; *FW* 101.15); and '4 Glacial periods' (VI.B.1.172; Wells 1922, 42). These link with the *Wake*'s preoccupation with historical (dis)continuities. He also records the discovery of Heidelberg Man and Piltdown Man in Sussex (VI.B.1.173; Wells 1922, 43–4), specimens of proto-human life, as well as the Neanderthals and 'Cro-Magnards', the first 'human' beings (VI.B.1.173; Wells 1922, 46, 51–2), all of which obviously connect with the *Wake*'s archaeological theme of historical objects (not least the Letter) discovered in the Irish bog and HCE as the giant interred in the landscape. Extremely significant, though, is that Joyce's notetaking from Wells is interrupted by the page of unsourced notes on Herder, Mommsen, Vico and Thucydides that I mentioned earlier. One can almost see that Joyce is having a brainwave when he reads Wells's opinion of the childlike mind of 'primitive man' whose reaction to the world around him is one of imaginative wonder:

> One needs to have been an imaginative child oneself to realize again how important, significant, portentous or friendly, strangely shaped rocks, lumps of wood, exceptional trees or the like may have appeared to the men of the Old Stone Age, and how dream and fancy would create stories and legends about such things that would become credible as they told them. Some of these stories would be good enough to remember and tell again. The women would tell them to the children and so establish a tradition. To this day most imaginative children invent long stories in which some favourite doll or animal or some fantastic semi-human being figures as the hero, and primitive man probably did the same—with a much stronger disposition to believe his hero real!
>
> (Wells 1922, 59–60)

Despite the stereotype that primitive people are incapable of rational thought, Wells evokes a process of cultural memory that sounded familiar to Joyce. The retelling of stories was already part of the *Wake*'s technique, from 'Roderick O'Connor' and 'Mamalujo' to the narrative of how Earwicker got his name in what was to become Chapter I.2. But it is the Vichian resonances that caught his attention. Joyce wrote down 'hero' (VI.B.1.174), which he later inserted on the *Transatlantic Review* proofs of 'Mamalujo' (Cornell-1; *JJA* 56:99). Wells's scientific account of human development thus resonated with Joyce because of its parallels with Vico's 'science', whose acts of symbolical interpretation grounded in reality led to the establishment and growth of human societies. While the Vichian connection resonated with Mamalujo, much of the Wells' notes on evolution fed into the development of HCE as father of the people.

The desire for origins is strong in *Finnegans Wake*, yet history's genealogies are never rectilinear. One constant in Joyce's career as a writer is his insistence on Irish 'civilization' as 'an immense woven fabric in which very different elements are mixed' together: 'What race or language ... can nowadays claim to be pure?' (*OCPW* 118), he asked in his 1907 'Ireland: Island of Saints and Sages' lecture. To prove his point, he listed the elements compounded in 'the old Celtic Stock': the Firbolgs, Milesians, Normans, Anglo-Saxons, Huguenots and Scandinavians (*OCPW* 114, 118–19). In explaining how the Danes did not leave Ireland after their defeat by Brian Boru, but were 'gradually assimilated into the community' (*OCPW* 113), he recognized that, contrary to the politics of racial purity, migration is a major historical factor in creating an ethnically hybrid population (see Nash 2015). *Finnegans Wake* exemplifies this process of ethnogenesis most clearly when it dwells on the Scandinavian influences on the making of the Irish nation. Here again Wells and evolutionary biology stimulated Joyce's thinking:

> We have to remember that human races can all interbreed freely and that they separate, mingle and reunite as clouds do. Human races do not branch out like trees with branches that never come together again. It is a thing we need to bear constantly in mind, this remingling of races at any opportunity. It will save us from many cruel delusions and prejudices if we do so. People will use such a word as race in the loosest manner, and base the most preposterous generalizations upon it. They will speak of a 'British' race or of a 'European' race. But nearly all the European nations are confused mixtures of brownish, dark-white, white and Mongolian elements.
>
> (Wells 1922, 70)

Recognizing the debate in 'Cyclops', Joyce recorded 'confusion of races' (VI.B.1.177) and attributes this new procreative agency to HCE (*FW-R* 28.3; *FW* 35.5).

Such evolutionary and genealogical diversification is central to the discussion that follows. In making the case for *Finnegans Wake* as a Revivalist work, I want to scope out how the book's preoccupation with the past developed out of those five early historical sketches from 1923 to arrive at a fuller consideration of how Joyce's last book presents the past. The target of this exploration is the *Wake*'s genealogical aesthetics, its preoccupation with the origin of the events that came to pass, but also with the reason why these events are never fixed discursively and politically. Drawing on Joyce's notebooks, the course of this exploration will be amplified with evidence as to how Joyce conceived of the *Wake*'s historical vision. A good point of departure from which to investigate the book's fashioning of the past is the *Wakean* year 1132.

The past, origins: 1132

For a long time, the arbitrariness of 1132 has puzzled critics who believed it was cabbalistic (Atherton 1959, 53) or gnostic in nature (Platt 2007, 116) or an allusion to the death of Finn MacCool, which the *Annals of the Four Master* date to 283 (which, multiplied by four, equals 1132) (McHugh 1976, 47). Mutating among others into a patent number (*FW-R* 238.24; *FW* 310.3), an address (*FW-R* 326.27; *FW* 420.23), the time of day ('twentyeight to twelve' [*FW-R* 483.32; *FW* 617.23], that is, 11:32) and the postmark on ALP's letter (*FW-R* 326.25; *FW* 420.20), I contend, however, that 1132 represents both the indeterminacy of origins and the not-yet-but-very-soon-after narrative of the *Wake*.

To qualify what I said a moment ago, the past in *Finnegans Wake* is not completely lost or inaccessible. It is there, but only just. Like Tir Na nÓg, it glimmers faintly in the distance: 'he had beheld the residuance of a delugion: the foggy doze still going strong, the old thalassocrats of invinsible empores' (*FW-R* 284.21–3; *FW* 367.24–5). To be sure, Mamalujo's historiographical ineptitude remains an obstacle: their vision of the past, of the time before the flood, is a delusion. Yet their role is important in underscoring the *Wake*'s – and Ireland's – historical complexity and pluriformity. The layering of historical times and periods is one of the book's most distinct characteristics. From ancient Ireland to the early twentieth century, historical periods are part of the fabric of the book.

At face value, the *Wake*'s genealogical aesthetics treat all history with equanimity, so that the book echoes popular conceptions of history in which any event that is beyond living memory is all just old, regardless of whether it happened 100 or 1,000 years ago: 'all of old right as anywas ever in very old place' (*FW-R* 456.29; *FW* 586.20–1). This erasure of historical difference stems from the fact that the view of the past is only dim, a condition that Joyce already introduced in his early sketches with Mamalujo's inability to remember and the inability of the narrator of 'Roderick O'Connor' to get his history straight. One might link this dimness of the past to the critical commonplace that *Finnegans Wake* is a dream, but that connection is not particularly helpful. Instead, the past is clouded in the *Wake* because of the imperfection of memory and the limitations of historiography. Historical documents are difficult to decipher, interpret and understand; historical interpretations of past events are contested. Mamalujo not only cannot remember precisely what happened, they also contradict other sources as well as each other (*FW-R* 302.27; *FW* 390.2–3).

The *Wake* thus seemingly enacts the conditions understood by postmodern historiography that the past can only be represented discursively (see, for example, White 1987, 48).[5] Although Joyce was acutely aware how bias – particularly nationalist bias – creeps into the historical account, most of the historical writing that Joyce read and used was, like most history at the time, positivist in its approach. His early encounter with Nietzsche no doubt influenced his thinking; *The Birth of Tragedy*, *The Joyful Wisdom* and a volume containing *The Case of Wagner, Nietzsche Contra Wagner, and Selected Aphorisms*, all published by T.N. Foulis between 1909 and 1911, were in his Trieste library. But in the years of 'Work in Progress', there is no evidence of Joyce's direct engagement

---

[5] For relevant Joyce criticism that draws on the methods of new historicism and postmodern history, see Fairhall (1993), Spoo (1994) and Hofheinz (1995).

with Nietzsche's historical relativism or that of any other thinker.[6] Conscious of history's 'infinite possibilities' (*U* 2.50–1), rather than its hermeneutic fluidities, he turned instead to the universalist, pre-positivist conceptions of history of Vico, Michelet, Quinet and Hegel. Joyce was clearly attracted by the paradox that there is mutability within history's immutability: history repeating itself with a difference. (Aptly, Tacitus, the first-century Roman historian, is rendered as 'Taciturn' [*FW-R* 13.37; *FW* 17.3].) Quinet's 'beautiful' sentence that punctuates *Finnegans Wake* captures this essence: the permanence of the landscape *versus* the transience (or permeability if you like) of political power. Within Vico's cycles lie the flotsam and jetsam of history characterized by language change (etymology), manners and customs, the constitution of laws and so on. Of these three, Vico had, not coincidentally, the most impact. Joep Leerssen (2008) understands *The New Science*'s preoccupation with *filologia*, the Greek word for 'erudition', as an exercise in cultural genetics. Insofar as 'philology investigates the certainties that are a product of the human mind', it deals with culture and all the 'things by which humans make their world recognizable, knowable, predictable'. In philology, Vico looks for the sources and seeks to understand the process behind culture. Thus, Vico formalized the idea of a genealogy going back to first principles and the idea that all culture is 'derived from a single primitive ethnic self-invention and self-articulation. Law-makers, poets and priests have aboriginally one and the same function' (Leerssen 2008, 17). Leerssen presents Vico as a proto-romantic, his work giving rise to philology as a discipline as well as providing the rationale for all European nationalisms. It is in this sense that Vico provided Joyce with a model with which he went 'rooting' through history.

Appropriately, Earwicker, working his land, is following 'his plough for rootles' (*FW R* 24.12; *FW* 30.15). As a metaphor, digging through the earth, looking for *roots*, is as important to *Finnegans Wake* as the Vichian cycles. In fact, cyclicality in the *Wake* is not a structurally simple device expressing universal timelessness. On the contrary, it functions as a marker of change: 'timing the cycles of events grand and national' (*FW-R* 11.19; *FW* 13.31–2). The cycles of history can bring the promise of renewal and regeneration: 'Teems of times and

---

[6] It is also worth nothing which other theoretical historians Joyce had in his library: Thomas Babington Macaulay, *Critical and Historical Essays contributed to the Edinburgh Review* (1874); Thomas Carlyle, *The French Revolution: A History* (two editions, 1888 and 1905); David Hume, *The History of England from the Invasion of Julius Caesar to the Revolution in 1688* (1818); W.E.H. Lecky, *History of European Morals* (undated); and Edward Gibbon, *The Decline and Fall of the Roman Empire* (1919), which he read for *Finnegans Wake* (VI.B.1.98, 101–2, 119–20). His reading of Metchnikoff and Stefan Czarnwoski's *Le Culte des héros et ses conditions sociales: Saint Patrick, héros national de l'Irlande* (VI.B.14.213–18) also shows a consistent regard for the social processes shaping human history. Joyce's interest in historiography was, to say the least, eclectic.

happy returns. The seim anew' (*FW-R* 169.6–7; *FW* 215.22–3). But they can also signify the past condemned to repeat itself; aptly, 'repeating itself' is Mamalujo's stock phrase (*FW-R* 298.7; *FW* 384.16). More to the point, the passing of time as marked through epochal stages also implies that there exists a time before the change, a moment outside history.

The 'before time' of the *Wake*'s opening passage, 'not yet, though venisoon after' (*FW-R* 3.9–10; *FW* 3.10), is an important element in the *Wake*. As the Edenic 'prefall paradise peace' (*FW-R* 24.13; *FW* 30.15), it is a time of assumed innocence. In narrative terms, it marks the period before Earwicker's encounter with the king's retinue – before he was known to everyone as Here Comes Everybody – which precipitated the rumours about his exposure in the park that led to his downfall. Historically, it is the time before anything had happened, when 'everything' was 'still possible' (Lernout 2007, 54). In Ireland, this time coincides with the period of the island's mythological people: the Parthalonians, Nemedians, the Firbolg, Thuatha de Danaan and the Fomorians, which *Finnegans Wake* calls the 'unimportant' people of ancient Ireland (*FW-R* 294.37–8; *FW* 381.5). This 'before time' is, however, not a just a time before written records and therefore before history proper began. Writing likely did not exist in Ireland in the period before Saint Patrick. Nonetheless, historians have traced the origins of Irish historiography to well before the fifth century to the period covered by the chieftains Ferdiad and Cuchulain. Even if early Irish genealogies are not reliable – they were tools by which clans legitimized their claim to power – they reveal a historiographical sensibility for origins (Ó Cróinín 2005, 182). Where much of the Irish Revival looked back to an idealized prehistoric mythology to forge the nation's identity, the *Wake* uses the 'before time' as a trope to indicate the passing of one era into another, which often comes about through conflict.

In that respect, the *Wakean* year 1132 fulfils a special function. Because of its ubiquity, the date has special significance. It lampoons the unreal nature of a golden age in which the memory of a better past contrasts with the social, political and economic deficiencies of the present (Erll 2011, 35; Foster 1993, 100). In the narrative, the date functions as a significant moment in the collective memory. Unlike 1798, for example, the year of the failed rising whose centenary is mentioned several times in Joyce's writing, the year 1132 is a red herring, designating a moment in Irish history for which nothing of any particular consequence happened in the course of Irish history. *The Annals of the Four Masters* (n.d.) record a series of minor invasions and conflicts between Munster and Connaught. The year 1132 is also the year Dermot MacMurrough became King of Leinster, Saint Malachy was appointed Bishop of Armagh (which marks the imposition of the Roman Liturgy on the Irish Church), and both Laurence O'Toole, patron saint of Dublin, and Henry II were born. However, the reason why Joyce would latch on to any of these events remains unclear. Lastly, again for reasons that are not apparent, both the *avant-texte* and the *Wake* itself (*FW-R* 95.2; *FW* 119.26) link 1132 with 432, the year of Saint Patrick's arrival seven centuries earlier, albeit only through a deliberate dissociation of history and time. This dissociation exists in the historical anachronism in the Mamalujo sketch, but also in the mystical 'synchronisms' of time (*FW-R* 224.8–9; *FW* 290.7–8). From the Cathay cycles, long periods without change, mentioned in Chapter I.5 (*FW-R* 91.93; *FW* 119.23) to Yeats's gyres (*FW-R* 228.3–4; *FW* 295.23–4), cyclicity and timelessness are closely associated in the *Wake*. It is no surprise that in this book, in which all worldly phenomena are rendered imprecise, 1132 is a temporal (and in several instances also a spatial) marker that, although indefinite in its own right, acts as a point of reference against which change and transformation are measured.

The date is first mentioned in the text in the pseudo-chronicle of Chapter I.1. The chronicle mimics the annals section of *Thom's Official Directory of Ireland*, directly echoing Joyce's earlier allusion in the 'Proteus' chapter of *Ulysses*; the 'Whallfisk' reprises the shoal of 'turlhyde whales', which stranded in the mouth of the Dodder in 1331 (*FW-R*, 11.21–2; *FW* 13.34; *U* 3.2–3).[7] The event spurs Stephen's historical imagination, as he pictures the genealogical link with 'my people' (*U* 3.4). The pseudo-chronicle chiastically lists four events in AD 1132 and AD 566 turning around a mysterious silence: '[Silent]' (*FW-R* 11.28; *FW* 14.6). This silence is a still point around which history flows backwards and forwards, indicating both epochal change and history repeating itself. The four events in the pseudo-chronicle represent four ages in the history of Dublin: 'Ublanium' (*FW-R* 11.22; *FW* 13.34 5), for Eblana, the Latin name for Dublin recorded in Ptolemy's *Geography c.* AD 140; 'Hurdlesford' (*FW-R* 11.27; *FW* 14.5) and 'Ballyaughacleeaghbally' (*FW-R* 11.21–2; *FW* 14.9–10) for Town of the Ford of the Hurdles, which is a transliteration of *Baile Atha Cliath*. Of unknown origins, *Ath Cliath* was the common name for any hurdle ford; *Baile* was added in reference to the ford in the capital, where the road from Tara to Wicklow likely crossed the river at what is now Father Mathew Bridge (Joyce 1910–13, I, 45–6, 363–4).[8]

---

[7] The *Wake*'s image of men crawling like ants around the whale comes from *Thom's Directory* (1904, 2092): 'They were from 30 to 40 feet long, and so thick that men standing on each side of one of them could not see those on the other'.

[8] A hurdle is a wattled frame used as a fortification in building a passage cross marshy land (*OED*, s.v. 'hurdle'; see also Joyce 1910–13, I, 362 and II, 199). The 'blay of her Kish' (*FW-R* 11.24–5; *FW* 14.2) suggests a wickerwork causeway (Joyce 1910–13, I, 362).

Finally, 'Dublin' (*FW-R* 11.35; *FW* 14.15), the city's English name, derived from Irish *duibhlin*, 'black pool', which is of Scandinavian origin (Joyce 1910–13, I, 363). Each of the four stages, furthermore, are loosely associated with the *Wake*'s characters. The pseudo-chronicle is critically more important for establishing *Wakean* historiography than as a parody of the *Annals of the Four Masters*. The chiastic form of the chronicle runs counter to normal chronological progression by which recorded history moves forward, while again underscoring historical indifference. The four states of Dublin do not correspond to the years 566 and 1132. Nor do they, with the exception of Ptolemy, link to any precisely dateable events or origins. What they do do is connect history, place and character in a form not unlike that of the 'dinnseanchas', the Irish poetic form that records how places got their names. Despite its irregular form, the pseudo-chronicle does, in other words, point to how the past is part of the city's cultural DNA.

History in *Finnegans Wake* is deeply flawed. Often specific in its allusion to historical events, the *Wake* is also indifferent to those events. Their superabundance creates a surfeit of history that cannot ever cohere. The endeavours to discover the laws of history by Vico, Hegel and other philosophers of history were an attempt to regulate and subsume the flotsam and jetsam of the past in a single universal system. Vico (1948, 53) believed that if it were possible to correctly assign the facts of the 'first origins' of nations, it would furnish him with the 'scientific principles' from which the rest of history could be understood. In *Finnegans Wake*, Joyce attempted to fuse the universal and the particular. But in contending with the uncertainties of history – the inchoateness of origins, the unpredictability of the future – Joyce ended up in a hermeneutic circle in which not enough particulars can be mustered to arrive at universals and universals fall apart because of the inconsistency and inadequacy of the particulars. In the *Wake*, the universal and the particular forces constantly rub against each other, creating a view of history as 'this grand continuum, overlorded by fate and interlarded with accidence' (*FW-R* 366.34–5; *FW* 472.30–1). A conception of the world in which predestination is disrupted by accident is particularly problematic with respect to Irish history. It is the nightmare of history all over again. While *Finnegans Wake* at times upholds the hopes and dreams for a new Irish nation able to fulfil its own destiny, the book also underlines the fragility of those ideals when history kicks back. As is well known, Joyce's representation of the Free State in *Finnegans Wake* is highly ambivalent; Ireland had freed itself from British rule, but it was not free of the nets of language and religion.

It is no surprise, therefore, that the *Wake* presents different takes on (the passing of) time. On the one hand, there is a preternatural sense of time concerned with time outside history; on the other, there are moments of significant epochal transformation, including the transition into history. The two most crucial of these moments staged in *Finnegans Wake* are the arrival of Saint Patrick and the Anglo-Norman invasion. The third take on time are the events that happened a long while ago, the history that is barely felt, the changes that barely register the deep effects they brought about. This indifference towards history manifests itself tropologically in the *Wakean* year 1132, the year in which nothing happened. Nevertheless, this nothingness can be politically charged too: 'Pastimes are past times. Now let bygones be bei Gunne's' (*FW-R* 207.12; *FW* 263.17–18). This is the nightmare of history re-enacted. Bygones cannot be just bygones when guns are at stake. In that sense, *Finnegans Wake* can be read as an attempt to think through the double problem of Irish history: the difficulty of awaking from the nightmare of history and the risks involved in doing so. Encapsulated within this is the problem of how to write the history of Irish history, a question that was not at the forefront of the Irish Revival because it involved incorporating the competing and contradictory voices of Celtic 'history' (the voices of pre-Christian myth and legend), British voices on Ireland, the voice of the Catholic Church, as well as the voices of the multiple factions within the Irish Revival itself.

The *Wake*'s vision of the past, furthermore, pulls in different directions between, on the one hand, the impossibility and undesirability of remembering and, on the other, the admonition not to forget. The double exhortation of ALP's 'Forget, remember' expresses an incertitude, one that she quickly resolves a few lines later with a plain 'Forget!' (*FW-R* 481.8; *FW* 614.22). Naturally, ALP's desire to forget is riddled with doubt as her own 'end' is near. Moreover, she is the *Wake*'s only character to question her past, agency and destiny: 'Have we cherished expectations? Are we for liberty of perusiveness? Whyafter what forewheres? A plainplanned liffeyism assemblements Eblania's conglomerate horde' (*FW-R* 481.5–7; *FW* 614.23–4). She also knows that in the squaring of the circle there is no real end, which makes forgetting impossible: 'It will remember itself from every sides, with all gestures, in each our word' (*FW-R* 481.2–3; *FW* 614.21–2). Moreover, the book as a whole insists on (the dangers of not) remembering: 'Forgetful of all save his vassal's plain fealty to the ethnarch' (*FW-R*24.17–18; *FW* 30.19–20), 'the unforgettable treeshade looms up behind the jostling judgments of those … malrecapturable days' (*FW-R* 47.11–12; *FW* 58.20–2), 'the identities in the writer complexus … will be best appreciated by never forgetting that both before and after the battle of the Boyne it was a habit not to sign letters always' (*FW-R* 91.13–16; *FW* 114.33–5), 'before I forget it don't forget' (*FW-R* 115.12–13; *FW* 144.22–3), 'forgetmenot' (*FW-R* 168.34; *FW* 215.8), 'remember all should I forget to' (*FW-R* 217.F1; *FW* 279.F1), 'United We Stand, even many offered. Don't forget' (*FW-R* 250.31; *FW* 325.5–6), 'The field of karnags and that bloasted tree. Forget not the felled' (*FW-R* 262.26–7; *FW* 340.7–8), 'Don't forget! The grand fooneral will now shortly occur. Remember' (*FW-R* 483.33–4; *FW* 617.25–6). There are many more examples. The *Wake*'s narratives reveal an unmistakable anxiety about forgetting, precisely because ascertaining and holding on to the memory of what happened is so difficult (ironically, Mamalujo are not very good at it), but also because remembering is both important and necessary to cope with the nightmare of history.

History is not only quintessentially unsettled in *Finnegans Wake*, it also takes on different forms. Within its universalist logic, the *Wake* may sometimes give the impression that history is a leveller in the endless cycle of rise and fall. The immutability expressed through the Quinet sentence eradicates the historically particular, downplaying difference and change in favour of what is permanent and timeless. Many of the *Wake*'s depictions of historical conflict are almost schematic. The nature or cause of the disagreement is rarely clear; neither are the consequences. There is just eternal strife, 'clashes' of 'wills gen wonts, ostrygods gagging fishygods' (*FW-R* 3.23; *FW* 4.1–2), with the occasional call to 'let us be tolerant of antipathies' (*FW-R* 207.12; *FW* 163.14). The allusion to Michael Gunn, the manager of the Gaiety Theatre, in 'let bygones be bei Gunne's' (*FW-R* 207.12; *FW* 263.18), calls to mind the innocent jousting of the pantomime. Likewise, the 'Willingdone Museyroom' turns historical representation into vaudeville. The animosities between the Mookse and the Gripes and the Ondt and the Gracehoper are the stuff fables are made on. And the violence that erupts at the wedding feast in Chapter III.3 is a slapstick brawl involving the 'fighting Irish' (Fox 2019). Humour notwithstanding, the schematic and grotesque nature of these incidents indicate the extent to which (as Bloom has it) 'Force, hatred, history, all that' (*U* 12.1481) belong to the Irish condition. The *Wake*, ultimately, imparts rather than glosses over this condition.

A case in point is the history/geography lesson in Chapter II.2. The language of retrospection is rosy, but the tone reveals a darker subtext:

> In theses places sojournemus, where Eblinn water, leased of carr and fen, leaving amont her shoals and salmonbrowses, whom inshore breezes woo with freshets, windeth to her broads. A phantom city, phaked of philim pholk, bowed and sould for a four of hundreds of manhood in their three and threescore fylkers for a price partitional of twenty six and six. By this riverside of our sunnybank, how buona the vista, by Santa Rosa! A field of May, the very vale of Spring. Orchards

here are lodged: sainted lawrels evremberried: you have a hoig view ashwald: a glen of marrons and of thorns: Gleannaulinn, Ardeevin: purty glint of plaising height. This Norman court at boundary of the ville, yon creepered tower of a church of Ereland, meet for true saints in worshipful assemblage, with our king's house of stone, belgroved of mulbrey, the still that was mill and Kloster that was Yeomansland, the ghastcold tombshape of the quick foregone on, the loftleaved elm Lefanunian abovemansioned, each, every, all is for the retro-spectioner. Skole! Agus skole igen!

(*FW-R* 207.30–208.10; *FW* 264.15–265.6)

The places they live in ('sojournemus') appear idyllic. The 'Norman court at the boundary of the ville' offers quite a picturesque view. The inclusion of *The House by the Churchyard* is no coincidence. Throughout the *Wake*, Joyce uses LeFanu's novel to evoke Chapelizod's bucolic setting. But this is all veneer. The idyllic past in Le Fanu's novel contrasts sharply with the disturbing world of duelling, double-crossing, deception and murder. Although heavily satirical, its world is that of the Anglo-Protestant Ascendancy and British military presence. Likewise, the geography lesson cannot completely keep the problematic Irish past under wraps. The 'retro-spectioner' is duped into seeing the beauty of this 'place in which we live', but the subtext is that of a divided nation that encompasses the system of Norman land division imposed after the conquest of Henry II and, crucially, Irish partition in 1921.

The cast of historical characters (again)

Turning back to the genetic origins of *Finnegans Wake*, it is worth asking what role the cast of historical characters from the early sketches played elsewhere in the book. With the important exception of Roderick O'Connor, they became an integral part of the *Wake*'s narrative and structural development (see Hayman 1990, 38–42). He eventually joined them with the Doodles, furnishing them with their own sigla. Their presence in the book takes on different forms. Saint Kevin, for instance, becomes an avatar for Shaun in his role as innocent child: Kevin with his 'cherub cheek' plays 'postman's knock around the diggings' (*FW-R* 21.26–8; *FW* 27.5–7). Kevin, in other words, not only doubles as Shaun but is directly linked with the archaeological recovery of the Letter (see *FW-R* 88.10–12; *FW* 110.32–5). Saint Patrick, by comparison, is embedded in the *Wake*'s texture, not unlike the initials of ALP and HCE. A name without the contours of a character, his appearance blends with that of other characters, events and attributes. He merges with Swift in 'Shamus Swiftpatrick, archfieldchaplain of Saint Lucan's' (*FW-R* 439.29–30; *FW* 564.22–3); places are named after him, as in 'the coast of … Saint Patrick' (*FW-R* 301.13–14; *FW* 388.13) and 'from Lismore to Cape Brendan, Patrick's' (*FW-R* 381.19–20; *FW* 491.11); and he designates historical periods, such as 'Prepatrickularly' (*FW-R* 243.25; *FW* 316.4), or anniversaries, as in 'K. O. Senpatrick's Day and the fenian rising' (*FW-R* 28.19–20; *FW* 35.24). As full-blown characters, however, they are also emblems of the Irish national past who are deeply connected with history and the *Wake's* genealogical exploration of origins and endings.

Roderick O'Connor plays a minor role in *Finnegans Wake*, although notebook evidence suggests that Joyce may have contemplated some presence for him. An early note, recorded not long after the sketch's composition, reads: 'Irish kings | Cimboeth to Rory (BC 289 — ?)' (VI.B.2.4). Suggesting an unbroken lineage, the note reflects the idea of epochal (dis)continuity that was the theme of the original sketch. The source of the note, William Bullen Morris's *The Life of Saint Patrick: Apostle of Ireland* (1908), and Joyce's creative adaptation further underscore this theme.[9] In the original passage, Morris notes that anyone perusing the Irish annals might think that the time from Cimboeth, who reportedly founded Armagh in 289, to that of Laoghaire, who was High King in Saint Patrick's time, is but 'a catalogue of wars, domestic and foreign' (Morris 1908, 144). Although pagan Ireland lived by the sword, it was not just a place of violence; rather, Ireland was well populated, prosperous and, while not exactly self-sufficient, it was thriving agriculturally. It was also on the overseas trade routes, the same routes that Saint Patrick brought to captivity. The question mark and the deliberate change of Laoghaire to Rory (for Roderick) indicates that Joyce was intent on showing history's end.

Roderick's sole mention in the *Wake* is, however, 'by Roderick's, our mostmonolith' (*FW-R* 419.8; *FW* 539.1). This is the name given in Chapter III.3 to the Wellington Monument, whose 'erectheion' (*FW-R* 419.0; *FW* 539.3–4) celebrates HCE as the original ancestor, the father of the people, and the moment his 'toils of domestication first began' (*FW-R* 419.34–5; *FW* 539.34). This moment is not only the foundation of Dublin but also the restitution of the Irish nation in the glory of its past greatness ('to seek again Irrlanding' [*FW-R* 419.23–4; *FW* 539.17–18]). There is an irony in that this 'domestication' is an act of subjugation, the colonizer placing his 'imperial standard by weaponright'

---

[9] For a further account of the Morris source, see Henkes (2014a, b).

(*FW-R* 419.25; *FW* 539.19–20), following the victory on the 'slaughterday of cleantarriffs' (*FW-R* 419.22–3; *FW* 539.28), recalling Brian Boru's victory at Clontarf as well as the Anglo-Irish trade wars (see Van Mierlo 2019). Joyce picked out Roderick's name, without context or comment, when he raided the 'Dublin Annals' in *Thom's Directory* with the help of an amanuensis in preparation for the revision of 'Haveth Childers Everywhere' in 1930 (VI.B.29.156). He also selected from *Thom's* the entry on the hoisting of the Imperial Standard (VI.B.29.157), when the new flag of the new British Union was flown for the first time at Dublin Castle on 1 January 1801. Roderick's presence in *Finnegans Wake*, although limited, is therefore also part of a contra-Revival genealogical line of descent from the Anglo-Irish invasion to the Act of Union.

The retrospective drive in Chapter III.3, recounting the events already narrated, proves to be important for the development of the cast of historical characters. In their cross-examination, Mamalujo are concerned that the young Kevin may have shooed away the hen that dug up the Letter (*FW-R* 374.28; *FW* 482.19). Questioning the Letter's legibility, its legitimacy and even the credentials of the one who found it ('an unelgible' [*FW-R* 374.29; *FW* 482.21]), they suspect that Kevin counterfeited the letter. With their interrogation, Mamalujo aim to establish that Kevin is Shaun's double, thus seeking to confirm Shaun's guileful role in the Letter's creation. Of course, the passage plays out de Valera's duplicity in the Anglo-Irish Treaty negotiations of 1921 and what is, within the *Wake*'s fictional universe, the competing versions of the Irish Treaty. Shaun responds, in an exceptionally lucid manner, that he does know Kevin, but he does not let on whether he knows anything about the document or not: 'If I do know sainted sageness? Sometimes he would keep silent for a few minutes and clasp his forehead, as if in prayer, and during that time he would be thinking to himself and he would not mind anybody who would be talking to him or crying stinking fish' (*FW-R* 374.30–3; *FW* 488.22–6). The language of 'sageness' and 'prayer' reprises that of the original Saint Kevin sketch, but the passage is, of course, a Shaunian charade. That Mamalujo believe Kevin to have practised 'psychical chirography' (*FW-R* 374.26; *FW* 482.17) gives new meaning to the original sketch and possibly explains Joyce's choice of placing it at the end of *Finnegans Wake*.

Often confused with calligraphy, 'chirography' is not just writing; it designates an individual's handwriting, regardless of the quality of the penmanship (Hackett and Girvin 1884, 14). A 'chirograph' also denotes a formal document, usually a deed or indenture, written or engrossed in duplicate on the top and bottom half of a single sheet of vellum; the parties named on the agreement would each retain one half of the document separated across the word 'chirographum' written across the middle of the page (Beal 2008, 72). From telecommunication (radio and telephone) to psychic messages, receiving communications from a different plane is central to Chapter III.3. In 'Haveth Childers Everywhere', Joyce incorporated material from Hester Travers Smith's *Psychic Messages from Oscar Wilde* (1923). Smith, an Irish spiritualist, had purportedly used automatic writing to communicate with the spirit of the dead writer, who shared his opinions on the work of modern writers like Galsworthy, Meredith, Shaw and Joyce himself, whom he had read through the eyes of the living (see Slote 1995, 112–15). As Slote indicates, Smith's work suited Joyce because Mamalujo are attempting to summon HCE's spirit, in effect to gain first-hand knowledge of his exploits and therefore the history of the nation. Kevin's chirography, however, is automatic writing as well as a covenant with a higher order. The link here is to Shaun's postal mission 'that is put upon [him] from on high' (*FW-R* 318.23; *FW* 410.1).

The narratives of *Finnegans Wake* always work through, and towards, revelation in a double movement, both equally impossible. One is genealogical, how things came to pass; but this history of origins as revealed through memory is problematic by default, because remembering and bearing witness are unreliable. The archaeological excavation and palaeographical interpretation of the Letter are its emblem. The other is universal, imaging the cyclical revolutions of history, seeking revelation in transcendental knowledge; but the desire for spiritual manifestation is problematic – even in the early work, '*claritas* is not as such transcendent' (Slote 2010, 15) – in that it implies a process of ontogenetics, something coming out of nothing. This is why revelation in the *Wake* is perennially ambiguous, an anti-revelation; and the end of time is always 'the seim anew' (*FW-R* 169.7; *FW* 215.23).

In Chapter III.3, Saint Patrick's historical persona and the narrative of his life are given its due as a national icon. The chapter includes references to his Anglo-Roman birth, his captivity and escape, his vision and return to Ireland to convert the heathens. In particular, the chapter inserts iconic moments from the life, such as the Wood of Fochlut (*FW-R* 372.10; *FW* 479.13, *et passim*), the woods of the Irish wolfhound near the western coast where Patrick was held captive; the heathen seafarers who force Patrick to suck their breastpaps (*FW-R* 372.39; *FW* 480.14); and the composition of Saint Patrick's Breastplate, the hymn the saint composed to protect him and his followers from danger (*FW-R* 182.37–40; *FW* 231.23–7). These moments grow into a symbolical-historical complex as Shaun channels Patrick's voice shortly after Mamalujo raise the question of the Letter ('Are you in your fatherick, lonely one?' [*FW-R* 371.32; *FW* 478.28]).

Shaun appears as in a trance, sensing he is in the Wood of Fochlut. Joyce's source, Flood's *Ireland: Its Saints and Scholars* (VI.B.3.9), describes Patrick's dream vision that 'induced' him 'to undertake the conversion of Ireland':

> I saw in the visions of the night a person coming from Ireland with innumerable letters, and he gave me one of them, and I read in the beginning of the letter 'The voice of the people of Ireland,' and I thought at that very moment that I heard the voice of those who were near the wood of Focluth, which is adjoining the Western Sea, and they cried out, as it were with one voice, 'We entreat thee, holy youth, to come and walk still amongst us,' and I was very much pricked to the heart, and could read no further, and so I awoke.
>
> (Flood 1917, 11–12)

Shaun's dream vision is not of his own holy mission to deliver the Letter, but of the coming of, and temptation by, a Scandinavian conqueror: 'Magnus Spadebeard ... welsher perfyddye. A destroyer in our port' (*FW-R* 372.38–9; *FW* 480.12–13). A Danish/Welsh hybrid, HCE brings destruction, subjugation and paganism, yet he is a new Christ rising. In narrative terms, Shaun will become HCE as the father's voice will take over from Shaun's in the final part of the chapter. In a trance-like state, Shaun chants his own version of Saint Patrick's Breastplate:

> – Hail him heathen, heal him holystone!
> *Courser, recourser, changechild, ... ?*
> *Eld as endall, earth ... ... ?*
> (*FW-R* 373.20–2; *FW* 481.1–3)

The coming of HCE fills Shaun with foreboding of inevitable change. Where the voices that Patrick hears call him back to Ireland, Shaun's vision is of a threat to his own position and existence; he is a changeling and through him the epochal change happens, while history courses onwards and loops back on itself. The Vichian language comes from Metchnikoff's *La Civilisation et les grandes fleuves historiques* (1889), the geographical investigation of the influence of rivers on history and civilization that was instrumental for the development of *Finnegans Wake* (VI.B.1.29; see Landuyt and Lernout 1995).

The idea of impending epochal change is both directly and indirectly woven into the passage. The word 'keeltappers' (*FW-R* 372.36; *FW* 480.9) harks back to Roderick O'Connor's 'heeltapping' (*FW-R* 295.2; *FW* 381.9), the last High King emptying the beer glasses of their dregs. ('Heel-tapping', according to the *OED*, also means the deliberate delaying of proceedings, which comprises

Shaun's tactics throughout his interrogation.) The psychoanalytical regression that Shaun undergoes in Chapter III.4 is foreshadowed in Chapter III.3 in what is a perfect example of cultural *mélange*. Among the many mentions of wolves, Joyce alludes to Shaun's dread of 'the dragon vice-father' (*FW-R* 373.9–10; *FW* 480.26), which is one of several phrases in this passage borrowed from Freud's 'The Wolf Man', which Joyce was reading in preparation for the later chapter (Ferrer 1985, 374, 378). But it is also an attribute of Saint Patrick, his using the shamrock to explain the Trinity to the pagans, that clinches the awareness of historical difference when Mamalujo feign to understand Shaun's dream: 'I have your tristich now. It recurs in three times the same differently' (*FW-R* 373.29; *FW* 481.10). Insofar as historical change is tantamount to events occurring and recurring, the Trinitarian enigma also applies to the *Wake*'s economy of characters. On the one hand, Shaun is 'Trinathan Partnick Dieudonnay ... The same. Three persons' (*FW-R* 371.30–3; *FW* 478.24–7). On the other, characters have different names, and different historical roles and attributes, in different epochs. So HCE evolves from Fenian warrior to modern toff: 'from the human historic brute, Finnsen Faynean, oceanyclived, to this same vulcanised hillsir from yours ... Mr Tuppling Toun of Morningside Heights' (*FW-R* 373.30–4; *FW* 481.12–15). The subtext of Mamalujo's name-calling is the allegation that HCE is a Fenian rebel; this is another instance in the *Wake* in which historical change is predicated on violence, which Mamalujo express through their perversion of the Holy Trinity: 'We speak of Gun, the farther' (*FW-R* 373.36; *FW* 481.19).

As the preceding discussion indicates, Mamalujo are the only characters from the historical cast who have a voice of their own – and a highly significant one at that. As the inquisitors, they are given a central role that creates narrative continuities within the book. One of these involves the search for the Letter's meaning again from Chapter I.5 and connects it with a question regarding the fundaments of historical interrogation. But as the courtroom drama unfolds, which Joyce modelled on the bathos of trial proceedings reported in the press, Mamalujo never get any the wiser about the Letter's contents. The examination unfolds at cross-purposes: the wires get crossed and the radio/telephone connection is echoey; Shaun (deliberately) mishears their questions:

— First, if yu don't mine. Name yur historical grouns.
— This same prehistoric barrow 'tis, the orangery.
— I see. Very good now. It is in your orangery, I take it, you have your letters? Can you hear here me, you, sir?

— Thorsends. For my darling. Typette!
— So long aforetime? Can you hear better?
— Millions. For godsends. For my darling dearling one. (*FW-R* 371.6–12; *FW* 477.35–478.5)

But the past itself is also fluid and ever-changing. The naming of historical grounds seemingly establishes a scholarly premise. But the historical grounds (as in soil or surface) are actually highly ambivalent and unstable. Generally, the midden heap can be read as the *Wake*'s omphalos, 'the starting point for understanding the Irish past' (McKenna 1999, 139). But, in this instance, the midden heap and orangery are two manifestations of the same topopgraphical feature. In Chapter I.5, the orangery, built on the location of the midden heap, was the place where during its demolition the 'orangepeel' was found thrown away 'by some unknown sunseeker or placehider *illico* way back in his mistridden past' (*FW-R* 88.8–9; *FW* 110. 29–31). In Chapter III.3, the orangery is the 'prehistoric barrow', which suddenly suggests an unxpected continuity in political history: Celtic landscape and Protestant history have somehow become entangled, the one circling back onto the other. One might perhaps see in this a recondite allusion to the role played by Anglo-Protestant scholars and intellectuals in the interpretation of Ireland's past. But in *Wakean* terms such impossible (one should say counter-historical) genealogy has its own logic. It was the logic of the spatiotemporal mixing that is present in the early Mamalujo writings. This is how mythologies are made: 'History as her is harped. Too the toone your owldfrow lied of. Tantris, hattrick, tryst and parting, by vowelglide!' (*FW-R* 377.20–1; *FW* 486.6–7). The fusion of Saint Patrick and Tristan is another instance of histories performing becoming entangled – becoming, literally, two in one. But with the allusion to the traditional symbol of the harp, the harping of history – the making of songs – is passed off as a mode of historiography that is at the same time noble and unreliable.

David Hayman (1990) has claimed a central position for the Tristan and Isolde legend in *Finnegans Wake*, but this centrality exists first and foremost within the book's deep genetic structure. As an archetypal narrative of the love triangle, the legend furnished Joyce with a triad of characters out of whom his own protagonists evolved: Isolde turned into Issy; King Mark first changed into a proto-male Pop before turning into HCE; and Tristan became an avatar of Shaun (Hayman 1990, 27–31). In the surface text, by comparison, the legend seems less central. The opening of *Finnegans Wake* famously alludes to Tristan's return from 'Armorica' (or Brittany) to Cornwall from where he will set off for Ireland to fetch Isolde for King Mark. The return is both an event yet to happen and an act of sexual violence. Similarly highlighting an act of sexual promiscuity, the scene of the 'old geeser who calls on his skirts' (*FW-R* 52.15; *FW* 65.5–6) in Chapter I.3 is a crude adaptation of Tristan and the two Isoldes. The legend relates how one day the pining Tristan sang a lay about Isolde. His friend Kanhedrin believed Tristan was referring to his sister, Isolde Blanchemains, and set up a marriage arrangement. Tristan was aware of Kanhedrin's mistake. But believing the Irish Isolde to be married to King Mark, he acquiesced to the fact that he would not see her again and agreed to marry the Breton princess. In Joyce's vignette, the 'old grum' (*FW-R* 52.27 and 30; *FW* 65.20 and 23) declares his love to his sweetheart, but she runs off with another fellow. But the old grum is not bothered, because he is fond of another girl as well, only to start fantasizing about 'canoodl[ing] the two' (*FW-R* 52.3; *FW* 65.26). Their imagined threesome in the 'dreamlifeboat' (*FW-R* 52.36; *FW* 65.30) reprises the infantile lovers' discourse from Joyce's original sketch: 'hugging two by two in his zoo-doo-you-doo, a tofftoff for thee, missymissy for me and how-cameyou-eenso for Farber, in his tippy, upindown dippy, tiptoptippy canoodle' (*FW-R* 52.36–8; *FW* 65.30–3).

Elsewhere in the *Wake*, Tristan and Isolde serve to adumbrate the relationship between Shaun and the Issy. This is the case in the Maidens' prayer to Shaun in Chapter II.1, promising (not) to wait for his return (*FW-R* 185.32–186.32; *FW* 235.09–236.18); in Shaun's admonition against unwanted pregnancy in Chapter III.2 (*FW-R* 344.30–345.37; *FW* 444.6–445.25); Isolde as bride in Chapter III.3 (*FW-R* 388.31–40; *FW* 500.21–30); and Issy taking the veil, a passage that picks up on the devotional theme in the 'Young Isolde' vignette from 1923 (*FW-R* 432.21–9; *FW* 556.1–11). The most crucial passage, however, is the Issy answer in Chapter I.6 in which the girl talks to her double about her lover Tristan/Shaun, remembering her excitement 'the day he carried me from the boat' (*FW-R* 116.39; *FW* 146.24) and practising in the mirror what she would say/do to him when meeting again. The passage reads like another version of that written in 1923, this time with elements from Isolde's double, Iseult Blanchemains, worked in. It also reprises some of the language of the original material as well as some of its stock elements, including another (imagined) kiss and poetry recitation: 'More poestries from Chickspeer's with gleechoreal music or a jaculation from the garden of the soul?' (*FW-R* 116.5–6; *FW* 145.24–6). But there is a new element as well: the memory of a lover, Don Holohan, a version of Michael Bodkin/Furey. Holohan's 'proof of love, up Smock Alley' (*FW-R* 117.36–7; *FW* 147.32) is far more sexually forward, however, than Molly's and Gretta's lovers ever were; he is also, of course, Hoppy Holohan from 'A Mother', who is a bit of a cad, and another Tristan. Like Joyce's first use of the Tristan and Isolde legend, the passage is an exercise in lovers' discourse; it starts with the question itself, which is a rendering of Philip Rosseter's 'What then is love but mourning'? This Jacobean song by James I's court lutenist, a lament on absent or unrequited love, harks back to Joyce's interest in Early Modern English lyricism; its diction and imagery also resembles that of *Chamber Music*. The Tristan and Isolde material, however, and its intertextual origin is also made to fit the *Wake*'s come-back-to-Erin motif ('Come big to Iran' [*FW-R* 115.10; *FW* 144.18]), which signifies both cyclical return as well as physical return from exile.

This cyclical return is also pertinent to Chapter II.4. However, what's of prime interest is that chapter's poetics of memory. The portmanteau motif 'rememboded' that punctuates their account signals Mamalujo's inability to produce a sensible understanding of the past. The anachronisms they produce are a form of non-history, emerging from a 'memory crisis' in which a surfeit of unusable facts, or too much history, creates a mnemonic deficit and makes meaningful history impossible (Terdiman 1993, 5–6, 14). Through this surfeit, the *Wake* registers the equivocal and traumatic nature of the Irish past.

In its original form, the Mamalujo material from 1923 already presented elements encapsulating that aspect. Mamalujo's ironic obsession with forgetting signals to undo the effects of history that involves the creation of a counter-history, which retrieves a more innocent state of affairs, a return to a 'before time' 'long long ago ... when my heart knew no care' (*FW-R* 300.25–9; *FW* 387.17–21). The language of the come-all-you is a significant marker of Joycean nostalgia. The proofs of the vignette's prepublication in the *Transatlantic Review*, however, added in the discourse of Roman law taken from the articles on 'Roman Law' and 'Vico' in the *Encyclopaedia Britannica*. These notes, and Joyce's use of them, focus on the *connubium*, the Roman term on which Vico comments extensively for the 'right of intermarriage' (*EB* XXIII, 530). Joyce filled the chapter with references as to how the Romans understood the family unit. Matt Gregory is the 'paterfamilias' (*FW-R* 299.29; *FW* 386.13); Johnny proves inadequate at 'backscratching' the 'materfamilias' of Mrs Dowager Justice Squalchman (*FW-R* 303.15–16; *FW* 390.36); while Lally, the constable, admonishes the Four to forget the past and 'the grand confarreation' (*FW-R* 302.34; *FW* 390.11).

This 'confarreation' is the wedding celebration in Chapter III.3, a primal scene of sorts that ends in utter chaos. As the *Encyclopaedia Britannica* explains, among the early Romans,

> the [wedding] ceremony was a religious one, conducted by the chief pontiff and the flamen of Jupiter, in presence of ten witnesses, representatives probably of the ten curies of the bridegroom's tribe, and was known as *farreum* or *confarreatio*. Its effect was to dissociate the wife entirely from her father's house, and to make her a member of her husband's; for confarreate marriage involved *in manum conventio*, the passage of the wife into her husband's 'hand' or power.
>
> (*EB* XXIII, 530)

The crux of the matter, which is important to Mamalujo, is that the family in Roman law does not correspond to the modern nuclear family, but is altogether more permeable and fluid. Thus, Joyce notes in Notebook VI.B.I, presumably with reference to HCE: 'family all too himself' (117). Joyce's note is on the following passage in 'Roman Law':

> The word *familia* in Roman law had at once a more extensive and a more limited meaning than it has in its English form. Husband, wife and children did not necessarily constitute an independent family among the Romans, as with us, nor were they all necessarily of the same one. Those formed a family who were all subject to the power – originally *manus*, later *potestas* or *jus* – of the same head (*paterfamilias*). The *paterfamilias* was himself a member of the family only in the sense in which a king is a member of the community over which he rules. He might have a whole host dependent on him, wife and sons and daughters, and daughters-in-law and grandchildren by his sons, and possibly remoter descendants related through males; so long as they remained subject to him they constituted but one family, that was split up only on his death or loss of citizenship. But if his wife had not passed *in manum* (a result apparently unknown among the patricians at this period), she did not become a member of his family: she remained a member of the family in which she was born, or, if its head were deceased or she had been emancipated, she constituted a family in her own person. Both sons and daughters on emancipation ceased to be of the family of the *paterfamilias* who had emancipated them. A daughter's children could never as such be members of the family of their maternal grandfather; for children born in lawful marriage followed the family of their father, while those who were illegitimate ranked from the moment of birth as *patresfamilias* and *matresfamilias*.
>
> (*EB* XXIII, 529–30)

Why Joyce decided to give Mamalujo a female identity remains unclear, but 'Roman Law' provides a partial, and retroactive, justification in that women could at least be the head of a household. The notebook, furthermore, makes clear that in applying the terms *paterfamilias* and *materfamilias*, Joyce did not just have their general meaning in mind; his note, 'bastard from birth | pater familias' (VI.B.1.117), alludes to the specific meaning by which illegitimate offspring automatically become the head of the family.

Rather than gender bending, the importance of these legal terms is part of a larger framework about property rights, which in turn bears on genealogy as well as race. A term that Joyce appropriates and that is of interest here is 'emancipation' (VI.B.1.117) or 'mancipation', a concept that regulates the exchange of 'movable *res mancipi*' (*EB* XXIII, 523), that is, property *in manu* of the paterfamilias, which included land and houses and everything that belonged to it, such as rights of way, aqueducts, slaves and oxen, horses, mules and donkeys. Mancipation also included, at least in plebeian families who were excluded from confarreation, the sale of a woman to a man for a nominal price payable to her paterfamilias (*EB* XXIII, 531). Joyce's reading supports and inflects a narrative concern that was already present in the writing. 'The emancipated statues' that are sold by the auctioneers (*FW-R* 299.40; *FW* 386.5) highlight what is at stake – or rather obfuscated – in the conveyancing of Dublin's assets. Bringing into play the statue of 'Mrs Dana O'Connell', the Four appear to question the legitimacy of what is presented as legal conveyancing. The account of the horse race slips in the word 'cattleraiders' (*FW-R* 300.10–11; *FW* 387.2), an allusion to the *Táin Bó Cúailnge* (Cattle Raid of Cooley), but also to the economic impact of colonial practices.

The archive illuminates this subtext of what is partially obscured in the published text. Instead of 'Noord Amrikaans and Suid African cattleraiders' (*FW-R* 300.10–11; *FW* 387.2), the proofs of the *Transatlantic Review* read: 'horses and priesthunters from the Curragh and confusionaries ^and the authorities^ over from England and American ~~visitors~~ cattleraiders (so they say)' (Cornell-2; *JJA* 56:100). This brings to mind the 'Roastbeef for old England' (*U* 6.393–94) passage in 'Hades' and the Irish agricultural movement's concern over the export of produce. At the same, the Joyce notebook that provided material for this passage opens up a context in which history repeats itself: '101 battles | cattleraiders | Fomorians back as Firbolg' (VI.B.1.105). In its origins, Ireland was not one nation, but came about as the result of successive invasions and political countermeasures by early kings to unite the country under one ruler. Joyce's source for these notes is, in essence, a potted history of Ireland's early colonizers, which was included in *The Handbook of the Ulster Question* (1923), a Free State pamphlet on the socioeconomic, political and cultural impact of partition. The references are to the return, as the Firbolg, of the mythical Fomorians, who had fled Ireland after their defeat, and to the victory of Conn of the Hundred Battles, the High King, over the Picts. Once the 'dominant race in Ulster', the territory of the Picts reached as far south as Tara. In defeating Conan MacAirt at the Battle of Crinna *c.* AD 250, Conn pushed the Picts out of central Ireland and established 'the authority of the kings of Tara over all Ireland' (*Handbook* 1923, 2).[10] The word 'cattleraiders' does not derive directly from the source. Joyce creatively conflates the Irish epic – which tells of the stealing of the Donn Cúailnge, the Brown Bull of Cooley, from the cattle lords of Ulster by Queen Medb (Maeve) and King Aillil of Connaught – with the 'raids' of the third- and fourth-century Picts on the western coasts of Britain and Scotland; in Latin, the Irish were named 'Scotti', which is believed to be an old Celtic word for 'raiders' (*Handbook* 1923, 4). The 'gallowglasses' (binoculars) through which the 'fellow' in the 'grey half a tall hat' looks at the race/raids completes the pattern. Also taken from the *Handbook*, the 'galloglass', or 'Gall-oglaich' were foreign soldiers who came from the Norse settlement in Argyle between 1250 and 1600, introducing the idea of a standing army of well-trained soldiers (*Handbook* 1923, 9).

That Joyce took these notes on early Irish migrations from a political pamphlet on the new Irish border may be coincidence. Nevertheless, the source is more than just fortuitous. (Joyce was familiar with this aspect of early Irish history for sure.) Thus we need to wonder what associations Joyce was making – which brings us back to Roman law and Vico if we consider the 'migratories' (*FW-R* 297.24; *FW* 384.2) that bring their messages to Mamalujo. The 'sea' birds – 'seahawk, seagull, curlew and plover, kestrel and capercailzie' (*FW-R* 297.15; *FW* 383.16–17) – that scream their glee over the waves at the start of Chapter II.4 designate the 'auspices', the practice of bird divination.[11] The *auspices*, however, refer to all forms and customs by which the Romans sought to sanction legal decisions by divine approval, including 'the taking of the auspices' during the marriage ceremony (Vico 1948, 12; see also *EB* XXIII, 530). It would seem, therefore, that, like Shaun's postal mission, Mamalujo receive their history from 'on high' (*FW-R* 318.23; *FW* 410.1). As diviners, or proclaimers, the 'auspices' become an attribute of the Four. Joyce recorded the word 'auspices' in the context of other Vichian material:

---

[10] See Braslasu and Lernout (2021) for the annotations on this source.
[11] Mamalujo also practises tree divination: 'listening ... to the solans and the sycamores' (*FW-R* 297.20–3; *FW* 383.22–384.1).

⌐auspices⌐   heroes
gentiles   dark
Livius   middle
...
Sure not to do incest?
la venere incerta
⌐plebean
⌐patrician
⌐12 tables (VI.B.1.96–7)

Most of the notes are basic to Vico and fairly self-explanatory. In early Roman society, the people were divided into classes based on citizenship rights, but irrespective of 'ethnographic descent' (*EB* XXIII, 527). The patricians enjoyed all rights, including the right to marry, draw up wills and take part in legislative and judicial assemblies, the *curiate comitia*. The gentiles, or *gentes*, are family clans with a common name and, usually, a common ancestor; they held common property, had their own burial places, and enjoyed their own customs and legal statutes. The plebeians were non-gentile freemen, comprising mainly immigrants from racially different origins, who, unlike the *clientes* who were attached to a patron clan, remained independent; their social sphere was not organized by gentile laws, but, as craftsmen, they formed their own traditions and regulatory alliances. Vico uses the term 'gentile' for all indigenous people regardless of place (although in line with Western discourse, he does usually distinguish the gentiles from Jews and Muslims), but the context of Joyce's notes is clearly Roman. The Law of the Twelve Tables is the first codified legal system that formalizes relationships in Roman society, explicitly excluding the plebeians from the auspices.

Apart from the use of 'auspices', the words have a throwaway presence in Mamalujo. Johnny is, ironically, 'the patrician' (*FW-R* 300.23; *FW* 387.15), while the 'plebeians' (*FW-R* 300.4; *FW* 386.29) are part of a rowdy, lowlife bunch that run riot at the horse race. The Law of the Twelve Tables becomes the 'twelve tables' around which the Four are sitting, dozing and 'droning along' (*FW-R* 301.34–5; *FW* 389.1–3). However, the unused entry, 'Sure not to do incest? | la venere incerta', furnishes an angle on the chapter that is of great interest. As a term, 'la venere incerta', which loosely translates as *illegitimate wedlock*, is Vichian (Vico 1843, 63). It belongs to Vico's argument about the importance of the institution of marriage, for the family is the cornerstone of a civilized nation. Vico uses the term in the 1725 edition only; in the later edition of 1744, the term has become 'la Venere bestiale', a term by which Vico means incest, for its derivation from Orpheus's description of the foul beasts of the ancient forest 'among whom bestial venery was practiced by sons with mothers and by fathers with daughters' (Vico 1816, I, 198; 1948, 87).[12] While Vico's revision does not change the gist of his argument, the earlier version appears more strident in its elucidation of the reasons why dominant nations, and dominant religions, have supplanted primitive nations. Whereas the 1744 edition issues the warning that sexual corruption weakens nations, because it undermines the patrilineal system by which power and possessions are kept within the family, the earlier edition sounds more explicitly Christian. Vico's insistence on the unifying powers of a common religious language, and a common language generally by which laws can be explained and understood, binds people in one nation. (This is the case, he writes, with the Christian churches, but not with that of the Jews, Muslims and Gentiles [Vico 1843, 63].) Without a common language, parents cannot teach their children to fear for God who forbids venial sin. Therefore, the Law of the Twelve Tables regulates marriage by divine authority, not simply to avoid sin but also to prevent intermarriage between patricians and plebeians, as this too would weaken the genealogical hold over power and property.

Mamalujo's concern with the auctioneers selling off the best Dublin houses makes sense in terms of preserving family lineage and patrimony. (Significantly, the date of the auction is both shifting and unusually specific: 1132, 1169 or 1798 [*FW-R* 303.17–18; *FW* 391.2].) Yet the Four's gender change undermines the patriarchal logic of historiography and genealogy, as does the representation of 'Powerscout and Dona', HCE and ALP, as 'our first marents' (*FW-R* 30115; *FW* 388.15–16). But, above all, the Earwicker family's incestuous behaviour – HCE exposing himself to the girls, Shaun's sexual overtures to Issy, and the brothers' gazing up at ALP's vagina – receive new meaning as well. Their relationships are not just sexually and morally transgressive but also politically and economically, going against the grain of progressive nation-building. While Joyce's Vichian notes remained unused and so, at best, only part of the *Wake's* subtext, Chapter II.4 does point to HCE's sexual impropriety in the drowning of 'poor Dion Cassius Poosycomb': 'because it was most improper and most wrong, when he attempted (well, he was shocking poor in his health, he said, with the shingles falling of him)' (*FW-R* 303.35–8; *FW* 391.23–6). The impropriety is not actually mentioned, but (say no more) the innuendo is understood by the listeners: 'sure, he was only funning' (*FW-R* 304.9; *FW* 392.2–3).

---

[12] Joyce's source is likely a detailed commentary on the first edition from 1725, one that includes a comment on the text by Livy that Vico quoted just a few pages earlier (Vico 1843, 60).

The notes also provide a subtext for the inclusion of Tristan and Isolde. Even though Mamalujo and Tristan and Isolde were genetically linked – the main point of connection being the Four's witnessing Tristan and Isolde's kiss – the process by which Joyce folded part of the original Tristan and Isolde vignettes into the Mamalujo chapter is rather crude. His purpose appears to have been to further sexualize the historical language of Mamalujo. Johnny MacDougal, for instance, becomes 'nothing if not amorous' (*FW-R* 303.20; *FW* 391.5; see 47481-123; *JJA* 56:189), a phrase lifted from Tristan and Isolde, of Mrs Dowager Justice Squalchman, the androgynous judge presiding over the marriage court-cum-auction house.

The kiss functions as a primal scene. In the Tristan and Isolde legend it represents a point of no return. The accidental drinking of the love potion has irreparable consequences that leads to the lovers' deception of King Mark and their elopement from the Cornish court. For Joyce, the kiss represents the precise nexus in the archetypal love triangle between passion and betrayal. Connected with sexual transgression, the kiss was already part of the 'Mamalujo' narrative via another Irish commonplace, Dion Boucicault's *Arrah-na-Pogue* (1864), a play set during the 1798 Rebellion in which the heroine, Arrah Meelish, hides the rescue plan for her imprisoned foster-brother in her mouth and passes it to him with a kiss. Originally, Joyce had ended the Mamalujo material with an invocation to Tristan and Isolde. In the early manuscripts, the song that the Four sing at the end ('auld luke syne' [*FW-R* 309.15; *FW* 398.26]) is followed by the apostrophe 'Hear, Isolde la belle! Tristan, sad hero, hear!' (47481-4; *JJA* 56:35) and the 'Anna Domini' poem about a boisterous gallant seducing his girl (47481-24-25; *JJA* 56:62–3). But instead of attaching the Tristan and Isolde material at the end, Joyce works it into the middle of the chapter.

The position of the tale about the 'strapping fine young modern old ancient Irish prisscess' (*FW-R* 307.19; *FW* 396.7–8) thus intimates its symbolic function. The first intent is to make space, as the Revival did, for legend within history. For Yeats, Lady Gregory and other members of the Revival, legend, myth and folklore preserved an authentic past that could not be found in other historical sources. In casting these narratives as a medium through which the past can speak, the Revival thus also adumbrated a central tenet of cultural memory, which recognizes the important value of symbol and ritual as a means of accessing the past (Coser 1992, 2–3). Similarly, Vico posited that poetry first emerged in primitive cultures to give 'sense and passion to insensate things' as a way of dealing with the incomprehensible; in poetry are found 'the historical meanings' that are 'natural', and of equal value to the 'vulgar wisdom of the lawgivers', as opposed to the 'esoteric wisdom' of the philosophers (Vico 1948, 64, 108). Thus Vico was not only an important precursor to the work of cultural memory, his ideas about the value of the symbolical had an influence on Joyce. Specifically, Joyce associated the origins of the poetic languages, the mute languages of the wild animals, with Tristan and Isolde in his reading of the 1725 edition of the *Scienza Nuova*:

> CAPO XXV *Guisa come formassi la Favella Poetica che ci è giunta.* § In cotal guisa della *Lingua muta* de' bestioni di *Obbes*, semplicioni di *Grozio*, solitarj di *Pufendorfio* incominciati a venire all'Umanità, cominciossi tratto tratto a *formare la Lingua di ciascheduna antica nazione*, prima delle volgari presenti, *Poetica*; la quale dopo lungo correre di secoli si trovò appo i popoli primieri ciascuna in tutto il suo corpo nel quale ci provenne, composta di tre parti, come ora l'osserviamo, di tre *spezie diverse*.
>
> (Vico 1843, 225)[13]

In an unused note that was clearly of conceptual importance, Joyce recorded: 'lingua muta (bestioni) | (T & I)' (VI.B.2.132). Primeval and universal, the discourse of love is ascribed to the 'imaginative universals' (Vico 1948, 340), the first tier in the evolutionary system of language that characterizes Vico's understanding of cultural progress.

In the Irish tradition, poetry is an ancient form of knowledge and history. In *Finnegans Wake*, Joyce puts his own inflection on this tradition, heralding the days of yore, while evincing the contradictory forces in the national past. We see this at work in a passage from the Mamalujo chapter that alludes to the reign of Sitric Silkenbeard, the Scandinavian king of Dublin defeated by Brian Boru at the Battle of Clontarf in 1014: 'that time of the dynast days of old konning Soteric Sulkinbored ... in old Hungerford-on-Mudway, where I first met thee oldpoetryck flied from me' (*FW-R* 305.5; *FW* 393.7–10). The Four Old Men here think back to another before time when the Scandinavians dominated Dublin. Throughout the *Wake*, Joyce recognizes the importance of Scandinavian influence on Irish identity; it happens here by a negation of traditional Irish historiography in which the indigenous high king finally triumphed over the foreign invader. What is particularly significant is that Mamalujo view Silkenbeard's 'dynast days' as a period of stability that they re-create in poetry. The 'old poetry trick' is the

---

[13] 'The mode in which the poetic language that has come down to us was formed. §. In this mode, from the mute languages of Hobbes's great beasts, Grotius's simpletons and Pufendorf's solitary beings, after they had emerged into humanity, the poetic languages of the ancient nations gradually came to be formed before our present vulgar languages. Hence, after the long passage of the centuries, the whole corpus of the language of each of these first peoples was composed of three parts, each different in kind, as we can now see' (Vico, quoted in Braslasu and Henkes 2019b).

poem-as-history. In other words, Joyce alludes here to the 'dinnseanchas', the Irish form of genealogical poetry on the origins and symbolism of place names, as well as the practice of Irish antiquarians who derived historical understanding from the physical landscape (Hofheinz 1995, 69). But he also marries the Irish tradition of topographical writing commemorating and interpreting places and events with Vichian historiography rooted in the poetic languages of the ancient nations.

What follows is the recitation of a piece of 'poetry' in which Tristan addresses Isolde:

> theeuponthus ... eysolt of binnoculises memostinmust egotum sabcunsciously senses upers the deprofundity of multimathematical immaterialities wherebejubers in the pancosmic urge the allimmanence of that which Itself is Itself Alone (hear, O hear, Caller Errin!) exteriorises on this ourherenow plane in disunited solod, likeward and gushious bodies with (science, say!) perilwhitened passionpanting pugnoplangent intuitions of reunited selfdom ... in the higherdiminsional selfless Allself, theemeeng Narsty meetheeng Idoless.
> (*FW-R* 30.6.14–21; *FW* 394.29–395.2)

In one sense, Tristan's love poem is a rationalization of his love for Isolde, which did not, of course, come about naturally but through chemical means, after he accidentally drank the love potion ('science, say!'). As a reflection on the substance of love, the poem is, in fact, an esoteric-cum-pseudoscientific dithyramb on the creation of the cosmos and all it entails, emerging from the immanence of a unitary godhead, the materiality of the world created from the immateriality of his will. We are back to the hermeticists' obsession with unlocking the secret to the universe, or the origin of everything, which Stephen referenced in *Ulysses*. The reference in 'Itself Alone' to Sinn Féin (Ourselves Alone) also makes this a poem about the creation of a free and united Ireland. The catalyst, however, is the kiss. As a sexual union, the 'perilwhitened passionpanting ... of reunited selfdom' is a rejection of partition. In other words, Mamalujo's vision, voiced through the Tristan and Isolde legend, was never just one of the past but also of the future. At the chapter's end, the Earwicker children, standing in for the children of Ireland, are set free: 'The way is free. Their lot is cast' (*FW-R* 310.17; *FW* 399.33).

Reviving places

Tristan's creation poem has its correlative in a more down-to-earth phrase that registers Mamalujo's intent, and that of *Finnegans Wake* as a whole, as Revivalist: 'how our seaborn isle came into exestuance' (*FW-R* 300.21; *FW* 387.12). The concern with origins, moreover, is explicitly connected with a desire to make Ireland great again: 'Eringrowback' (*FW-R* 301.37; *FW* 389.4–5). Joyce left few periods or events from the Irish past unmentioned in *Finnegans Wake*, yet what is striking – and largely unnoticed – is the book's nostalgic tenor in representing a past that is remarkably, and perhaps paradoxically, idyllic. Yet the tenebrous world of the *Wake* finds an appropriate vehicle in the idyll whose settings exist in the twilight zone of reality. The book's preoccupation with 'dreams of yore' (*FW-R* 305.28; *FW* 393.36), its insistence on looking back to an unspoilt past, points to a deliberate conceit not unlike that of the Irish Revival and its celebration of the Irish land. It does so, too, in the awareness that the 'natural landscape of the county was irrevocably altered' (O'Callaghan 2014, 99). The citizen's complaint about the deforestation of Ireland in *Ulysses*, for instance, is countered in *Finnegans Wake* with a celebration of the trees of Ireland. What follows from this, however, is that the *Wake*'s treatment of history is as much about time as it is about space.

This final section will probe some of the idyllic and nostalgic features of *Finnegans Wake* by looking at Joyce's treatment of the landscape as well as his interest in eighteenth-century Dublin. The relevance of this time and place has also not been noted in the rich historicist readings of Joyce's final book. Nevertheless, the Irish eighteenth century, associated with the Parliament of Henry Grattan, marks for Joyce, as well as many Revival figures, a golden age of civil politics and public debate (Nolan 1995, 86). Yet the political ideals of the period, expressed in the right to Ireland's self-determination, were thwarted by the 1798 Rebellion and the abolition of the Irish Parliament. The Act of Union was Britain's retaliation and excuse for Ireland's inability to govern itself.

As is apparent from my earlier discussion of 1132 and origins, the book abounds with references to unspoilt landscapes and locations: 'she pulls a lane picture for us in a dreariodreama setting, glowing and very dividual, of old dumplan as she nosed it, a homelike cottage of elvanstone' (*FW-R* 63.30–3; *FW* 79.27–9); 'Vieus von DVbLIn ... the Turnpike under the Great Elm (with Mearingstone in Foreground' (*FW-R* 226.21–3; *FW* 293. 12–14); 'my little grey home in the west, in or about Mayo' (*FW-R* 372.1; *FW* 479.2–3); 'This seat of our city it is of all sides pleasant, comfortable and wholesome' (*FW-R* 419.39–40; *FW* 540.3–4). Some of these evocations echo the discourse of eighteenth-century travel writing or the visual language of seventeenth- and eighteenth-century landscape painting as it idealizes, or *idyllizes*, the scenery. Fittingly, a description of the topography of Dublin in Chapter I.1, hailed as 'how charmingly exquisite!'

(*FW-R* 10.37; *FW* 13.6), reminds the speaker of an engraving he has seen on the wall in HCE's pub; reality resembles representation. The opening of Chapter III.1 especially is noted for its picture-perfect setting:

> Methought as I was dropping asleep somepart in nonland of where's please (and it was when you and they were we) I heard at zero hour as 'twere the peal of vixen's laughter among midnight's chimes from out the belfry of the cute old speckled church tolling so faint a goodmantrue as nighthood's unseen violet rendered all animated greatbritish and Irish objects nonviewable to human watchers save 'twere perchance anon some glistery gleam darkling adown surface of affluvial flowandflow as again might seem garments of laundry reposing a leasward close at hand in full expectation. And as I was jogging along in a dream as dozing I was dawdling, arrah, methought broadtone was heard and the creepers and the gliders and the flivvers of the earthbreath and the dancetongues of the woodfires and the hummers in their ground all vociferated, echoating, *Shaun! Shaun! Post the post!* with a high voice and, O, the higher on high the deeper and low.
>
> (*FW-R* 313.17–29; *FW* 403.30–404.9)

The setting is Chapelizod, a suburb west of Dublin on the edge of Phoenix Park, which doubles as the Garden of Eden. In Joyce's imagination, the idyllic characteristics of this space are compounded with the settings in Sheridan LeFanu's *The House by the Churchyard* ([1863] 1899), which Joyce read (or re-read) in spring 1924 (VI.B.1.62-64).

Le Fanu's novel is a rather peculiar work, and not just for its gothic leanings. The novel is full of references to ghosts. But, as its mystery unfolds, *The House by the Churchyard* resolves any suggestion of supernatural activity when it turns out that Charles Archer, believed to be murdered, is alive and lives under the assumed of Paul Dangerfield. The narrative of this uncovering is, fittingly, framed around an unsettling conflict between idyll and modernity, between rural calm and ruination. Le Fanu's conceit in his depiction of eighteenth-century Chapelizod is making the place deliberately quaint and other. The narrator, Charles de Cresseron, reminds his reader several times that the events he is relating happened 'about a hundred years ago'; consequently, the customs, fashions and language of which he tells are now 'quite passed away' (Le Fanu [1863] 1899, 1). This deliberate eschewing of modernity is, on the one hand, a narratological device: as the narrator explains, technologies such as the telegraph and the railway that assisted Victorian police with the detection of crime were not available in 1767 (Le Fanu [1863] 1899, 238). On the other hand, and more directly relevant to the *Wake*, in setting the narrative in the eighteenth century, Le Fanu calls to mind the old social order in colonial Ireland and the hegemony of the Anglo-Protestant middle class that was irrevocably waning (see Mishler 2018, 172, 194).

But, while much of the quiet and calm of Chapelizod that de Cresseron remembered from his youth no longer existed, the quaintness of the setting is deceptive. The novel abounds in allusions to the idyllic landscape, such as this one:

> The morning was fine – the sun shone out with a yellow splendour – all nature was refreshed a pleasant smell – rose up from tree, and flower, and earth. The now dry pavement and all the row of village windows were glittering merrily – the sparrows twittered their lively morning gossip among the thick ivy of the old church tower – here and there the village cock challenged his neighbour with high and vaunting crow, and the bugle notes soared sweetly into the air from the artillery ground beside the river.
>
> (Le Fanu [1863] 1899, 15)

Not too dissimilar from Joyce's setting in *Finnegans Wake*, this pastoral view of Chapelizod is disrupted by the gruesome events and the duplicity of the characters. Not only is murder at the centre of the plot, the narrative expounds on a large range of crimes and misdemeanours: toxic pride (the duel between Cluffe and Puddock), false impersonation (Mary Matchwell poses as Mrs Nutter to claim her late husband's inheritance), medical malpractice and extortion (Surgeon Dillon charging 500 guineas to perform the questionable trepanning on Sturke) and attempted murder (Dangerfield seeking to eliminate Sturke to protect his secret).

The temporal and cultural displacement in Le Fanu as well as the disruption of the novel's pastoral world Joyce likely found compelling (Mishler 2018, 172, 177). His notes point sharply at the lost customs and language that Le Fanu's prologue dwells on (VI.B.1.63–4). In the passage quoted earlier from 'Night lessons', Joyce makes direct use of the old Chapelizod village as a 'remnant of the past' (Mishler 2018, 185):

> This Norman court at boundary of the ville, yon creepered tower of a church of Ereland, meet for true saints in worshipful assemblage, with our king's house of stone, belgroved of mulbrey, the still that was mill and Kloster that was Yeomansland, the ghastcold tombshape of the quick foregone on, the loftleaved elm Lefanunian above mansioned, each, every, all is for the retro-spectioner.
>
> (*FW-R* 208.4–10; *FW* 264.29–265.06)

Mishler (2018, 184) points out that, apart from incorporating the author's name, the passage loosely alludes to Le Fanu's topographic descriptions. Joyce's 'retrospectioner', according to Mishler, is Le Fanu's narrator, who looks back from the 1860s to 1767. He also looks at, or into, a spectral past whose contours are only vaguely visible. The historian as nostalgist, however, sees 'Ereland' (Ireland, as well as before land, from 'ere', *before, formerly* or *first* [*OED*]) not only as a land lost in time but also as a nation whose history and origins are multiple and contested.

The premodern landscape links with the traditional poetic response to landscape in dinnseanchas and aisling poetry. As Katherine O'Callaghan (2014, 108) has pointed out, the *Wake* follows the Irish tradition in which the landscape 'bear[s] witness to the past'. In one respect, Joyce pares back the physical landscape to its most rudimentary, mythological dimensions by portraying HCE as the giant interred in the landscape, ALP as the river, Shem and Shaun as the tree and stone on the riverbanks. At the same time, the *Wake* delights in using place names that are poetic and imaginary, part of an Irish landscape that reads like an ancient manuscript (Heaney 1980, 132). Most instances refer to actual places, albeit often in portmanteau form ('from Mullinahob and Peacockstown … Tankardstown … Raystown and Harlockstown … Cheeverstown … Loughlinstown and Nutstown … by the Boolies' [*FW-R* 77.12–18; *FW* 97.3–10]; 'Kong Gores Wood' [*FW-R* 269.18; *FW* 348.21. Others are legendary or mythological (the 'Woods of Fogloot'/'Woods of Foglut' [*FW-R* 371.37; *FW* 478.34]) or are made up ('Lucalizod' [*FW-R* 25.38; *FW* 32.16], 'Neuilands' [*FW-R* 269.13; *FW* 348.16].) The linguistic unfixing of place names in the *Wake* is not purely a game, however, but matches ancient topographical practices; the shifts, for instance, in Dublin's four historical appellations – Eblana, the Ford of the Hurdles, Baile Atha Cliath and Dublin – suggest a poetic licence in the naming of places.

Place, like time, is fluid in *Finnegans Wake*. The a/synchronicity of historical events finds its parallel in the telescoping of places into one another, from the 'doubling' of Dublin and Ireland (Dublin, Laurence County, Georgia [*FW-R* 3.7; *FW* 3.8]) and 'New South Ireland' (*FW-R* 62.38; *FW* 78.26) to Phoenix Park, which geographically encompasses Dublin, Ireland, Europe and the world. Other places are configured in topographic constellations, such as the twenty-nine Dublin churches (*FW-R* 469.27–34; *FW* 601.21–8). Far from being random, this preoccupation with location and dislocation is associated with Mamalujo, intimating a close connection between history, geography and memory: 'as question time drew nighing and the map of the souls' groupography rose in belief within their quarterings' (*FW-R* 370.10–11; *FW* 476.32–4).

Their 'souls' groupography', coincidentally, sounds like a form of psychogeography, the late twentieth-century preoccupation with unravelling place in psychological and geographical terms (see Debord 1956). Maps in *Finnegans Wake* function as a psychogeographic instrument to represent and come to terms with the past (although in orthodox *Wakean* fashion not always to good effect). Instead of individual experiences, however, maps capture the collective memory; they belong to the category of material objects that, in the theories of Maurice Halbwachs, generate the structural link that makes transgenerational collective memory possible (Halbwachs 1992, 234–5; Erll 2011, 18). The 'planet's melomap', for example, is a map of melodies that records the 'lay of the vilest bogeyer … the world has ever had to explain for' (*FW-R* 33.28–9; *FW* 42.15–16). (While the allusion is to 'The Ballad of Persse O'Reilly', the ballad as a type of folk song was celebrated as a gateway to an authentic past by Revivalists.) In 'Night lessons', the children learn to read maps using the compass to find the point α, ALP's vagina, the origin from which all life emanated (*FW-R* 221.29–222.1; *FW* 287.8–15).

But it is the 'relief map' (*FW-R* 439.11; *FW* 564.10) in Chapter III.4 that requires special consideration. The map describes the topography of Phoenix Park (and HCE's bum) in three-dimensional form and lists the prominent features in the landscape, the location of buildings, as well as the spot where HCE *relieved* himself. The map helps to lay bare the park as contested territory, unambiguously identified as 'this royal park' (*FW-R* 439.31; *FW* 564.35); the only buildings named are those of colonial power: the Viceregal Lodge and the Chief Secretary's Residence, which stand on either side of the Chesterfield Road that bisects the park. The genteel scenes in the park again echo those in *The House by the Churchyard* in which 'rustic cavalries' are out riding, enjoying 'pretty dears' and the leafy shade of the trees just outside Chapelizod. But beneath this idyllic scene is a dark undertone of violence. Mixing history and hysteria, the 'hystorical leavesdroppings' of the local amateur historian and guide, 'Sir Shamus Swiftpatrick, Archfieldchaplain of Saint Lucan's' (*FW-R* 439.29–30; *FW* 564.31–3), include the most atrocious events the park has ever seen: the murder of Lord Cavendish, the Chief Secretary for Ireland, by the Invincibles (*FW-R* 439.26–7; *FW* 564.29–30). In the same location, 'a scarlett pimparnell now mules the mound' (*FW-R* 439.26; *FW* 564.30), a sinister figure biding his time to commit 'feud fionghalian' (*FW-R* 439.27; *FW* 564.30), that is, murder.[14]

---

[14] McHugh (2006, 564) glosses Ir. 'fingail' as *fratricide*, but various sources give its meaning as the murder of a relative or 'kin-slaying' (Williams 2018, 264). The narrative is about Shaun's desire to usurp HCE.

Ultimately, Mamalujo's 'soul's groupography' – their attempt to write the history of the Irish race – falls apart. First of all, the 'relief map' is an ambivalent device. Mapping was a colonial tool introduced in Ireland during the Elizabethan period (O'Callaghan 2014, 99) and 'relief' was in short supply during the Famine because of Britain's intractable liberal trade policies. Earlier, the narrator points up the 'dimeshow advertisers [who] advance the temporal relief plea' (*FW-R* 130.2–3; *FW* 163.13–14) as a political sideshow offering opportunities for the gombeen men to improve themselves. Second, and more concretely, Mamalujo find themselves complete lost in the 'donkers' (*FW-R* 441.12; *FW* 566.31). The signpost (that is, the Wellington Monument) by which they try to orient themselves is no help at all because it defies accurate topography; not only are its distances warped, the sign points to itself, inverting all topographical logic. The landscape becomes its own nightmare.

However, there is counterpoint in this drama of the landscape, which constitutes a revival of place of sorts, and that is in the replanting of trees. Not coincidentally, the Phoenix Park relief map includes a tree, which is at once a symbol of hope (olive tree), wisdom (Ir. 'ollvav', *sage*) and life (virility): ''Tis a tree story. How olave, that firile, was aplantad in her liveside' (*FW-R* 439.20–1; *FW* 564.21–2). The presence of this tree in *Finnegans Wake* is archetypal. It designates, on the one hand, the sexual economy of the Earwicker family. The conjugal relations between HCE and ALP are, of course, the narrative focus in Chapter III.3, but it is the 'quicken bole' with its 'triliteral roots' (*FW-R* 392.5–18; *FW* 504.25–505.4) or 'overlisting eshtree' (*FW-R* 391.17; *FW* 503.30) that, in its symbolic overdetermination (Fordham 2007, 239), provides the gnostic locus of their wedding. On the other hand, the tree in *Finnegans Wake* is (so to speak) deeply rooted in Irish history. In 'Cyclops', the reason why John Wyse Nolan and the citizen bewail the loss of Irish forests at the hand of colonial settlers is because of the spiritual importance of the tree in Ireland; traditionally safeguarded by the ancient bardic order, the tree was a site of 'indigenous knowledge and practices' (O'Callaghan 2014, 99). Furthermore, systematic felling to provide fuel and timber for Queen Elizabeth's navy also had an economic impact, harming native industries that relied on wood (Foster 1989, 6). Yet deforestation continued well into the nineteenth century. As the successive Land Acts of the 1870s and 1880s effected a socioeconomic revolution, outgoing landlords saw in timber a way to make some quick cash before departing, while former tenants focused their activity on increasing food production (Magner 2011, 4). By 1904, when only 1 per cent of the land was covered in forest, policy was slowly changing towards preservation and reforestation; at the same time, however, the felling of trees to create land for farming on former estates was continuing unabated (Magner 2011, 1, 5; Keenan 2006, 75-6).

An early note evokes the once-luscious forests of Hibernia, 'Hib. forested' (VI.B.2.157), and does so in the context of aisling poetry. Joyce's source is an essay on 'Celtic nature poetry' in Alfred Perceval Graves' *Irish Literary and Musical Studies* (1913) (see Henkes 2014a, 2014b; Braslasu and Henkes 2019b). The *Wake* personifies the fear of the ancient trees at the prospect of their eradication: 'All the trees in the wood they trembold ... when they heard the stoppress from Domday's Erewold' (*FW-R* 458.20-2; *FW* 588.32-4). In 1934, Joyce read and took extensive notes from a short scientific paper by H.M. Fitzpatrick called 'The Trees of Ireland – Native and Introduced', published in 1933 by the Royal Dublin Society (see Rose 1995, 150-68). This resulted in a symbolic planting of trees in *Finnegans Wake*, offsetting the wrongs of history, in a way that is less ironic than the 'tree marriage' passage in 'Cyclops' (see O'Callaghan 2014, 109). One might think of the trees in *Finnegans Wake* in the way Joyce included rivers in the Anna Livia chapter: to make his book lusher and more verdant, like the ancient country.

Although coming fairly late, Joyce had been interested in trees much earlier in the book's composition history.[15] Apart from the oak, the two trees that feature regularly in *Finnegans Wake* are the ash and the elm. The mountain ash (also known as rowan or quicken) belongs to the noble trees, the highest class in the Old Irish Tree list of the Brehon Laws (Magner 2011, 2). It has sacred properties, associated with, among others, fertility. As I alluded to earlier, Joyce uses the ash as an archetypal symbol; the 'quickenbole' is the 'ouragan of spaces' (*FW-R* 391.35; *FW* 504.14), the origin of species (the locus of the original marriage) as well as the prime space in which all geography and history are contained. The Earwicker children inhabiting the 'preeminent giant' (*FW-R* 391.37; *FW* 504.15) act out another primal scene. While the girls play family (their 'woody babies' are growing up in its branches [*FW-R* 392.3; *FW* 504.22]), the boys re-create their vision of ALP's symbol/vagina in II.2, 'climbing to her crotch for the origin of spices' (*FW-R* 392.7-8; *FW* 504.27-8). The elm, by contrast, is a tree of a lesser order, belonging to the class of commoners; it is mentioned more frequently in the *Wake* as a fixture in the landscape. Among others, the 'stalworth elm' in Le Fanu's Chapelizod, which 'has not grown an inch these hundred years' (Le Fanu [1863] 1899, 3), appears as 'the loftleaved elm Lefanunian abovemansioned'

---

[15] An index from an unidentified source on trees in VI.B.1.61-6, for example, lists different kinds of wood used in the manufacturing of common products, from gunstocks to toothpicks.

in the passage I quoted earlier from Chapter II.2 (*FW-R* 208.9; *FW* 265.4-5). Significantly, the elm is also the tree associated with Shaun.

Joyce's reading of Fitzpatrick's paper may not seem hugely significant; he raided the paper for names of trees, which he then placed in his text in four separate passages (see Rose 1995, 154-5).[16] He was, however, building on pre-existing thematic concerns as he strategically incorporated the Fitzpatrick material to link the *Wakean* family with the pre/colonial landscape. True to the subtitle of Fitzpatrick's paper, 'Native and Introduced', the first passage (*FW-R* 79.31-4; *FW* 100.11) suggests HCE as the invader; to the native oak and 'noble fir', he is the 'liquidamber' and 'balsam poplar', trees that were artificially introduced (see Fitzpatrick 1933, 598-9). But, as Fitzpatrick makes clear, Ireland's mild climate, and in many places its rich limestone soil ('Limestone Road' [*FW-R* 79.33; *FW* 100.13]), make the country suitable to the cultivation of many non-native species. Through Joyce's eyes, we can read this as an allegory of Ireland's pliancy in absorbing foreign influences. The second passage (*FW-R* 127.11-26; *FW* 159.34-160.16) continues this theme in Shaun's own disquisition, in his guise as Professor Jones, on the 'genus' of certain species, their classification and origin. The passage is a clear pastiche of Fitzpatrick's prose. Shaun's purpose appears to be to declare 'Alderman Whitebeam is oaky-o', that is, HCE is OK/like an oak, Ireland's sacred tree. His speech is concerned with keeping 'its boles clean' and 'a pure stand' (deriving from Fitzpatrick's description of the common yew tree's 'clean bole', which makes them decorative in formal gardens, and the 'pure stand' of the balsam fir, that is, not mixed with other types of conifer [1933, 335, 605]), but again many of the trees he mentions are imports. Shaun's discourse, furthermore, slips into the overtly sexual ('pure stand', 'as plane as a lodgepole', 'olivetian') highlighting HCE's virility and reproductive prowess ('those selfsown seedlings', from Fitzpatrick's observation about the self-proliferation of the Monterey cypress, introduced around 1838 [1933, 161]). The third passage is Maidens' prayer passage in Chapter II.1, a counterpart to Shaun's Lenten Sermon in Chapter III.3. The Issy girls promise to look after 'what's nicest and boskiest of timber trees' (*FW-R* 135.37-8; *FW* 235.15). Their thanksgiving, however, is an admission of sexual promiscuity, as they promise to write 'lovesick letterines' (*FW-R* 186.3; *FW* 235.22) while exposing themselves to voyeurs in the garden. Also in II.1, the final passage (*FW-R* 194.39-195.8; *FW* 246.36-247.11) is only very short, with just two borrowings from Fitzpatrick; it introduces Shem as

---

[16] Joyce's notes from Fitzpatrick are in VI.B.36.206 and VI.B.46.120x-121. The first page, 120x, is a missing leaf following p. 120 reconstructed by Rose (see 1995, 156-62).

'the chastenot coulter', combining chestnut with Coulter, a reference to Thomas Coulter (1793–1843), the Irish botanist noted for the specimens of rare fir and pine trees that he collected in California. The element that links the four passages is fertility through sexual promiscuity, which adds a layer of irony to the pious nationalist treatments of the trees/forests of Ireland.

The Joycean genome

Whether it is Ireland's ancient forests or the eighteenth-century Dublin landscape, Joyce's treatment of topography in *Finnegans Wake* once again involves bringing 'prehistoric scenes' back to mind (*FW-R* 298.40–299.1; *FW* 385.19). As an expressive mode, nostalgia is important in Joyce's final work to represent the past. This is not to say that nostalgia is treated without irony. Like no other work in Irish literature before or since, the *Wake* enacts the messy, contested national past. The book neither imagines a perfect national past, nor projects an ideal vision about the future state of Ireland. As such, the disquieting forces behind the nightmare of history remain real. Nonetheless, the *Wake* highlights at every turn just how *present* the past is. The *Wake* is a Revivalist work by making the cultural desire for origins a central conceit, even if it enacts the impossibility of uncovering those origins. Its failure to do so has its parallel in Stephen's inability to fly by the nets of language, nation and religion. Not the outcome, but the process is important. The *Wake*'s aesthetic and political value exists in bringing this dichotomy to the fore. All of Joyce's work performs such an anatomy of the conditions that made Ireland what it was during Joyce's lifetime. Frequently, this anatomy goes against the grain of conservative strands within the Irish Revival. On the one hand, Joyce was intent on upending nationalist pieties. On the other, he creatively sought the means to see Ireland differently, beginning with *Chamber Music*. His verse offered resistance to conventional Irish modes of expression, yet it is also quintessentially Irish in that it connects with the tradition, and nostalgic tone, of the come-all-you. *Exiles* and certain stories in *Dubliners* redefined Irish identity in terms of the realities of the Irish diaspora, seeking to revise what it meant to be 'native'.

Dubliners has not featured extensively in this book, but its stories are complicit in upending the nationalist pieties that Joyce lambasts in *Stephen Hero* and *A Portrait*. Joyce's disdain for the people of Dublin, described with an economy of style and naturalistic frankness, serves (as he said) a moral purpose; its focus are the socioeconomic realities that underpin life in Ireland of which the exile theme is only one symptom. In Joyce's non-fiction, and later in *Ulysses*, questions about political economy show Joyce's alignment with the practical voices in the Irish Revival who defend socioeconomic self-reliance as a means to gaining political emancipation.

But before Joyce took this public turn, he explored a personal path. The manner in which he transformed *Stephen Hero* into *A Portrait* is crucial to our understanding of how he came to see the question of identity. The revisionism of *Exiles* became the core of his autobiographical fiction. As Joyce explored the edges of what counts as an authentic Irish experience, he turned to alternative traditions – one European, the other medieval and scholastic – to formulate an aesthetic theory that was at once rarefied and effective in explaining how 'the reality of experience' (*P* 253) is transformed into a work of art that meaningfully addresses 'the interminable ambivalence involved in defining national identity in linguistic terms' (Castle 2001, 198) as well as cultural terms. Observation, imagination and memory are key components in Stephen's aesthetic theory and praxis as well as in Joyce's notetaking with which the theory is closely correlated.

Where the early fiction articulated a subjective position centred on the artist whose ambition it is to rise above the conditions that made him, *Ulysses* expresses scepticism that such an ambition could ever be realized. But while *Ulysses* registers this impossibility, Joyce provided Stephen with an expanded set of intellectual tools – theosophy and the philosophy of Otto Weininger among others – to probe his cultural and political environment. Joyce's own probing of his environment took a turn as well. Before *Ulysses*, his notetaking had intermittently turned to Irish subject matter; now his research of Irish history became more prominent and sustained. The result was a novel in which the past is very much present – a novel that also shows the vestiges of a cultural memory project. Its action takes place in the recent past. It undoubtedly shows a modern Dublin, but also a Dublin suspended in time, re-created from memory and external sources; certainly, in 1922, Irish readers would have looked at 1904 as a before time. In a similar way, *Ulysses*' characters, Stephen among them most prominently, shape a collective conscience by engaging, individually and collectively, in remembering the past. But where memory is intangible, remembering is a concrete (if involuntary) act that takes place in a tangible sociocultural context. Consequently, 'versions of the past change with every recall, in accordance with the changed present situation' (Erll 2011, 8). It is thus that *Finnegans Wake*, concerned with the twinned notions of remembering and forgetting (Erll 2011, 8–9), is a cultural memory project par excellence.

It is also thus that Joyce's work, especially when we consider its genealogy, is a cultural project. The nature of Joyce's engagement with the historical and cultural legacy of Ireland only becomes truly apparent when we look at his work not as a unifying statement about the conditions that produced it, but as a changing and changeable response that evolved over time. Each of the preceding chapters delineate a stage in the forging of the uncreated conscience of the Irish race: a project that explored the creation of a culturally, politically and economically emancipated Ireland. That project reached its high point (although not its millenarian end point) in *Finnegans Wake*. The ideological value of Joyce's work does not lie in his vision of a future Ireland, but in the mechanisms of how a nation's self-image is made. Cultural historians call this collective process 'cultural memory'. This book calls it 'cultural genetics' to evince how culture and the literary work intersect in the making of that work. Within the notes and drafts of Joyce's work, we find not only the genetic codes of his aesthetic creations but also those of his engagement with the world around him.

Bibliography

Note: Joyce's works in the editions listed below are referenced in-text according to the page/line number conventions that are in standard use in Joyce studies, that is, page numbers for *D*, *SH*, *P*, *E*, *Letters I-III*, *PSW* and *OCPW*; chapter and line number for *U*; page and line number for *FW-R* and *FW*; and volume and page number for *JJA*. Manuscripts are additionally cited using the cataloguing convention/shelfmark of the holding institution, except for the Buffalo Notebooks. These are referenced with their Buffalo catalogue number and notebook page number (e.g. VI.B.10.91) when the text is quoted from the Brepols edition (Joyce 2001–2004) or from *JJA* when no edited version exists. All transcriptions are my own (again with exception of the Buffalo Notebooks included in the Brepols edition) and may differ from previous transcriptions published in Scholes and Kain (1965), Joyce (2018) and elsewhere. Manuscripts from the National Library of Ireland collections are available online at https://catalogue.nli.ie/Collection/vtls000194606/CollectionList (Joyce Papers 2002) and http://catalogue.nli.ie/Record/vtls000252560 (Pre-'Work in Progress': *Finnegans Wake* Drafts). The Joyce Correspondence (Joyce 2021) and Yeats Intelex letters (Yeats 2002) are cited in the text with their database number. All URLs in the bibliography as well as those in the text correctly point to live websites at the time of going to press. For Joyce's personal library, I have consulted the LibraryThing James Joyce Legacy Library at www.librarything.com/legacylibraries/profile/JamesJoyceLibrary.

A.C.H. 1919. 'Chamber Music – Old and New'. *Poetry: A Magazine of Verse* 14 (May): 98–103.
Allen, Nicholas and Terence Brown. 2011. 'Publishing after Partition, 1922-30', in Hutton and Walsh, pp. 70–88.
Annals of the Four Masters. n.d. Comp. by Emmy Ryan, in *CELT: Corpus of Electronic Texts* (Cork: University College Cork), https://celt.ucc.ie/published/T100005B.html.
Assmann, Jan. 1995. 'Collective Memory and Cultural Identity', *New German Critique*, 65: 125–33.
Atherton, James S. 1959. *The Books at the Wake: A Study of Literary Allusions in James Joyce's Finnegans Wake* (Carbondale, IL: Southern Illinois University Press).

Aubert, Jacques. 1991. 'Réflexions sur Joyce et l'occultisme', in *Studies on Joyce's Ulysses*, eds Jacqueline Genet and Wynne Hellegouarc'h (Caen: Presses universitaires de Caen), pp. 119–29, https://doi.org/10.4000/books.puc.240.

Barry, Kevin. 2000. 'Introduction', in Joyce 2000, ix–xxxii.

Bate, Walter Jackson. 1961. *From Classic to Romantic: Premises of Taste in Eighteenth Century England* (New York: Harper Torchbooks).

Beal, Peter. 2008. *A Dictionary of English Manuscript Terminology, 1450–2000* (Oxford: Oxford University Press).

Benstock, Bernard. 1984. '*Exiles*', in *A Companion to Joyce Studies*, eds Zack Bowen and James F. Carens (Westport, CT: Greenwood Press), pp. 361–86.

Benstock, Bernard. 1985. *James Joyce* (New York: Frederick Ungar Publishing Co.).

Berensmeyer, Ingo, Gert Buelens and Marysa Demoor. 2019. 'Introduction', in *The Cambridge History of Literary Authorship*, eds Ingo Berensmeyer, Gert Buelens and Marysa Demoor (Cambridge: Cambridge University Press), pp. 1–10.

Bernecker, Sven. n.d. 'Memory Knowledge', *ProtoSociology: An International Journal and Interdisciplinary Project*, www.protosociology.de/Download/Bernecker-Memory.pdf, pp. 1–15.

Bielenberg, Andy. 2009. *Ireland and the Industrial Revolution: The Impact of the Industrial Revolution on Irish Industry, 1801–1922* (London: Routledge).

Braslasu, Viviana-Mirela and Robbert-Jan Henkes. 2019a. 'From Luther to Steiner and the Scienza Nuova in Notebook VI.B.7', *GJS* 19, www.geneticjoycestudies.org/articles/GJS19/GJS19_Braslasu_Henkes.

Braslasu, Viviana-Mirela and Robbert-Jan Henkes. 2019b. '*Finnegans Wake* Notebook VI.B.2 Nativities, August-September 1923', *GJS* 19, www.geneticjoycestudies.org/articles/GJS19/GJS19_Henkes_Braslasu.

Braslasu, Viviana-Mirela and Robbert-Jan Henkes. 2019c. 'The Lost Notebook VI.D.2: A Preliminary Digital Edition', *GJS*, www.geneticjoycestudies.org/articles/GJS19/GJS19_Henkes_Braslasu.

Braslasu, Viviana-Mirela and Geert Lernout. 2021. 'Source Emendations in *Gem Thief*, Notebook VI.B.1: *Topography of Ireland* and *Handbook of the Ulster Question*', *GJS* 21, www.geneticjoycestudies.org/static/issues/GJS21/GJS21_Braslasu_Lernout_1.pdf.

Brown, Richard. 1985. *James Joyce and Sexuality* (Cambridge: Cambridge University Press).

Budgen, Frank. 1972. *James Joyce and the Making of Ulysses and Other Writings* (London: Oxford University Press).

Bury, John B. 1905. *The Life of St. Patrick and His Place in History* (London: Macmillan).

Bushell, Sally. 2009. *Text as Process: Creative Composition in Wordsworth, Tennyson, and Dickinson* (Charlottesville, VA: University of Virginia Press).

Callanan, Frank. 2010. 'James Joyce and the *United Irishman*, Paris 1902-3', *Dublin James Joyce Journal*, 3: 51–106.

Campbell, Mary. 1988. *Lady Morgan: The Life and Times of Sydney Owenson* (London: Pandora Press).
Campbell, Matthew. 2012. 'The Unconsortable Joyce: *Chamber Music*', in Conner, 51–77.
Castle, Gregory. 2001. *Modernism and the Celtic Revival* (Cambridge: Cambridge University Press).
The Catholic Encyclopedia. 1908. (New York: Robert Appleton Company), www.newadvent.org/cathen/.
Collison Black, R.D. 1960. *Economic Thought and the Irish Question, 1817–1870* (Cambridge: Cambridge University Press).
Colum, Mary. 1947. *Life and the Dream* (Garden City, NY: Doubleday).
Colum, Mary. 2013. *The Selected Works*, ed. Denise A. Ayo, http://marycolum.com.
Colum, Padraic. 1922. 'With James Joyce in Ireland', *New York Times*, 11 June, 52.
Colum, Mary and Padraic. 1959. *Our Friend James Joyce* (London: Victor Gollancz).
Conner, Marc C. 2012. 'The Poetry of James Joyce Reconsidered', in *The Poetry of James Joyce Reconsidered*, ed. Marc C. Conner (Gainesville, FL: University Press of Florida), pp. 1–32.
Coser, Lewis A. 1992. 'Introduction: Maurice Halbwachs, 1877–1945', in Halbwachs, 1–34.
Coyne, William P. 1902. *Ireland: Industrial and Agricultural* (Dublin: Browne and Nolan).
Crispi, Luca. 2009. 'A Commentary on James Joyce's National Library of Ireland "Early Commonplace Book", 1903–1912 (MS 36,639/02/A)', *GJS*, 9, www.geneticjoycestudies.org/articles/GJS9/GJS9_Crispi.
Crispi, Luca. 2010. 'Reading and Writing Ireland's Past and Future: James Joyce (1882–2012)', *The Stinging Fly*, 17(2): 53–61.
Crispi, Luca. 2011. 'A First Foray into the National Library of Ireland's Joyce Manuscripts: Bloomsday 2011', *GJS*, 11, www.geneticjoycestudies.org/articles/GJS11/GJS11_Crispi.
Crispi, Luca and Sam Slote (eds). 2007. *How Joyce Wrote Finnegans Wake: A Chapter-by-Chapter Genetic Guide* (Madison, WI: University of Wisconsin Press).
Crowley, Ronan. 2015. 'Things Actually Said: On Some Versions of Joyce's and Yeats's First Meeting', in McCourt, 31–53.
Crowley, Ronan and Dirk Van Hulle (eds). 2016. *New Quotatoes: Joycean Exegenesis in the Digital Age* (Leiden: Brill Rodopi).
Curran, C.P. 1968. *James Joyce Remembered* (London: Oxford University Press).
Davis, Graham. 2000. 'The Irish in Britain, 1818–1939', in *The Irish Diaspora*, ed. Andrew Bielenberg (Harlow: Longman), pp. 19–36.
Deane, Vincent. 2001a. 'Introduction to VI.B.3', in Joyce 2001–2004, 4–13.
Deane, Vincent. 2001b. 'Introduction to VI.B.33', in Joyce 2001–2004, 4–20.
De Biasi, Pierre-Marc. 1996. 'What Is a Literary Draft? Toward a Functional Typology of Genetic Documentation', *Yale French Studies*, 89: 26–58.

De Biasi, Pierre-Marc. 2011. *Génétique des textes* (Paris: CNRS Éditions).

Debord, Guy. 1956. 'Theory of the Dérive', trans. Ken Knabb. *Situationist National Online*. www.cddc.vt.edu/sionline/si/theory.html.

Debray-Genette, Raymonde. 1977. 'Génétique et poétique: Esquisse de méthode', *Littérature*, 28: 19–39.

Deming, Robert H. (ed.). 2007. *James Joyce: The Critical Heritage*, 2 vols (London: Routledge).

Deppman, Jed. 1995. 'Hallow'd Chronicles and Exploytes of King Rodericke O'Conor from Joyce's Earliest Draftes to the End of Causal Historie', in Hayman and Slote, 179–202.

Deppman, Jed. 2007. 'A Chapter in Composition: Chapter II.4', in Crispi and Slote, 304–46.

Dictionary of Irish Biography. n.d. Eds James McGuire and James Quinn. Cambridge: Cambridge University Press; Dublin: Royal Irish Academy, https://dib.cambridge.org.

Donoghue, Denis. 1986. *We Irish: Essays on Irish Literature and Society* (Berkeley, CA: University of California Press).

Downes, Gregory. 2002. James Joyce, Catholicism and Heresy: With Specific Reference to Giordano Bruno, PhD thesis, University of St Andrews.

Eglinton, John. 1906. *Bards and Saints* (Dublin: Maunsel & Co.).

Eglinton, John and Frederick Ryan. 1904. 'Introductory', *Dana: A Magazine of Independent Thought*, 1(1), 1–4.

Eliot, T.S. 2014. 'Tradition and the Individual Talent', in *The Perfect Critic, 1919–1926*, eds Anthony Cuda and Ronald Schuchard, vol. 2: *The Complete Prose of T. S. Eliot: The Critical Edition* (Baltimore, MD: Johns Hopkins University Press; London: Faber and Faber), pp. 105–114.

Ellis, Havelock. 1905. *Studies in the Psychology of Sex: Sexual Selection in Man* (Philadelphia: F. A. Davis).

Ellmann, Richard. 1950. 'Joyce and Yeats', *Kenyon Review*, 12: 618–38.

Ellmann, Richard. 1954. *The Identity of Yeats* (London: Macmillan).

Ellmann, Richard. 1967. *Eminent Domain: Yeats among Wilde, Joyce, Pound, Eliot and Auden* (New York: Oxford University Press).

Ellmann, Richard. 1982. *James Joyce*, rev. edn (Oxford: Oxford University Press).

Encyclopædia Britannica. 1910–11. 11th edn. 29 vols (Cambridge: At the University Press).

Erll, Astrid. 2011. *Memory in Culture*, trans. Sara B. Young (Basingstoke: Palgrave Macmillan).

Fairhall, James. 1993. *James Joyce and the Question of History* (Cambridge: Cambridge University Press).

Falc'her-Poyroux, Erick. 2014. 'The Great Irish Famine Songs', *Revue Française de Civilisation Britannique/French Journal of British Studies*, 19(2): 157–72, https://journals.openedition.org/rfcb/277.

Fargnoli, A. Nicholas and Michael Gillespie. 2016. 'Introduction', in Joyce 2016, 1–14.

Fellowes, Edmund Horace. 1921. *The English Madrigal Composers* (Oxford: Clarendon Press).

Ferrer, Daniel. 1985. 'The Freudful Couchmare of /\d: Joyce's Notes on Freud and the Composition of Chapter XVI of "Finnegans Wake"', *JJQ*, 22: 367–82.

Fitzgerald, William George. 1923. *The Voice of Ireland* (Dublin: Virtue and Co.).

Fitzpatrick, Benedict. 1921. *Ireland and the Making of Britain* (New York City: Funk & Wagnalls).

Fitzpatrick, H.M. 1933. 'The Trees of Ireland – Native and Introduced', *Scientific Proceedings of the Royal Dublin Society*, 20(41): 597–656.

Flood, J.M. 1917. *Ireland: Its Saints and Scholars* (Dublin: Talbot Press).

Flynn, Catherine. 2019. *James Joyce and the Matter of Paris* (Cambridge: Cambridge University Press).

Fordham, Finn. 2007. *Lots of Fun at Finnegans Wake: Unravelling Universals* (Oxford: Oxford University Press).

Foster, R.F. 1989. *Modern Ireland, 1600–1972* (London: Penguin).

Foster, R.F. 1993. *Paddy and Mr Punch: Connections in Irish and English History* (London: Allen Lane, The Penguin Press).

Foster, R.F. 1998. *W.B. Yeats: A Life. I: The Apprentice Mage* (Oxford: Oxford University Press).

Fox, Brian. 2019. 'Sots, Songs, and Stereotypes: 1916, the Fighting Irish, and the Irish American Nationalism in *Finnegans Wake*', *JJQ*, 56(1/2): 45–61.

Frawley, Oona. 2014. 'Introduction: James Joyce, Cultural Memory, and Irish Studies', in Frawley and O'Callaghan, 1–9.

Frawley, Oona and Katherine O'Callaghan. 2014. *James Joyce and Cultural Memory*, vol. 4, eds Oona Frawley and Katherine O'Callaghan (Syracuse, NY: Syracuse University Press).

Freitag, Barbara. 1997. 'From George Moore to Brian Moore: Irish Writers Making a Fetish of Exile', in *Exiles and Migrants: Thresholds in European Culture and Society*, ed. Anthony Coulson (Brighton: Sussex Academic Press), pp. 72–82.

FWEET. n.d. *Finnegans Wake* Extensible Elucidation Treasury, comp. by Raphael Slepon. fweet.org.

Garratt, Robert F. 1989. *Modern Irish Poetry: Tradition and Continuity from Yeats to Heaney* (Berkeley, CA: University of California Press).

Garratt, Robert F. 2014. 'History and Trauma in Joyce's *Ulysses*', in Frawley and O'Callaghan, 27–45.

Geertz, Clifford. 1973. *The Interpretation of Cultures: Selected Essays* (New York: Basic Books).

Geheber, Philip Keel. 2015. 'A Return to Revivalist Myth in *Finnegans Wake*', in *The Power of Form: Recycling Myths*, eds Ana Raquel Fernandes, José Pedro Serra and Rui Carlos Fonseca (Cambridge: Cambridge Scholars Publishing), pp. 170–83.

Geheber, Philip Keel. 2016. 'Assimilating Shem into the Plural Polity: Burrus, Casseous, and Irish Free State Dairy Production', in *Along the Krommerun: Selected Papers from the Utrecht James Joyce Symposium*, eds Onno Kosters, Tim Conley and Peter de Voogd (Leiden: Brill), pp. 127–39.
Gibbons, Luke. 2015. *Joyce's Ghosts: Ireland, Modernism, and Memory* (Chicago: University of Chicago Press).
Gibson, Andrew. 2002. *Joyce's Revenge: History, Politics, and Aesthetics in Ulysses* (Oxford: Oxford University Press).
Gibson, Andrew. 2013. *The Strong Spirit: History, Politics, and Aesthetics in the Writings of James Joyce, 1898–1915* (Oxford: Oxford University Press).
Gibson, Andrew and Len Platt. 2006a. Introduction, in Gibson and Platt, 1–29.
Gibson, Andrew and Len Platt (eds). 2006b. *Joyce, Ireland and Britain* (Gainesville, FL: University of Florida Press).
Gifford, Don. 1982. *Joyce Annotated: Notes for Dubliners and A Portrait of the Artist as a Young Man*, 2nd edn (Berkeley, CA: University of California Press).
Gifford, Don and Robert J. Seidman. 1989. *Ulysses Annotated: Notes for James Joyce's Ulysses* (Berkeley, CA: University of California Press).
Gilbert, Stuart. 1961. *James Joyce's Ulysses: A Study* (New York: Vintage).
Gorman, Herbert. 1949. *James Joyce: A Definitive Biography* (London: John Lane, The Bodley Head).
Gregory, Lady. 1970. *Gods and Fighting Men: The Story of the Tuatha de Danaan and of the Fianna of Ireland* (Gerrards Cross: Colin Smythe).
Gribbon, H.D. 2012. 'Economic and Social History, 1850–1921', in *Ireland under the Union, II, 1870–1921*, ed. W.E. Vaughan, vol. 6: *A New History of Ireland* (Oxford: Oxford University Press), pp. 260–356.
Hackett, Francis. 1918. *Ireland: A Study in Nationalism* (New York: Huebsch).
Hackett, Fred H. and Ernest A. Girvin. 1884. *Pure English: A Treatise on Words and Phrases, or Practical Lessons in the Use of Language* (San Francisco, CA: Samuel Carson; New York: C.T. Dillingham).
Halbwachs, Maurice. 1980. *The Collective Memory* (New York: Harper Colophon Books).
Halbwachs, Maurice. 1992. *On Collective Memory*, ed. Lewis A. Coser (Chicago, IL: University of Chicago Press).
Hall, Stuart. 1999. 'Cultural Studies and its Theoretical Legacies', in *The Cultural Studies Reader*, ed. Simon During, 2nd edn (London: Routledge), pp. 97–109.
Handbook of the Ulster Question: Issued by the North Eastern Boundary Commission. 1923. (Dublin: Stationery Office).
Hart, Clive. 1962. *Structure and Motif in Finnegans Wake* (Evanston, IL: Northwestern University Press).
Hartmann, Martin. 1896. *Metrum und Rhythmus: Die Entstehung der arabischen Versmasse* (Giessen: J. Ricker).
Hayman, David. 1990. *The 'Wake' in Transit* (Ithaca, NY: Cornell University Press).
Hayman, David. 1999. 'Epiphanoiding', in Slote and Van Mierlo, 27–41.

Hayman, David. 2007. 'Male Maturity or the Public Rise & Private Decline of HC Earwicker', in Crispi and Slote, 250–303.
Hayman, David and Sam Slote. (eds). 1995. *Probes: Genetic Studies in Joyce* (Amsterdam: Rodopi).
Heaney, Seamus. 1980. *Preoccupations: Selected Prose, 1968–1978* (London: Faber and Faber).
Henkes, Robbert-Jan. 2011. 'On the Verge of the *Wake*: Joyce's Reading in Notebook VI.B.10', *Joyce Studies Annual*, 1: 122–61.
Henkes, Robbert-Jan. 2014a. '2 Weeks in the Life of James Joyce as Gleaned from his 1923 Notebook VI.B.2 Nativities', *GJS* 14, www.geneticjoycestudies.org/static/issues/GJS14/GJS14_Henkes_2weeks.pdf.
Henkes, Robbert-Jan. 2014b. '2 More Weeks in the Life of James Joyce as Gleaned from his 1923 Notebook VI.B.2 Nativities', *GJS* 14, www.geneticjoycestudies.org/static/issues/GJS14/GJS14_Henkes_2moreweeks.pdf.
Henry, O. 1916. *The Four Million* (London: Hodder and Stoughton).
Herr, Cheryl. 1986. *Joyce's Anatomy of Culture* (Urbana, IL: University of Illinois Press).
Herrick, Robert. 1906. *The Poems of Robert Herrick*, ed. John Masefield (London: E. Grant Richards).
Herring, Phillip F. (ed.). 1972. *Joyce's Ulysses Notesheets in the British Museum* (Charlottesville, VA: University Press of Virginia).
Herring, Phillip F. (ed.). 1977. *Joyce's Notes and Early Drafts from Ulysses: Selections from the Buffalo Collections* (Charlottesville, VA: University Press of Virginia).
Hofheinz, Thomas C. 1995. *Joyce and the Invention of Irish History: Finnegans Wake in Context* (Cambridge: Cambridge University Press).
Hogan, Patrick Colm. 1995. *Joyce, Milton, and the Theory of Influence* (Gainesville, FL: University of Florida Press).
Hutton, Clare. 2006. 'Joyce, the Library Episode, and the Institutions of Revivalism', in Gibson and Platt, 122–38.
Hutton, Clare and Patrick Walsh (eds). 2011. *The Irish Book in English, 1891–2000*, vol. 5: *The Oxford History of the Irish Book* (Oxford: Oxford University Press).
Janik, Allan. 2001. Preface, in Weininger, ix–xi.
Jones, Ellen Carol. 2014. 'Ghosts through Absence', in Frawley and O'Callaghan, 125–44.
The Joyce Project: James Joyce's Ulysses Online. n.d. Ed. John Hunt, www.joyceproject.com.
Joyce, James. 1955. *Stephen Hero*, eds Theodore Spencer, John J. Slocum and Herbert Cahoon (New York: New Directions).
Joyce, James. 1966. *Letters of James Joyce*, eds Stuart Gilbert and Richard Ellmann, 3 vols (New York: Viking).
Joyce, James. 1969. *Dubliners: Text, Criticism, and Notes*, eds Robert Scholes and A. Walton Litz (New York: Viking).
Joyce, James. 1977. *A Portrait of the Artist as a Young Man: Text, Criticism, and Notes*, ed. Chester G. Anderson (Harmondsworth: Penguin).

Joyce, James. 1977–1978. *The James Joyce Archive*, eds Michael Groden et al. (New York: Garland).

Joyce, James. 1991. *Poems and Shorter Writings*, eds Richard Ellmann, A. Walton Litz and John Whittier-Ferguson (London: Faber and Faber).

Joyce, James. 1992. *Selected Letters of James Joyce*, ed. Richard Ellmann (London: Faber and Faber).

Joyce, James. 2000. *Occasional, Critical, and Political Writing*, ed. Kevin Barry (Oxford: Oxford University Press).

Joyce, James. 2001–2004. *The Finnegans Wake Notebooks at Buffalo*, eds Vincent Deane, Daniel Ferrer and Geert Lernout (Turnhout: Brepols).

Joyce, James. 2010. *The Restored Finnegans Wake*, eds Danis Rose and John O'Hanlon (London: Houyhnhm).

Joyce, James. 2016. *Exiles: A Critical Edition*, eds A. Nicholas Fargnoli and Michael Patrick Gillespie (Gainesville, FL: University Press of Florida).

Joyce, James. 2018. *James Joyce Digital Archive: Ulysses and Finnegans Wake*, eds Danis Rose and John O'Hanlon, jjada.ie.

Joyce, James. 2021. *James Joyce Correspondence*, eds Dirk Van Hulle et al. (Antwerp: University of Antwerp), jamesjoycecorrespondence.org.

Joyce, P.W. 1910–13. *The Origin and History of Irish Names of Places*, 3 vols (London: Longmans, Green; Dublin: M.H. Gill).

Joyce, Stanislaus. 1950. *Recollections of James Joyce*, trans. Ellsworth Mason (New York: James Joyce Society).

Joyce, Stanislaus. 2003. *My Brother's Keeper: James Joyce's Early Years*, ed. Richard Ellmann (Cambridge, MA: Da Capo Press).

Jurt, Joseph. 2007. 'Génétique textuelle et génétique sociale', in *La Création en acte: Devenir de la critique génétique*, eds Paul Gifford and Marion Schmid (Amsterdam: Rodopi), pp. 41–50.

Kane, Chris. 2013. 'James Joyce and Matthew Kane', *James Joyce: Online Notes*, 5, www.jjon.org/jioyce-s-people/kane.

Keenan, Desmond. 2006. *Post-Famine Ireland: Social Structure – Ireland as it Really Was* (Xlibris).

Kenner, Hugh. 1974. 'The Portrait in Perspective', in *Joyce: A Collection of Critical Essays*, ed. William M. Chace (Englewood Cliffs, NJ: Prentice Hall), pp. 29–49.

Kettle, T.M. 1910. *The Day's Burden: Studies, Literary and Political* (London: T. Fisher Unwin).

Kettle, T.M. 1911. *Home Rule Finance: An Experiment in Justice* (Dublin: Maunsel & Co.).

Kiberd, Declan. 1996. *Inventing Ireland: The Literature of the Modern Nation* (London: Vintage).

Kristmannsson, Gauti. 2015. 'Ossian, the European National Epic (1760–1810)', EGO: Europäische Geschichte Online, http://ieg-ego.eu/en/threads/models-and-stereotypes/anglophilia/gauti-kristmannsson-ossian-the-european-national-epic-1760-1810.

Landuyt, Inge and Geert Lernout. 1995. 'Joyce's Sources: Les Grands Fleuves Historiques', *Joyce Studies Annual*, 6: 99–138.

Lassman, Eli Z. 2008. '"Scribbled Words": The Usage of the *Ulysses* Notebooks in "Proteus" and "Aeolus"', *JJQ*, 45(2): 301–22.

Latham, Sean. n.d. 'General Introduction to *Dana: An Irish Magazine of Independent Thought*', in Modernist Journals Project, https://modjourn.org/general-introduction-to-dana-an-irish-magazine-of-independent-thought/.

Leerssen, Joep. 2008. 'Introduction: Philology and the European Construction of National Literatures', in *Editing the Nation's Memory: Textual Scholarship and Nation-Building in Nineteenth-Century Europe*, eds Dirk Van Hulle and Joep Leerssen (Amsterdam: Rodopi), pp. 13–27.

Le Fanu, J. Sheridan. [1863] 1899. *The House by the Churchyard* (London: Macmillan).

Leinster Leader. 1916. 'Arterial Drainage. The River Barrow', 25 November, www.kildare.ie/ehistory/index.php/arterial-drainage-the-river-barrow.

Lernout, Geert. 1990–91. 'Woman the Inspirer – Wagner in VI.B.3', *A Finnegans Wake Circular*, 6: 1–12.

Lernout, Geert. 2007. 'The Beginning: Chapter I.1', in Crispi and Slote, 49–65.

Lernout, Geert. 2010. *Help My Unbelief! James Joyce and Religion* (London: Continuum).

Levin, Harry. 1960. *James Joyce: A Critical Introduction*, rev. edn (New York: New Directions).

Litvack, Leon B. 1996. 'The Psychology of Song; the Theology of Hymn: Songs and Hymns of Irish Migration', in *Religion and Identity*, vol 5: *The Irish World Wide: History, Heritage, Identity*, ed. Patrick O'Sullivan (London: Leicester University Press), pp. 71–89.

Longley, Edna. 2015. '"The Rhythm of Beauty": Joyce, Yeats and the 1890s', in McCourt, 55–73.

Lowe-Evans, Mary. 1989. *Crimes against Fecundity: Joyce and Population Control* (Syracuse, NY: Syracuse University Press).

McCarthy, Andrew. 2011. 'Publishing for Catholic Ireland', in Hutton and Walsh, 244–63.

McCourt, John. 2015a. 'Introduction: Joyce, Yeats and the Revival', in McCourt, 7–29.

McCourt, John, ed. 2015b. *Joyce, Yeats, and the Revival*. Special issue of *Joyce Studies in Italy*, 4.

MacDuff, Sangam. 2020. *Panepiphanal World: James Joyce's Epiphanies* (Gainesville, FL: University Press of Florida).

McGreevy, Thomas. 1941. 'James Joyce', *Times Literary Supplement*, 25 January, 43, 45.

McHugh, Roland. 1976. *The Sigla of Finnegans Wake* (Austin, TX: University of Texas Press).

McHugh, Roland. 2006. *Annotations to Finnegans Wake*, 3rd edn (Baltimore, MD: Johns Hopkins University Press).

McKenna, Bernard. 1999. '"This same prehistoric barrow 'tis, the organgery": Duelling and Dual Communities', in *Finnegans Wake, LIT: Literature, Interpretation, Theory*, 10(2): 131–47.

McKenzie, D.F. 1999. *Bibliography and the Sociology of Texts* (Cambridge: Cambridge University Press).

McMahon, Timothy J. 2008. *Grand Opportunity: The Gaelic Revival and Irish Society, 1893–1910* (Syracuse, NY: Syracuse University Press).

Magner, Donal. 2011. *Stopping by Woods: A Guide to the Forests and Woodlands of Ireland* (Dublin: Lilliput Press).

Malamud, Randy. 1999. '"What the Heart Is": Interstices of Joyce's Poetry and Fiction', *South Atlantic Review*, 64: 91–101.

Metchnikoff, Léon. 1889. *La Civilisation et les grands fleuves historiques* (Paris: Hachette).

Miller, Kerby A. 1985. *Emigrants and Exiles: Ireland and the Irish Exodus to North America* (New York: Oxford University Press).

Miller, Kerby A. 1990. 'Emigration, Capitalism, and Ideology in Post-Famine Ireland', in *Migrations: The Irish at Home and Abroad*, ed. Richard Kearney (Dublin: Wolfhoud Press).

Mishler, Katie. 2018. '"A Phantom City, Phaked of Philim Pholk": Spectral Topographies and Re-Awakenings in James Joyce's *Finnegans Wake*', *Joyce Studies Annual*: 161–94.

Mitterand, Henri. 2004. 'Genetic Criticism and Cultural History: Zola's Rougon-Macquart Dossiers', *Genetic Criticism: Texts and Avant-Textes*, eds Jed Deppman, Daniel Ferrer and Michael Groden (Philadelphia: University of Pennsylvania Press), pp. 116–31.

Moore, George. 1925. *Hail and Farewell!* 2 vols (London: Heinemann).

Moore, George. 1903. *The Untilled Field* (Leipzig: B. Tauchnitz).

Moore, Thomas. 1856. *The Poetical Works: Collected by himself, complete in one volume* (Philadelphia, PA: J.B. Lippincott).

Morris, William Bullen. 1908. *Life of Saint Patrick, Apostle of Ireland, with a Preliminary Account of the Sources of the Saint's History*, 6th edn (London: Burns & Oates).

Mullin, Katherine. 2003. *James Joyce, Sexuality and Social Purity* (Cambridge: Cambridge University Press).

Nash, Catherine. 2015. *Genetic Geographies: The Trouble with Ancestry* (Minneapolis, MN: University of Minnesota Press).

Natali, Ilaria. 2008a. '"This diverting chase of the presumable": Procedures of Rewriting in the Dossier of *A Portrait of the Artist as a Young Man*', *GJS* 8, www.geneticjoycestudies.org/articles/GJS8/GJS8_Natali.

Natali, Ilaria. 2008b. *The Ur-Portrait: Stephen Hero ed il processo di creazione artistisca in A Portrait of the Artist as a Young Man* (Firenze: Firenze University Press).

Natali, Ilaria. 2011. 'A Portrait of James Joyce's Epiphanies as a Source Text', *Humanicus*, 6: 1–25.
Nelson, James G. 1989. *Elkin Mathews: Publisher to Yeats, Joyce, Pound* (Madison, WI: University of Wisconsin Press).
'New Books'. 1878. *The Irish Monthly*, 6: 639–41.
Nikolova, Lolita. 2018. *Cultural Genomics and the Changing Dynamics of Cultural Identity: The Scholarly Bond of Archaeology, Genealogy, and Genomics* (New York: Nova Science).
Nolan, Emer. 1995. *James Joyce and Nationalism* (London: Routledge).
Nora, Pierre. 1989. 'Between Memory and History: Les Lieux de Mémoire', *Representations*, 26: 7–24.
O'Callaghan, Katherine. 2014. 'Joyce's "Treeless Hills": Deforestation and its Cultural Resonances', in Frawley and O'Callaghan, 95–111.
O'Ceallaigh Ritschel, Nelson. 2001. *Productions of the Irish Theatre Movement, 1899–1916* (Westport, CT: Greenwood).
O'Connor Morris, William. 1901. *Present Irish Questions* (London: Grant Richards).
Ó Cróinín, Dáibhí. 2005. 'Ireland, 400–800', in *Prehistoric and Early Ireland*, ed. Dáibhí Ó Cróinín, vol. 1: *A New History of Ireland* (Oxford: Oxford University Press).
O'Dea, Dathalinn. 2017. 'James Joyce the Regionalist: *The Irish Homestead*, Dubliners, and Modernism's Regional Affect', *Modern Fiction Studies*, 63(3): 475–501.
Ó Dochartaigh, Pól. 2004. 'The Source of Hell: Professor Pokorny in *Ulysses*', *JJQ*, 41: 825–29.
O'Hanlon, John Canon. n.d. *Lives of the Irish Saints, with Special Festivals, and the Commemorations of Holy Persons, Compiled from Calendars, Martyrologies, and Various Sources, Relating to the Ancient Church History of Ireland*, 9 vols (Dublin: James Duffy and Sons).
O'Hara, Alexander. 2018. *Columbanus and the Peoples of Post-Roman Europe* (Oxford: Oxford University Press).
O'Rourke, Fran. 2011. 'Joyce's Early Aesthetic', *Journal of Modern Literature*, 34(2): 97–120.
O'Sullivan, Patrick. 1997. 'Introduction: The Creative Migrant', in *The Creative Migrant*, vol. 3, *The Irish World Wide: History, Heritage, Identity*, ed. Patrick O'Sullivan (London: Leicester University Press), pp. 1–27.
Paterson, Adrian. 2012. '"After Music": *Chamber Music*, Song, and the Blank Page', in Conner, 117–42.
Platt, Len. 1998. *Joyce and the Anglo-Irish: A Study of Joyce and the Literary Revival* (Amsterdam: Rodopi).
Platt, Len. 2007. *Joyce, Race and Finnegans Wake* (Cambridge: Cambridge University Press).
Plunkett, Horace. 1904. *Ireland in the New Century* (London: John Murray).
Pokorny, Julius. 1917. 'Perlen der irischen Literatur', *Irische Blätter*, 1: 342–60, 625–34.

Reizbaum, Marilyn. 1995. 'Weininger and the Bloom of Jewish Self-Hatred in Joyce's *Ulysses*', in *Jews and Gender: Responses to Otto Weininger*, eds Nancy A. Harrowitz and Barbara Hyams (Philadelphia, PA: Temple University Press), pp. 207–13.

Rimbault, Edward F. 1847. *Bibliotheca Madrigaliana: A Bibliographical Account of the Musical and Poetical Works published in England during the Sixteenth and Seventeenth Centuries* (New York: Burt Franklin).

Rose, Danis. 1982. *Chapters of Coming Forth by Day* (Colchester: A Wake Newslitter Press).

Rose, Danis. 1995. *The Textual Diaries of James Joyce* (Dublin: The Lilliput Press).

Rose, Danis. 2013. 'i..o.l: A Preface to Finn's Hotel', in James Joyce, *Finn's Hotel*, ed. Danis Rose (Dublin: Ithys Press).

Rose, Danis and John O'Hanlon. 1979. 'Specific Use of Yeats' *A Vision* in *Finnegans Wake*', *A Wake Newslitter*, n.s. 16(3): 35–44.

Rose, Danis and John O'Hanlon. 1989. 'The Name of the Book', *A Finnegans Wake Circular*, 4(3): 41–50.

Rose, Danis and John O'Hanlon. 1993. 'Commentary', in *The Lost Notebook: New Evidence on the Genesis of Ulysses*, eds Danis Rose and John O'Hanlon (Edinburgh: Split Pea Press), pp. xi–xxxvii.

Rose, Danis and John O'Hanlon. 2018. 'Finn's Hotel: Details of the Various Draft Stages', in Joyce, http://jjda.ie/main/JJDA/F/FF/fdra/fhda.htm.

Russell, George. 1961. *Letters of AE*, ed. Alan Denson (London: Abelard-Schumann).

Said, Edward. 2001. *Reflections on Exile and Other Literary and Cultural Essays* (London: Granta).

Sass, Louis. 2001. 'Deep Disquietudes: Reflections on Wittgenstein as Antiphilosopher', in *Wittgenstein: Biography and Philosophy*, ed. James C. Klagge (Cambridge: Cambridge University Press), pp. 98–155.

Saunders, Max. 2010. *Self Impression: Life-Writing, Autobiografication, and the Forms of Modern Literature* (Oxford: Oxford University Press).

Scholes, Robert. 1992. *In Search of James Joyce* (Urbana, IL: University of Illinois Press).

Scholes, Robert and Richard M. Kain (eds). 1965. *The Workshop of Daedalus: James Joyce and the Raw Materials for A Portrait of the Artist as a Young Man* (Evanston, IL: Northwestern University Press).

Schuchard, Ronald. 2008. *The Last Minstrels: Yeats and the Revival of the Bardic Arts* (Oxford: Oxford University Press).

Scott, Bonnie K. 1975. 'John Eglinton: A Model for Joyce's Individualism', *JJQ*, 12(4): 347–57.

Senn, Fritz. 1965. 'Esthetic Theories', *JJQ*, 2: 134–36.

Sheehy, Ian. 2010. '"A Deplorable Narrative": Gladstone, R. Barry O'Brien and the "Historical Argument" for Home Rule, 1880-90', in *Gladstone and Ireland: Politics, Religion and Nationality in the Victorian Age*, eds D. George Boyce and Alan O'Day (Basingstoke: Palgrave Macmillan), pp. 110–39.

Shelley, P.B. 1890. *An Address to the Irish People, reprinted from the original edition of 1812*, ed. Thomas J. Wise (London: Published for the Shelley Society by Reeves and Turner).
Shelley, P.B. 1977. *Shelley's Poetry and Prose: Authoritative Texts, Criticism*, eds D.H. Reiman and S.B. Powers (New York: Norton).
Sigerson, George. 1904. 'Irish Influence on European Literature', in *Irish Literature*, eds Justin McCarthy et al. (New York: Bigelow, Smith), vol. 4, pp. vii–xiii.
Slote, Sam. 1995. 'Wilde Thing: Concerning the Eccentricities of a Figure of Decadence in *Finnegans Wake*', in Hayman and Slote, 101–22.
Slote, Sam. 2004/6. 'Prolegomenon to the Development of Wakean Styles: New Acquisitions at the National Library of Ireland', *JJQ*, 42/43(1/4): 21–30.
Slote, Sam. 2010. 'Stephen's Nietzschean Ethics', in *James Joyce: Metamorphosis and Re-Writing*, ed. Franca Ruggieri (Rome: Bulzoni), pp. 15–26.
Slote, Sam. 2013. *Joyce's Nietzschean Ethics* (Basingstoke: Palgrave Macmillan).
Slote, Sam. 2016. 'The Economy of Joyce's Notetaking', in Crowley and Van Hulle, 163–70.
Slote, Sam and Wim Van Mierlo (eds). 1999. *Genitricksling Joyce* (Amsterdam: Rodopi).
Smedley, Frank E. 1855. *Harry Coverdale's Courtship, And All That Came of It* (London: Virtue, Hall, and Virtue).
Spielberg, Peter and Luca Crispi. 2010. *Joyce Catalog* (Buffalo, NY: University of Buffalo), https://library.buffalo.edu/jamesjoyce/catalog/.
Spoo, Robert. 1994. *James Joyce and the Language of History: Dedalus's Nightmare* (New York: Oxford University Press).
Sturge Moore, T. 1922. 'The Story of Tristram and Isolt in Modern Poetry', *The Criterion*, 1(1): 34–49, and 1923, 1(2): 170–87.
Sullivan, James P. 2008. 'Padraic Colum's "James Joyce as a Young Man"', *JJQ*, 45: 339–47.
Symons, Arthur. 1989. *Selected Letters, 1880–1935*, eds Karl Beckson and John M. Munro (London: Macmillan).
Terdiman, Richard. 1993. *Present Past: Modernity and the Memory Crisis* (Ithaca, NY: Cornell University Press).
Terrinoni, Enrico. 2007. *Occult Joyce: The Hidden in Ulysses* (Newcastle: Cambridge Scholars Publishing).
Todhunter, John. 1905. *Sounds and Sweet Airs* (London: Elkin Mathews).
Tymoczko, Maria. 1994. *The Irish Ulysses* (Berkeley, CA: University of California Press).
Valente, Joseph. 2004. 'Joyce's Politics: Race, Nation, and Transnationalism', in *Palgrave Advances in James Joyce Studies*, ed. Jean-Michel Rabaté (Basingstoke: Palgrave Macmillan), pp. 73–96.
Van Hulle, Dirk. 2014. *Modern Manuscripts: The Extended Mind and Creative Undoing from Darwin to Beckett and Beyond* (London: Bloomsbury).
Van Mierlo, Chrissie. 2017. *James Joyce and Catholicism: The Apostate's Wake* (London: Bloomsbury).

Van Mierlo, Chrissie. 2019. 'Joyce's Trade Wars: The Politics of Provenance in Finnegans Wake', in *Modernism and Food Studies: Politics, Aesthetics, and the Avant-Garde*, eds Jessica Martell, Adam Fajardo and Philip Keel Geheber (Gainesville, FL: University Press of Florida), pp. 196–210.

Van Mierlo, Wim. 2016. 'James Joyce and the Middlebrow', in Crowley and Van Hulle, 141–62.

Vico, Giambattista. 1816. *Principi di Scienza Nuova, d'Intorno alla comune natura delle Nazione*, 6th edn, 3 vols (Milano: Giovanni Silvestri).

Vico, Giambattista. 1843. *Principi di una Scienza Nuova d'Intorno alla commune natura delle Nazioni: Secondo l'edizione del MDCCXXV*, ed. Giuseppe Ferrari, 2nd edn (Milano: Società Tipografica de' Classici Italiani).

Vico, Giambattista. 1948. *The New Science: Translated from the Third Edition (1744)*, trans. Thomas Goddard Bergin and Max Harold Fish (Ithaca, NY: Cornell University Press).

Wakeman, W.F. n.d. *The Tourists' Picturesque Guide to Ireland*, 8th edn (Dublin: Printed at 'Official Guide').

Ward, Patrick. 2002. *Exile, Emigration and Irish Writing* (Dublin: Irish Academic Press).

Webb, Timothy. 1982. '"Planetary Music": James Joyce and the Romantic Example', in *James Joyce and Modern Literature*, eds W.J. McCormack and Alistair Stead (London: Routledge and Kegan Paul), pp. 30–55.

Weininger, Otto. 1903. *Geschlecht und Charakter* (Vienna and Leipzig: Wilhelm Braumüller).

Weininger, Otto. 1904. *Über die letzten Dinge, Mit Einem Biographischen Vorwort von Moriz Rappaport* (Wien and Leipzig: Wilhelm Braumüller).

Weininger, Otto. 1912. *Sex and Character: Authorised Translation from the Sixth German Edition* (London: William Heinemann).

Weininger, Otto. 2001. *A Translation of Weininger's Über Die Letzten Dinge (1904/1907): On Last Things*, trans. Steven Burns (Lewiston: Edwin Mellen Press).

Wells, H.G. 1922. *A Short History of the World* (London: Cassell & Company).

White, Hayden. 1987. *The Content of the Form: Narrative Discourse and Historical Representation* (Baltimore, MD: Johns Hopkins University Press).

Williams, Mark. 2018. *Ireland's Immortals: A History of the Gods of Irish Myth* (Princeton, NJ: Princeton University Press).

Witen, Michelle. 2018. *James Joyce and Absolute Music* (London: Bloomsbury).

Woolf, Virginia. 2002. *Moments of Being*, ed. Jean Schulkind, new edn (London: Pimlico).

Wordsworth, William. 1965. *Selected Poems and Prefaces*, ed. Jack Stillinger (Boston, MA: Houghton Mifflin).

Yeats, W.B. 1986. *The Collected Letters of W. B. Yeats:* vol. 1: *1865–1895*, eds John Kelly and Eric Domville (Oxford: Clarendon Press).

Yeats, W.B. 1989a. *Yeats's Poems*, ed. A. Norman Jeffares (London: Macmillan).

Yeats, W.B. 1989b. *Prefaces and Introductions*, ed. William H. O'Donnell (New York: Scribner).

Yeats, W.B. 1994. *The Collected Letters of W. B. Yeats:* vol. 3: *1901–1904*, eds John Kelly and Ronald Schuchard (Oxford: Clarendon Press).

Yeats, W.B. 1999. *Autobiographies*, eds William H. O'Donnell and Douglas N. Archibald (New York: Scribner).

Yeats, W.B. 2000a. *The Collected Letters of W. B. Yeats:* vol. 2: *1896–1900*, eds Warwick Gould, John Kelly and Deirdre Toomy (Oxford: Clarendon Press).

Yeats, W.B. 2000b. *Later Articles and Reviews: Uncollected Articles, Reviews, and Radio Broadcasts written after 1900*, ed. Colton Johnson (New York: Scribner).

Yeats, W.B. 2002. *The Collected Letters of W. B. Yeats: Intelex Electronic Edition*, ed. John Kelly (Oxford: Oxford University Press).

Yeats, W.B. 2007. *Early Essays*, eds George Bornstein and Richard J. Finneran (New York: Scribner).

Yeats, W.B. 2010. *Early Articles and Reviews: Uncollected Articles and Reviews Written between 1886 and 1900*, eds John P. Frayne and Madeleine Marchaterre (New York: Scribner).

Zweig, Stefan. 1964. *The World of Yesterday: An Autobiography* (Lincoln, NE: University of Nebraska Press).

Index

Abbas, Joachim 109–10
Abbey Theatre, *see also* Irish Literary Theatre 33n, 100, 159
The Academy and Literature 83–4
Adrian IV 135
AE 25, 35–8, 71, 81, 107, 110
Aillil, King 190
Aldrich, T.B. 25
Allingham, William 15, 38
Annals of the Four Masters 19, 153, 155, 160, 171, 174, 176
Aquinas, Thomas 15, 17, 24, 39, 44–5, 51, 85, 96–8
Archer, William 41
Ardill, Rev. John Roche 144
Aristotle 15, 17, 24, 43–4, 46, 82, 85, 168n
Arnold, Matthew 25, 147
The Athenaeum 149

Ballsbridge 84
Bannow Bay 135
Barrett, Michael 123
Barry, Kevin 31, 64n
Battle of the Boyne 95, 139, 177
Battle of Waterloo 158, 178
Beach, Sylvia 3, 10
Beardsley, Aubrey 82, 84
Bérard, Victor 3
Berkeley, George 41, 100, 114, 144–6
Berlitz school 59–60, 67
Bernecker, Sven 102
Besant, Annie 107n, 108
Best, Richard 12, 122
Binyon, Laurence 147
Blackrock 84
Blake, William 25
Blanchardstown 163
Boccaccio, Giovanni 25
Boehme, Jacob 114
Bonaparte, Napoleon 95, 158
The Book of Kells 163
The Book of the Dead 166

Boru, Brian 101, 136, 151, 154–5, 170, 181, 194
Bottomley, Gordon 147
Boucicault, Dion 193
Bourdieu, Pierre 8
Bray 84
Brehon Laws 138, 202
Brittany 149, 185
Bruno, Giordano 109
Bryce, James 120
Buchanan, George 25
Budd, G.W. 43
Budgen, Frank 117
Burke, Edmund 89
Burney, Charles 43
Bury, J. B. 3, 145, 146
Bushell, Sally 134n
Byrd, William 15, 93
Byrne, J.F. 89, 90
Byron, George Lord 25, 27n, 150
Bywaters, Frederick 143–4

Cape Clear Island 152
Carleton, William 119
Carlyle, Thomas 173
Casey, Joseph 83–4, 89, 123
Cashell 135
Catholic Church, *see also* Catholicism 29, 34, 56, 58, 63, 71n, 88, 96–7, 109, 135, 142, 144, 159n, 162–4, 175, 177
Catholic Encyclopedia 96, 97
Catholicism, *see also* Catholic Church 8, 12, 14, 19–20, 27n, 30, 34, 60, 61, 91, 92n, 96–7, 99, 101, 134, 141, 150–2, 162, 165, 177
Cavalcanti, Guido 89
Celticism 13–6, 19, 24, 31–2, 38, 47, 71, 89, 121–2, 139, 141, 142, 146, 149, 153, 170, 177, 185, 190, 202
Chamber Music 2, 5, 14–16, 22, 23–29, 38–39, 43–51, 91, 157, 187, 204
Chapelizod 22, 162, 179, 197–8, 200, 202

Chaucer, Geoffrey 25
Childers, Erskine 166
Church of Ireland 123
Civil War 21, 55, 101, 136–7, 151
Clancy, George Stephen 89–91
Clonmacnoise 154–5
Clonard 135
Clontarf 63, 155, 181, 194
Collinstown 136
Colonialism 3, 5, 10, 16, 18, 19, 22, 27, 54, 63, 91, 95, 100, 116n, 127, 139, 161, 189, 198, 200, 201, 203
Colum, Mary 13, 49, 99–100
Colum, Padraic 13, 34n, 36–7, 42–3, 49, 84n, 131
Connaught 134–5, 174, 190
Conway, Mrs 'Dante' Hearn 83, 84
Cork 126, 152, 153
Corkery, Daniel 30
Cornwall 185, 193
Cosgrave, Vincent 89
Cosgrave, W.T. 100
Courtney, Margaret 25
Cousins, Gretta 84
Cousins, James 37, 84
Coyne, William P. 126n
Crispi, Luca 45n, 82, 90n, 133n, 136
The Criterion 147, 174
Critical writings 13, 32, 36, 51, 64, 68, 71n, 93, 105, 109n, 123, 124, 155, 170
   'The Day of the Rabblement' 14, 24, 32–4, 47, 70
   'Fenianism' 124, 129
   'Ireland at the Bar' 24
   'Ireland: Island of Saints and Sages' 24, 63, 68, 96, 128, 170
Cuchulainn 142
Cullen, Cardinal Paul 56n, 164
cultural genetics 1–3, 7–9, 14, 20, 129, 167–8, 173, 205–6
cultural memory 9–11, 15, 18, 21–2, 78, 88, 101–2, 107, 123, 129, 140, 153, 158, 164, 166, 169–72, 174, 182, 187, 193–4, 199–200, 205–6
cultural studies 3–4, 7–9, 11
Curran, C.P. 42, 59, 60
Czarnowski, Stefan 173n

The Daily Express 32
The Daily Mail 136
The Daily Sketch 144
Dana 31–2
Dante Alighieri 25, 34
Davenant, Sir William 73
de Biaisi, Pierre-Marc 4
De Valera, Éamon 162, 181
Debussy, Claude 147
Derry 153
Descartes, René 115
Dinnseanchas 21, 176, 195, 199
Dixon, R.W. 48
Dolmetsch, Arnold 15, 41–3
Donnybrook 89
Donoghue, Denis 87
Dowland, John 15, 25, 42, 45, 93
Dowson, Ernest 25
Dublin 10, 14, 21, 23, 31, 33–6, 47n, 48, 55, 58, 60, 67–8, 70, 72, 80, 83n, 90–1, 92n, 101, 104n, 105, 108, 110, 122, 128, 134–5, 136–7, 140, 153, 155, 158n, 162, 175–6, 180–1, 192, 194, 196–7, 199, 204–5
Dubliners 14, 16, 38, 50, 53, 55, 56, 58, 64, 79, 81–2, 84, 98, 101, 104, 204
   'After the Race' 79
   'The Boarding House' 64, 79
   'Clay' 64
   'Counterparts' 79
   'The Dead' 12, 51, 94n, 69, 70, 94n, 187
   'Eveline' 53, 60, 65, 68, 79, 94n
   'Ivy Day in the Committee Room' 79–80, 94
   'A Little Cloud' 16, 53, 64, 67–8, 80, 93
   'A Mother' 187
   'A Painful Case' 79, 94n
Dun Laoghaire 155
Dundalk 137
Dundrum Bay 153
Duns Scotus, John 96–7

Easter Rising 55, 101, 123, 129, 151, 154, 161
economics 10, 13, 16, 31, 53–6, 59–64, 66, 70–2, 89, 91, 98, 102n, 121, 124–9, 131, 150–1, 169, 174, 189–90, 192, 201, 204–6
Edward VII 94
Eglinton, John 31–2, 34, 36n, 99
The Egoist 103

Eliot, T.S. 87
Elizabeth I 73, 201
Elizabethan 5, 15, 25, 26–9, 43–4, 47, 49, 51, 90–1, 201
Ellis, Havelock 156n
Ellmann, Richard 23, 30, 32, 34, 57, 84n, 134
emigration 11, 16–17, 53–7, 60–7, 70–2, 75, 77, 126, 128, 153, 170, 190
Emmett, Robert 119
Encyclopaedia Britannica 119n, 120, 122–3, 167, 168n, 187–8
Epiphanies 2, 6–7, 17, 39, 49–50, 51, 74, 78–85, 87, 90, 93, 109, 114–15, 133, 168
esotericism 3, 107–8, 148, 166, 171, 194–5
Esposito, Bianca 83, 84
Esposito, Michele 84
Esposito, Vera 83, 84
Exiles 1, 5, 14, 16–17, 53, 55–8, 65, 67, 68–74, 94n, 113, 148, 204–5
exogenetics 5–7, 82, 83, 87, 89, 103

Fairhall, James 7n, 10, 172n
famine 16, 54, 61, 63, 99, 102, 124, 201
Farr, Florence 41–2
Fenian Brotherhood, *see* Irish Republican Brotherhood
Ferdiad 174
Ferguson, Samuel 38, 99
Field, Michael 147
Finn MacCool 121, 142, 147, 171
Finnegans Wake 2–3, 5, 6, 14, 19–22, 24, 50, 55, 63, 65, 81, 88, 92, 94n, 97, 122, 126, 129, 131–203, 204–6
Firbolg 91, 139, 170, 174, 189–90
Fisher Unwin, T. 49n
Fitzgerald, William George 100n
Fitzharris, James 155
Fitzpatrick, Benedict 136n
Fitzpatrick, H.M. 202–3
Flood, J.M. 136n, 141n, 143n, 159, 183
Flynn, Catherine 45
Fomorians 28n, 174, 189–90
Fordham, Finn 134, 168
Foster, R.F. 34n, 35n, 67, 70
Foulis, T.N. 172
Fox, Brian 123, 178
The Freeman 100n

The Freeman's Journal 34, 36, 47, 63n, 122
Freitag, Barbara 58–9
The Future 26n

Gaelic League 30, 118, 128
Galsworthy, John 182
Galvani. Luigi 86–7
Garratt, Robert F. 47, 88, 116
Gassendi, Pierre 115
Geertz, Clifford 9, 167
genealogy 1, 4–7, 9, 17, 20–2, 53, 79, 91–2, 102, 113, 139, 140, 155, 158, 161, 162, 164, 167–73, 174, 175, 180–2, 185, 189, 192, 195, 206
genetic criticism 1–2, 4, 7–9, 22
Giacomo Joyce 81
Gibbon, Edward 173n
Gibbons, Luke 7n, 95, 101, 199
Gibson, Andrew 3, 7n, 10, 12, 27n, 71, 101, 102n, 116n, 128n
Gibson, W.W. 48
Gilbert, Stuart 107
Gladstone, William 120, 123
Glandore Harbour 153
Glendalough 141–3
Gogarty, Oliver St. John 12, 37, 42, 89
Gonne, Maud 36, 58
Gordon, Michael 89
Gorman, Herbert 24, 30, 45–6, 82n, 83
Gosse, Edmund 45
Grattan, Henry 89, 196
Graves, Alfred Perceval 49n, 202
Gregory, Lady Augusta 10, 13–14, 24–5, 29, 32, 35–7, 57–8, 121–2, 139–40, 144–5, 165, 193
Griffith, Arthur 13, 129
Gunn, Michael 177–8
Gwyn, Nell 73

Hackett, Francis 67, 124–6, 128
Halbwachs, Maurice 11–12, 166n, 200
Hall, Stuart 9
Harnett, Sheila
Hart, Clive 133
Hartmann, Martin 45–6
Hauptmann, Gerhart 33
Hawkins, John 43
Hayman, David 6, 82n, 133, 161n, 185
Healy, Michael 89
Heaney, Seamus 90
Hegel, G.W.F. 131, 173, 176

Heidegger, Martin 86n
Henry II 135, 175, 179
Henry S. King & Co. 45n
Henry, Father William 89
Henry, O. 149
Herbert, George 25
Herder, Johann Gottfried 167, 169
Hermes Trismegistus 167n
hermeticism 106–10, 195
Herr, Cheryl 3, 7n, 9, 159
Herrick, Robert 25, 26, 28
Herring, Phillip F. 6
Hind, C. Lewis 83
Hirn, Irjö 3
historiography 10, 20–1, 102–3, 119–21, 123, 131, 133–4, 153–4, 160, 166–7, 169, 172–4, 176, 185, 192, 194–5
Hofheinz, Thomas C. 19n, 172n
'The Holy Office' 24–5, 56
Home Rule 55, 62, 71, 102n, 118, 120, 126
Homer 105, 167n
Horton, W.T. 107n
Hume, David 173
Hyde, Douglas 12, 122, 165

Ibsen, Henrik 31, 33, 35, 89, 113
Identity 2, 8–9, 11, 14–18, 21, 24, 27, 30, 53, 56, 58, 63, 66, 71, 77–8, 90, 91–2, 101, 105, 115–16, 129, 153, 159n, 163, 168, 174, 189, 194, 204–5
Irische Blätter 122
The Irish Catholic 150
Irish Civil War 21, 55, 62, 101, 136–7, 151
Irish folklore 25, 29, 32, 38, 47, 165, 168, 193
Irish Free State 20, 62, 100, 131, 136, 138, 151, 162, 176, 189
The Irish Homestead 31, 58, 60, 65, 79, 102n, 128–9
The Irish Independent 36
Irish legend 19, 29, 32, 91, 136, 145n, 153, 165, 177, 193, 199
Irish Literary Theatre, *see also* Abbey Theatre 11, 12, 14, 32–4, 36–37, 84
Irish myth 13, 19, 38, 118, 121–2, 138, 139–40, 144, 146–7, 151, 156, 163, 165, 174, 177, 190, 193, 199
Irish Republican Army 120, 151
Irish Republican Brotherhood 116, 119–20, 122–4, 129, 180, 184

Irish Revival 2, 9–10, 12–15, 18–21, 24, 25, 30–2, 36, 47–8, 71n, 77, 92, 94n, 99–100, 102, 105, 109, 118–19, 129, 134, 139–41, 146, 151, 159, 161, 165, 169, 171, 174, 177, 181, 193, 195–6, 200, 201, 204–5
The Irish Times 36, 63n, 137, 150–1
Isis Unveiled 108, 162

Jacobean 15, 25, 49, 91, 187
James I 93, 187
James II 95, 139
Jespersen, Otto 3
Jesuits 36, 89
Jesus Christ 82, 84, 89, 105, 107–8, 183
Jolas, Eugene 10
Jonson, Ben 15, 25, 46
Joyce, James 1–9, 10, 12–15, 16, 25–7, 29–32, 34–7, 38–39, 41–3, 46–7, 49, 50, 53, 55, 56, 57–60, 66–7, 70, 72, 74, 75, 77, 78, 79, 81–4, 87, 93, 102, 104, 106–7, 112–13, 115, 117, 121, 123, 129, 131–4, 141, 145, 158–9, 164, 165–6, 168, 169, 172, 173, 179, 182, 189, 193, 202–3, 204
Joyce, John Stanislaus 16, 60, 84, 88, 148
Joyce, Margaret Alice ('Poppie') 89
Joyce, Nora 51, 55, 58–60, 89, 101, 141, 153, 158n
Joyce, Stanislaus 24, 32n, 42n, 50–1, 58–9, 81, 93, 103, 107
Jurt, Joseph 8

Kain, Richard M. 83, 89
Kane, Matthew F. 155
Keating, Seán 149
Kegan Paul, Trench, Trübner & Co. 45n
Kells 135
Kelly, H.P. 95
Kelly, John 84
Kenner, Hugh 78–79
Kerry 136, 154
Kettle, Thomas 30, 47, 67, 72, 98, 102n
Kildare 136
Kilkenny 98
Killala 155

language 25–7, 50, 51, 54, 59, 89, 90–1, 112, 116, 128, 139, 170, 173, 176, 192, 194–5, 197–8, 204

Lawrence, D.H. 112
Le Caron, Major Henri 119–20, 122–3
Le Fanu, Sheridan 22, 179, 197–9, 202
The Leader 62, 129, 137
Leary, King 146, 163
Lecky, W.E.H. 173n
Leinster 135–6, 139, 154–5, 174
The Leinster Leader 125
Lessing, Gotthold Ephraim 115n
Lewis, Wyndham 115
Limerick 124, 126–7
The Little Review 4, 103
Livy 192n
London 15, 23, 35–36, 41, 48n, 58, 59–60, 67, 83–4, 93, 94, 98, 134, 143
London Irish Literary Society 119, 121
Longford 154–5
Lovelace, Richard 25
Lowe-Evans, Mary 65

Mac Lochlainn, Muirchertach 135, 136
MacAirt, Conan 190
Macaulay, Thomas Babbington 173
MacMurrough Kavanagh, Art 135–8
MacMurrough, Dermot 135, 138, 156, 174
MacNeill, Eoin 122
Macpherson, James 167
Maitland, Margaret 160
Malamud, Randy 26
Malthus, T.R. 61, 124
Mananaan MacLir 28n
Mangan, James Clarence 25, 36, 51, 93, 119
Manuscripts and notebooks
 'Alphabetical Notebook' (Cornell 25) 17, 54, 87–98, 103, 104
 British Museum Add. MSS 136–40, 142–3, 146–50, 152–3, 155, 158, 160, 163, 193
 British Museum *Ulysses* notesheets 98n, 113, 117
 Buffalo Notebooks
  VI.A. ('Scribbledehobble') 148, 156
  VI.B.1 134n, 167–71, 173n, 183, 189, 191, 197–8, 202n
  VI.B.2 159, 161n, 180, 194, 202
  VI.B.3 136n, 141–3, 148–50, 159, 183, 203n
  VI.B.8 150n
  VI.B.10 136–8, 144, 147–8, 151, 159, 166, 168
  VI.B.14 97, 144, 173n
  VI.B.25 142
  VI.B.29 181
  VI.B.36 203n
  VI.B.45 144
  VI.B.46 203n
  VI.X.1 136n
 Cornell MSS 82, 170, 189
 'Early Commonplace Book' (NLI 36,639/2/A) 24, 43–6, 56, 80, 82–5, 118
 Paris-Pola Notebook, *see* 'Early Commonplace Book'
 'Subject Notebook' (NLI 36,639/3) 4, 18, 98, 103–24
 Pre-'Work in Progress' (NLI 41,818) 148–54. 156–7, 164
 'Proteus' (V.A.3) 104
Marsden, Dora 112, 166
Martyn, Edward 33–4
Masefield, John 48
Mathers Anna 41
Mathews, Elkin 15–16, 47–9
Maunsel & Co. 58, 94
Mayo 155, 196
McCarthy, J. Huntley 121
McCarthy, Justin 13, 119, 121
McKenzie, D. F. 7, 9, 185
Mead, G.R.S. 108
Meath 135, 136, 154
Medb, Queen 190
Meredith, George
Métchnikoff, Léon 131, 167, 173, 183
Meyer, Kuno 122
Michelet, Jules 131, 173
Milesians 170
Miller, Kerby A. 61, 66
Mitterand, Henri 8
Mizen Head 152
Mommsen, Theodor 167, 169
Moore, George 12, 33–6, 71, 83, 94n, 99
Moore, Thomas 25, 54–5, 142
Moran, D. P. 12, 30, 64n
The Morning Leader 41
Morris, William Bullen 160n, 161n, 180
Mullin, Katherine 65, 94n, 190n

Mullingar 74
Munster 174
mysticism 29, 31, 109, 110, 114, 141

Nash, Thomas 15, 93
Natali, Ilaria 81
The Nation 47, 48
nationalism 2–3, 8–13, 17, 24, 27, 30–1, 36, 38, 54–8, 64, 66, 70–1, 75, 77–9, 88–9, 91, 94, 98, 100, 105–6, 118–29, 131, 135, 139, 146, 150, 164, 165, 172–3, 204
Nemedians 174
Nero 138
Nibelungenlied 99
Nietzsche, Friedrich 112, 154, 172–3
Nolan, Emer 7, 30, 100–1, 169
Nora, Pierre 116

O'Brien, R. Barry 119–21
O'Callaghan, Katherine 196, 199, 201
O'Connell, Daniel 107
O'Connor Morris, William 13, 119–20
O'Connor, Roderick 19, 21, 133, 134–8, 180–1
O'Donnell, William 84
O'Donoghue, D.J. 119
O'Hanlon, John 147n, 158n
O'Hanlon, John Canon 141, 143
O'Leary, John 123
O'Sullivan, Patrick 66–7
occultism 106–7, 148
Olcott, Henry S. 107n
Orpheus 167n
Ossian 122, 144–5, 167

Palgrave, F.T. 48
Palladius 144
Paris 18, 32, 35, 55, 58, 59, 71, 72, 75, 81, 83–4, 94, 97, 107, 123, 129, 138
Parnell, Charles Stuart 56n, 88–9, 118, 120–1, 150, 156, 164
Parthalonians 139, 174
Percy, Thomas 15
personal library 3, 9, 31, 102n, 103, 107, 119n, 172, 173n
Phoenix Park 119, 155, 197, 199–201
Piccolo della sera, Il 123
Pius IX 56

Platt, Len 30, 102
Plunkett, Horace 89n, 124
Pokorny, Julius 121–2
Pola 66–7
Pomes Penyeach 50, 69
   'She Weeps over Rahoon' 69
'A Portrait of the Artist' 31, 79, 107, 109
A Portrait of the Artist as a Young Man 1–2, 5, 14–15, 17–18, 26–7, 39, 44, 46, 50, 51, 56, 68, 75, 78, 79, 81, 84, 85–95, 98, 116, 118, 204–5
Pound, Ezra 4, 10, 26, 28, 47, 103
Prezioso, Roberto 89
Protestantism 8, 12, 29, 32n, 60, 100, 101, 151, 179, 185, 198
Prout, Father 164
Ptolemy 127, 175–6
Pugh, T.W. 101

Quinet, Edgar 131, 167, 173, 178
Quinn, John 37

Ramacharaka, Yogi 107
Random House 101
Ranelagh 72
Rathmines 84
Richardson, Dorothy 136
Rimbault, Edward F. 43–4
Roberts, George 58
Robinson, Lennox 49n, 100
Rogers, Marcellus 89
Rose, Danis 133, 147n, 158n, 203n
Rosseter, Philip 187
Rossetti, D.G. 25
Roucati, Venanzio 89
Russell, George, *see* AE

Said, Edward 9, 66
Saint Brigid 141
Saint Columba 141, 146, 159
Saint Columbanus 96–7, 141n, 159
Saint Columcille, *see* Saint Columba
Saint Dympna 19, 150, 160
Saint Faro 96
Saint Fiacre 96–7
Saint Finnian 63
Saint Fridianus 97
Saint Fridolinus 97

Saint John of the Cross 109
Saint Kevin 19, 21, 133, 141–4, 145, 150, 155, 158, 160n, 161, 162, 163n
Saint Laurence O'Toole 135, 175
Saint Malachy 174
Saint Mansuetus of Toul 63
Saint Martin 160
Saint Patrick 3, 19, 21, 122, 133, 141, 144–6, 154, 158, 160n, 162–4, 174–5, 177, 179–80, 182–4
Sandycove 60
Sandymount 39, 84, 114
Sarsfield, Patrick 137n
Scholes, Robert 80–1, 83, 85, 89
Scotland 97, 127, 139, 190
Scott, Walter 139
Sedulius Scottus 63
Sendivogius, Michael 109
Senn, Fritz 115
Shakespeare, William 25, 40, 73, 99, 105, 107, 115
Shaw, G.B. 182
Shelley, Percy Bysshe 25, 39, 85–6, 89, 92–3
Sigerson, George 99
Sinn Féin 94, 129, 195
Sinnett, A.P. 107
Skeffington-Sheehy, Francis J.C. 89
Slote, Sam 7, 86n, 133n, 166, 182
Smedley, Frank E. 148–9
social class 27n, 35–6, 38, 59–60, 72, 90, 92n, 118, 150–1, 191, 198
Song of Solomon 25
Sordino, Conte Francesco 89
Spenser, Edmund 27, 99
Spoo, Robert 7, 101, 172n
Stein, Gertrude 112
Stephen Hero 2, 5, 17–18, 26, 39, 50–1, 56, 59, 74–5, 78–85, 88–91, 93, 98, 115–16, 204–5
Strongbow 135
Sturge Moore, T. 147
Sutcliffe, G.E. 109n
Svevo, Italo 112
Swedenborg, Emanuel 109–10, 166
Swift, Jonathan 100, 180, 200
Swinburne, A.G. 147
Symons, Arthur 16, 25, 47–50, 84n
Synge, J.M. 15, 33n, 48, 58, 82, 83–4, 156

Táin Bó Cúailnge 189
The Talbot Press 159
Tara 75, 94, 107, 138, 145–6, 154, 155, 159, 175, 190
Tennyson, Alfred Lord 25, 26n, 73, 147
The Academy and Literature 83–4
The Kenyon Review 34n
theosophy 13, 18, 105, 106–10, 118, 205
Thom's Directory 55, 175, 181
Thompson, Edith 143–4
Thompson, Francis 25
Thompson, Percy 143
Thornton, Ned 83n
Thucydides 167, 169
Tipperary 126, 127, 149
Todhunter, John 48
Tolstoy, Leo 33
Tone, Wolf 166
Torbridge, George
Traherne, Thomas 109
Trallee 136
Transatlantic Review 164, 170, 187, 189
Travers Smith, Hester 182
Trieste 54, 58–9, 63, 66–7, 89, 95, 128, 131
Tristan and Isolde 19, 21, 99, 147–9, 152, 156, 160, 185–7, 193–95v
Tuatha de Danaan 139
Turle, James 43
Tymockzko, Maria 33n
Tynan, Katharine 38, 48, 49n
Tynan, Patrick J.P. 119
Tyrone 98

Ultonius 97
Ulysses 2, 4, 5, 7, 12, 14, 18–19, 24, 32, 39, 55, 57, 62, 64, 77–9, 81, 83, 88, 89, 92, 94, 96, 98, 99–129, 131–2, 138, 150, 155, 158, 159, 165, 195, 205
'Circe' 106, 112, 115n
'Cyclops' 22, 31, 54, 61, 64, 109n, 121, 127–8, 151, 171, 196, 201–2
'Eumaeus' 63, 98, 119, 138
'Hades' 63, 103, 106, 127, 189
'Nestor' 95, 106, 116
'Oxen of the Sun' 27n, 105, 113
'Penelope' 138, 187
'Proteus' 41, 97, 103, 106, 109, 115, 117, 122, 175

'Scylla and Charybdis' 12, 73, 99, 106–7, 113
'Telemachus' 103
'Wandering Rocks' 10
The United Irishman 34, 36, 119

Vaughan, Henry 25
Verlaine, Paul 25, 44–5
Vico, Giambattista 20–1, 113, 131, 166–70, 173, 176, 183, 187, 190–95
Virtue, Hall and Virtue 148
Vizetelly, Henry 3

Wagner, Richard 33, 147
Wales 183
Wallis Budge, E. A. 3
Walshe, Louis 89
War of Independence 55, 64, 101
Ward, Patrick 55, 64
Waterford 126, 135
Weaver, Harriet Shaw 3, 10, 103, 134
Webb, Timothy 92–3
Weininger, Otto 18, 105–6, 110–17, 118, 122, 205
Wells, H.G. 169–71
Wexford 127, 135
Wicklow 90, 92, 175
Wilbye, John 43
Wilde, Oscar 71, 73, 182
Wilmot, John 25
Witen, Michelle 45

Wittgenstein, Ludwig 112
Woolf, Virginia 79
Wordsworth, William 41, 80n
'Work in Progress' 3, 21, 50, 132–4, 144, 158, 160–1, 166, 168, 172
  'Here Comes Everybody' 19, 133, 157–8
  'Mamalujo' 133, 147, 152–7, 158, 160, 164, 168, 170, 175, 193
  'Roderick O'Connor' 19, 21, 133, 134–40, 141, 154, 159–62, 170, 172, 183
  'Saint Patrick' 19, 21, 133, 141n, 144–6, 162–3, 185
  'Saint Kevin' 19, 133, 140–4, 146, 147, 152, 154, 162
  'Tristan and Isolde' 19, 133, 146–52, 153, 157, 164, 185, 193

Xanthippe 73

Yeats, W. B. 10–16, 19, 23–5, 27–39, 41–2, 44–5, 47–9, 51, 58, 64, 77, 82–4, 92, 99–101, 110, 121, 123, 142–3, 146–7, 165, 166, 175, 193
Young Ireland 124

Zola, Émile 8
Zurich 59–60, 67

www.ingramcontent.com/pod-product-compliance
Lightning Source LLC
Chambersburg PA
CBHW071830300426
44116CB00009B/1502